Fodor's

EXPLORING

PROVENCE

Fodor's Travel Publications, Inc.
New York • Toronto • London • Sydney • Auckland

Published in the United States by Fodor's Travel Publications, Inc.
Published in the United Kingdom by AA Publishing.

ISBN 0–679–03089–1
First Edition

Fodor's Exploring Provence

Author: Nick Hanna
Series Adviser: Christopher Catling
Joint Series Editor: Susi Bailey
Copy Editor: Lynn Bresler
Original Photography: Adrian Baker
Cartography: The Automobile Association
Cover Design: Louise Fili, Fabrizio La Rocca
Front Cover Silhouette: Catherine Karnow

Special Sales
Fodor's Travel Publications are available at special discounts for bulk purchases (100 copies or more) for sales promotions or premiums. Special editions, including personalized covers, excerpts of existing guides, and corporate imprints, can be created in large quantities for special needs, For more information, contact your local bookseller or write to Special Markets, Fodor's Travel Publications, 201 East 50th Street, New York, NY 10022.

Printed and bound in Italy by Printers S.R.L., Trento
10 9 8 7 6 5 4 3 2 1

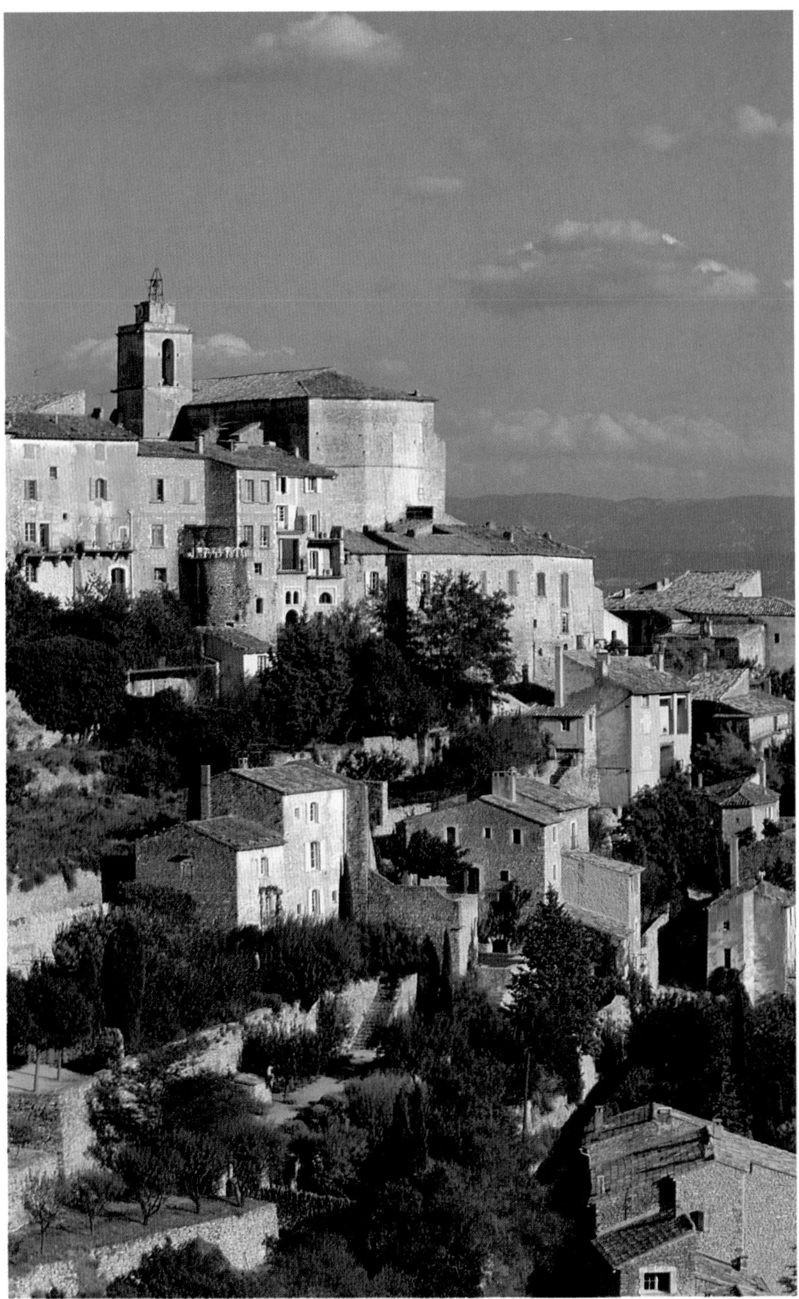

Nick Hanna specializes in travel writing and photography. He is the author of AA/Thomas Cook *Singapore & Malaysia* and his articles and photographs appear regularly in a number of national newspapers and magazines. He has also written on the marine environment, scuba diving, and tourism issues.

How to use this book

This book is divided into five main sections:

- ❑ Section 1: ***Provence Is***
  discusses aspects of life and living today, from rural architecture to summer festivals
- ❑ Section 2: ***Provence Was***
  places the region in its historical context and explores those past events whose influences are felt to this day
- ❑ Section 3: ***A to Z Section***
  is broken down into five regional chapters, and covers places to visit, including walks and drives. Within this section fall the Focus-on articles, which consider a variety of topics in greater detail
- ❑ Section 4: ***Travel Facts***
  contains the strictly practical information that is vital for a successful trip
- ❑ Section 5: ***Hotels and Restaurants***
  lists recommended establishments in Provence, giving a brief résumé of what they offer

How to use the star rating
Most places described in this book have been given a separate rating:

►►►	**Do not miss**
►►	**Highly recommended**
►	**Worth seeing**
	Not essential viewing

Map references
To make the location of a particular place easier to find, every main entry in this book is given a map reference, such as 176B3. The first number (176) indicates the page on which the map can be found, the letter (B) and the second number (3) pinpoints the square in which the main entry is located. The maps on the inside front cover and inside back cover are referred to as IFC and IBC respectively.

Contents

Quick reference

This quick-reference guide highlights the features of the book you will use most often: the maps; the introductory features; the Focus-on articles; the walks and the drives.

Maps and plans

Provence Is

Quick reference

Françoise Prébois
Françoise Prébois was born in La Charité sur Loire (Nièvre), and came to Provence at the age of 18 when she married an *arlésian*.

She studied cinema and is a graduate of the IDHEC. As a movie director/documentary maker for television, she has made many programs on Argentina. She works occasionally as a subtitle translator, and divides her time between Paris and her home in Vaucluse.

My Provence

by Françoise Prébois
Some places are like people: you fall head-over-heels in love with them and there's something irrational in the sensual pleasure a sky, a sound, or a fragrance can suddenly arouse in you. Thirty years ago I arrived here from the damp slopes of the Loire Valley, accustomed to the soft light on the river, the tranquil green meadows — and the oppressive reserve of the people. Provence stunned me at first with the abstraction of its arid rocky landscapes and its outrageous extremes — the raw sun, the icy savagery of the mistral, the steely blue skies, the blood in the arenas, the liters of pastis — and the glibness of the people. But however real all this excess *à la* Pagnol may be, the Provence that is now near to my heart is far removed from the clichés. It is more secretive, more sensual.

You have to have walked in the Fontvieille hills to appreciate what perfume is; you have to have strolled in Sénanque of an evening to grasp the deep mystery of stark Romanesque monasteries. And you have to have driven along the little road from Noves to St-Rémy where the clear-cut outline of the Alpilles surges suddenly into view; no other landscape will ever be so exhilarating, so serenely melancholy, so ideal. These are secret journeys of the soul. Reason alone cannot explain them — any more than it can explain that exquisite sense of living in the land of the gods.

Pierre Coste
Pierre Coste was born in Arles and studied humanities in Montpelier and Aix. He also spent some time in Liverpool, England, as a French language assistant.

On his return to France he did his military service in Algeria and then took a variety of jobs. He worked for the cultural affairs department at Arles Town Hall, and now writes regularly for the monthly local Arles-Magazine. He now lives in Fontvieille.

My Provence

by Pierre Coste
For a long time I didn't believe Provence existed. I thought of it as Arcadia — an ancient, idyllic, French-style Greece, a land of myths and stories. I really believed that the stones that cover La Plaine de la Crau had, as the legend goes, been cast by Zeus to protect Heracles from the Ligurians. In the Alpilles, under a spring sky cleansed to a brilliant blue by one of those mistrals that can go to your head, I was so dazed I expected to see a faun leap out from behind an olive tree, or a nymph playing in a stream (in fact it was the irrigation canal!). But they never appeared and I gave up on them, disappointed.

Then I looked for Provence in Provençal books — in Giono or in Bosco. As for movies, I despised Pagnol's because they portrayed an all too accurate picture of ourselves at a time when, dreaming of Paris, I found our Provençal accent vulgar and our concerns petty. (Once again I was wrong!) Next I delved into the charming Daudet and into Mistral, the "humble student of the great Homer." Yes, they had portrayed Provence — but why, I asked, should I not look at it for myself, to see it as it really was, all around me?

So that is what I did. And I found it was worthy of all the books and all the movies: a flight of flamingos over the Beauduc lagoons, a sunset on Les Baux, an icy sky over Mont Ventoux, a lavender field near Manosque, or a secret rocky inlet near Cassis…

PROVENCE IS

Despite the picture-postcard images of mellow landscapes, in reality Provence is rugged and mountainous, with arid, wind-blown terrain alternating with the lush river valleys.....

Mountains, rivers, gorges In the northeast corner of Provence the craggy peaks of the Alpes de Haute-Provence tower above glaciated valleys, such as the Vallée de l'Ubaye, the dramatic mountain passes often cut off by deep snow in winter. To the south, these alpine heights adjoin the Mercantour *massif* on the border with Italy and lead down into the upper valleys of the Var, Tinée, Roya, and Vésubie rivers. *En route* to the coast these torrents have created chasms through the pre-Alps, which shelter the hinterland and the Riviera resorts.

To the west, the Verdon river has carved out of the limestone of the Plateau de Valensole one of the great natural wonders of the region, the Grand Cañon du Verdon. The Plateau de Valensole and the Plan de Canjuers to the south of the Verdon are among the least populated regions in Provence, desolate, wild areas dominated by *garrigue* (scrubland).

The Durance loops down from the Alps through the heartland of Provence before disgorging into the Rhône. During the summer its stony bed is all but dried out, but in the spring the melting snow transforms it into an impressive, foaming torrent several hundred yards across.

Above the broad curve formed by the Durance are the Petit and Grand Lubéron ranges, reaching their peak at the Mourre Nègre (3,690 feet.). The wide-open, arid plains of the Plateau de Vaucluse beyond the Lubéron are fractured by chasms and fissures that lead down to a vast network of subterranean rivers through which rainwater is carried to spectacular resurgent springs such as the Fontaine-de-Vaucluse.

Rising up to the north of the Plateau de Vaucluse is the imposing bulk of Mont Ventoux, with its barren summit at 6,263 feet dominating the

Spring blossoms on the slopes of the Dentelles de Montmirail

surrounding landscapes. Flanking it to the east is the Montagne de Lure, with the unusual mini-peaks of the Dentelles de Montmirail displaying a jagged profile to the west.

To the south of the Durance's leisurely arc lie the southern Provençal ranges — Ste-Victoire above Aix, Ste-Baume behind Marseille, and Mont Faron overshadowing Toulon harbor.

The western boundary of Provence closely follows the Rhône, a major artery for communication and transportation in Provence since antiquity. Alluvial deposits on either side of the river have created the fertile valleys of the Comtat Venaissin and the plains of la Crau and Petite Crau near its delta. Separating the Crau and the Petite Crau is the rugged Alpilles chain.

On either side of the delta, the Grand Rhône and Petit Rhône embrace the marshy wilderness of the Camargue — along with the rest of the Rhône valley, the Camargue is subject to periodic flooding which can have devastating effects.

Three of the most distinctive geographical features of the present-day coastline are the Cap Canaille (which has the highest cliffs in France) and the unusual *massifs* of the Esterel and the Maures.

The "mud-eater" *mistral* Provence has many winds but the most famous is the *mistral*, whose course is shaped by the mountains and rivers of the region. Originating in the north or northwest, the *mistral* is channeled down the Rhône valley and blasts across mid-Provence and the coast before dissipating itself on the Alpes-Maritimes. The *mistral* (in Provençal: the *mangio fango* — the "mud-eater") has a profound effect, drying out the soil and clearing up the atmosphere, creating luminous blue skies in its wake. It knocks off roof tiles and sets doors banging, getting on everyone's nerves. Folk wisdom claims that it blows in cycles of three days (a *mistral* blowing for nine days is not unknown) if it starts up by day; if it begins at night it may last only "as long as it takes to bake bread." Generally, it blows for between 100 and 150 days a year.

Top: view of the Camargue
Below: canoeists work their way through the Ardèche gorges

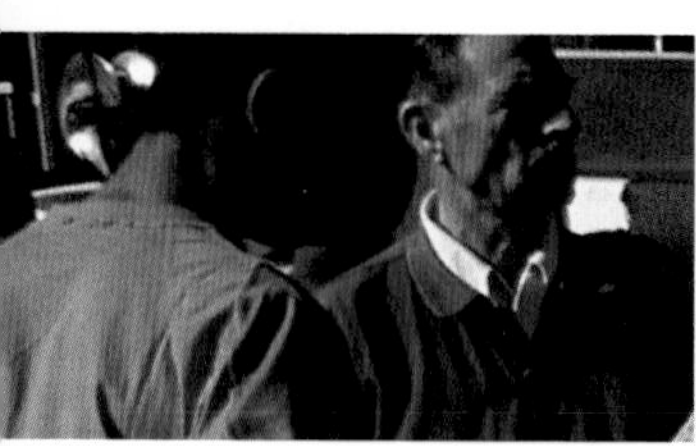

The people of Provence are mostly Mediterranean in temperament and looks, but they also have their own distinct character based on a strong regional identity and sense of independence. After decades of neglect the Provençal language — a symbol of a shared identity — is undergoing a revival.....

The Provençals Who are the real Provençals, and what are they like? Generations of writers and travelers have tried to provide answers and more often than not come up with patronizing generalizations. Victor Hugo considered them typically Mediterranean and hot-blooded ("in Paris one quarrels, in Avignon one kills"), while almost everyone from Stendhal to Lawrence Durrell thought they embodied the *mañana* attitude — lazy, unhurried, ready to put off work until *demain* or (more likely) *après demain*. This reputation is no doubt partly due to the difficulties newcomers experience getting locals to work on their houses — a story line that has been mined from the days of Lady Fortescue (who settled near Grasse in the 1930s) through to Peter Mayle in the 1980s.

Alphonse Daudet was first responsible for portraying the Provençals as whimsical, comic characters through his Tartarin novels, and the enormously popular books and movies of Marcel Pagnol have reinforced this stereotype of the light-hearted, playful Provençal who spends all day doing nothing more serious than playing *boules* and drinking *pastis*.

There may be a grain of truth in these caricatures but in reality Provençals are far more serious and hard-working — although they also know how to enjoy themselves. They also have a reputation for surliness and distrust of outsiders (natural enough, one would think, in a region that has seen so many invasions — including invasion by tourism), but once the ice is broken they become welcoming and hospitable.

In rural areas, villages are bound together by a strong sense of community and old-fashioned values (among the older generation, at least) combined with a healthy respect and love for the Provençal countryside. Although regular church-going is no longer universal, Catholicism is deeply ingrained. Alongside their religious beliefs, the Provençals have retained many customs and rituals, some dating back to antiquity, and a healthy dose of superstitious beliefs.

The Provençal language Although Provençal is no longer widely spoken, the distinctive regional accent is easily recognizable and tells you that you are conversing with a true Provençal — if you can understand what he or she is saying behind the thick nasal twang (where *vin* becomes *ving*, *demain* becomes *demang* and so on) which is often rendered even more incomprehensible by high-speed delivery.

Dual French–Provençal road signs are now common

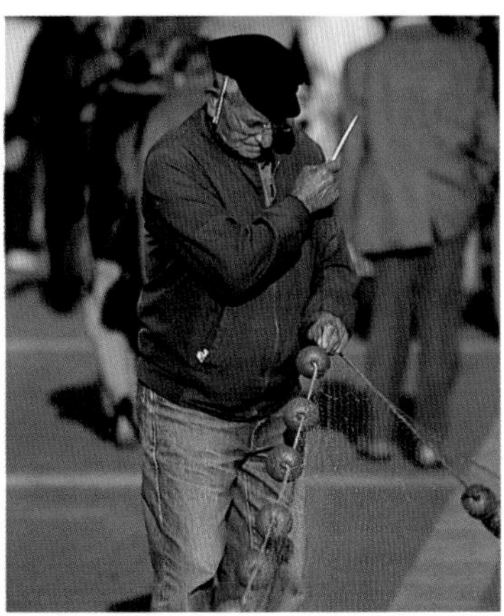

A disappearing lifestyle: fisherman in Bandol

The Provençal language has been in decline since the 16th century, despite the efforts of the poet Mistral, who collated his giant Provençal dictionary and published a popular journal, *L'Aïoli*, in an attempt to revive it in the late 19th century. Today, however, there are signs that the sense of regional identity is becoming stronger once more and Provençal is now an option in many schools. Nearly every rural village now has its name on the road sign in both French and Provençal.

In the postwar years the younger generation deserted many of the old ways, lured away from the traditional lifestyle by the bright lights (and work) in the big cities. But now another generation is taking a far greater interest in their linguistic heritage. Curiously, one of the strangest manifestations of young Provençals seeking out their roots has emerged from Marseille, where learning Provençal has become the latest craze among second-generation immigrants.

Local folklore has become a way of asserting their identity and sense of belonging, a trend that has developed hand in hand with the rise of ragamuffin music — a blend of reggae and rap, into which they sometimes weave old Provençal songs. One local ragamuffin band even starts off its performances with the symbolic rallying cry of "Aïoli!" Mistral would have been both horrified and delighted.

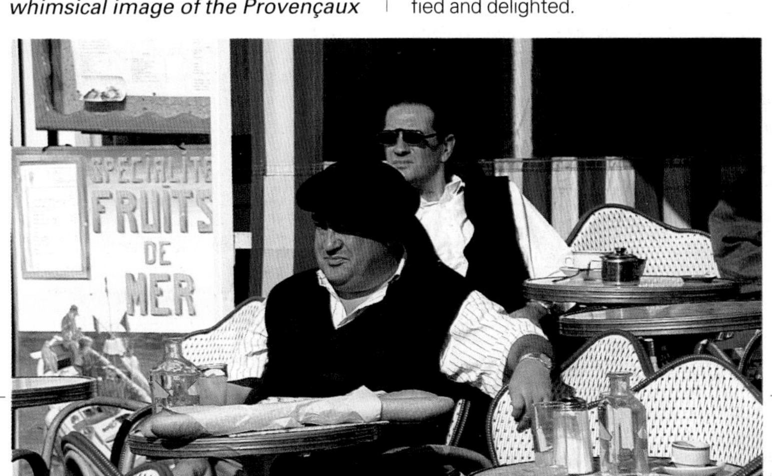

Drinking pastis *all day long — the whimsical image of the Provençaux*

Rural architecture

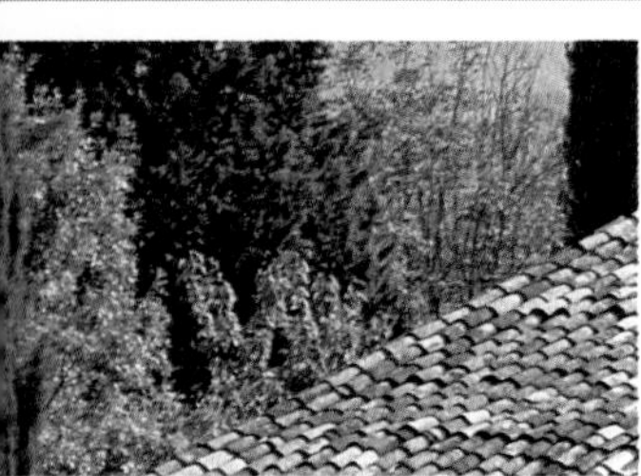

■ In contrast to the futuristic ambitions of public buildings in Nice, Marseille, or Nîmes, in rural areas of Provence one architectural form remains supreme — the Provençal country house. Although it has some elements in common with an Italian villa or a Spanish hacienda, the Provençal country house is as different from these as it is from a Normandy farmhouse.....■

Perfect adaptation The Provençal house has evolved to cope with the often harsh extremes of the climate in this part of France, the strong sunlight of summer and the bitingly cold winter winds. Its thick walls, sometimes buttressed, merge into the terrain and usually have no windows on the north side and just enough openings on the other three sides to let in light. A perfect example of thermal insulation, the house is well designed to stay cool in summer and warm in winter.

In regions where the *mistral* predominates (most of Provence between the Alps, the sea and the Rhône) the house is usually oriented north–south with a slight turn to the east so that the front of the house is sheltered from the northwesterly *mistral*.

Tiled roofs The characteristic curved roof tiles of the Provençal house are Greek in origin. Their shape (which is tapered at one end) probably comes from being molded on the thigh of the potter. Traditionally made by hand, they were fired in the kilns at Aubagne, Biot, Moustiers, Vallauris, and Apt. The Provençal roof is usually finished off with a *génoise*, a double or triple row of tiles embedded under the eaves.

Definitions First of all there is the *mas*, which could mean anything from a country house to a farm or even a barn. Typically, the Provençal *mas* is a large, low-lying farmhouse which sprawls outward and encompasses stables, storerooms, dovecots, and even sheep pens under one roof. It has evolved and been added to over many generations. In the Camargue and the Crau, it was often built around an enclosed courtyard — again, for protection from the *mistral*.

Then there is the *bastide*, which could also be a farm but was more likely to be a country house, with decorative elements such as balconies, exterior stone staircases and sculpted lintels. It was usually two stories high, with a third floor adorned by oval "eyebrow windows" (in Provence known as *oeils de boeuf* — bull's eyes). Unlike the long, low sloping roof of the *mas*, the *bastide* roof had four slopes.

The *bastidon* ("little *bastide*") preserved the same proportions on a smaller scale.

Interiors Inside, the *mas* was often divided in two by a corridor with one side for the owner and the other for the *bayle* (farmer or steward). Terracotta tiles were used on the floors, with roofbeams made from whole treetrunks — left round in *mas*, squared off in the *bastides*.

❑ "In August, in our region, just before evening, a powerful heat sets the fields ablaze. The whitewashed, beaten soil radiated against the low wall of the abandoned sheepfold. The heart of the house remained cool, however. There remained in this retreat some reserves of shade and freshness that were fed at night and which, during the heat of the day, were a great resource." Henri Bosco, *Le Mas Théotime*. ❑

> ❑ "The village mason understands the compass card, the direction of the rains, the orientation of the light, the cardinal points, the character of the people who will come: with all these insights, the mason then builds the house." Jean Giono ❑

A typical example of a mas *(below) and (top) a closeup view of its roof*

As well as wall ovens and open hearths, kitchens nearly always had their *pétrins* (wooden trunks that were used for leavening bread dough) and *panatières* (a wooden cage hung on the wall, used for storing bread), both of which might be elaborately carved in the Arlesian style. Another distinctive Provençal feature is the *radassie* in the drawing-room, a three- or four-seater settee with armrests between the seats.

■ **Farming and forestry still play an essential role in modern Provence. Fields and forests cover nearly 80 percent of the region and support 45,000 farms and smallholdings. Together with secondary industries (such as food-processing), the land provides employment for 15 percent of the working population.....■**

A bountiful harvest One of the strengths of agriculture in Provence is the enormous diversity of the produce grown, a cornucopia that includes lavender from the mountains, chestnuts from the forests, flowers from the greenhouses of the Côte d'Azur, rice from the Camargue, *les primeurs* (early crops of fruits and vegetables) such as cherries, strawberries, melons, asparagus, and peaches from the fertile plains...not to mention sunflowers, olives, grapes, apples, tomatoes.

❏ Provence produces 52 percent of all the olives in France, 50 percent of table grapes, and 30 percent of its melons, tomatoes, and apples.

Changing patterns Despite the buoyant state of agriculture at present, some forecasts predict that by the end of the century the peasant lifestyle will have all but disappeared and that the number of farmers will have halved to just 20,000 or fewer. Pressures from developers, particularly in coastal areas, have forced many farmers off the land — in the Alpes-Maritimes, the number of farmers has declined from 44,000 in 1929 to just 5,200 today. High land costs are another factor, with prices leaping by a third in recent years in some areas (particularly the Var).

Adaptation Agriculture in Provence is having to adapt to competition within the European Union, and to modernize. Greater emphasis is now being placed on food processing (which has a higher added-value), better marketing, on new varieties of fruit and vegetables (there are 12 applied plant-breeding stations in the region) and on other innovations, such as biological pest control to reduce crop losses, and new irrigation schemes.

Other farmers are moving in different directions, many of which are connected to tourism and the realization that the rural environment is a valuable attraction in its own right. Some are restoring old olive oil mills, not only so that they can process oil but also to draw visitors. Others are developing "gourmet routes" through their localities, with farms selling food specialities (*produits de la ferme*). In the Alps, they are even studying the possibility of introducing bison — not only would they be a tourist attraction, but their meat sells at premium prices.

Horticulture The main centers for horticulture in Provence are the Var and the Alpes-Maritimes, which between them grow more than 300 varieties of ornamental plants and cut flowers including mimosa, tulips, roses, carnations, and 30 different types of palm tree.

❏ Provence grows around 172 million roses and 188 million carnations annually, 60 and 90 percent respectively of the total French production. ❏

Viniculture The patchwork of vineyards which give the Provençal countryside its characteristic appeal is also undergoing change, notably the upgrading of vine stocks to

❏ The largest area of vineyards in Provence is in the Vaucluse (144,950 acres), followed by the Var (93,775 acres) and the Bouches-du-Rhône (34,600 acres). ❏

produce better quality wines. In the Bouches-du-Rhône, for instance, ordinary *vin de table* accounted for nearly 70 percent of production 15 years ago; now it is more like 20 percent, with many more vineyards having gained the coveted *Appellation d'Origine Contrôlée* (AOC) status (see also Regional Wines, pages 94–95). Another phenomenon is overseas winemakers buying vineyards in Provence — in the Var alone, nearly 50 *domaines* have recently been taken over by outside investors, injecting new capital and new ideas into this important sector of the economy.

Lavender is one of many crops that Provence produces in abundance

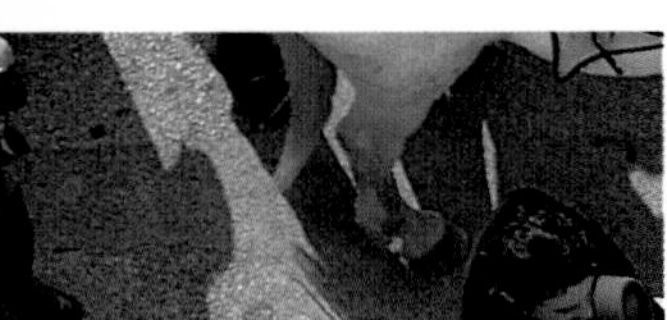

■ With something in the region of 500 festivals encompassing around 4,000 separate events, Provence in the summertime is justifiably called 'The Land of Festivals'. The following is but a sample of the cultural riches the region has to offer.....■

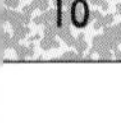

Traditional festivals Many of the traditional village festivals revolve around the natural calendar and the bounty of the earth and the sea. Others have their roots deep in Provençal folklore. Whatever the reason, the day will usually involve a procession of some sort in traditional costumes, accompanied by pipes and drums, culminating in a vast feast with *pastis* and wine flowing freely, when a good time is had by one and all.

❑ In the St. Eloi processions, horses with their bridles and Saracen-style harnesses ablaze with ribbons and pompons pull chariots piled high with wheat, followed by men and boys on horseback and women and children in horse-drawn carts in Provençal costumes. ❑

On May 1 the cowboys of the Camargue, the *gardians*, put on a rodeo in the arena in Arles for the *Fête des Gardians*, while at Pentecost the old sheep migrations between the mountains and the plains are celebrated in the *Fête de la Transhumance* in St-Rémy. St-Tropez has its noisy and ebullient *bravades* on May 16 (in honor of St. Tropez himself) and June 15 (to celebrate seeing off the Spanish fleet in 1637), while on May 24 and 25 gypsies from all over Europe arrive for the *pèlerinage* (pilgrimage) to les Stes-Maries-de-la-Mer.

In June the atmospheric *procession dai limaca* (in thanksgiving for the olive harvest) takes place in Gorbio and the highly colorful Tarasque festival (last weekend in June) unrolls in Tarascon. The Feast of St. John, June 24, is celebrated in numerous villages.

St Eloi is one of the most popular saints in Provence, and festivities in his honor (or those fêting St. Roch, another popular saint) take place between mid-June and early September in dozens of villages.

August sees the *Fête de la Lavande* in Sault, the *Fête du Muscat* in Beaumes-de-Venise, and the *Fête de la Veraison* with medieval pageantry to celebrate the grapes maturing in Châteauneuf-du-Pape. In September the Camargue rice harvest is celebrated in Arles, the apple harvest in Peyruis, and the *vendange* (wine harvest) in numerous towns and villages.

Cultural festivals Provence has numerous outstanding venues which resonate during summer evenings to the classics, jazz, and folk music — or simply act as a superb backdrop to theater and dance performances. What better stage could there possibly be than the grand arenas of Arles and Nîmes, the forecourt of the Palais des Papes in Avignon, or the exquisite Roman theater in Orange? And then there are smaller, more intimate locations — the charming medieval tower which gave Simiane-la-Rotonde its name, the cloisters of the various churches or cathedrals, the enchanting *théâtres de verdure* (open-air "green theaters") set among ruins in Draguignan, Villefranche, and elsewhere. Another dramatic spot is the

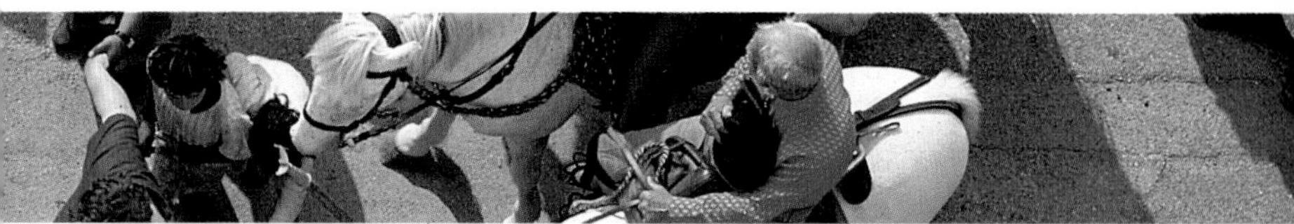

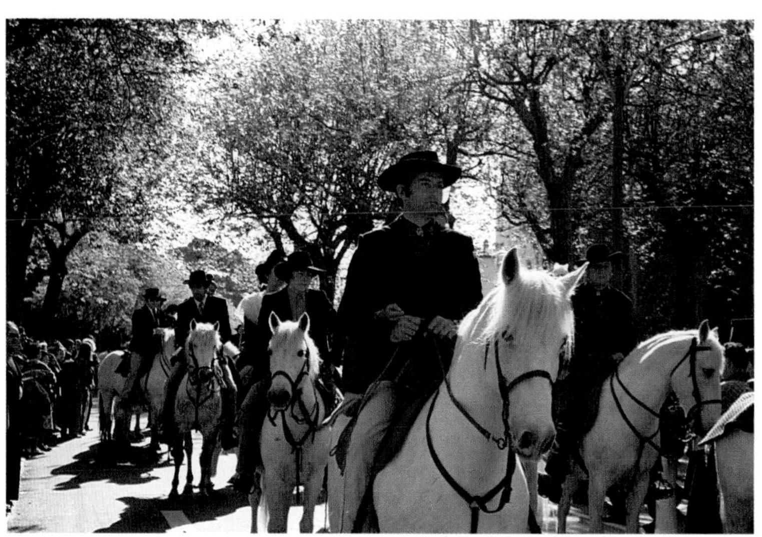

The gardians *of the Camargue parade on their famous white horses*

ruined château in la Tour-d'Aigues, which plays host to the Sud-Lubéron summer festival. Add to this a line-up that includes performers of international caliber and the stage is set for a creative extravaganza which lasts all summer long.

July and August are the busiest months, with jazz festivals in Nice, Toulon, and Aix; an international folklore festival in Cavaillon; theater, jazz, and classical music in Gordes; music, dance, and theater at Fontaine-de-Vaucluse and l'Îsle-sur-la-Sorgue; folklore in Marseille; classical music at the Organa festival in St-Rémy-de-Provence and in Cassis; and early music in Entrevaux and Simiane-la-Rotonde. In Orange, *Les Nuits d'Été du Théâtre Antique* encompasses everything from pop to jazz, with the renowned *Chorégies* (opera and classics) taking place in the same superb setting.

And then there is the big festival in Avignon (with literally hundreds of theater performances, movies and concerts from mid-July onward) as well as dance and photography in Arles.

❑ Over 300 towns and villages have some kind of festival during the summer. Complete listings can be found in the booklet *Provence — Terre de festivals*, available at tourist offices. ❑

■ Tourism plays an essential part in the Provençal economy, as it has done for the last 160 years since foreigners first started vacationing on the Côte d'Azur. Today, around 24 million tourists annually contribute between 36 and 39 billion francs to the region.....■

Early tourism Tourism on the Riviera started in the 1830s when the English aristocracy started building luxury mansions in which to escape the winter fog of England. In the interwar years Coco Chanel popularized sunbathing, and the season switched to the summer — a phenomenon that intensified after World War II with the emergence of mass tourism. By the mid-1970s millions of people were vacationing on the coastline but inland Provence still remained largely unspoiled, discovered only by more adventurous visitors.

Tourism today The Alpes-Maritimes (which includes the Côte d'Azur) is today the most popular destination for foreigners, followed by the Vaucluse, the Bouches-du-Rhône, Var, and the Alpes de Haute-Provence. Conversely, the French (who constitute three fourths of all visitors to Provence) favor the Var and the Alpes de Haute-Provence, followed by the Bouches-du-Rhône, the Vaucluse, and the Alpes-Maritimes — which may tell you something if you want to avoid your own neighbors.

❑ On average around three million people visit the museums of the coast each year, with a third of that total accounted for by the Musée Océanographique in Monaco alone — making it the eighth most popular attraction in the whole of France. ❑

The number of people who visit the Côte d'Azur (just over eight million annually) is equivalent to the number of tourists who visit Greece or the entire Caribbean, and the coast accounts for around 25 billion francs out of total tourism revenues for Provence of between 36 and 39 billion francs. Despite these seductive figures, tourism on the coast is in crisis. There is a huge over capacity of hotel rooms, and the changing patterns of international tourism are also having an effect: due to increased awareness of the dangers of sunbathing, fewer people are taking beach vacations. No longer content simply to fry their brains (*bronzer à idiot* as the French say), vacationers want more things to do, they want better value for money, and they want to experience the real Provence.

Harborside swimming, Monte-Carlo

Cultural tourism is now being more heavily marketed, emphasizing the extraordinary artistic legacy of the Côte d'Azur, which is blessed with no fewer than 80 museums, running the gamut from Impressionist paintings to Picasso and Chagall, perfume and honey to wine and wildlife. Many are being upgraded (such as the recently re-opened Matisse museum in Nice) and new ones are being opened (such as the proposed Musée des Merveilles in Tende).

The tourist industry also suffers from a huge seasonal imbalance, with over three million people coming to Provence in August alone when the French go on holiday. Business tourism is seen as part of the solution — particularly in spreading tourism over a longer period — and it already accounts for around 300,000 people drawn to congresses in state-of-the-art conference facilities such as the Acropolis in Nice or the massive new Centre des Expositions in Monaco, due to open in 1996/7.

The rich natural and cultural heritage has always been the main drawcard in inland Provence, but with increasing numbers of people now wanting to hike, bike, or simply do their own thing discovering the mountains and valley byways, the authorities are eager to tap into this market and promote rural tourism. Since 1990 they have embarked on a coordinated program that includes supplying management expertise for rural communities who want to diversify into tourism. It also provides grants to upgrade hotels and restaurants and for renovating houses in historic villages.

Initiatives such as these are not only good news for rural communities but also point the way forward for better quality tourism and a sustainable future for this important sector of the Provençal economy.

Tourism is now a big money-spinner in coastal resorts

■ Horror stories of the polluted Côte d'Azur were once commonplace but the seas are once again safe to swim in. The challenge now is managing conflicting demands on the coastline — such as recreation, aquaculture and development — and maintaining the health of marine ecosystems. At the same time, Provençe is mobilizing its marine industries to place itself at the forefront of global developments in undersea technology.....■

The coast Huge efforts have been made to clean up beaches in recent years and the quality of bathing water has improved enormously, although, given the fact that the Mediterranean is an enclosed sea, Provence is still dependent on neighboring countries taking similar action. A large proportion of beaches on the coast have been awarded the European Blue Flag. To achieve this, they must not only pass the strictest water quality controls but also meet required standards in 25 other areas (such as having safe access, lifeguards, first aid posts, and so on). Around Nice an astonishing 22 beaches have been awarded the Blue Flag, as have at least 24 in the Antibes area — but if the big public beaches are not your cup of tea there are plenty of secluded coves to be discovered where the water quality is also excellent.

❏ The first experimental fish farm was instituted at the Paul Ricard Oceanographic Institute on the Ile des Embiez, where they now breed half-a-million sea bass annually. The Institute was also the first to develop microbacteria that eat crude oil — knowledge that was put to good use in the *Exxon Valdez* disaster in Alaska in 1989. ❏

Mussels are now farmed extensively

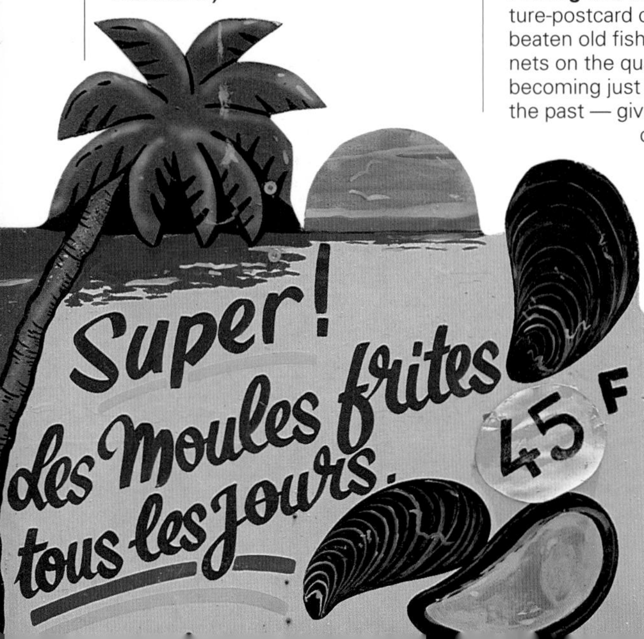

Fishing and aquaculture The picture-postcard cliché of the weather-beaten old fisherman mending his nets on the quayside is in danger of becoming just that — a snapshot of the past — given the decline in the coastal fishing in Provence. In the Var, for instance, there are now only 300 fishing boats left. Overfishing, lack of investment, and EU directives to reduce fishing fleets have all had an impact. Faced with declining catches, many fishermen are now turning to fish-farming. At present, there are just

Clean seas have become a major priority for Provençal authorities

over 20 fish farms but there is enormous potential for aquaculture in Provence, with plenty of suitable coastal sites. The most popular species are sea bass and sea bream (both of which taste no different from their "wild" cousins) and mussels.

Marine parks Provence has so far only one official marine park, the 750-acre Côte Bleue reserve offshore from Carry-le-Rouet, west of Marseille. Many more are needed to act as nurseries to replenish declining fish populations. Since 1989, ten marine species in danger of extinction have been protected, and there is a five-year moratorium (until 1997) on catching black groupers of which very few remain (these big fish have been the victims of overzealous spear fishermen for decades).

❑ COMEX, based in Marseille, is acknowledged as a world leader in offshore engineering and underwater robotics. They have recently developed a hydrogen mixture, called heliox, which allows divers to reach hitherto undreamt of depths of between 1,000 feet and 2,150 feet underwater. ❑

Marine research Provence is one of the world's leading research centers for ocean engineering, with 54 companies in this area alone. In total nearly 300 enterprises are involved in marine technology, with projects ranging from the manufacturing of remote-control deep-sea robots, catamarans, or passenger submarines to submarine cable maintainance and the development of pollution-control techniques.

■ **The sunny South of France has allied itself with America's Golden State and, despite the huge cultural differences between these two high-profile regions, it is with some justification that Provence likes to think of itself as "the California of Europe".....** ■

A far-flung alliance On May 6, 1991 an agreement was signed in Sacramento, twinning Provence-Alpes-Côte d'Azur (PACA) with California, a union based on similarities in climate, technological development, industry, agriculture, and tourism. Some of these connections may seem far-fetched to a Provençal peasant tending his vineyards or an Angelino cruising down Sunset Boulevard (although Hollywood was twinned with Cannes long ago) but the twinning has already borne fruit in the form of exchanges in research, training, technology, and other areas — including waste management and hydroelectric power. Strategically, PACA sees itself as the southern gateway to the European Union in the same way that California is the gateway to the Pacific basin.

Science parks Launched in the 1970s, Sophia-Antipolis (Greek for "city of wisdom" — the new Antibes) was France's first science park and is still the largest in the country. Covering 12,500 acres in the landscaped hills behind Antibes, it is going to expand by half as much again. Currently there are around 980 enterprises in this futuristic complex, employing 16,000 people: this is expected to reach 1,500 businesses with a total of 30,000 employees by the year 2010. In addition to the multinational companies working in high-technology areas such as telecommunications, biotechnology, and robotics, Sophia-Antipolis has training and research centers specializing in solar energy, molecular biology, and information sciences.

Although it was Sophia-Antipolis that

❏ If you are flying into Provence on a European airline, there is a good chance your airline reservation will have been routed through one of Sophia-Antipolis' huge computer systems: not only is it the global reservation center for 15,000 Air France terminals worldwide, but it is also the home of Amadeus, the giant computer network which links together passenger reservations for SAS, Lufthansa, Air France and Iberia. ❏

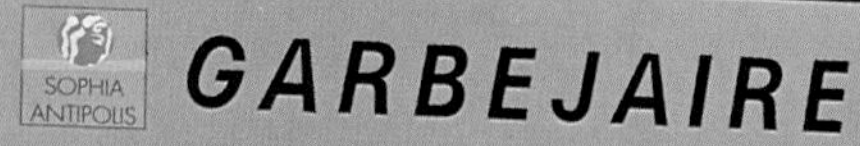

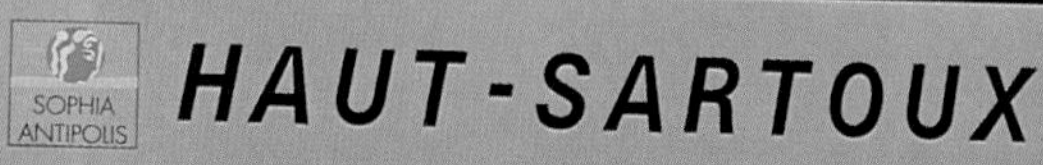

Signposts point the way to the future in Sophia-Antipolis

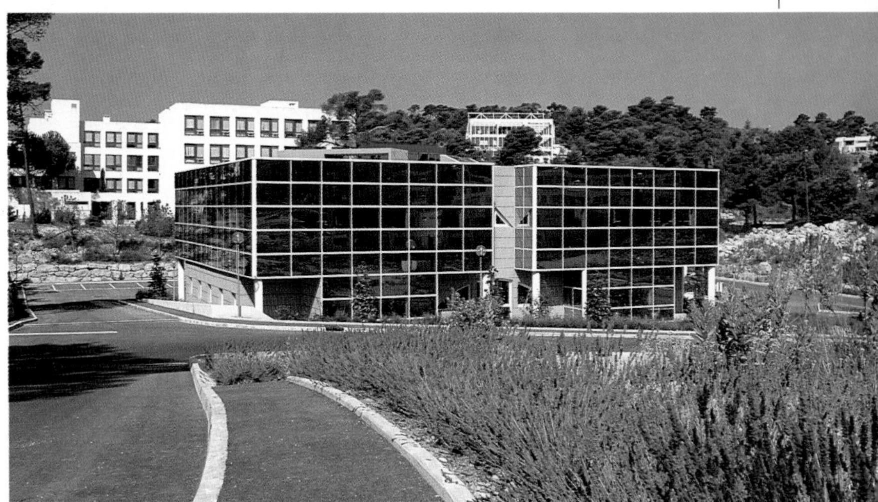

first sparked the comparisons with California's Silicon Valley, in fact Provence now has five other major science and technology parks. These are on the outskirts of Marseille, Toulon, Aix, Manosque, and Avignon. With all this activity, it is perhaps not surprising to discover that Provence is classed as the most important region in the country for high-technology research outside Paris. It has the fastest growth rate for business creation in France, especially in the high-tech fields, and currently numbers more than 8,000 research workers and 18,000 research technicians.

Ultimately, the regional authorities aim to link the six science parks together into a powerful network which will propel the region along the so-called "high technology route" to future prosperity. Since the creation in 1987 of the southern European "high technology route," which links together eight of the most dynamic regions around the Mediterranean, the planners are confident that Provence will fulfill its intention of becoming the technological heart of southern Europe.

Sophia-Antipolis is the largest science park in France

❑ The six main science parks and their specializations are:

Sophia-Antipolis: electronics, telecommunications, information technology.
Toulon-Var-Technopole: mechanical and acoustic engineering.
Marseille-Provence-Technopole: robotics, biotechnology, electronics.
Manosque-Cadarache: industrial robotics, chemical analysis.
Avignon-Montfavet-Agroparc: agrotechnologies.
Arbois-Europole: information sciences, electronics. ❑

■ Dances such as the *farandole* are an important part of the Provençal identity, and not just something staged for tourists' cameras. Similarly, the folk art of making *santons* (little saints) is rooted in ancient traditions.....■

Dances and costumes Traditional costumes are often worn during village fêtes and festivals. For women, the costume consists of a full skirt and a long-sleeved, black blouse over which a pleated shirt or lace shawl is worn. There are several different types of headgear (usually embellished with lace, velvet, or delicate embroidery), always worn on top of a high bun. For men, a white shirt is set off by a lace tie or ribbon and a velvet waistcoat, with canvas pants supported by a wide woolen belt. They can wear either black felt hats with raised brims or a straw hat.

The best-known Provençal dance is the *farandole*, which is performed by young men and women in traditional costume at village festivals. It is accompanied by a six-beat rhythm on the *tambourin*, a small drum made from calfskin and decorated with colored ribbons or cords. The *tambourinaire* hangs the tambourine on his right side and with his left hand he holds a small three-holed flute known as the *gaboulet* with which he plays a piercing tune.

Santons Nativity scenes with small figures known as *santons* (little saints) first appeared in Provence in the 17th century and were originally made from wood, wax or cork. When churches were closed after the Revolution, a potter from Marseille, Jean-Louis Lagnel, conceived the idea of mass-producing *santons* in clay, so that every family could have a Christmas crèche. Soon the range of figurines produced came to include Provençal characters (the innkeeper, the shepherd, the baker, and so on) bringing their gifts to the Christ child, with the nativity setting transposed to a typical Provençal village. Today, *santonniers* still make these traditional figures, usually in clay (sometimes in wood), often with hand-painted finishes and wearing miniature costumes.

Santons *are a Provençal tradition*

PROVENCE WAS

■ The first traces of human habitation in Provence are found, curiously enough, in some of the Côte d'Azur's most sophisticated resorts — this coastal area must have appealed as much to Cro-Magnon man as it does to visitors today.....■

❑ There are no cave paintings in Provence to compare with those at Lascaux in the Dordogne, but in 1991 a local diver discovered a partially submerged cave in one of the *calanques* near Cassis with a number of paintings (depicting horses, bison, and deer) thought to be around 20,000 years old. It has to be said, however, that these may yet prove to be a hoax – see panel, page 123. ❑

Early hunters The earliest evidence of settlements in Provence dates back 400,000 years and comes from the site known as Terra Amata, just behind the old port in Nice. Unearthed in 1966, Terra Amata revealed several encampments built by Cro-Magnon man: these nomadic hunters had found the perfect spot for a camp at the mouth of the Vallée de Paillon, where there was a freshwater spring next to a small, sheltered beach. Primarily hunters of deer and elephant, the inhabitants built small, circular huts from branches, each with its own central hearth. Paleolithic remnants have also been found near Menton, notably the skull of "Menton man" which is believed to date back around 30,000 years. The skeletons were covered in sea shells and necklaces, coinciding with the first use of burial grounds in the late paleolithic period.

From hunters to shepherds During the neolithic era, beginning around 6000B.C., there was a shift toward growing crops and the domestication of wild sheep. The people who lived

The first Greek settlers landed at Massalia (Marseille) in 600B.C.

Ligurian legacy: carving in Vallée des Merveilles and (top) bories

in Provence at this time are known as the Ligurians, although their origins are uncertain. Some say they arrived from the east, others from the Iberian peninsula. Either way, during the neolithic and the Bronze Age which followed, the Ligurians started to build villages, constructing dry-stone huts known as *bories* and trading with the outside world. Although none of the *bories* that survive today is this old, the Ligurians left huge standing stones (dolmens) and the impressive rock engravings of the Vallée des Merveilles.

Arrival of the Celts and the Greeks

Sometime between the 8th and the 4th centuries B.C. the Celtic tribes began descending on Provence, bringing with them iron tools and building the first of their fortified hilltop settlements or *oppidi*. Intermarrying with the local Ligurians, the Celts started to build up powerful alliances and gradually trading links across the Mediterranean region began to blossom, particularly with Asia Minor.

❑ Greek traders from the island of Rhodes are attributed with having given Provence's greatest river its current name: *Rhodéenne* is an adjective still in use to describe the plains alongside the Rhône. ❑

Driven by the desire to establish new trading colonies, and by the depletion of their agricultural lands, Phocaeans (they came from Phocis in Asia Minor) set up their first Greek settlements at Massalia (Marseille) around 600B.C., providing a bridgehead for the arrival of Greek civilization on the European mainland. The Celto-Ligurians welcomed the Greeks as trading partners, exchanging metals (such as copper, gold, tin, and silver) and foodstuffs for Greek vases and other artifacts.

The Greeks introduced the cultivation of cherries, olives, figs, walnuts, and vines (although vines and olives were both already present in Provence, neither had been cultivated to yield fruit). The Greeks confined themselves to trading up the Rhône and the Durance and along the coast, setting up a series of ports such as Antipolis (Antibes), Athenopolis (St-Tropez), Citharista (la Ciotat), Nikaia (Nice), and Olbia (Hyères).

The peaceful arrival of the Greeks was not to be repeated when the Romans descended on Provence with full military force in the second century B.C. They stayed for about 600 years and their legacy is a series of monuments that are unparalleled elsewhere in Northern Europe outside Italy.....

The cohorts march in After Rome had conquered Spain in 206B.C., securing the land route across Provence was the next priority. They were given the perfect excuse in 124B.C. when the Greeks of Massalia appealed for help against the Celto-Ligurian Salyens, who were threatening them from their base at Entremont. The Romans came in force, with Sextius Calvinus leading a whole army to pacify the Salyens. Once that had been achieved, the Romans decided to stay permanently, founding their first settlement in Provence at Aquae Sextiae, the present city of Aix-en-Provence.

A Roman bust, Vaison-la-Romaine

The Roman "Provincia" In 118B.C. Narbonne was founded and became the capital of the Roman territory, which extended from the Pyrenees to the Alps and north as far as Lyon.

Roman remains at St-Rémy-de-Provence

Only the Alpes-Maritimes were left more or less under Phocaean control. This new province (or *Provincia*, from where the present-day name of Provence derives) was known as *Gallia Narbonensis*.

The barbarian invasions Rome's stranglehold on southern Gaul was not yet complete. From 115B.C. onward the region was subject to attacks by several northern tribes, most notably the Teutoni. They were finally defeated by Marius in a battle below Montagne Ste-Victoire near Aix in 102B.C.

❑ After the defeat of the Teutoni pockets of local resistance to Roman rule continued through until 14B.C., when the last of the Alpine tribes were subdued. This final subjugation of the *Provincia* was marked by the building of the *Trophée des Alpes* at la Turbie, a monumental symbol of Roman power. ❑

The downfall of Massalia In the civil wars that followed the conquest of Gaul by Julius Caesar in 51B.C., the inhabitants of Massalia made a huge mistake in not taking the side of Caesar against Pompey. In 49B.C. Caesar took his revenge by laying siege to the city and ruining its trade, stripping Massalia of its territory

along the coast of the Alpes-Maritimes. Caesar promoted Arelate (Arles) in its place, and before long Massalia was also eclipsed by Aix, Nîmes, and Fréjus.

❑ The main settlements during this era developed alongside the major Roman roads (the Via Agrippa, which went north through Avignon and Orange from Arles, and the Via Aurelia, which linked Italy with Arles via Cimiez, Fréjus, and Aix) and in the Rhône valley. ❑

Pax Romana The next 400 years saw the blossoming of Roman civilization in Provence, particularly under the Emperor Augustus, Caesar's great-nephew. Augustus established colonies, ruled by veteran legionnaires, in Apt, Arles, Avignon, Carpentras, Digne, Fréjus, Glanum, Riez, and Vaison. These settlements grew into prosperous cities with baths, theaters, arenas, aqueducts, temples, and bridges. Arts and culture thrived, and Provence paid its way by supplying the Roman Empire with grain, oil, and even ships.

Early Christianity Legend has it that Christianity arrived on the shores of Provence with the "boat of Bethany" (see page 141), and St. Trophimus is also said to have arrived in Arles at around the same time. Christianity received a major boost under the Emperor Constantine and the first Church council was held in Arles in A.D.314. About a hundred years later, the great monasteries of the Îles de Lérins and St-Victor in Marseille were founded.

Top: Pont du Gard. Below: the theater at Vaison-la-Romaine

Dark Ages to feudalism

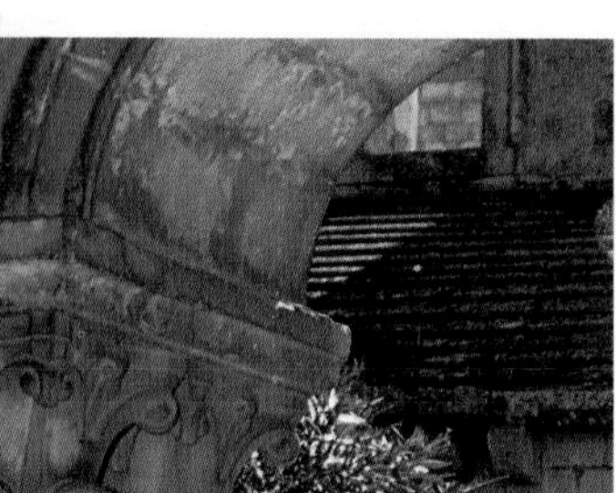

■ After the collapse of the western Roman empire in the 5th century, Provence suffered from numerous invasions and went through a period of anarchy and decline. Once the invaders had been driven out, a period of stability followed, during which troubadours roamed between the powerful courts of the local *seigneurs* and Romanesque architecture flourished. But feudal squabbles continued.....■

Wars and bloodshed Since the beginning of the 5th century the Visigoths had been making raids on Arles, and by the time the Roman empire disintegrated they were in control of all the land south of the Durance. At the same time the Burgundians had established their domination to the east and north. Neither of these new overlords lasted long, since they were ousted by the Ostrogoths from Italy. In turn, they were succeeded in A.D.536 by the Franks, who carved up the territory into semi-autonomous regions. During these troubled times life was hard in Provence, with land being appropriated and populations declining through bloodshed, famine, and disease.

The time of the troubadours was a golden age for Provence

Saracen invasions The 8th century saw the emergence of the Islamic powers, with Arab armies sweeping up through Spain and over the Pyrenees into France. The Arabs (or Saracens, as they became generally known) got as far north as Poitiers before being defeated by the Frankish General Charles Martel in 732. Martel took advantage of the Saracen retreat to sweep down through Provence between 736 and 740 to reassert Frankish control, mercilessly sacking Avignon, Marseille, and Aix. Provence was once more under Frankish rule, and by the end of the century had been integrated into the empire of Charlemagne.

With the demise of Charlemagne's empire in 843, Provence passed through the hands of various rulers before being made in 855 into a kingdom, which also encompassed territory farther north in the Rhône basin (such as Lyon). This was of little help to the Provençals, who still had to contend with invasion by the Normans in 859 and the constant threat from the Saracens.

The Counts of Provence A new age of stability and prosperity dawned in Provence when Guillaume le Libérateur (William the Liberator) finally expelled the Saracens in 1032. Provence began to develop its independence during the years that followed, with the local lords

❑ After their rout by Martel, the Saracens switched tactics. They harassed Provence from the coast, successfully establishing several outlaw bases (notably at la Garde-Freinet in the Massif des Maures, from where they terrorized the surrounding countryside for around 200 years) and laid siege to Marseille in 838 and Arles in 842. ❑

(*seigneurs*) controlling their own fiefdoms. The country began to emerge from the Dark Ages, helped along by the Benedictine monasteries that became centers of learning, and agriculture and vineyards thrived. With the Mediterranean no longer controlled by the Saracens, trade links grew (particularly with Spain, Italy, and the Orient) and the Rhône became a major artery for commerce with northern Europe, leading to increased wealth for Marseille, Arles, Avignon, and Orange. Commerce on the coast benefited enormously from the Crusades, which started in 1095. In the courts of the feudal barons, the troubadours made their first appearance. These roaming entertainers were welcomed in the baronial castles where they performed popular songs of the day, usually about love.

In 1125 Occitania was divided up between the counts of Toulouse (who ruled west of the Rhône and north of the Durance) and the counts of Barcelona (who controlled most of the land south of the Durance). However, the never-ending game of shifting alliances and squabbles between fiefdoms continued. The counts of Forcalquier fought on, as did the notorious *seigneurs* of les Baux.

Les Baux was a powerful feudal stronghold in the 12th century

❑ Linguists call the language spoken between the Alps and the Pyrenees at this time the *langue d'oc*, to distinguish it from the *langue d'oïl* which was the dialect in the north of France (*oc* and *oïl* were the words for "yes" in each region). The *langue d'oc* spread across the whole of southern France, an area dubbed Occitania. Provençal was one of many regional dialects spoken within Occitania. ❑

Union with France

■ Under the House of Anjou, Provence drew closer to France but was still largely autonomous. During the 14th century the popes settled in Avignon, but by the beginning of the 15th century the popes had gone and in 1481 the last of the Angevins bequeathed his kingdom to France, heralding the end of independent Provence.....■

The House of Anjou Count Raymond-Bérenger V of Barcelona managed to bring some degree of stability to the warring fiefdoms in Provence during the 13th century, and imposed a unified system of law and administration based on Catalan practice. Several of his daughters made illustrious marriages. The most important was the union in 1246 of his youngest daughter, Beatrice, to Charles of Anjou, brother of the French king (later St. Louis). Charles became Count of Provence when Beatrice inherited the region from her father, and this ushered in nearly 200 years of Angevin rule.

At the beginning of the 13th century the French had embarked on a crusade against the Cathars in Languedoc (a heretical Christian sect otherwise known as the Albigenses), sacking Avignon into the bargain as punishment for loyalty to Toulouse (see page 52). The Counts of Toulouse were forced to turn over their territories north of Avignon, the Comtat Venaissin, to placate King Louis IX. In 1274 France handed over the Comtat Venaissin to the Holy See in Rome, an event that was to lead to an extraordinary era in Provençal history.

❏ Under the Angevins the boundaries of Provence changed. Sault, Gap, les Baux, and Marseille were brought into the fold, while Nice, Puget-Théniers, and Barcelonnette became part of the Duchy of Savoy (and remained so for nearly 500 years). ❏

The Avignon popes In 1309 Pope Clement V decided to shift the center of papal power away from strife-torn Italy closer to his native France. He moved to Carpentras in the Comtat Venaissin, and his successor, Pope John XXII, moved the papal

René of Anjou's castle at Tarascon

court to Avignon in 1316, beginning more than 100 years of what the Italians called "the Babylonian Captivity." It was indeed a time of avarice and debauchery but the city also witnessed a flowering of the arts and culture, the founding of the university, and the construction of dozens of churches and chapels as well as the grandiose Palais des Papes. Started by the third pope, Benedict XII, this was greatly expanded by his successor, Clement VI, who was also responsible for buying Avignon from Queen Joan. Altogether seven popes presided over this glittering court before the papacy reverted to Rome.

The last of the Angevins While the popes at Avignon feuded with Rome, the rest of the country was suffering a succession of disasters, notably the first great plague (1348) and political instability and wars brought about by the death of Queen Joan in 1382. A semblance of normality returned under Louis II of Anjou, and on his death in 1434 sovereignty was transferred to René of Anjou, who passed into popular legend as Good King René.

❑ One of the greatest blows to Provençal cultural autonomy was the hated Edict of Villers-Cotterêts, passed by François I in 1539: this decreed that French would henceforth be the official language in schools, churches, and the administration. It dealt a death blow to the Provençal language and is still cited today by Provençal nationalists. ❑

Top: detail, Palais des Papes, Avignon. Above: Pope Benedict XII

Union with France René's heir, his nephew Charles III, inherited the throne in 1480 but died a year later without an heir, bequeathing Provence to Louis XI of France. In 1482 the *parlement* in Aix approved the union but the French monarch immediately set about eroding the powers of the Provençal *États-Généraux* (States General), beginning a process of assimilation which signalled the end of an independent Provence.

In the face of Provençal opposition the French crown was forced to take a more conciliatory line because the region was still a crucial buffer zone with Italy. In 1486 a treaty was signed, designed to ensure the autonomy of Provence and its legal institutions and local customs. This was gradually weakened by successive edicts, however, and Provence surrendered its autonomy to the centralized state. Union swiftly became unification.

■ During the 16th century the reformist ideas of Calvin took a firm hold in Provence, where Protestantism became a symbol of rebellion against royal control as much as it was a protest against the old Catholic order. Repression was followed by a further loss of autonomy for Provence — and the third and deadliest outbreak of the plague.....■

The Vaud heresy The Vaudois were the first sect to suffer the wrath of the established church against Protestantism. The Vaudois lived quietly in the villages of the Petit Lubéron until the 1540s, when the *parlement* at Aix ordered a crackdown. During five days in April 1545 blood ran through the village streets as 3,000 people were massacred and 600 sent to the gallows.

This was the beginning of half-a-century or more of bloodshed and mayhem as the Catholic church resisted the "heretical" ideas of the Reformation.

The spread of Protestantism Calvin's doctrines appealed to the Provençals not only as a reaction to the bloated Church hierarchy but also as an expression of opposition to the French state. Reformers sacked the cathedral in Orange, destroyed the abbey at St-Gilles, and pillaged churches throughout Haute Provence. The backlash brought more violence (with massacres at Barjols, Sisteron, and Orange) and atrocities continued until the arrival of the plague in 1580 put a temporary stop to hostilities.

Trouble continued to ferment when the Huguenot Henri de Navarre became heir to the

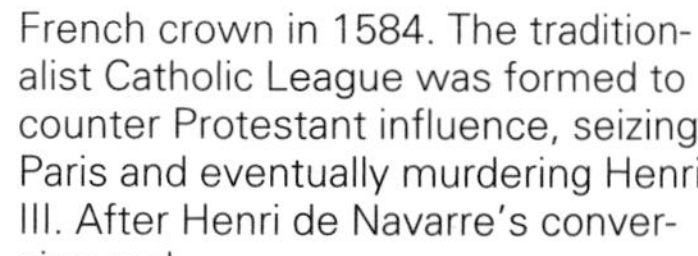

French crown in 1584. The traditionalist Catholic League was formed to counter Protestant influence, seizing Paris and eventually murdering Henri III. After Henri de Navarre's conversion and

Fort St-Nicolas, a symbol of Louis XIV's power over Marseille

❑ Outside the cities and ports, Provence stagnated. In the countryside the peasantry eked out a living based on cereals, sheep, vines, and the recently introduced art of raising silkworms, which provided the raw material for a nascent textile industry. ❑

accession to the throne (as Henri IV) he issued the Edict of Nantes, in 1598, which guaranteed the right of worship to Protestants.

Louis XIII and Louis XIV With the assassination of Henri IV in 1610, Louis XIII came to the throne and the influence of the French state increased under the statesmanship of Cardinal Richelieu, who further whittled away the powers of the regions. Richelieu overrode the *parlement* in Aix by imposing his own agents, the *intendants*, who collected taxes and had control over military and fiscal affairs. The *États-Généraux* (States General), having resisted contributing to the royal purse, were simply banned from holding parliamentary assemblies.

Dissension continued, notably in Marseille which rebelled in 1659: Louis XIV quickly repressed the uprising, and built the Fort St-Nicolas so he could monitor what he called "*ce peuple violent et libertin.*" (these violent and libertine people). In 1685 Louis XIV revoked the Edict of Nantes, and thousands of Protestants fled fearing reprisals.

❑ The Vaudois' beliefs originated with Pierre Valdo, who had founded a sect in Lyon as a reaction against the excesses of the avaricious papacy. Drawing on elements of Manichaeism (which had also been central to the Cathar heresy), they preached poverty and a rejection of the ecclesiastical hierarchy. ❑

Above: victims of the 1720 plague
Top: members of Louis XIV's family

Early 18th century Despite his hostility toward Marseille, Louis XIV made it a free port and at the beginning of the 18th century it prospered in trade with the Near East. Unfortunately this also led to the third and worst outbreak of the plague in 1720, carried by a ship from the East, during which 100,000 died in Provence — 50,000 from Marseille alone, half the population of the city.

Maritime commerce also led to the creation of great wealth and the construction of some of the magnificent *hôtels particuliers* (private mansions) in Avignon, Aix, and Marseille. A boom in shipbuilding (principally in Marseille, Toulon and la Ciotat) led to massive deforestation of areas such as Mont Ventoux.

The Revolution and after

■ The upheavals of the Revolution and its aftermath were as keenly felt in Provence as they were elsewhere in France. Despite hopes to the contrary, under the First Republic ancient "Provence" disappeared as an entity in its own right as new *départements* were created .....■

Discontent and Revolution The decadence of the Sun King's court, followed by corruption and the abuse of privileges under Louis XV and Louis XVI, led to widespread discontent throughout France where the economic gap between rich and poor was creating hardship, unemployment, and famine. Provence was no exception, particularly since the loss of the silk harvest and a steep drop in the price of wine in 1787. The following year, a heavy frost wiped out a large percentage of the olive groves in the region, and in 1789 there was widespread rioting over the price of bread. As the Bastille was being stormed in July 1789, the people of Provence followed suit and looted and pillaged châteaux and churches. Guillotines were set up in the streets of Marseille, and aristocrats were lynched in Aix.

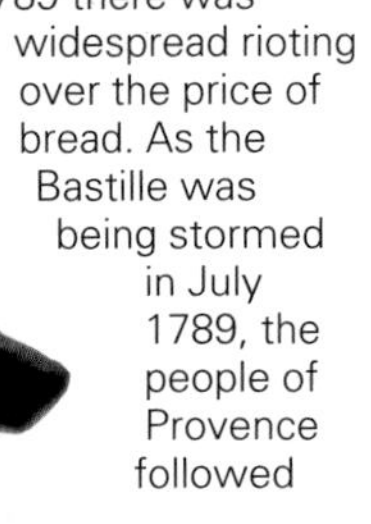

❑ In 1792 the *Féderés* (National Guard) from outlying regions were summoned to Paris to defend it from counter-revolutionaries. Five hundred Marseillaise marched to the capital singing Rouget de Lisle's *Hymn to the Army of the Rhine* (composed for the war against Germany several months earlier). This stirring song instantly became known as the *Marseillaise*, now France's national anthem. ❑

The aftermath The enthusiastic reception for the Revolution in Provence was partly because the Provençals hoped to regain privileges lost during the preceding centuries. Unfortunately the Jacobin-dominated National Assembly proved to be even more centralist than the *ancien régime*. In 1790, local government was dissolved and the region divided into three *départements*: the Bouches-du-Rhône (capital, Aix and after 1800 Marseille); the Var (capital, Toulon) and the Basses-Alpes (capital, Digne). A year later the Vaucluse was created and in 1793 the annexation of Nice led to the addition of the Alpes-Maritimes.

In the White Terror unleashed in 1795 following the execution of Robespierre, thousands died in Provence, as elsewhere. After

Napoléon (left) brought defeat to the English fleet in Toulon (top) when it came to the aid of the Royalists

Napoléon's surprise *coup d'état* in 1799 order was restored but Provençals showed little enthusiasm for the Napoleonic wars that followed. With the defeat of Napoléon in his Russian campaign, Provence also lost much of the Alpes-Maritimes *département,* which was handed over to Sardinia at the Congress of Vienna in 1814.

A year later, Napoléon escaped from exile on Elba and marched up through Provence before being conclusively defeated at Waterloo and sent further afield, to remote St. Helena. The restoration of the Bourbons after Waterloo led to further bloodshed between royalists and republicans in Provence, but their eventual replacement on the French throne in 1830 by the "Citizen King," Louis-Philippe, created little interest in the south, which had endured its share of civil unrest and tumult.

Thousands died in Provence after Robespierre's execution

France's national flag, originally from Martigues

The 1848 Revolution Continuing discontent over harsh economic conditions led to the overthrow of Louis-Philippe and the creation of the Second Republic in 1848. This was supported in Provence, but the election of Louis-Napoléon in 1850 and his subsequent coronation as emperor was bitterly contested. Many areas, particularly in the Provençal Alps, turned once more to armed revolt. In the reprisals that followed thousands were shot or deported.

❑ As well as the national anthem, France also acquired its national flag from Provence during the Revolution. The red, white and blue tricolor adopted by the revolutionaries had previously been the flag of the small town of Martigues, west of Marseille. ❑

Changing pace

■ Improved communications and economic growth began to transform Provence as it emerged from isolation in the 19th century. The discovery of the Riviera coastline, first by aristocratic tourists, then by writers and artists, placed it firmly on the international map. Although development was brought to a halt by two world wars, the pattern had been set for the 20th century.....■

Rural depopulation In the second half of the 19th century the foundations were laid for profound changes in the pattern of life in Provence. Marseille rose to become France's premier port largely due to a booming trade with the newly acquired colonies (such as Algeria) and the Far East after the opening of the Suez Canal in 1869. Traditional industries, such as sugar refining and the manufacture of "Marseille soap," expanded alongside new activities such as shipbuilding.

Although Provence remained essentially rural in nature, increased economic activity was already starting to affect village life. Migrations to the cities began, and land was turned over, for example, to horticulture in the Var and orchards in the Rhône valley. Extensive vineyards were planted, although the devastating onslaught of phylloxera in the 1870s destroyed vast areas. The development of light industries signaled the end of many traditional rural activities such as silk production, tanning, and dyeing.

❑ The arrival of the railway along the coastline in the 1860s, connecting Paris with Marseille and Italy, marked the real beginning of the winter tourist season on the Côte d'Azur. ❑

W. Somerset Maugham, one of the postwar crowd

Writers and artists Provence also witnessed a linguistic and literary revival under the auspices of the Félibrige, founded by Frédéric Mistral and a group of like-minded poets and writers in 1854. Harking back to the "golden age" of the troubadours, the Félibrige mounted a spirited defense of Provençal culture in the face of constant erosion by the French state.

Early 20th century This saw an acceleration of demographic changes, such as rural depopulation and the arrival of immigrants from around the Mediterranean to work in the coastal cities. The economic gap between the booming coastal region and deprived inland areas increased.

A second generation of artists (among them Matisse, Dufy, Bonnard, Derain, and Vlaminck) descended on the coast, exchanging gray northern skies for the dazzling Mediterranean light. The *belle*

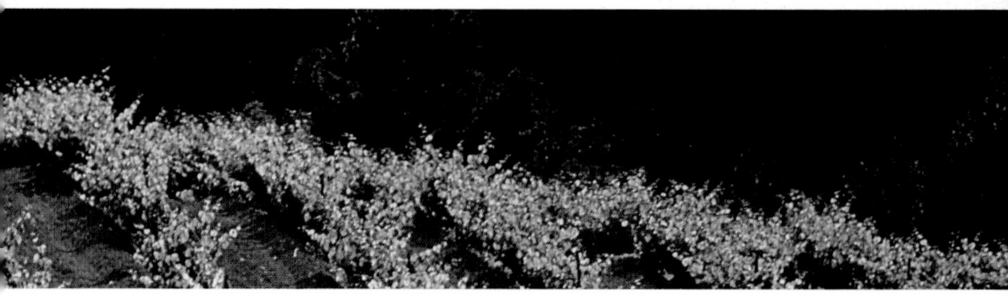

époque mansions of the Côte d'Azur marked a new era in architecture, financed by the thriving tourism industry. The effects of World War I were largely felt in the north of France but conscription drained Provençal villages of their already dwindling manpower. After the war tourism was quickly reestablished and a new wave of talent (in the form of writers and *literati* such as Gertrude Stein, Anaïs Nin, Somerset Maugham, Katherine Mansfield and others) discovered the joys of the Riviera high life. Picasso and Jean Cocteau also spent time on the coast.

World War II During World War II Provence was part of the "free" zone controlled by the Vichy government in the south, but once the Allied counteroffensive began in 1942, the Germans marched on Marseille and Toulon. Resistance groups were particularly active in the Vaucluse and the Provençal Alps, where reprisals and deportations followed their courageous harassment of enemy forces.

❑ At this time Provence's greatest artist, Paul Cézanne, was painting the landscapes around his home town of Aix or on the coast at l'Estaque near Marseille. Van Gogh came south to capture the brilliance of the southern light on canvas — and eventually to go mad and be hospitalized, first in Arles and then in St-Rémy. ❑

Two months after the D-Day landings on the beaches of Normandy in 1944, the Allied forces landed on the beaches between St-Raphaël and St-Tropez. Within a month they had swept the Germans back and by September 15 most of Provence had been liberated.

Cézanne's house and studio, Aix

Recovery and growth

■ Provence was slow to recover from World War II. With the arrival of mass tourism on the Riviera and the establishment of heavy industries near Marseille, the economy picked up, but growth was still largely confined to the coast. Mass immigrations led to the emergence of unsavory right-wing political groups.....■

Postwar years World War II had taken a heavy toll on the infrastructure of Provence, particularly in cities such as Toulon, Marseille, and Avignon. In the Alpes-Maritimes, where there was heavy fighting, particularly along the Italian border, whole communities were devastated. Towns such as Breil, Sospel, and Lantosque lost almost half their populations; Castillon lost all but 47 of its 300 inhabitants.

Recovery after the war was slow, and the task of rebuilding cities such as Marseille was jeopardized by a decline in international trade. Nice airport opened in 1946 (with flights to Paris, Brussels, and Stockholm) but tourism did not pick up again until two years later, partly because the beaches had to be cleared of mines and concrete blocks put there by the Germans as obstacles to the Allied landings.

❑ The delineation of the boundaries of Provence-Alpes-Côte d'Azur (PACA) in the 1950s created one of the largest regions in France, covering about 12,000 square miles, nearly 6 per cent of the country's total land mass. ❑

Expansion and growth In the 1950s work began on the *autoroute* Esterel–Côte d'Azur and the right-wing Médecin dynasty rose to power in Nice, heralding the end of socialist politics in the south. When Algeria regained its independence in 1962 hundreds of thousands of colonists returned to France. Derisively known as the *pieds noirs*, they brought with them racist attitudes which were fueled by the French government's policy of encouraging immigration from North Africa.

The 1960s saw massive expansion of the petrochemical industries around the Étang de Berre and Fos-sur-Mer, west of Marseille. Oil refineries sprang up thanks to the South European oil pipeline and huge tanker terminals were built. Coincidentally, the first marina opened in Cannes in 1964.

In inland Provence massive irrigation schemes such as the Canal de Provence and the development of hydroelectric power helped to slow the decline in the agricultural and industrial economy, although rural depopulation continued to accelerate. This trend was slowed to some extent by an influx of newcomers, artists, potters, and hippies who rebuilt old village houses in their quest for the rural idyll.

The first preplanned ski resort, Isola 2000, opened in the 1970s in the Alpes-Maritime. Tourism on the coast went into overdrive, and the fragile Mediterranean seaside became overrun with concrete. Hideous buildings such as the controversial Marina Baie-des-Anges disfigured the coast and rapidly became a byword for insensitive development on the Riviera.

❑ The population of Provence escalated dramatically in the postwar years: from 1.5 million inhabitants in 1870 it had grown to 2 million by 1950, 3 million by 1960, and nearly 4 million by 1982. Today it stands at 4.4 million. ❑

Originally established in 1956, the regional administration of Provence-Alpes-Côte d'Azur (PACA, which includes the Hautes-Alpes) was put on a new footing in the 1970s with the creation of the *Conseil Régional* (Regional Council), which had its first assembly in 1974. In 1982, power was decentralized to the *Conseil Général* (General Council) of each *département*, with responsibilities covering education, transport, economic development, the environment, and social and cultural affairs.

In the 1980s Jean-Marie Le Pen's fascist *Front National* party started to gain a foothold in the south, swept along by a tide of anti-immigrant sentiments and economic recession. Their particular stronghold has been around Marseille, where roughly half of the 200,000 North African immigrant population now lives.

Top: the autoroute *at Marseille*
Above: a townscape (Bollène) that reflects the changes of recent years

The 1980s also saw a new influx to rural areas, with crumbling old farmhouses and the like being snapped up as second homes by Parisians and foreigners. But shuttered windows in the winter months showed that the benefits were short-term, and many rural communities struggled to adapt to rising unemployment.

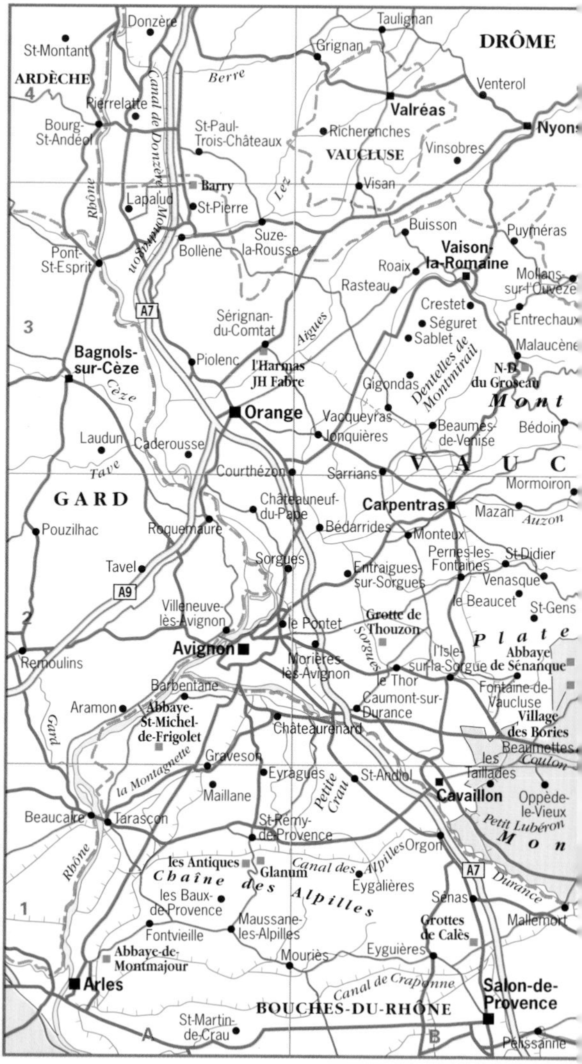

A view over Bonnieux and the Lubéron region

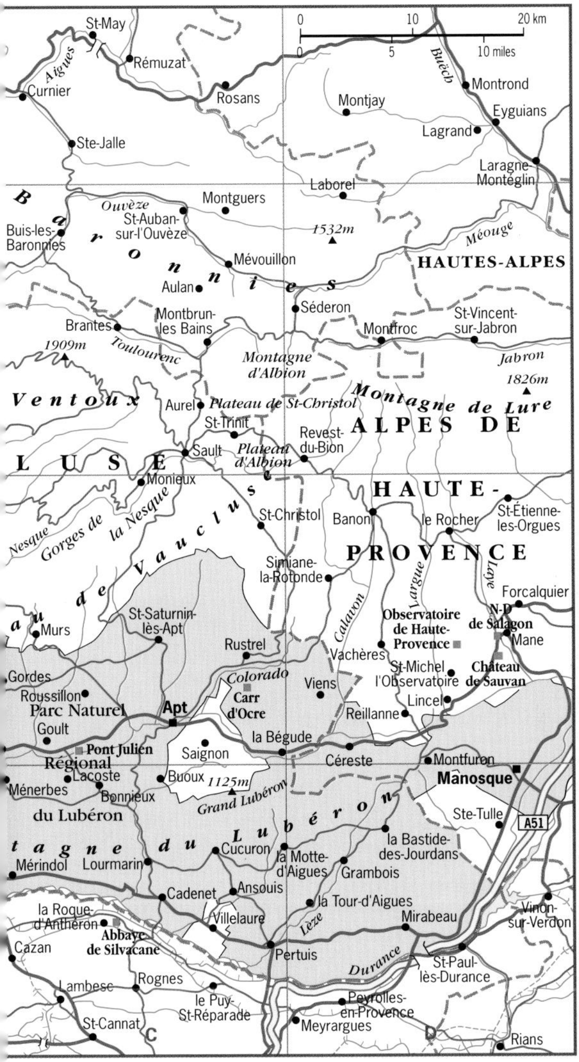

VAUCLUSE

Vaucluse Despite being one of the smallest *départements* in France, Vaucluse can boast attractions that range from grand Roman monuments to sleepy wine villages, from the red ocher cliffs of Roussillon and Rustrel to mighty Mont Ventoux.

Mont Ventoux and the north Rising like a sentinel at the northern gateway to the Vaucluse, Mount Ventoux is the highest peak between the Alps and the Pyrenees. The ascent to the top is one of the most awesome in Provence and the views will take your breath away – sometimes almost literally, since the winds come from all directions of the compass. The *mistral*, howling down from the north, has reached record levels of 140mph at the summit. Legend has it that this is the origin of the mountain's name (from *ventour*, the Provençal for windy)

Lavender, sage, rosemary, and thyme — the constituents of herbes de Provence — are on sale in a variety of packages and containers throughout the Vaucluse

but it may also be that the barren limestone summit, often covered in snow, gave rise to *ven top*, meaning white mountain in Celtic.

To the west of Mont Ventoux lies the jagged curtain of peaks known as the Dentelles de Montmirail, with enchanting wine villages such as Gigondas, Rasteau, and Beaumes-de-Venise nestling under the flanks of the Dentelles. On the other side of the Dentelles, the town of Vaison-la-Romaine straddles the Ouvèze river. On the right bank of the Ouvèze are the remains of a prosperous Roman settlement, partly built over by the 18th-century town which is now the heart of Vaison. On the left bank of the river, the medieval village encircles a dramatic ruined castle which further enhances the appeal of this popular spot.

Roman ruins are much in evidence in the historic town of Orange, sprawling beneath the St-Eutrope hill, whose northern slopes accommodate the multiple tiers of the ancient theater. Its magnificent backstage wall, one of the best preserved in Europe, provides a dramatic setting for summer choral performances. Orange, too, has its *arc de triomphe*, another imposing legacy from the time when the town was an important staging post on the Roman highway up through the Rhône valley to northern Gaul.

From Orange it is but a short hop to Châteauneuf-du-Pape, rising amid a sea of vineyards that produce the full-bodied Rhône wines which have earned this small village an international reputation.

Avignon and the plateau de Vaucluse Heading south again, Avignon presents an unpromising façade, girded by industrial suburbs — unless you arrive by river steamer (as did Dickens and Robert Browning) and witness the ramparts with the Palais des Papes rising behind them like a medieval tableau. Within the ramparts is a different city, a feisty, lively place infused with cultural riches during the summer season and always full of fascination. Even if some are disappointed by the famous bridge, no one can fail to be awed by the Palais des Papes, part-church, part-fortress, and undoubtedly one of the most extensive feudal castles in the world.

Across the river Villeneuve-lès-Avignon has considerable charm, as does the attractive town of l'Îsle-sur-la-Sorgue further to the east of Avignon. The river that runs through it rises at Fontaine-de-Vaucluse on the edge of the Vaucluse plateau. The funnel-shaped cavern out of which the spring rises lies at the foot of towering cliffs over 650 feet high, with the river running down a beautiful valley through the village and on down to the Rhône. The site was originally known as *Vallis Clausa* ("the closed valley"), which later became Vaucluse, and eventually gave its name to the entire *département*.

This enchanted valley cast a spell on the great humanist poet Petrarch, but to experience it as he did you would be wise to avoid the peak summer months, especially as the source itself is at its most dramatic not during the main tourist season, but during the winter and spring.

Fluorescent traces added to rivers far away have shown the source has a huge catchment area, covering about 50 square miles from Mont Ventoux to the eastern extremes of the Vaucluse plateau.

On the southern escarpment of the plateau, to the east of the *fontaine*, the village of Gordes is perched some 1,000 feet above the Coulon valley in a spectacular setting which also attracts considerable crowds. Hidden away behind the village in a lavender-scented valley is the 12th-century Abbaye de Sénanque, whose pure silhouette, stripped down to the essentials, echoes the spirituality of the Cistercian monks who built it.

Another way of life, another bewitching testament to the past, is reflected in the remarkable Village des Bories behind Gordes. In Provence there are some 5,000– 6,000 *bories* (drystone huts), the majority of which are in the Vaucluse.

The Lubéron And so to the Lubéron, where the conversion of old houses has turned this corner of Provence into one of the most fashionable addresses for foreigners and Parisians. No matter, since there are still many wild and unspoiled corners, secret valleys, and lovely villages to be explored. Most of the region is part of the Parc Naturel Régional du Lubéron.

On the southern flanks of the Lubéron the vegetation becomes more Mediterranean in character, hinting at the coastal hinterlands which start below the Durance, the natural boundary marking the southernmost extent of the Vaucluse.

Some of the drystone huts in the extraordinary Village des Bories near Gordes. The reason for their construction is still debated

The Sabran family home, commanding the hilltop above Ansouis village

►► Ansouis 45C1

Ansouis is built on a rocky spur dominated by the castle keep of the **Château de Sabran►►**, home of the Sabran family for the last 800 years. From the north the château displays an impregnable exterior — part of the original fortress — but, as you circle it, it changes to reveal an 18th-century mansion façade with gardens and terraces shaded by chestnut trees. The interior of the château (open afternoons except Tuesday; admission) is furnished in a way that reflects this dual identity: the ground floor displays a collection of arms and armor, while upstairs Flemish tapestries and Italian Renaissance furniture predominate. From the second floor balcony you get a good overview of the elegant garden (no visits). The 18th-century Provençal kitchen (still in use today) features several very fine hand-crafted pieces.

Adjoining the château, the church of St-Martin contains busts of St. Delphine and St. Elzéar (see panel).

Down at the end of the village veteran diver Georges Mazoyer has assembled his **Musée Extraordinaire►** (open afternoons except Tuesday; admission) featuring minerals, fossils, shells and paintings of underwater life and a little "Blue Grotto" built into the vaults.

A celebrated celibate couple
In 1298 Charles II of Naples hatched a plan to unite two grand families loyal to his cause by arranging the marriage of Eléar de Sabran to Delphine de Signes. Unfortunately Delphine, brought up in a convent, had already taken a vow of chastity and would go ahead only on the basis that Elzéar took a similar pledge — which he duly did. They maintained this virtuous relationship until Elzéar died. Delphine survived another 37 years, living a life of poverty and devoting herself to good works, with many visions and miraculous healings attributed to her. Both were later made saints.

► Apt 45C2

A busy market town proclaiming itself not only capital of the Lubéron but also world capital of crystallized fruits, Apt has been a prosperous urban center since Roman times.

Its principal monument is the old **Cathédrale Ste-Anne►** (closed Monday and Sunday afternoon), famous for its ancient crypt, on two levels, which is said to house the bones of Ste Anne. The saint is depicted in a fine set of 14th-century stained-glass windows at the end of the apse; her shroud is displayed among the reliquaries in the *trésor* (closed Sunday, Monday and holidays).

Next door to the church is the 16th-century **Tour de l'Horloge**, which straddles the rue des Marchands: on Saturday mornings this old shopping street and all the neighboring thoroughfares overflow with the stalls of Apt's lively **market**. Other sights include the **Musée Archéologique** (open daily except Tuesday and Sunday) and the **Maison du Pays du Lubéron►** (closed Sunday all year, Saturday in winter) which houses an information center, a paleontology museum (admission) geared toward children, and a bookstore.

Protecting the Lubéron

■ Created in 1977, the Parc Naturel Régional du Lubéron now covers around 350,000 acres in the Vaucluse and the Alpes de Haute Provence. The greater part of it lies in the Vaucluse.....■

The natural setting Between Manosque and Cavaillon the Durance river, flowing westward toward the Rhône, takes a mighty loop within which the Lubéron range lies. Stretching 40 miles from east to west, the mountains are divided in two by a wooded valley, the *combe de Lourmarin*. To the west is the Petit Lubéron, while to the east the Grand Lubéron reaches its summit of over 3,300 feet at the Mourre Nègre.

One of the most striking features of the Lubéron *massif* is the contrast: to the south, the rich agricultural land sloping gently down to the Durance is characteristically Mediterranean, to the north the steep ravines and abrupt cliff faces are cooler, and forested with downy oaks.

Wildlife The variety of natural features in the Lubéron has created a species-rich environment where plants such as the fragrant Etruscan honeysuckle, aspic lavender and downy rockroses thrive. Predators that have all but disappeared in the rest of Europe — such as Bonelli's eagle, the white Egyptian vulture, the eagle owl, and the migratory eagle Circàete Jean Le Blanc — retain a precarious foothold here.

The human impact The most startling evidence of early habitation are the curious *bories*, or drystone huts, which can be seen dotted about the countryside. Although some were built as recently as the 18th century, many date back to the Iron Age.

The Middle Ages left the Lubéron with numerous *villages perchés* (perched villages) strategically positioned high above the valley floors. Surrounded by an intricate network of cultivated land, many of these villages (particularly those on the northern slopes) went into a decline with the changing agricultural patterns of the last century.

Revitalized by an influx of Bohemians and artists during the 1950s who rebuilt ruined houses, the Lubéron villages now face a new threat to their identity, that of being swamped by tourism.

On the mule train
Walking tours off the beaten track through some of the most evocative scenery in the Parc Naturel Régional du Lubéron are organized in conjunction with the *Maison du Parc* in the *Voyages au Naturel* program. Your luggage is transported by mule on these seven-day tours, which take place from April through October. Contact the Lubéron Regional Park, 90 74 08 55.

Living projects
As well as conducting scientific studies on the natural environment and publishing information for visitors, the *Maison du Parc* (which administers the park from Apt) carries out restoration projects in rural areas and has created nature trails and other attractions. In particular, you can visit the Sentier du Conservatoire des Terrasses en Culture (Open Air Terrace Museum) at Goult (see page 75), the botanic trail through the Forêt des Cèdres (near Bonnieux) and the Sentier des Ocres (Ocher Trail) at Roussillon (see page 83).

Top: rockroses
Left: unmistakable but rarely seen, the white Egyptian vulture

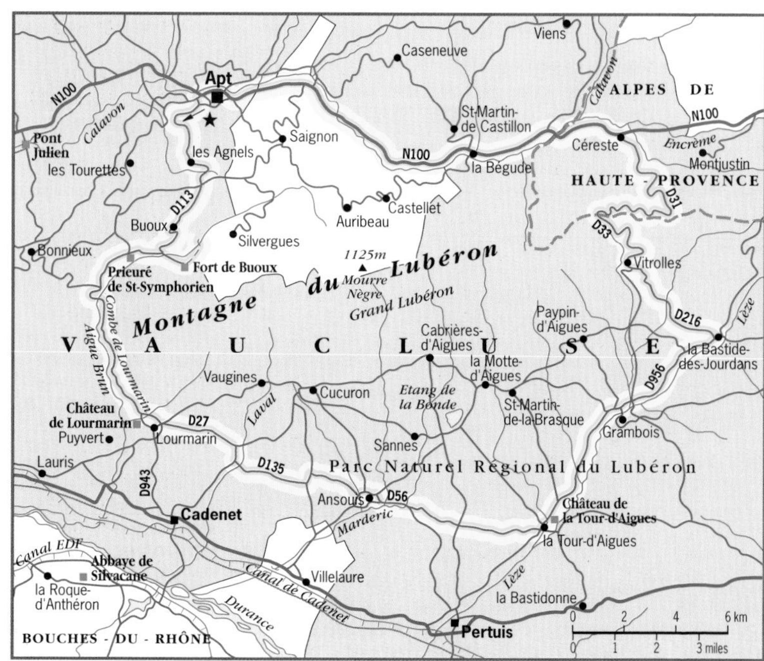

Drive Grand Lubéron

This drive encompasses one of the most beautiful valleys in the Lubéron as well as the principal châteaux of the Sud-Lubéron, before traversing the *massif* to return to Apt. Although only 50 miles, allow all day if you plan to visit the châteaux or walk up to the Fort de Buoux.

From Apt, take D113 to the tiny hamlet of Buoux, surrounded by fields of lavender. Continue past here and the road descends further into the wild and beautiful **Vallon de l'Aigue Brun▶▶**. The **Fort de Buoux▶▶**, reached via a steep footpath, commands a magnificent view of the Vallon de l'Aigue Brun — hence its strategic importance, since this was once the main pass across the Lubéron. First occupied by the Ligurians, then the Romans, the site was fortified in the 13th century.

Back on D113 the elegant bell tower of the 12th-century **Prieuré de St-Symphorien** (not open to visitors) rises above the treetops on your left.

Follow D943 through the *combe de Lourmarin* until you come to **Lourmarin▶** itself at the mouth of the valley. This lively town was once the home of Albert Camus, who moved here after winning the Nobel Prize for Literature in 1957. On the edge of the town is the imposing **Château de Lourmarin▶▶** (open daily except Tuesday in winter; admission). The older part of the château was built between 1495 and 1525; the "new" part was begun in 1540.

Abandoned in the 19th century, the château was salvaged in the 1920s by a wealthy Lyonnais industrialist, Robert Laurent-Vibert, who hired a team of 40 artisans for the four years it took to complete the restoration. At his untimely death in 1925 the château was bequeathed to the Academy of Arts, Agriculture, Science and Belles Lettres at Aix and a foundation set up to encourage talented young French people. The older part now houses an arts library and accommodations. The Renaissance wing contains a collection of old Provençal and Spanish furniture as well as souvenirs from Laurent-Vibert's travels in Egypt, Indonesia, Morocco, and Russia.

Leaving Lourmarin behind, take D27 and then D135 to Ansouis (see page 48), passing through the Côtes du Lubéron vineyards flanking the foothills of the Lubéron *massif*. From Ansouis, take D56 and then follow signs to **la Tour-d'Aigues**. In the middle of this large market town is one of the most astonishing Renaissance ruins in Provence, the remains of the **Château de la Tour-d'Aigues▶▶**, built in the latter half of the 16th century. Early engravings show it to have been a hugely ambitious palace.

The southern slopes of the Lubéron massif, *overlooking the Durance valley*

In 1780 it was badly damaged by fire, and then finally torched during the Revolution in 1792. Now, the ruins accentuate the dimensions and make a spectacular backdrop for the performances held here as part of the Sud-Lubéron Summer Festival. The cellars of the château contain several exhibitions (open daily, closed Tuesday afternoons and Saturday and Sunday mornings out of season; admission) including the **Musée du Pays d'Aigues** and the **Musée des Faïences.**

From la Tour-d'Aigues follow D956 toward la Bastide-des-Jourdans and turn left on D216 for the sleepy hamlet of Vitrolles. The road then becomes the D33 as it winds up over a pass in the Grand Lubéron and then down to Céreste. In contrast to the valley of the Aigue Brun, the mountain here is cloaked in *garrigue* scrub and oak forests. Return along N100 to Apt.

The Avignon Festival
Founded as a drama festival in 1947 by Jean Villar, in 1967 the festival brief was widened to include movies, music, and dance, and at the same time fringe events (*le festival off*) became increasingly popular. Today, around 120,000 people descend on Avignon for this sellout arts extravaganza, which takes place from mid-July onward for one month. For details contact the Bureau de Festival d'Avignon, 8 bis rue de Mons, 84000 Avignon (tel. 90 82 67 08).

▶▶▶ Avignon 44A2

Introduction Avignon has always evoked extreme reactions from visitors. On the one hand it is a major center for art and culture, a lively, innovative city that over the centuries served as a channel for the influence of the Italian Renaissance on the rest of France, nurtured the Provençal literary group the Félibrige, and gave birth to one of the country's most celebrated cultural events, the annual Festival of Dramatic Arts. It is an inevitable "must see" on every tourist itinerary.

On the other hand Avignon has never been a likeable city, provoking detestation from many a traveler since medieval times. Petrarch called it a living hell, "the sewers of the earth;" Henry James loathed it at first sight, and Lawrence Durrell railed against it in his novel *Monsieur.* In the summer months the place is full of outsiders who flock here to mine the gold dust of tourism with no apparent care for the city and its rich heritage.

And yet, unlovable though it may be, Avignon has a magnetism that was recognized long ago, in the Provençal proverb, *Quau se lèvo d'Avignoun, se lèvo de la resoun* (He who takes leave of Avignon takes leave of his senses).

The Rocher des Doms, overlooking the confluence of the rivers Rhône and the Durance, was occupied in neolithic times but, despite flourishing as a river port, the settlement was eclipsed by Arles and Nîmes in the Roman period and sank into relative obscurity. By the 12th century it had grown into a large town and, surrounded as it was by feuding baronies, Avignon declared itself a sovereign state and ruled its own affairs. The first ramparts were erected and trade prospered largely thanks to the rebuilding of the bridge over the Rhône, which was then the only route between Italy and Spain upriver from the sea.

Avignon made a strategic mistake in allying itself with the Albigensians (followers of the heretical Cathar sect,) in the 13th century, as a consequence of which Louis VIII razed the city in 1226 and pulled down its defenses. However, it was also as a result of the Albigensian Crusade that the papacy acquired a large slice of Provençal territory which became known as the Comtat Venaissin. The papal court decamped *en masse* to Avignon in 1309

Standing forlornly on the last remaining arches of Avignon's famous bridge, the Chapelle St-Nicolas is part-Romanesque, part-Gothic

Trompe-l'oeil paintings on the east side of the place de l'Horloge depict scenes from the city's past

and stayed for the next 100 years or so.

Avignon in this period was a thriving city of between 30,000 and 40,000 people, a large proportion of whom were under holy orders in the numerous convents, churches, and chapels that had been built. The university, founded in 1303, housed thousands of students and the best Sienese artists were summoned to embellish the pontifical palaces. The city became a refuge for exiles — including a sizable Jewish community — but its open doors also attracted criminal outcasts and adventurers and the city's name became a byword for filth, debauchery, overcrowding, and vice. The Italians, envious of the loss of the wealthy papal court, declared it the "second Babylonian Captivity."

In 1377 Ste. Catherine of Siena persuaded the seventh pope, Gregory XI, to return to Rome, where he fell sick and died. The Italian cardinals seized the chance and forcibly elected an Italian pope, but when the French cardinals returned to Avignon they elected another pope, Clement VII, thus setting off the Great Schism, which saw pope and anti-pope struggle for supremacy and control of the Church's income for the next 40 years.

After this issue was finally resolved with the election of Martin V in 1417, Avignon remained papal property and was ruled by the cardinal legates until 1791, when the Comtat Venaissin became part of France during the Revolution.

Before the Revolution, Avignon had been an important publishing center, thanks to freedom from French censorship laws, and the printing presses continued to roll through the 1800s, helping to foster the growth of the nascent Félibrige movement (see pages 60–61). Its cultural influence was firmly reestablished in recent times with the creation in 1947 of the annual Avignon Festival.

The many steeples defining Avignon's skyline led Rabelais to call it la ville sonnante *— the ringing city*

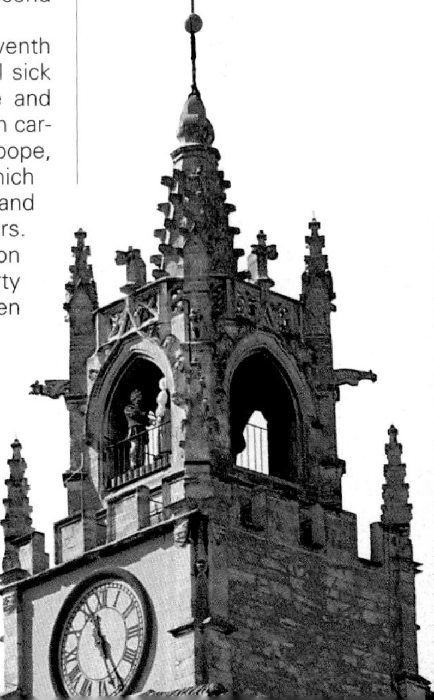

Walk Exploring Avignon

Around the periphery of the town center there are numerous interesting back streets with fine old mansions, churches and other sights. Allow 2–3 hours for this circular walk from place de l'Horloge.

From place de l'Horloge, head west toward rue St-Étienne. At the beginning of this street are some of the few Roman relics from early Avignon, stone blocks dug up from what was the place du Forum (now place de l'Horloge) and part of a Roman arcade. At No. 18, the ironwork balconies of the house are discreetly embellished with balloons to mark the spot where Joseph de Montgolfier invented the hot-air balloon.

Follow the street down to place Crillon, where the lovely façade of the old **La Théâtre Comédie**►► (built in 1734, restored in 1979) faces the Porte de l'Oulle. Take a small passageway (rue Mazan, beside the theatre) to reach rue Joseph Vernet. Along the street there are several impressive 18th-century façades, as well as the **Chapelle de l'Oratoire** (now an exhibition center), the **Musée Calvet** (see page 58) and the **Musée Requien** (see page 58).

Cross over the cours Jean-Jaurès onto rue Henri Fabre. Continue down the rue des Lices, where, on your left, is the immense, unusual Almône générale► **(General Almshouse),** built between 1546 and 1557. Only the central portion remains, a three-story arcade with a fine sundial (1789) on the top floor. The building is now part of the neighboring École des Beaux Arts.

Turn right into the **rue des Teinturiers**►►, one of Avignon's oldest and most picturesque streets. Immediately on your right is the remains of the Chapelle des Cordeliers. Just past here is the **Chapelle des Pénitents-Gris**►. Towards the end of the street are several derelict waterwheels which powered the textile factories after

Carved panel, Église St-Pierre doors

which it is named. Retrace your steps and turn left into rue de la Masse, then into rue du Roi René. On the left is the **Chapelle Ste-Clair**, supposedly the location of the first meeting between Petrarch and Laura (see panel on page 58). Toward the end of rue du Roi René there is a cluster of lovely old mansions, including the **Hôtel d'Honorati de Jonquerettes** (No. 12), the **Hôtel Fortia de Montreal** (Nos. 8 and 10) and the elegant Italianate **Hôtel Berton de Crillon** (No. 7).

Backtrack briefly and turn down rue Collège de la Croix, cross two pedestrianized shopping streets through the arches of rue Bernheim-Lyon, to arrive at place Jerusalem. This was the heart of the old Jewish ghetto, once encircled by walls, although now only the synagogue remains. Just beyond here, place Carnot is dominated by the Gothic façade of the **Église St-Pierre**►; the magnificent carved walnut doors date from 1551.

Hidden away behind the church (take the alleyway leading off from the beginning of rue des Sciseaux d'Or) is the **Musée Théodore Aubanel**► (open mornings only) which celebrates the life and times of one of the leading lights in the Félibrige: the museum houses a collection of old printing equipment and a number of rare documents and first editions.

Continue down rue Banastèrie until you reach the **Chapelle des Pénitents-Noir ►►**. Nestling incongruously alongside the walls of Avignon's present-day prison, the delightful baroque façade is ornamented with a relief showing cherubs holding the head of John the Baptist, encircled by rays of sunshine piercing through the clouds.

Take rue Migrenier and then a series of steps which lead up to the **Rocher des Doms**►►, one of the most peaceful parks in the city, scattered about with fountains and statues — and a sundial that tells the time by your shadow. From the belvedere, there are views across the Rhône to Villeneuve-lès-Avignon.

Steps lead back down the other side of the park past the Palais des Papes to place de l'Horloge.

Fountain, Rocher des Doms

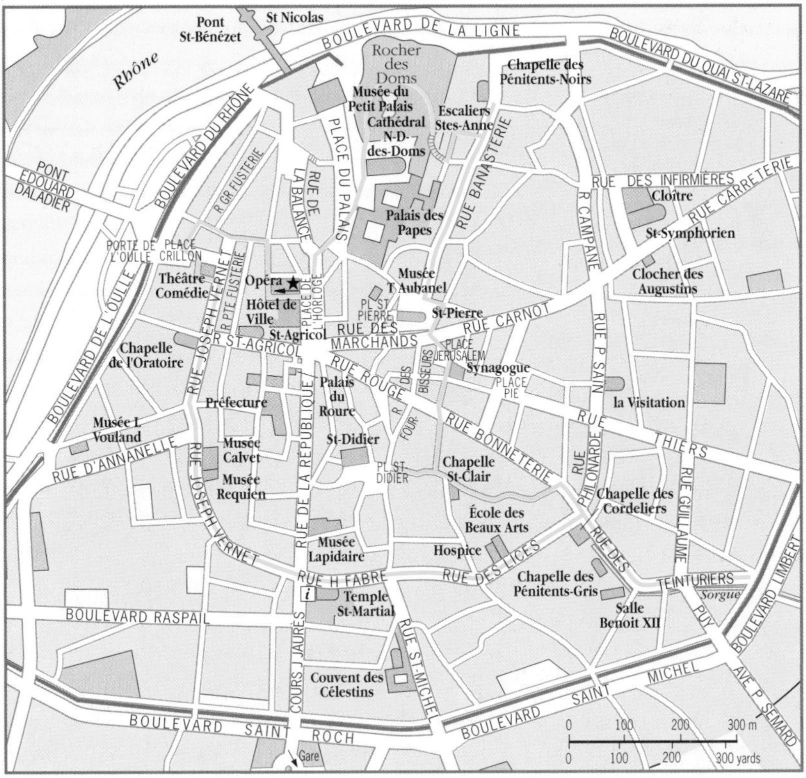

The shepherd boy's bridge In 1177 a shepherd boy called Bénézet was told by a voice from the sky to leave his sheep and go and build a bridge over the Rhône. Initially hesitant, Bénézet set off for Avignon with an angel disguised as a pilgrim. The bishop laughed at him, and sent him to the provost who, equally derisive, told him that if he could lift a huge stone he could build the bridge. This Bénézet did, hefting it down to the river bank. The awestruck crowd started donating money for the bridge. It was completed in 1185.

What to see The central core of Avignon lies within its 14th-century walls, although this represents just a small part of the city, which sprawls several miles eastward toward the *autoroute de soleil.* The walls are nearly 3 miles long but unfortunately only one small section of the rampart (adjacent to the Porte du Rhône) is accessible.

Projecting from the city wall by the Porte du Rhône is one of Avignon's most photographed landmarks, the **Pont St-Bénézet▶▶** (open daily; admission). On the second pier, the Chapelle St-Nicolas is part Romanesque, part Gothic. Since it was first built, the bridge has been swept away several times by the Rhône; in the 17th century the Avignonais finally abandoned it to fate.

At the heart of the city is the **place de l'Horloge▶**, a huge square shaded by plane trees and overrun with cafés. Toward late afternoon it comes alive with a pageant of street musicians, jugglers, and portrait painters. An antique carousel spins round in front of the **Hôtel de Ville,** whose clock tower gave the square its name.

To the south of place de l'Horloge is the **Église St-Agricol▶** (not open for visits), the oldest church in Avignon after the cathedral.

North of place de l'Horloge is the **place du Palais▶**, once a densely populated area which was cleared on the orders of Benedict XII, who feared that his enemies would be able to sneak up to the palace walls through the houses.

Looming above the square is the gigantic **Palais des Papes▶▶▶** (open daily; admission; guided tours in English available). Inside this veritable fortress there is a maze of rooms, galleries, passageways, and chapels; pillaged of all its furnishings during the Revolution, you have to use a great deal of imagination to envisage the decadent, luxurious living that went on inside. In 1810 it was converted into a barracks and the soldiers hacked off many of the murals to sell to collectors. Turned over to the Historic Monuments Board in 1906, it has been under restoration ever since.

Passing through the reception area in the old guardroom, you emerge into the Courtyard of Honor. On the left is Benedict XII's austere, military-style Vieux Palais and, on the right, Clement VI's Gothic-style Palais Neuf.

Decorative paneling brightens up the antique carousel in place de l'Horloge

Busy outdoor cafés overflow into the place de l'Horloge

The usual route through the building goes first to the Consistory Hall in the Vieux Palais, where ambassadors and dignitaries were received. The original frescoes were destroyed by a fire in 1413, and replaced with fragments of Simone Martini's frescoes (dated *c.*1340) from the Cathedral porch. Portraits of the nine popes line one of the walls. Leading off this room is the Chapelle St-Jean, with frescoes by Matteo Giovanetti (painted 1346–1348). On the floor above is the Grand Tinel, or banqueting hall, a huge, 100 feet. long room with beautifully restored paneling in the shape of an inverted ship's keel on the ceiling.

Past here is the papal Antechamber, hung with Gobelin tapestries, and then the papal Bedchamber, decorated with murals. Through here you come to one of the loveliest rooms in the palace, the Chambre du Cerf, which was the pope's private study. The delightful frescoes depict scenes of hunting and fishing against a panorama of the forest which encircles the room: most likely painted by Giovanetti, the frescoes were commissioned by Clement VI. From here the route leads through to the Grand Chapelle (or Chapelle Clementine), bigger even than the banqueting hall.

At the top end of the Place du Palais is the **Musée du Petit Palais▶▶▶** (closed Tuesday; admission). Once a cardinal's residence, it was converted in 1958 to house two important collections — medieval works formerly in the Calvet Museum and those from the Campana collection in the Louvre. The former consists of 600 sculptures and around 60 paintings, including important works by the 15th-century Avignon school, particularly the Requien Altarpiece by Enguerrand Quarton. The most important works, however, are the 13th–16th-century Italian paintings from the Campana collection.

Beneath the bridge
Only four of the 22 original arches remain of the bridge that is immortalized in a popular song as the Pont d'Avignon. The bridge once spanned two branches of the Rhône (and the île de la Barthelasse between them) to connect with Villeneuve-lès-Avignon. Although the song as it has come down to us celebrates dancing "*sur le pont*", in reality it was "*sous*" (beneath) the bridge on the island, where there were once dance halls.

Dragons and eagles on the façade of the Hôtel des Monnaies come from the coat of arms of Cardinal Borghèse, who built it in 1619

The myth of Laura
Petrarch was born in Arezzo but his family was exiled in 1302 and eventually came to Avignon in 1314. It was outside the Chapelle SteClair in 1327 that he first caught sight of Laura, who was to become his muse for the next 15 years: he continued to pour his heart out long after she died in 1348. Laura was Laure de Noves, who was already married to Hugo de Sade at the time Petrarch met her

Next to the palace is the **Cathédrale Notre-Dame-des-Doms▸**, built between 1140 and 1160 but added to many times since. Worth noting in the interior is the Romanesque dome and the splendid Tomb of John XXII attributed to the English sculptor Hugh Wilfred. Opposite the Palais des Papes is the **Hôtel des Monnaies▸** (the old mint, now the music conservatory), which boasts a flamboyant 17th-century façade.

Avignon has a number of other museums, displaying some engrossing exhibits. Housed in one of the grandest mansions of the city at 65 rue Joseph Vernet is the **Musée Calvet▸▸** (closed Tuesday; admission) – its remarkably wide-ranging collection encompasses everything from Egyptian mummies to tapestries, wrought-iron work, Greek and Roman vases, and Dutch, French, Italian, and Flemish paintings spanning the 16th to the 19th centuries.

In comparison, there is a strong Provençal theme to the exhibits in the **Palais du Roure▸▸** (visits at 3:30P.M. on Tuesday or on request from the concierge). Built in 1469 on the site of an old tavern, the mansion belonged to the Baroncelli family and from 1891 to 1899 Baron Folco de Baroncelli-Javon worked here with Mistral editing their Provençal journal, *L' Aïoli* (see page 61).

It now houses a center for Provençal studies and a large collection of Provençal costumes, *santons,* and antique furnishings.

Some superb examples of Provençal *faïence* are on display in the **Musée Louis Vouland▸** (open Tuesday to Saturday in summer, Wednesday to Saturday winter; admission). Finally, there is the **Musée Requien** (open Tuesday to Saturday) which houses a small natural history collection and the **Musée Lapidaire** (closed Tuesday) with sculptures and stone carvings across the centuries housed inside the 17th-century chapel of a former Jesuit College.

Just over the river from Avignon is the town of **Villeneuve-lès-Avignon▸▸**. In the 14th century the cardinals at the papal court built themselves houses here to escape the noise and bustle of Avignon; it still maintains a peaceful, village-like atmosphere and has several interesting and worthwhile places to visit. Foremost among these is the **Chartreuse du Val-de-Benediction▶▶▶** (open daily; admission), which was the largest and most important Carthusian monastery in France until the Revolution, when art treasures were sold off and the outlying properties taken over by homeless families.

Since the beginning of this century the buildings have been gradually repurchased and restored. Of its former treasures, all that remains are the 14th-century frescoes by Matteo Giovanetti in the refectory chapel. Also worth noting is the ornate tomb of Innocent VI in the church. In 1973 parts of the monastery were taken over by the *Centre International de Recherche de Création et Animation* (CIRCA), which promotes a wide range of contemporary artistic and cultural activities, with workshops and exhibitions all year round (open daily).

On the hill above the Chartreuse is the **Fort St-André▶**, a massive citadel flanked by watchtowers. Inside the twin-turreted gateway there are a series of vaulted barrack rooms, including one with a bread oven so that the soldiers could withstand a long siege without missing their *baguettes*.

On the right of the gateway are the ruins of the **abbey of St-André**, destroyed during the Revolution and now a private residence with lovely Italianate gardens. Apart from the small Romanesque chapel of **Notre-Dame-de-Belvezet** on the west side, most of the rest of the fort's interior is a jumble of ruined houses (the old village of St-André) but from several vantage points there are fine views of Avignon, Mont Ventoux, and the Rhône Valley.

A similar panorama unfolds from the top of the 125 feet **Tour Philippe le Bel▶** (closed Tuesday and February; admission), also built to keep watch on Avignon and to protect the French end of the Pont St-Bénézet.

In the town center the **Église Notre Dame▶** has a well-conserved cloister (now used as a summer festival venue) and once housed a superb 14th-century *Madonna and Child* carved out of ivory: this rare work — and many others — now resides in the nearby **Musée Municipal▶▶** (open daily; admission).

An ancient vase provides a focal point in the lovely gardens of the abbey of St-André

The cowboy baron
The eccentric Marquis Folco Baroncelli-Javon left his native city of Avignon in 1890 to lead the life of a *gardian* in the Camargue. In 1905 he went to Paris to see Buffalo Bill Cody's Wild West Show, and invited Cody and his American Indian companions down to the Camargue. The Indians pitched their wigwams around Baroncelli's home and a lassoing competition took place between Buffalo Bill's cowboys and the *gardians*. Some of the gifts that the Indians gave Baroncelli can be seen in the Musée Baroncelli in les Saintes-Maries-de-la-Mer.

Cypresses and pines protect the elegant rose parterre in the St-André gardens

Mistral and the Félibrige

■ **You can't go far in Provence without coming across the name of Frédéric Mistral, the region's most famous poet. Plaques inscribed with his verses are found everywhere from remote beauty spots to bustling town centers, and many a street or park is named in his honor. But Mistral was more than just a poet; he helped spark what was to become a major revival of Provençal language and literature in the 18th century.....■**

The patrician figure of Frédéric Mistral at the age of 76, pictured with his family

Close to home
"Frédéric Mistral neither sought nor wished for metropolitan success, and was content to spend his long life quietly and happily in Provence, in the very village community in which he had been born. Occasionally he would visit Paris but Mistral was not happy away from Provence, and there he lived out his dedicated life...there are few lives of great writers, perhaps few recorded lives of human beings, as fortunate and enviable as that of Frédéric Mistral, voluntarily circumscribed within the limits of the halcyon landscape into which he had the superlative good fortune to be born." James Pope-Hennessy, *Aspects of Provence*

Mistral was the only poet in a minority language ever to be awarded the Nobel Prize

Early talent Frédéric Mistral was born on September 8, 1830 in the Mas de la Juge, his parents' farm just outside the village of Maillane near St-Rémy-de-Provence. He went to school at the abbey of St-Michel-de-Frigolet and then in Avignon, where his interest in his native language (his mother was a Provençal speaker) was awakened by Joseph Roumanille.

After finishing law studies in Aix, Mistral moved back to Maillane to help his father with the farm and devote himself to poetry. At the age of 21 he had already embarked on what was to become his most famous work, the epic poem *Miréio*.

The founding of the Félibrige Soon afterward he joined together with a group of like-minded poets to form the Félibrige, an association dedicated to the rebirth of Provençal (the name itself comes from *félibre*, meaning doctor, although why they chose this name remains a mystery). The seven (Roumanille, Mistral, Brunet, Giera, Aubanel, Mathieu, and Tavan) had their first meeting in the Château Fort-Segugne on May 21, 1854. A year later Roumanille and Mistral launched the annual *Armanan*

Provençau, the first journal to be written in Provençal.

Mistral's cause was helped enormously by the publication in 1859 of *Miréio*, which made him instantly famous. This tragic poem tells the story of a beautiful young girl who falls in love with a man whom her parents consider unsuitable; she runs away to seek help from the Holy Marys at les Saintes-Maries-de-la-Mer in the Camargue but dies on the beach from a broken heart.

By now established as the region's greatest writer, Mistral began work on a monumental encyclopedia, *Le Trésor de la Félibrige*, which was to become the most important reference work on Provençal culture ever published. He also published the second of his major epics, *Calendau*, which tells the story of a young fisherman from la Ciotat who falls in love with a waternymph. In 1876 Mistral married and moved into a house opposite his mother's in Maillane (where he lived until his death in 1914).

In the 1890s Mistral and the Félibrige founded a museum in Arles devoted to Provençal arts and culture (the Museon Arletan) and started a new, more popular journal called *L'Aïoli*. In 1904 he became one of the first recipients of the Nobel Prize for Literature.

Provençal revival The romanticism and nostalgia of the Félibrige for the chivalrous days of the troubadours was embodied in their poetry and their impassioned defense of a lifestyle which they saw being gradually eroded by progress and the imposition of the French language by the central state in Paris.

The greatest achievement of the Félibrige was to create a huge revival of interest in Provençal traditions, legends, and folklore which has ensured their continuance today. Their greatest failing was never to engage on the political level (unlike their cousins the Basques) and thus to allow "Occitania" to be eventually eclipsed by French culture.

Mistral has been almost deified by his admirers since his death; when he was alive he attended the unveiling of a bronze statue of himself in the Forum at Arles. Showing that his feet were still firmly planted on the ground despite the veneration bestowed on him, Mistral commented that the statue looked like a passenger waiting for a train to come in the station. "All he needs is a suitcase!" said the man who will always be remembered with honor and gratitude in Provence.

The countryside
"There are gardens of beans, orchards with apples, pears, and peaches, cherry trees that catch your eye, fig trees that offer you their ripe figs, round-bellied melons that beg to be eaten, and beautiful vines with bunches of golden grapes — ah, I can almost see them!" *The Memoirs of Frédéric Mistral*

Mistral, age 62, soon after he began his Provençal journal, L'Aïoli

Muscat Festival
The best time to visit Beaumes is during the annual Wine Festival (July/August) when all the local vineyards set up stalls at various points around the village and everybody wanders, glass in hand, happily trying out one after the other. To soak it all up, other stalls sell goats' cheeses, *foie gras* pâté, and local specialties such as melon with Muscat or melon sorbet with Muscat.

►► Barry 44A4

This extraordinary cave-village is one of the best preserved in Provence. From the parking area, a track leads past a series of houses that look like someone has slapped the front half of a stone cottage onto a cave dwelling. That is exactly what did happen, since the inhabitants didn't need to build a whole house or even a roof and simply adapted the caves to their needs by carving most of the internal rooms out of the rockface.

Nevertheless, they were at constant risk from rockslides. After several villagers had been killed in the 19th century, the entire population abandoned Barry and moved down the hill to St-Pierre on the plain.

► Beaumes-de-Venise 44B3

Best known for the subtly flavored Muscat wines that bear its name, Beaumes has been producing this nectar since the Middle Ages — the Popes at Avignon owned a 175-acre vineyard here in the 14th century and Anne of Austria, visiting in 1660, presented the church with a set of liturgical vestments in recognition of the villagers' winemaking skills.

Built around a rocky cliff at the southern flank of the Dentelles range, Beaumes-de-Venise is named after the grottos that dot the hillside where the first inhabitants lived (the Provençal word for grotto is "*baume*"). The suffix "de-Venise" refers to the fact that the village was part of the ancient territory of the Comtat Venaissin.

Above the village, the ruins of the 12th-century **château** loom over the ancient streets. These are now private property, but follow the Grand Rue up through the village to come across some of the old grottos that riddle the rocks beneath the castle walls.

Bollène 44A3

This unassuming town has grown rapidly from a mere market garden center to a major urban center with the development of the nuclear facilities on the nearby Donzére-Mondragon canal. Climb up to the viewpoint next to the parish church of St-Martin and this huge industrial conglomeration is all too easily visible to the north of town. Beyond the church is a park dedicated to Louis

Built on the site of an ancient priory, St-Martin dates from the 11th century

Pasteur, who discovered an inoculation against swine fever while staying here (in a house on avenue Pasteur) in 1882.

Hidden away down the back streets in the rue de St-Sacrament is the excellent **Centre de Documentation Provençale**, which has more than 1,800 works on every aspect of Provençal life as well as tapes, records, and books for sale (open Saturday afternoons or by appointment, call 90 30 19 549).

The River Lez, which runs through the town, has not been kind to Bollène. In 1413 the river broke its banks and destroyed the town's main bridge, the Chapel Notre-Dame du Pont alongside, and drowned quite a few people. The chapel and bridge were rebuilt, only to be swept away again in 1745. Bollène was again seriously flooded in 1951, and in 1993 water levels reached a record 8 feet in the streets.

The inhabitants of this troglodyte village at Barry made their living smuggling salt and matches into neighbouring Dauphiné during the 18th century

►► Bonnieux *45C1*

Hugging the northern flank of the Lubéron, Bonnieux is a large and lively village which rises up steeply toward the old church and cemetery at its summit. From the terrace surrounding the church there are sweeping views across the valley and neighboring *villages perchés*.

Halfway up Bonnieux's main street, rue de la République, an ancient bakery has been converted into the **Musée de la Boulangerie►** (open daily except Tuesday in summer, Saturday and Sunday only in winter (closed January–March); admission). The museum covers just about everything there is to know about bread-making from harvesting the wheat onward.

Just near Bonnieux on D149 heading northward is the **Pont Julien►►**, one of the best-preserved Roman bridges in Provence. The triple-arched bridge was probably built around 300B.C. and named after the nearby town of *Apta Julia* (now Apt).

An ancient bread oven in the Musée de la Boulangerie in Bonnieux

Buoux *45C1*

See page 50

Characteristic blue-and-white faïences, *which contained herbal remedies, in the old pharmacy of Carpentras's Hôtel-Dieu*

▶▶ Carpentras *44B2*

Carpentras has been famous as a market center since the 5th century B.C. when a Celtic tribe known as the Meminiens set up their stalls on a busy cross roads just outside of the present town. Later, Greeks and Phoenicians came upriver from Marseille to buy wheat, honey, goats, sheep, and skins. Under the Romans the town prospered, although little remains from this period except a small triumphal arch. In the 14th century Clement V, having been proclaimed Pope by King Phillip, chose Carpentras as his second main residence outside Avignon.

From the 14th century onward Carpentras was one of the four main refugee centers in the Comtat Venaissin (the others were Cavaillon, Avignon, and L'Isle-sur-la-Sorgue) for Jews fleeing persecution under Philippe le Bel in France. Despite the best efforts of a succession of bishops in later centuries, (notably Mgr d'Inguimbert, who commissioned the Hôtel-Dieu), Carpentras went into economic decline. Its fortunes were only revived with the building of a canal from the Durance in the 19th century. The desert-like *garrigue* around the town blossomed into fruit and vegetable gardens which today supply early season produce (principally grapes, cherries, and strawberries) for the tables of France.

Every Friday there is a huge market that spreads throughout the town; from November to April truffles change hands at enormous prices in the **place Aristide Briand**; and the town is well known for *berlingots* (mint-flavored caramels).

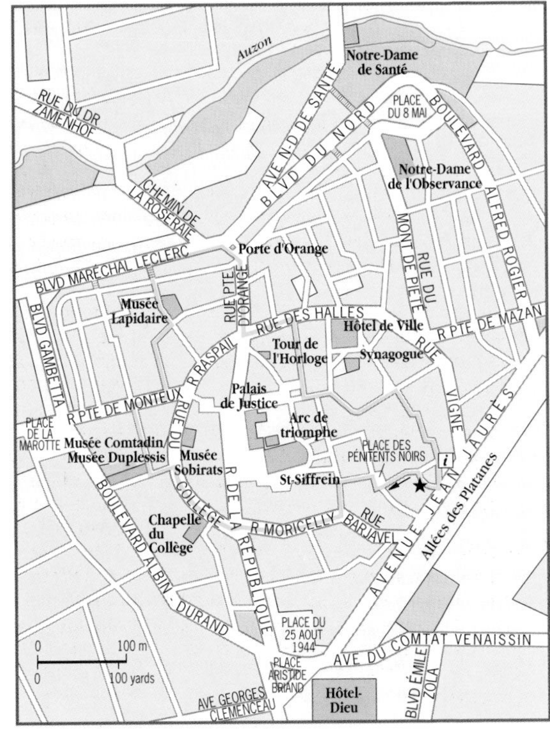

Walk Carpentras

Allow around two hours for this walk, which delves into some of the town's hidden corners. *See map opposite.*

Start at the tourist office and follow the rue Vieux Juiverie into rue de la Fornaque. Directly opposite you will find a magnificent, carved doorway, typical of the Provençal style of the period. The two Atlas-type figures supporting the portico are from the school of Pierre Puget.

Turn back up the rue des Marins, at the top of which in the place des Pénitents Noirs is the disused old chapel of the Pénitents Noirs. Turning down rue Moricelly you find many fine old mansions, in particular those at Nos. 71–83 and at No. 57.

The rue Moricelly leads you into the place Ste-Marthe, with a pretty fountain in the middle; to one side of the square is an even more ancient fountain embedded in a stone post.

Continue down rue du Collège, with the *college* (grammar school) itself on your left. The mid-17th-century chapel is now used for art exhibitions.

Weave your way left into rue Eysseric et Pascal, right into rue Joseph Fornery and into rue Piquepeyre. On your right the immensely tall, misshapen wall forms part of an old Carmelite monastery. The Franchini family have spent the last 30 years restoring it. Make your way through the back streets to the Porte d'Orange (see page 67).

From the gateway, walk up rue Porte d'Orange and turn left to rue Place de l' Horloge. Almost immediately on your right is a small passageway leading into a courtyard: the attractive ceiling here was discovered as recently as 1990. It dates from the 14th century and traces of a fire that took place in the 18th century can still be seen. Inside the courtyard, look up to admire the intricate ironwork of the 16th-century Bell Tower.

Continue down rue Place de l'Horloge and then turn right; at the end take rue Gaudibert-Barret and then left down rue Serpentine (one of the city's oldest and smallest streets) to return to the tourist office.

Stall-holder in the market

The vivid coloration of the stained glass in Carpentras cathedral shows it to have been heavily restored since the 15th century

What to see In the middle of the downtown pedestrian zone is the **Cathédrale St-Siffrein,** no great beauty to behold, mixing together as it does architectural styles from many different periods. The interior contains work by Mignard, Parrocel, and Duplessis, and, most notably, gilded wooden sculptures by Jacques Bernus.

Next to the cathedral is the **Palais de Justice** (ask at the tourist office for details of guided tours), formerly the Archbishop's Palace, commissioned by Cardinal Bichi in 1640. Tucked away behind the cathedral and the Palais de Justice is a **Roman arc de triomphe▶** which was built under Augustus in the 1st century A.D. to commemorate victory over the Franks. Built at the same time as the triumphal arch in Orange, it is not nearly as tall and only one arch of the original three remains. However, the smaller scale allows you to get a much closer look at the bas-relief sculptures of the enslaved captives on the east and west faces. It is a pity that this arch, the only Roman relic in Carpentras, is so hemmed in and concealed by the buildings around it.

Rebuilt many times over the centuries, the cathedral lacks a unifying style

Another monument which is remarkable for being so inconspicuous is the **Synagogue▶** (open Monday to Friday) on the place de l'Hôtel de Ville. The original synagogue was built in the 14th century but eventually became too small to serve the population of over 2,000 Jews who lived in the surrounding ghetto. When the synagogue was rebuilt in 1741 Bishop d'Inguimbert gave permission only on the condition that it was no higher than the cathedral — hence its position today, almost dwarfed by the surrounding houses. The oldest synagogue in France, the richly decorated interior of the *salle de culte* (restored in 1954) testifies to the wealth of the Jewish community in Carpentras.

Carpentras has a handful of museums (all open daily

except Tuesday) of no great distinction but on a rainy day you can take your choice between the municipal collections that are displayed in the **Musée Comtadin** (folkloric mementoes) with the **Musée Duplessis** (local 16th- and 17th-century paintings) on the floor above. Nearby are the **Musée Lapidaire** (prehistoric and Gallo-Roman finds) and the **Musée Sobirats** (a furnished period mansion).

On the south side of the tree-lined boulevard that encircles the center is the imposing **Hôtel-Dieu▶**, built in the 18th century by Monseigneur d'Inguimbert and still in use as a hospital. Once inside, the most delightful part of the Hôtel-Dieu is the ancient **pharmacy▶▶** (open Monday, Tuesday and Thursday 9–11:30; admission). Almost unchanged since the 18th century, this is one of the best-preserved antique pharmacies in the whole of France. It contains an excellent collection of *faïences* as well as pestles and mortars, brass scales, and all the other paraphernalia of the apothecary's trade. The room is decorated with landscape panels painted by Duplessis.

On the other side of town is the impressive **Porte d'Orange▶▶**, the last remaining tower of the ramparts, which were built between 1357 and 1395 on the orders of Pope Innocent IV. They originally consisted of 32 towers and four gates but sadly they were nearly all demolished from 1840 onward in the name of "urban expansion". This huge, 90 feet high tower is unusual in that it is *ouverte à la gorge* ("open-throated"), which means that it was open at the back so that troops could easily be replenished from the town. From the top (collect the key from the tourist office if you wish to climb the tower), there are views across Mont Ventoux and the Plateau de Vaucluse.

The *boule aux rats*

On the southern side of the cathedral is a flamboyant Gothic doorway which was known as the Porte Juive, through which Jews entered in order to be baptized. Above the doorway is one of the cathedral's most famous curiosities, the *boule aux rats*. The symbolism of this globe covered with rats has never been satisfactorily explained: it may be a play on the town's name in Latin, *carpere ras* (the nibbling rat); it may represent the Christian world being overrun with sin and hereticism; or be connected with the dreaded plague that swept the country in the 14th century.

Family values, as portrayed on a poster in the synagogue

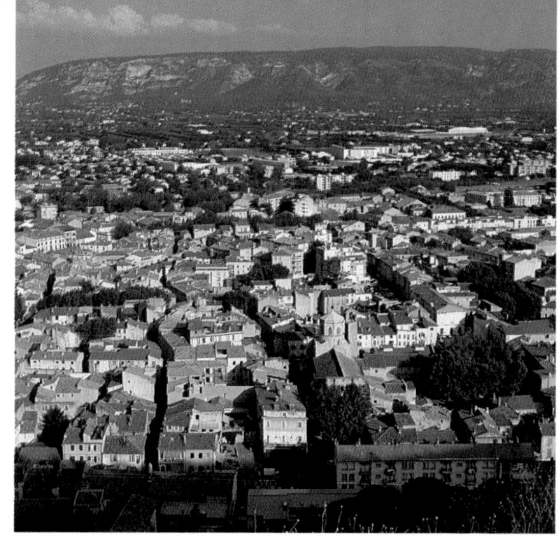

The view from Colline St-Jacques, where Cavaillon was founded by the Celto-Ligurians before it moved down to the plains in the Roman era

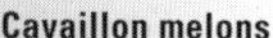

Cavaillon melons
In 1864 the writer Alexandre Dumas, who was very fond of melons, heard that the library at Cavaillon couldn't afford to stock his books so he agreed to supply them with copies in exchange for an annual rent of twelve melons, which were sent to him in Paris. The melons he so enjoyed were the heavy, oval-shaped cantaloupe melons. Since then many new varieties have been introduced, the most popular being the small Charentais melon, which aficionados consider to be absolute nectar.

► Cavaillon *44B1*

Surrounded by market gardens irrigated by the Durance and the Coulon, Cavaillon is one of the biggest agricultural towns in France. And by the end of your stay, you will be left in no doubt that this is the melon capital of France — there is even a Brotherhood of the Knights of the Order of the Melon. This prosperous town also grows an enormous quantity of prime fruit and vegetables — something for which it has been known since Roman times.

The only relic of the Roman era is a small **triumphal arch►**, built in the 1st century A.D. It was moved stone-by-stone to its present position at the foot of the Colline St-Jacques in 1880. The town's other main monument is the **Cathédrale St-Véran►**, an elegant Romanesque structure dating from the 12th century with a charming cloister on the south side. Nearby in the rue Hébraïque is the old **Synagogue►**, sole remnant of the large Jewish population who lived in the surrouding ghetto before the Revolution. The ornate interior is masterly; beneath the Worship Room the ancient bakery has been converted into a small museum.

Cavaillon also has an **archaeological museum** (closed Tuesday; admission) inside the chapel of the old Hôtel Dieu on Grand Rue.

► Châteauneuf-du-Pape *44A2*

The fame of this small town revolves around the wines that bear its name. The first vineyards were planted here in the 14th century by the Avignon popes, one of whom, John XVII, also built a castle at the summit of the village as a summer residence. The **Château des Papes►** was set on fire in 1562 during the Wars of Religion and then finally blown up by the retreating Germans in 1944. The two remaining walls give a good idea of the scale of the original château and from its hilltop vantage point there are fabulous views down the Rhône valley.

At the bottom of the village, in the **Musée du Père Anselme►** (open daily), there is an interesting display on winemaking through the centuries.

■ The relatively small area of just over 7,500 acres of vineyards surrounding Châteauneuf-du-Pape on the left bank of the Rhône produces one of the world's most prestigious and well-known wines.....■

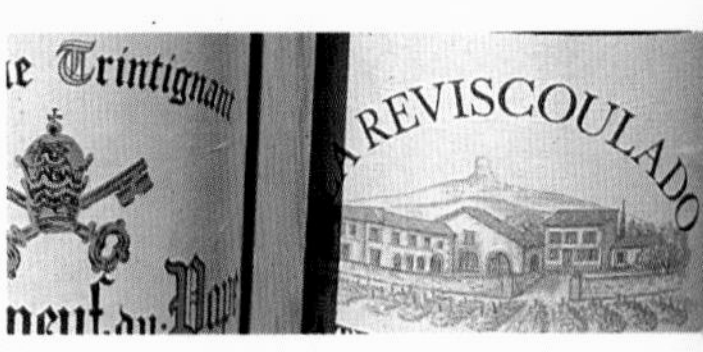

Hot rocks As you approach the vineyards you will notice something curious — there is no soil visible at all, only a sea of smooth pebbles between the vines. This alluvial shingle has a beneficial effect, magnifying the heat of the sun on the grapes by day and keeping them warm long into the night. This superheated microclimate and the wide spacing between the vines produces a wine with the highest minimum strength (12.5 percent alcohol) of any French wine.

The first *appellation contrôlée* Châteauneuf's most distinguished grower was the late Baron Le Roy de Boiseaumarie, who initiated a series of quality controls in 1923; these later became the standard for the national system of *appellations contrôlées*.

Unlike most Côtes du Rhône winemakers, whose product uses just one variety of grape, growers here can choose from up to 13 different types. The result may differ slightly from grower to grower but is a characteristically deep red, full-bodied wine with a strong bouquet. There are plenty of opportunities for visiting vineyards in the region, among the best-known of which are the Château Le Nerthe, the Château de Beaucastel, the Château Rayas, the Château de la Gardine, and the Domaine des Fines Roches.

The annual production of Châteauneuf is over 13 million bottles of wine, of which only 700,000 are white — this elegant, pale wine with a subtle bouquet is something of a rarity and well worth trying while you are here.

Festive tastings The annual *Fête de la Vraison* (which is held to celebrate the grapes' achieving maturity) takes place at the beginning of August when all the producers set up their stalls in the streets of the village. The business of winetasting is much easier and more fun than wine— accompanied as it is by dancing, processions, and a medieval pageant.

Quaffing cardinals
Such was the fame of Châteauneuf wines at the time of the Avignon popes that when Urban X suggested moving the papacy back to Rome he met with deep opposition from his cardinals, who were reluctant to leave an area producing such exquisite vintages. On hearing this, Petrarch commented that "the princes of the church value the wines of Provence and know that French wines are rarer at the Vatican than Holy Water."

Opportunities for tasting the famous wines are never far away in Châteauneuf-du-Pape

Probing the depths
The first attempt to explore the Fontaine de Vaucluse was made in 1878, when a spelunker reached 75 feet. Jacques Cousteau sent the remote control *Télenaute* down to 348 feet in 1967, and in 1983 a second probe, the *Sorgonaut*e, reached 803 feet but exploded on another attempt a year later. The bottom was finally reached in August 1985, when the minisub *Modexa* settled on the sandy bed at 1,010 feet A high-performance probe, the *Spélénaut*e, went down in 1994 to venture into the passageways that disappear back into the mountain.

▶ Crestet *44B3*

This charming little village, which derives its name from the rocky crest on which it is built, is one of the most unspoiled perched villages in the region. With no shops or cafés, there is little to do except enjoy a leisurely stroll through the cobbled alleyways and admire the ancient wooden doorways of the old houses. There is a minuscule square with a bubbling fountain and a 12th-century church, behind which a path leads up between rocks and wild fig trees to an old **château** (no visits).

▶ Cucuron *45C1*

The village of Cucuron lies on the southern flank of the Grand Lubéron and is the starting point for the 6 mile-long trail to the Sommet du Mourre Nègre.

A short distance from the church in the rue de l'Église is the **Musée Marc Deydier▶▶** (open daily, afternoons only in low season). Aside from the usual displays of Gallo-Roman finds and old agricultural tools, the prize exhibits are photographs of the village taken around the turn of the century by Marc Deydier, the town clerk after whom the museum is named. The graphic quality and extraordinary clarity of these superb photographs (reprinted from some of the 2,618 negatives in store) is matched only by their value as a vivid ethnographic record of everyday life in Cucuron, depicting charcoal-making, harvesting with steam tractors, and street scenes.

▶▶ Dentelles de Montmirail *44B3*

See pages 72–73

▶▶ Fontaine-de-Vaucluse *44B2*

In the summer months this little village is swamped with thousands of visitors drawn to the fabled fissure where the River Sorgue rises from the depths and disgorges at a rate that makes it one of the most powerful resurgent springs in the world. People used to come to pay homage to Petrarch, who lived here between 1337 and 1353, but now it is the source itself that exerts such a strong fascination, pouring forth in the peak months at a rate of between 3,500 and 7,000 cubic feet per second.

The source is a mile from the center of the village,

There is little to disturb the peace in Crestet apart from the sound of running water

reached by a path along the riverbank, which in former days must have been a blissful walk: now it is a circus of street musicians, T-shirt-vendors and souvenir sellers, with numerous restaurants and bars built out over the water (even in the 1950s the writer James Pope-Hennessy complained that "all has been commercialized and made vulgar...I confess to feeling beside Petrarch's fountain, as I have felt in Venice, that here was one place to which I had come a hundred and fifty years too late").

A handful of museums and exhibitions have sprung up along this path, among which is **Le Monde Souterrain de Norbert Casteret**► (open daily; closed Monday and Tuesday, February to April and September to November; closed December; admission). Guided tours focus on the history of caving and the specimens collected over the years by France's most celebrated speleologist.

At the exit you will find yourself in a vast underground concrete souvenir center, at the other end of which is the **Moulin à Papier Vallis Clausa**►, which displays the ancient papermaking equipment which was once powered by waterwheels on the banks of the Sorgue. On the other side of the path the excellent **Musée de la Résistance**►► (open daily; admission) is an evocative tribute to the men and women of the Resistance and to the hardships of life in wartime France. The most recent exhibit to open is the **Musée Historique de la Justice et des Châtiments**► (open daily; admission), which houses a macabre collection of instruments of torture, death and imprisonment (including a genuine guillotine) personally assembled by one of the country's last executioners, M. Meyssonnier. A more gentle evocation of the past can be found back down in the village at the **Musée Pétrarque**► (closed Tuesday; admission).

A riverside view of Fontaine-de-Vaucluse

Petrarch and the source
"Here I have the Fountain of the Sorgue, a stream that must be numbered among the fairest and coolest, remarkable for its crystal waters and its emerald channels. No other stream is like it; none other is so noted for its varying moods, now raging like a torrent, now quiet as a pool... I would speak of this more at length, were it not that the rare beauties of this secluded dale have already become familiar far and wide through my verses." Petrarch, 1347

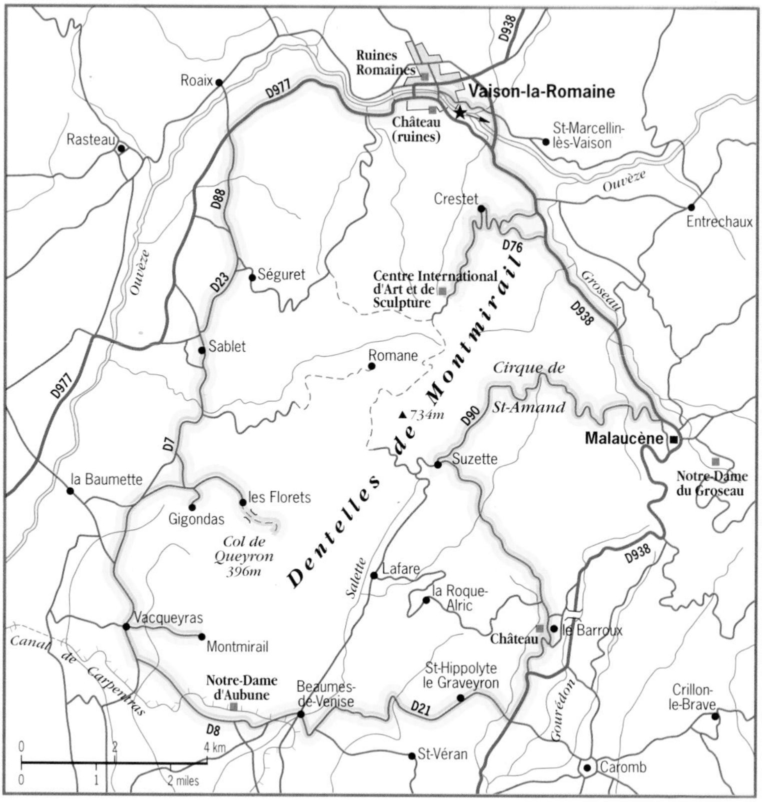

Dentelles

This round tour from Vaison-la-Romaine skirts the jagged limestone pinnacles of the Dentelles and encompasses many charming hill villages, several of which are famous for their wines. Allow 5–6 hours.

Leave Vaison-la-Romaine by D938 toward Malaucène. After about 2–3 miles turn right to **Crestet** (see page 70), then follow the signs for the **Centre International d'Art et de Sculpture▶▶**. Surrounded by dense woods, the Centre is housed in the former studio of sculptor François Stahly where artists explore the theme of art and nature. The *Chemin de Sculptures* is a magical walk through the pine and oak trees, where sculptures in stone, wood, and iron appear as if growing from the ground, on either side of the marked trail.

Return to the main road and continue on to **Malaucène** (see page 76). Follow the boulevard back in the direction of Vaison but take a left turn on D90, following signs for Suzette and the Dentelles.

After passing through vineyards and fields of sunflowers, the road begins to wind up through the forest, and shortly the Dentelles can be seen on your left.

Turn left at the tiny hamlet of Suzette and cross the valley to reach **le Barroux**. The 12th-century **château▶** (open daily July, August, September, afternoons in June and October; admission) was sacked during the Revolution and abandoned until restoration work began in 1929. Burned by the Germans in 1944, it

Serrated pinnacles of the Dentelles

burned for 10 days and the long struggle to restore it again began in the 1960s. The château is well worth visiting, particularly the curious dog-leg chapel — impenetrable rock forced a change of building direction.

Follow D938 towards Carpentras, turning right after 2 miles to **Beaumes-de-Venise** (see page 62). From Beaumes take the Vacqueyras road and turn right just outside Beaumes to **Notre-Dame d'Aubune►**. This small Romanesque chapel lies on the southern slopes of the Dentelles beneath a series of terraces cultivated for centuries.

Continue on to **Vacqueyras.** Its only claim to fame (apart from its wines) used to be a statue of Rambaud de Vacqueyras, a famous Provençal troubadour. His statue was stolen, alas, a few years ago and has never been replaced. From here you can detour to the sulphur springs at **Montmirail**, fashionable enough to warrant a casino next to the *station thermal* in the 19th century when over 1,000 guests a year (including Mistral) took the waters here.

Take D7 on to **Gigondas** (see page 74). Turning right out of the village, follow signs for the **Dentelles de Montmirail**. The road soon becomes an unpaved track, at the top of which is a parking lot with signs for the foot-path to the pass, the **Col de Queyron►**, at the center of the Dentelles' peaks.

Return to Gigondas and continue, via Sablet, to **Séguret►►**. Almost in ruins by the 1950s, Les Amis de Séguret set about breathing life back into it by restoring many of the monuments and reinvigorating local crafts and culture. There is a Provençal folk-lore festival in August.

Return to Vaison by following D88 and D977.

Vineyards shelter in the shadow of the Dentelles

An old château dominates Gigondas

APARE
The Sentier du Conservatoire des Terrasses en Culture (Open Air Terrace Museum) is the result of several years' research and on-site work by an organization known as APARE (*Association pour la Participation et Action Regionale*), formed in 1979. APARE's first project was to restore a small shepherd's hut in the Montagne de Lure. Since then it has organized hundreds of summer camps with volunteers working on projects relating to the heritage and environment of Provence.

The thick drystone walls of the bories *near Gordes*

► Gigondas *44B3*

A small village with a reputation for strong, full-bodied red wines, Gigondas has little in the way of sightseeing but plenty of opportunities for the serious imbiber to try what many consider to be one of the best wines in Provence. Around the main square there are at least half-a-dozen *caves* within weaving distance of each other, including the Caveau de Gigondas which stocks bottles from 40 different Gigondas *domaines*.

►►► Gordes *44B3*

Seen from afar, houses seem to cling precariously to the hillside terraces that lead up steeply to the center of Gordes. In the heart of the village is a 15th-century château whose profile is visible from miles away.

Gordes was set to become yet another victim of rural depopulation and decline until 1938 when the Cubist painter André Lhote fell for its charms and gave it a new lease on life. The village's future as a center for art and tourism was sealed in 1970 when the Hungarian artist Victor Vasarély opened a permanent exhibition dedicated to his works in the château. The **Musée Vasarély►** (open daily, closed Tuesday except July and August; admission) follows the development of his famous geometric designs from early works through many permutations to the creation of his *alphabet plastique*. Even if Vasarély doesn't appeal to you, it is worth visiting the first floor of the château to see the magnificent Renaissance fireplace in the Grand Salle, which was built in 1541.

In an area as rich in historical relics as Provence, perhaps none is as curious and compelling as the fascinating **Village des Bories►►►** (open daily; admission) 2.5 miles outside Gordes. Reached down a narrow, winding lane enclosed on either side by stone walls and *garrigue* scrub, the *bories* seem to grow out of the landscape around them, with the thick walls of the enclosures merging into the dwelling houses, which are joined by yet more walls to other, smaller huts, which housed livestock and were used for storage.

The *bories* were built using an ingenious technique whereby each layer of flat stone slightly overlaps the next to create a corbeled vault, which is then topped off with flagstones. No mortar was used in the construction of these sturdy dwellings. Similar drystone huts exist elsewhere in Europe, some of them dating back to neolithic times. In Provence there are probably between 5,000 and 6,000, with the majority found in this part of Vaucluse. Often seen in fields (where they are used as shepherds' huts), some have been converted into modern homes.

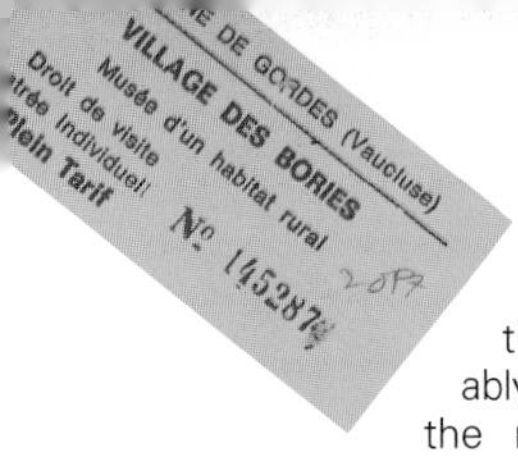

The integration of architecture and the environment is complete, but what is astonishing is that this particular group of *bories* is thought to have been built in the 18th or even the 19th century — making them contemporary with the Renaissance château in the village. The question as to why they were built here at this time (to escape the plague?) remains unanswered.

Also in the vicinity of Gordes is the **Abbaye de Sénanque▶▶▶** (open daily March–October, mornings only November–February; admission). One of three Cistercian monasteries in Provence, the 12th-century abbey makes an extraordinary impression rising from the lavender fields in a lonely valley 2.5 miles north of the village. As well as an exhibition on the monks' way of life (several of whom have now reoccupied the monastery after a period when it was used as a cultural center) there is a lovely cloister and, if you're lucky enough, your guide will sing a Gregorian chant in the church, where the purity and clarity of the acoustics are extraordinary.

▶ Goult *45C2*

Just off N100, which runs parallel to the Lubéron range, is Goult, the site of the unusual **Sentier du Conservatoire des Terrasses en Culture▶** (Open Air Terrace Museum) where you can ramble around a well-marked trail explaining the nature and function of ancient hill terraces and the intricate techniques of drystone walling.

Alongside the traditional shelters and cabins many old (and increasingly rare) varieties of olive and almond trees have been planted at the Open Air Terrace Museum.

Hillside terracing
Many of the hillside terraces, which once covered large areas of the Provençal hills, and are very labor-intensive to maintain, have fallen into disuse, largely due to the mechanization of farming. However, terracing has unique qualities as a growing environment: resistance to erosion and fire, and the microclimate is of great benefit to plants. Now, attempts are being made to grow specialized crops (such as kiwi fruits, raspberries, and Japanese artichokes) on terraces, and traditional plantations of apricot, almond, olive, peach, and fig trees are being irrigated to increase yields.

The serene Abbaye de Sénanque, set among oak trees and lavender

Antiques to go
L'Isle-sur-la-Sorgue is the "antiques capital" of Provence, with over 200 antique dealers scattered throughout the town. The main concentration is in the "Antiques Village" next to the train station, where stalls are spread throughout several old warehouses. In July and mid-August the town holds an antiques fair.

The search for antique bargains in l'Isle-sur-la-Sorgue

▶▶▶ l'Isle-sur-la-Sorgue *44B2*

Soon after the start of its journey from Fontaine-de-Vaucluse down to the Rhône at Avignon, the River Sorgue briefly divides around an island on which sits l'Isle-sur-la-Sorgue, a charming town that has built its fortunes on the river that runs through it.

No one is sure when the inhabitants of the village decided to dig three canals through their island estate, but in the Wars of Religion they put their mastery of the river to good use by flooding the surrounding plains so that they were out of reach of cannon fire. Later they built a whole series of waterwheels across the canals, their paddles powering what was to become a hive of industry including grain, oil and paper mills, tanneries, and textile and silk works.

The wealth these enterprises brought to the town is evident in the riches displayed in the baroque **Notre-Dame-des-Anges▶▶** in the center of town. The magnificent interior is mostly the work of 17th-century artists of the Avignon school. Also worth seeing is the 18th-century **Hôtel-Dieu▶** with its intricate wrought-iron gates and ancient pharmacy (ask for the concierge at the main gate to be allowed inside) and the **Hôtel Donadú de Campredon▶** (open daily; admission) which hosts temporary art exhibitions — in the past, these have included works by Miró, Matisse, Dufy, and Poliakoff.

Unless you are hunting for antiques (see panel), the main pleasure in visiting l'Isle-sur-la-Sorgue lies in strolling through the streets watching the soothing waters running beneath small ironwork bridges and past terraces and balconies replete with flowering plants. Of the 64 waterwheels that once existed only a handful remain: on the **Quai des Lices** and **Quai Berthelet** three of these magnificent wheels have been restored, and alongside **rue Jean-Theophile** and **rue Jean Roux** some of the remaining moss-encrusted paddlewheels still revolve slowly and steadily to the rhythm of the waters.

▶ Lacoste *45C1*

This hilltop village on the northern flank of the Lubéron is still a fashionable address for Parisian *résidences secondaires* despite (or perhaps because of) its heritage as the home for many years of the notorious Marquis de Sade (see panel). Dating back to the 11th century, the **château▶** used to be one of the grandest in the region. Pillaged in the Revolution, it fell into ruins and stayed that way until the current owner, a retired teacher named André Bouër, began his lifelong and quixotic task of restoring it; 40 years later, it is clear he still has a long way to go (M. Bouër sometimes gives guided tours).

▶ Lourmarin *45C1*

See pages 50–51

▶ Malaucène *44B3*

An attractive town encircled by a boulevard of plane trees, Malaucène is the major base for hiking, horseriding, and biking expeditions up nearby Mont Ventoux. Four **fortified gates** mark the entrances into the old town: follow rue St Étienne and rue du Château up past the crumbling old clock tower (which was used as a lookout point during

Still slowly turning under their mossy burdens, the paddle-wheels of l'Isle-sur-la-Sorgue are nearly 200 years old

the Wars of Religion) to reach the belvedere created from the ruins of the ancient château.

►► Mazan *44B2*

Some four miles east of Carpentras is Mazan, the sort of town you could easily pass by without giving it a second glance. However, behind its solid gateways the center of the town (which mostly dates from the 16th and 17th centuries) is a delight to explore and there are many architectural details — statues in niches, fountains, and ancient doorways — to savor as you wander around the peaceful streets.

Opposite the church, a bell tower marks the Chapelle des Pénitents-Blancs, which now houses the **Musée Mazan►** (open daily except Tuesday, June–September). Although there is little that is dramatic here (apart from a chilling skeleton from the 4th century of a young woman who was killed by a stone from a catapult, which left a gaping hole in the front of her skull), it is clear that the people of Mazan have raided their attics — their treasures seem to speak to us from across history in a way which a grand museum could never do.

The miscreant marquis
The Marquis de Sade, author of *120 Days of Sodom* and *Justine*, was born in Paris in 1740. His debaucheries forced him to leave the city when he was 31 for Lacoste, where he spent much of his wife's money embellishing the château. His sexual preferences have come to be called sadistic after his name and earned him the death sentence in 1772, when he fled to Italy in the company of his wife's sister. He lived at Lacoste between his numerous prison sentences until his death, in 1814, in a lunatic asylum at Charenton.

▶▶ **Ménerbes** *45C1*

The layout of this village on the northern flank of the Lubéron is inevitably compared with the shape of a ship, with its narrow promontory projecting like a prow out over the valley. Walking up through the village toward the promontory you pass the Mairie (Town Hall) and a 17th-century **bell tower** on your right, with the archway between them framing a picture-postcard view of the Lubéron. Past here there is a 14th-century **church** (with more lovely views from the old cemetery) and the ruins of an ancient **citadel**.

Ménerbes probably has the highest profile of all the Lubéron villages in media terms, with many celebrities using it as their Provençal *pied-à-terre*. President Mitterrand, Jane Birkin, and Dora Maar (Picasso's mistress during the 1930s) have all had homes near here, as at one time — before the rubbernecking tourists became too much for him — did Peter Mayle, best-selling English author of *A Year in Provence* and *Toujours Provence.*

▶▶ **Oppède-le-Vieux** *44B1*

Built on a limestone pinnacle set against the dramatic backdrop of the steep north-facing slopes of the Petit Lubéron, this evocative village is still partly in ruins and not (as yet) overrun by the trinket trade.

Oppède-le-Vieux was once a thriving community clustered around the base of the castle, but this was pillaged during the Revolution and the village itself went into a decline after the Comtat Venaissin was handed back to France, finally being abandoned altogether in 1910 when the remaining inhabitants moved down the hill to Oppède-les-Poulivets.

Recolonized by artists during the 1940s, some houses have been restored, but in the upper half of the village it is sometimes difficult to tell where houses end and ruins begin. Overgrown pathways wind up between ancient archways to the summit where there is an old **church** with massive flying buttresses and, farther on, the ruins of the **château** itself (take great care because there are many dangerous unprotected drops).

Stonework merges into the natural surroundings in Oppède-le-Vieux

▶▶▶ Orange 44A3

Once an important Roman city, Orange has always been considered the gateway to Provence — initially as a major settlement on the Via Agrippa which followed the Rhône valley and, later, the first stop on the train lines and roads that led south into the sunshine.

Despite the construction of the *autoroute du soleil* just to the west, traffic on N7 still thunders past one of Orange's most famous monuments, the Arc de Triomphe, before engulfing the city and making navigation around the outer boulevards somewhat hazardous. It is a relief to know that almost the entire downtown is pedestrianized, creating a pleasant environment with many squares linked together where you can wander from café to café under the shade of the plane trees.

After the Roman era the town passed through the hands of various feudal lords, including the House of Baux from 1173 to 1530. It was then inherited by René de Nassau, whose strongly Protestant family turned Orange into a refuge for dissenters amidst the surrounding sea of Catholicism. Maurice de Nassau fortified the town in the early 1600s but to no avail, since it was then razed by Louis XIV after war had broken out between the king and Maurice's nephew, William of Orange, who led the Netherlands to victory against Spain and secured Dutch independence in 1648. In 1678 the House of Orange regained the town, but it was ceded back to France under the treaty of Utrecht in 1713.

Whether the town of Orange gave its name to the Dutch royal family or vice versa is by no means clear, but what is certain is that the Dutch connection was bad news for the town's heritage, since Maurice de Nassau pulled down the Roman monuments to use the stone for his fortifications: only by chance did the theater survive because its massive rear wall was needed as part of the defenses.

The top-heavy Arc de Triomphe in Orange celebrates Rome's victory over the Celtic tribes

Resisting Rome

Once a Celtic settlement, Orange met its downfall when the inhabitants defeated the Roman legions, in a huge battle in 105B.C. Three years later the legions returned under General Marius to exact their revenge, almost entirely wiping out the town. It was not inhabited again until 35B.C., and this time it was by veterans of the Second Gallic Legion, who were given the territory in return for their part in Caesar's conquest of Gaul. They set about building a prosperous, well-ordered town, complete with theater, gymnasium, temples — and of course the Arc de Triomphe, which symbolized their victory over the barbarians.

The fully restored tiers of seating in Orange's Théâtre Antique can hold up to 10,000 spectators

Today Orange is an industrial and market garden center and a strategic base for the French Air Force who have been established at Caritat, east of the town, since 1936. Tourism has formed part of the economy since amateur historians started coming here in the last century to see two of the finest Roman monuments in Provence.

The first of these is the superb **Théâtre Antique▶▶▶** (open daily, guided tours in English at 11A.M. in summer; admission includes entry to the museum). Considered to be one of the best-preserved theaters in the Roman world, the main focus of interest is the enormously impressive stage wall.

Standing 120 feet high and measuring 338 feet from end to end, the wall testifies to the important role that the theater must have played in the lives of the citizens of the colony. Decorated with columns, marbles, statues, and mosaics, it is said to have been described by Louis XIV as "the finest wall in my kingdom." Hidden passageways within the wall allowed the stagehands and actors to move around unseen and the huge wooden stage was fitted out with traps so that actors and props could disappear and reappear at will. Above the central "Royal Door" stands a statue of Augustus; dating from the 1st century, it has been reconstructed from fragments.

The semicircular auditorium (or *cavea*) is built into the slope of the St-Eutrope hill and could hold up to 10,000 spectators — graded according to rank, as shown by the inscription found on one of the lower tiers "EQ. G III," i.e., *Equus Gradus III,* "third row for knights."

Outside the main theater, excavations have uncovered a number of other structures which may have been part of a forum or a temple complex.

The second important monument is the magnificent **Arc de Triomphe▶▶**. Like its counterpart in Paris, it has also

been left stranded in the middle of a traffic circle — in this case, on N7 (which follows the route of the Via Agrippa from Arles to Lyons) just to the west of town.

Built about 20B.C. to commemorate the Second Gallic Legion's victories, the triple archway is one of the oldest of its kind in existence and — despite the erosion of some features — one of the best preserved. The three arches are flanked by columns and echoed by the three horizontal planes, including the unusual double attic. On the north face of the arch the reliefs depicting captured trophies and Roman naval supremacy (prows of galleys, oars, anchors, and tridents) are easily visible, although you will need either binoculars or exceptional eyesight to interpret details of the battle scenes on the topmost attic, which is about 65 feet from ground level. Originally topped off with a bronze chariot drawn by four horses, the archway was dedicated to Tiberius some time after it was built.

In the first-rate **Musée Municipal▶▶** (open daily; admission), the light and airy rooms on the ground floor trace the history of Orange and display fragments and friezes recovered from the theater. Old engravings and prints show the theater before it was restored — neglected, overgrown, and sprouting houses inside and around the periphery, many of them built from the stones of the theater itself.

Outside the museum, the rue du Pontillac passes beneath an archway set in a large chunk of Roman wall which may have once encircled the *forum*. In the middle of town is the Romanesque **Cathédrale Notre-Dame** with the grand **Hôtel de Ville** just next to it.

The best views of Orange are from the **Colline St-Eutrope**, reached either by car or on foot. In front of the ruined foundations of a fortress there is an orientation table with views of the city and the Rhône valley beyond.

From orgies to operas
Roman theaters were used for a wide variety of entertainments, which could include anything from circus performances to lottery competitions. Drama, however, was the main focus, with Roman comedies proving more popular than heavyweight Greek tragedies. In the Middle Ages mystery plays were performed but it was not until the end of the 19th century that the theater at Orange entered its heyday again with the staging of a festival of choral music and opera which became known as the *Chorégies*. This (principally popular opera) festival continues today, with the addition of a repertoire of pop, jazz, and classical music throughout the summer months.

Roman legionnaires battle it out against the Celts in a detailed frieze on the Arc de Triomphe

►► Pernes-les-Fontaines 44B2

Like its neighbor l'Isle-sur-la-Sorgue 7 miles to the south, Pernes-les-Fontaines has achieved prominence thanks to the harnessing of water. In Pernes' case, the languid stream of the Nesque was channeled from the 15th century onward into a series of fountains which today give the town its own particular appeal. There are now 36 in all, ranging from the ancient (**la fontaine Reboul,** over 400 years old) to the sublime (**la fontaine de Cormoran**, dating from 1761) to the ridiculous (**la fontaine Villeneuve**, built in 1952 and reputedly so hideous that moss has been allowed to grow all over it; only the old villagers can remember what's underneath).

Apart from the fountains, Pernes ("les Fontaines" was added only in 1936) has one or two outstanding sights worthy of a stop. The first is the lovely 16th-century **Porte Notre-Dame**►► which has a small chapel, **Notre-Dame-des-Graces**, built onto one of the piles of the bridge. Stepping down to the walkway beside the Nesque, you will discover a photogenic cameo of the bridge, the chapel, and the keep framing the town's clocktower.

An absolute must is a visit to the interior of the **Tour Ferrande**►► (on request from the tourist office; admission). Inside the tower is a series of frescoes thought to date from around 1285, making them possibly the oldest in France, although their origins are a mystery. Some are being restored, but the tower should remain open.

A blood-red legend
The soft rock of Roussillon is red either because of the combination of oxides in the quartz, or because, many years ago, a young troubadour, Guillem de Cabestaing, came to sing at the court of Raymond of Avignon, the lord of Castel-Roussillon, and fell in love with his pretty young wife Seremonde. The old man went out hunting but returned to ambush the lovers, killing the handsome Guillem and, unbeknown to his wife, serving up his heart at a banquet. Discovering this, Seremonde threw herself from the cliffs in Roussillon, forever staining the ground red with her blood.

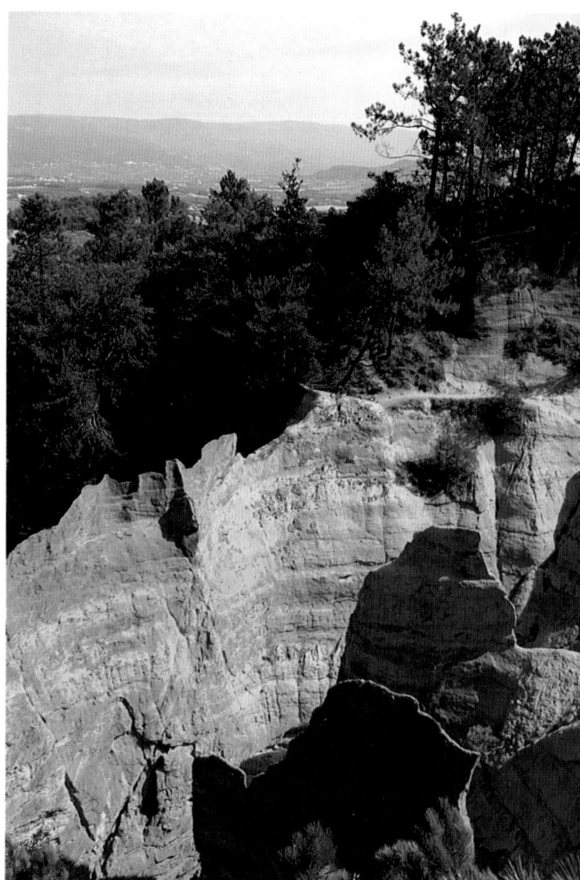

The eroded cliffs of the Chausée des Géants (Giants' Causeway) display the many hues of the ocher upon which Roussillon was built

The Sentier des Ocres (Ocher Trail) at Roussillon passes through old mine workings and quarries

► Rasteau 44B3

The vineyards that slope gently downward from the village of Rasteau produce a naturally sweet wine (similar to the Beaumes-de-Venise) but Rasteau is also one of the leading villages in the *Côtes du Rhône* appellation, with a famous wine route, the Route Orange, passing its doorstep. There is a ruined 12th-century château, but it is wine that attracts visitors, particularly the **Musée du Vigneron** (daily in summer, afternoons and weekends in winter; closed Tuesday) on the road out toward Roaix.

►►► Roussillon 45C2

It is hard to walk around this photogenic hill village without obscuring someone's video lens or tripping over art students sketching in the streets and alleyways.

Roussillon owes its unusual aesthetic appeal to the many different shades of ocher (17 in all, we are told) that have been used as if from an artist's palette to tint the village houses in intense colors ranging from golden yellow to blood red. Of course the villagers didn't plan it that way; they simply used the nearest available materials — the ocher rocks which for many centuries formed the basis of an important mining industry here.

Ocher has been used for coloring since prehistoric times and when the Romans occupied nearby *Apta Julia* they were quick to spot the potential of the extensive deposits around Roussillon. Commercial exploitation began in earnest in 1780, with ocher powders shipped all over the world from Marseille. At the beginning of this century over a thousand people were employed here and nearly everyone in the village was an *ocrier*. The decline set in with the discovery of synthetic dyes and by 1930 the industry had all but collapsed.

Ocher was mined either in tall, underground galleries or in the open air. The former are closed for safety reasons but you can wander at will through the disused quarries at the end of the village where there is a **Sentier des Ocres►►** (Ocher Trail) with information signboards.

► Rustrel 45C2

Although it shares a common heritage with nearby Roussillon founded on ocher mining, Rustrel is not in itself particularly compelling. However, the old quarries on the southern side of the Doua valley nearby, known as the Provençal **Colorado►**, are popular with hikers.

The Colorado walk
To reach the ocher quarries, head back from Rustrel toward Apt and take D22 to Gignac: shortly you will see a signpost on the left for Colorado. From the main parking lot there is a slightly confusing network of footpaths leading off through the woods, but just head away from the road and within a few minutes you will arrive at the quarries, a fantastic landscape of richly toned colors. Bear eastward in order to reach the towering red pillars known as the *cheminées des fées* (chimneystacks of the fairies).

Lavender honey, scented sachets, essential oils, and dried lavender are among the many products from this aromatic plant on sale at a roadside stall near Sault

► Saignon 45C2

Way above the Calavon valley, Saignon is slung like a hammock between two rocks — on one of which are the remains of an old castle and, on the other, the parish church. Approaching Saignon from the direction of Apt, it is easy to see why it has been a natural fortress since Celto-Ligurian times: the towering rocks on which the village is built would be enough to dissuade any attacker. Today it is a typically peaceful Provençal village with nothing more demanding of your attention than an old clock tower, a pretty square with a fountain in the middle and washingtroughs off to one side, and an unusually broad-beamed, 12th-century church.

St-Didier 44B2

Lined with plane trees, the main street in St-Didier ends up at a medieval gateway and church behind which a small square leads into the **Château de Thézan►**. This 15th-century building was converted in 1863 into a hydrotherapy center which today is renowned for the treatment of nervous diseases; it isn't open to the public but you can peek into the courtyard to see the Renaissance doorways and windows of the main facade.

The power of healing is also at the center of the nearby **Hermitage of St-Gens►**, past the neighboring village of le Beaucet on D39 (see panel).

St. Gens

On the right-hand side of the nave in the Hermitage of St-Gens is the rock in which St. Gens was apparently buried after his death, with numerous crutches and walking-sticks propped up nearby as testimony to the efficacy of his miracles. Behind the hermitage a path leads up to a spring which St. Gens caused to gush out of the rock. A procession in his honor (he is the patron saint of farmers) is held here every May.

► St-Saturnin-les-Apt 45C2

Set on the southern slopes of the Vaucluse plateau, the village today is mostly known for its cherries, olive oil, asparagus, honey, and truffles. Its violent past, however, is all too evident in the ruins of the 11th-century **château,** which sprawls across the rocks above the village; at the top of these atmospheric ruins is a small Romanesque **chapel** from where there are magnificent views across the surrounding countryside (the chapel itself is closed). Back down in the village, the remnants of past fortifications are evident in the **Portail Ayguier** (1420) and later additions such as the **Tour du Portalet**, the **Porte de Rome,** and **Porte de Roque**.

▶▶ Sault *45C3*

Set on a rock spur at the eastern end of the Vaucluse plateau, Sault may not be famous as a gastronomic center but, nonetheless, the products of the surrounding countryside play a prominent role in its economy: first, there are the rare mushrooms and truffles from the oak woods (*saltus*) which gave the village its name. Then there is nougat, a Provençal specialty made here by the Boyer family for generations. Add to this lavender honey (a lavender festival is held here in August) and a highly regarded local *saucisson (sausage)* and you will realize why the Wednesday markets are patronized by people from far and wide.

In the old quarter of Sault there are several fine old mansions, the remains of a feudal château, a 12th-century church, and a municipal museum.

Nearby To the south of Sault is the inhospitable Plateau d'Albion, which houses a massive French Air Force base together with underground bunkers concealing the country's strategic nuclear missiles. From Sault to Carpentras D942 runs westward through the Gorges de la Nesque, a deep canyon which cuts through the calcerous rock of the Vaucluse plateau. Perhaps the most dramatic point is the 1,000 feet high **Rocher du Cire** (the Wax Rock) 7 miles from Sault which was the inspiration for Mistral's poem *Calendau.*

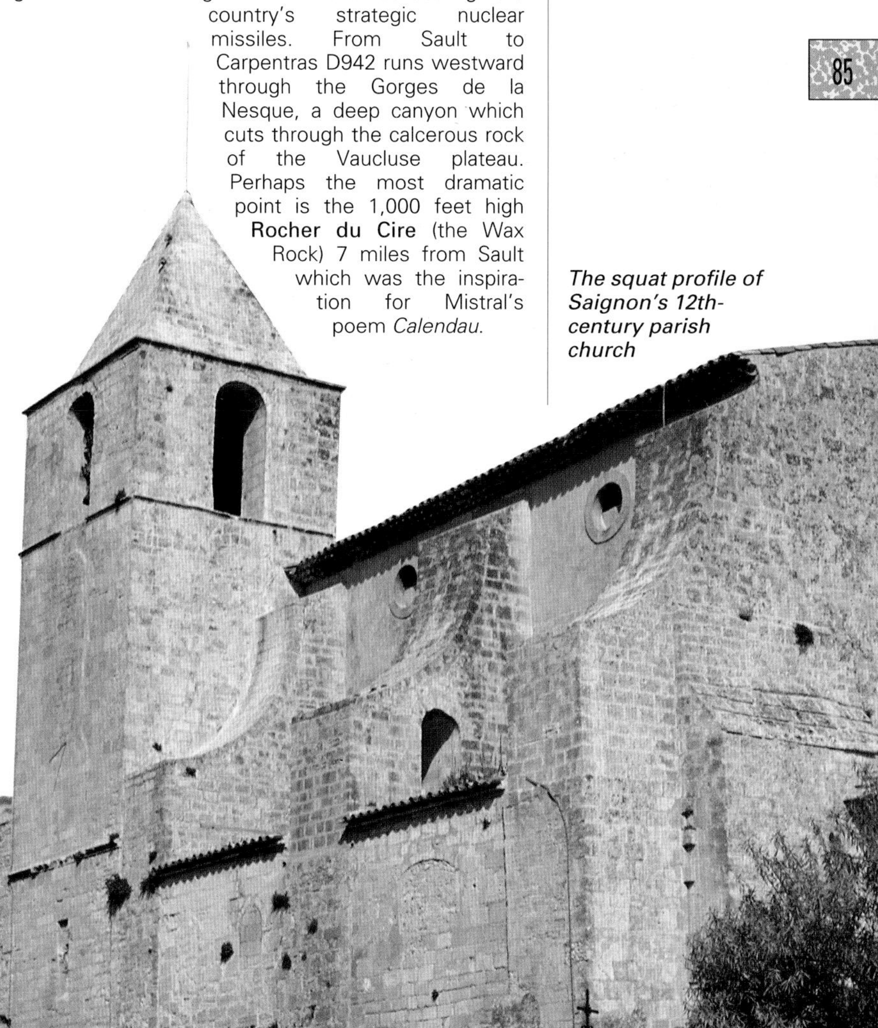

The squat profile of Saignon's 12th-century parish church

Camus at le Thor
Notre-Dame-du-Lac had a powerful effect on Albert Camus; the building's massive solidity conjured in his mind a bull at bay: "The bull sinks his four hooves into the sand of the arena. The church of Le Thor moves no more, by the force of stone: but reflected in the waters of the Sorgue this strength is purified, and becomes intelligence: it embraces the sky at the same time as anchoring itself in a bed of rocks near the stomach of the earth. On the Thor bridge I sometimes felt the fleeting taste of an unmerited happiness. Sky and earth were reconciled at that point." *La Postérité du Soleil*

►► Séguret 44B3

See page 73

► Sérignan-du-Comtat 44A3

The principal attraction of this small village 5 miles from Orange is the **Harmas de J-H Fabre►►** (open daily except Tuesday; admission). Jean-Henri Fabre was the son of a Languedoc peasant who rose to become one of the most eminent entomologists of the 19th century. Fabre's prodigious output of published works (which encompassed algebra, chemistry, astronomy, and geology as well as entomology) includes the famous *Souvenirs Entomologiques,* which earned him the nickname of the "Virgil of Insects."

When he bought a house on the outskirts of Sérignan-du-Comtat, he built a high wall around the garden and planted thousands of species of herbs and flowers, creating a botanical wilderness where he could study insects and plants to his heart's content. He christened it the *Harmas*, from the old Provençal word *herme* meaning a plot of untended land. He lived here until his death in 1915 at the age of 92.

Although Fabre was primarily an entomologist, a visit to the Harmas is about much more than just bugs and butterflies: on the first floor, for instance, there is a selection of his wonderfully delicate watercolors of the fungi of the Vaucluse, of which he painted 700 in all. Alongside editions of his 95 published works are letters from Mistral and Darwin and his collection of coins. Upstairs in his study the glass cabinets that line the wall contain shells, fossils, and minerals, while on top his colossal herbarium of France and Corsica contains some 325,000 specimens. Fabre's minute desk with his collecting satchel nearby gives the impression he just stepped out yesterday.

The gardens, which are still much the same as Fabre

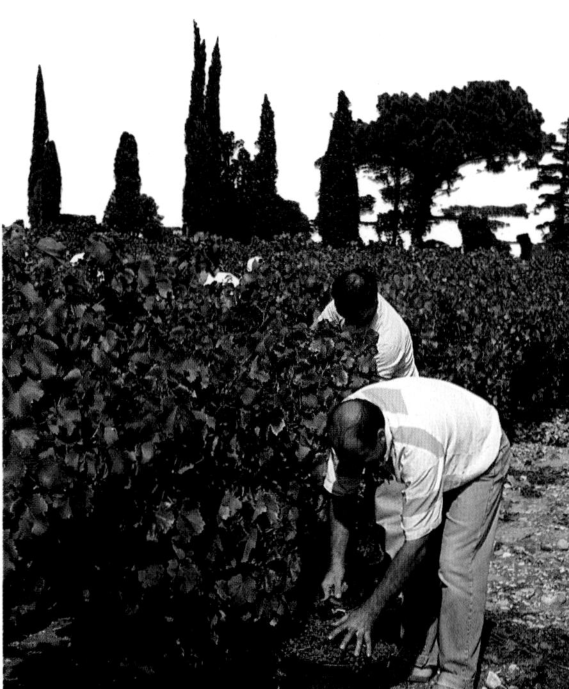

Harvest time in the vineyards surrounding Suze-la-Rousse

left them (complete with home-made insect traps), are best appreciated in April or May.

Suze-la-Rousse *44A3*

This village near Bollène has become the vinological capital of Provence thanks to the conversion of its 12th-century castle into the **Université de Vin** (open daily, conferences permitting). The lavishly equipped château runs courses on all aspects of wine, from marketing to winetasting, mostly aimed at professionals but open to the serious amateur. There is a huge library with a comprehensive collection of books on every subject related to wine.

House walls and quarry walls merge in the upper village of les Taillades

► les Taillades *44B1*

It is worth a quick detour off the Apt–Cavaillon road to see the upper half of this village, a rather bizarre assemblage of rocks and houses which has arisen because the old village was built on top of a quarry. Park in the square next to the post office and walk up to the old church at the top, passing by the Théâtre des Carrières (summer performances) and a number of dwellings where it is difficult to distinguish between house and rock.

On the D31 in the modern villages the lovely paddle-wheel on the Canal de Carpentras, which once powered a flour mill.

► le Thor *44B2*

Apples and the white dessert grape Chasselas were once the traditional mainstays of this modest market town in the Sorgue valley. On the banks of the Sorgue is one of the most impressive Romanesque churches in the Comtat, **Notre-Dame-du-Lac►►.**

Completed at the end of the 12th century, it marks the transition between the Romanesque and the Gothic, with the Gothic influence evident in the vaulting of the nave (one of the earliest examples of its kind in Provence). The west portal is finely detailed and shelters a wooden statue of the Virgin with what it is described as a "Provençal haircut."

Nearby Two miles north of le Thor is the **Grotte de Thouzon►►** is one of the prettiest cave systems in Provence. Discovered in 1902 while a quarry was being excavated in the side of the Thouzon hill, its 755 foot-long gallery was almost immediately opened up to visitors. Unlike many grottos, the gallery is almost horizontal (so it is an easy walk) and has some near-perfect examples of fistulous stalactites (known as "macaronis"), thin and transparent "draperies," and small internal pools called "gours." (Guided tours daily in summer, Sunday afternoons in winter; admission.)

Surrounded by vineyards, the Université de Vin is housed in a 12th-century château

la Tour-d'Aigues *45D1*

See page 50

Herbs and herbal lore

■ The intensity of the Mediterranean sun beating down on the hillsides of Provence forces wild, aromatic herbs to increase their yield of essential oils — thus making them more pungent, more efficacious in the many herbal remedies or recipes for which the region is celebrated.....■

Shepherd sorcerers The Provençal shepherd has long been considered a kind of sorcerer, a plant magician who is thoroughly conversant with the wild herbs of the hills and their healing properties. He knew that the sap from marsh mallow was good for healing cuts, that the juice of snails could strengthen rotten nails. He would cure the wounded foot of a sheep by transferring the illness to a patch of turf — at sunset. His knowledge of plants, of where they were to be found and when they should be picked, was legendary.

Many country people in Provence still cure themselves with age-old remedies such as "red oil," which is made from the flowers of St. John's wort (hypericum) mixed with olive oil and used in the treatment of wounds and burns. Sage is a popular cure-all and used for everything from hangover cures (in sage soup) to steam baths for acne.

Garlic is a well-known antiseptic (cut a clove in half and rub it on the skin as an antidote to bee stings) and useful for "cleansing the blood." It is also used as a remedy for corns, worms, and warts. Thyme can be used to protect against respiratory infections and coughs — it is also supposedly an aphrodisiac.

Many of these cures are now being revived thanks to the current fashion for treatments such as herbalism, aromatherapy, and other forms of natural healing.

Herbs in all their various forms provide an aromatic souvenir of Provence

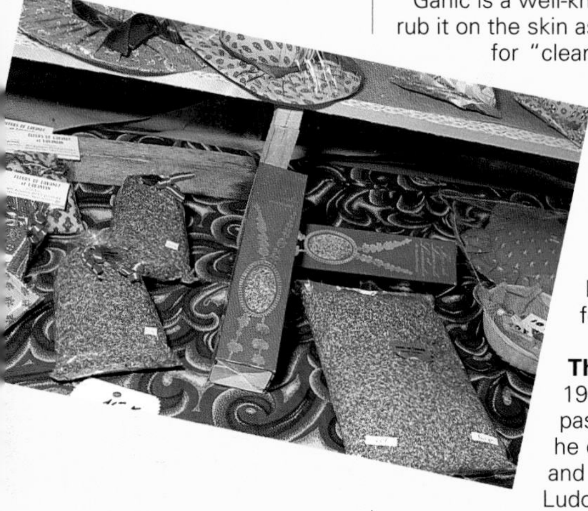

The Plant Magic Man In the early 1970s the writer Lawrence Durrell was passing through the Arles market when he came across a stall selling fresh herbs and herbal cures run by a local man called Ludo Chardenon. Driven to desperation by eczema, Durrell bought an herbal tea and was astonished when his painful condition cleared up in ten days: the infusion had succeeded where the top doctors of London and Paris had failed.

Durrell befriended Ludo Chardenon, and wrote a feature on his life story for the *International Herald Tribune* in 1972, christening him "the Plant Magic Man." A decade later Durrell persuaded the "Plant Magic Man" to write a book of his recipes, which is still in print today: *In Praise of Wild Herbs — Remedies and Recipes from Old Provence* (Century Publishing) is a fascinating compendium containing cures for everything from acne to worms, covering

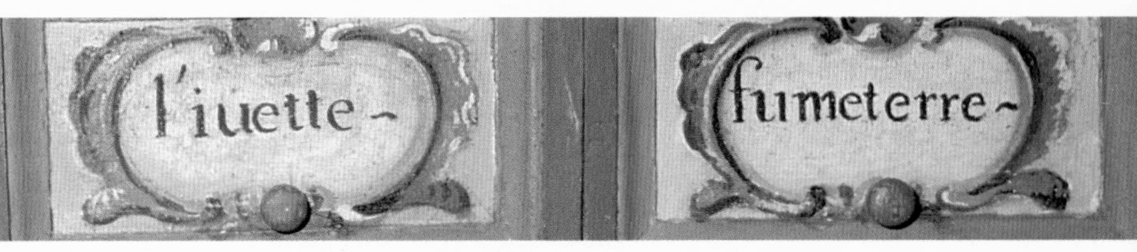

aging, baldness, cellulite, obesity, rheumatism, stress, and much more in between.

Lavender and lavandin The scent of lavender is one of the most characteristic aromas of Provence; rare is the souvenir shop that does not have bundles of scent bags stuffed with its fragrant flowers. The Romans treasured it for its soothing qualities, and added it to their baths (hence the name, from *lavare*, "to wash" in Latin). Today it is used in everything from soaps to expensive perfumes.

The main growing area for lavender in Provence is the so-called "mauve triangle" between Sault, Banon, and Séderon, which accounts for 70 percent of national production (the other main growing area is on the other side of Mont Ventoux, north of Nyons in the *département* of the Drôme).

The first lavender distillery started up in the 1880s to supply lavender essence for the apothecaries of Apt and Carpentras. After World War I, systematic cultivation began in response to demands from the *parfumeurs* of Grasse and by 1929 there were 47 stills around Sault, producing 22,000 pounds of essential lavender oil. Only a handful of distilleries now remain.

Most bouquets and other products that you buy in the shops are made using lavandin, a hybrid lavender that grows prolifically at low altitudes. The most highly scented and highly prized lavender is *lavande fine*, which grows at higher altitudes and carries its own Appellation d'Origine Contrôlée (AOC) like wine; at around 400 francs to the kilo, it is ten times more expensive than lavandin.

The dying fields
Although it has not yet struck the Vaucluse, a deadly fungus is killing off the fields of fine lavender in the neighboring *département* of the Drôme. Since 1985, plants have been withering and turning gray due to a tiny fungus, *Fusarium*, which it is thought might be flourishing because of climatic changes. Lavender prefers arid conditions, and too much spring rain in recent years has upset the balance. Recently scientists met at Nyons in the Drôme to try and solve the problem; if they don't come up with a solution soon, a whole way of life will be lost.

The Roman legacy is highly visible in Vaison-la-Romaine

▶▶▶ Vaison-la-Romaine *44B3*

Over the centuries, the inhabitants of Vaison have moved backward and forward between the two banks of the River Ouvèze. The first settlement was the Celtic stronghold on top of the hill when Vaison was the regional capital of the Voconces people. Conquered by the Romans in the 2nd century B.C., the inhabitants moved down to the more fertile plains on the other side of the river and lived alongside the Romans in what then became *Vasio Vocontiorum*. Accorded the status of federated city, the town prospered and its population grew to 10,000 inhabitants: luxurious villas, a theater, baths, an aqueduct, and a bridge were constructed.

Vaison became a bishopric in the 4th century and the building of the cathedral began in the 6th century; the latter was one of the casualties of the Frankish invasions which devastated much of the town. In the 12th century Count Raymond of Toulouse built a castle on the site of the old Celtic fortress and gradually people moved away from the Roman town to the greater safety of the *Haute Ville*.

Vaison became part of the Comtat Venaissin in the 1300s, remaining papal property until the Revolution. In the 19th century the inhabitants were on the move again, drifting back down to the left bank and leaving the *Haute Ville* to fall into ruins.

As they started to rebuild the town they uncovered parts of the Roman town, although it was not until 1907 that excavations began in earnest. Spread over an area of 32 acres, the **Roman ruins▶▶** (open daily; admission charge also includes cathedral cloister — see below) lie in two halves on either side of the place Abbé Sautel and the tourist office in the center of town.

To the east is the *Quartier de Puymin*, built around the base of a hill. On entering, you immediately find yourself in the middle of a huge villa, the Maison des Messii; next door is the *Portique du Pompée*, a public courtyard with gardens and a pool. Built into the north slope of the hill, the **theater▶** held around 6,000 people and was probably constructed about the 1st century A.D. Restored in the last century, it yielded several fine statues which are now in the **Museum▶▶** alongside most of the other important finds from the excavations.

On the other side of the road excavations are still going on in the *Quartier de la Villasse*. A Roman street leads down to the city baths and another huge villa. This has become known as the *Maison au Buste d'Argent*, after the silver bust of the owner which was found here, and included mosaic floors and two gardens with pools. Next door is the *Maison au Dauphin*, also with private gardens and baths.

Leaving the Quartier de la Villasse at the exit next to the baths, a pathway alongside the excavations brings you to the former cathedral of **Notre-Dame-de-Nazareth▶▶**

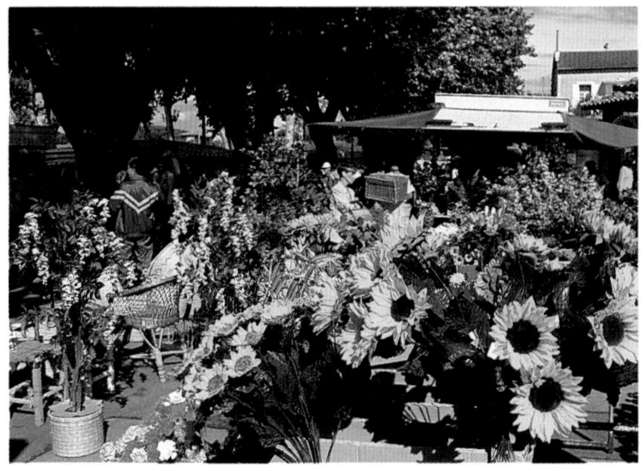

Vaison's colorful market spreads over the lower town every Tuesday

which many consider to be one of the finest Romanesque monuments in Provence. On the north side, the lovely 12th-century **cloister▶** has several finely carved pillars supporting the arcades.

The two halves of Vaison are connected by a 55 foot Roman bridge, from where a road leads up through the fortified gateway into the narrow streets of the **Haute Ville▶▶**. Deserted at the beginning of the century, many of its houses have been carefully restored and a handful of discreet craft shops and art galleries can be found among the cobbled streets and fountains. There are views back down to the town and across to Mont Ventoux from the ruins of the 12th-century château.

Gourmet days
Every November Vaison hosts *Les Journées Gourmandes* — "five days in the Provençal autumn dedicated to the most subtle of pleasures" – which brings together winemakers, restaurateurs, bakers, cheesemakers, and growers in an extravaganza of eating and drinking. The best of local food and wines are displayed, tasted, discussed — and simply enjoyed. Full details from the Maison du Tourisme et du Vin, place du Chanoine Sautel, 841110 Vaison-la-Romaine (tel. 90 36 02 11).

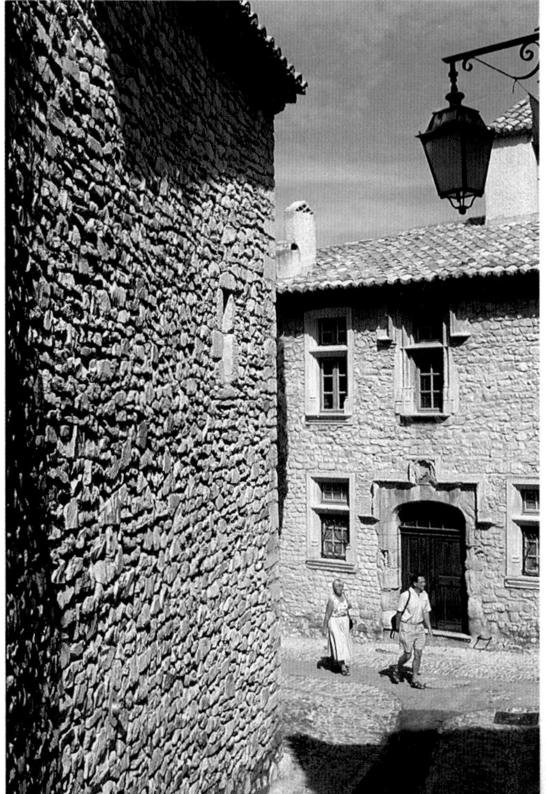

The cobbled streets of the Haute Ville *lead up to the ruins of an old château*

Memorial to British cyclist Tommy Simpson, Mont Ventoux

Petit-St-Jean
Valréas is the setting for a spectacular and colorful festival on June 23 each year, when the town celebrates *La Nuit du Petit-St-Jean.* Over 300 participants in full costume march through the streets by torchlight up to the Château de Simiane for the enthroning of "petit St-Jean," represented by a four-year-old child who becomes the protector of Valréas for the following year. The spectacle dates back many centuries and was originally a pagan ceremony in honor of the Sun, Water, and Fire, later to be transformed by the church into a summer solstice celebration.

▶ Valréas *44B4*

Valréas sometimes appears with *"l'Enclave des Papes"* tacked on after its name, a description that harks back to when Pope John XXII acquired this territory with the aim of expanding the Comtat Venaissin northward. Unfortunately, King Charles VII heard of this plan and forbade the sale of further land, leaving Valréas and the surrounding villages isolated.

When the *départements* of France were created in the 18th century, Valréas opted to remain part of the Vaucluse (and hence part of Provence) even though it was then, as it is now, encircled by the *département* of the Drôme.

Valréas today is a pleasant town ringed by a boulevard of plane trees, its economy mostly dependent on the cardboard industry and — somewhat more enticing — the production of Côtes du Rhône wine, asparagus, and lavender.

Within the medieval town center the most imposing monument is the mainly 18th-century **Château de Simiane▶** housing the town hall and contemporary art shows in the summer.

There are several fine old mansions to be seen in Valréas, as well as the Romanesque church of **Notre-Dame-de-Nazareth▶** which has a particularly interesting doorway on its south side.

▶ Venasque *44B2*

Overlooking the Carpentras plain, Venasque is another village whose commanding position makes its value as a

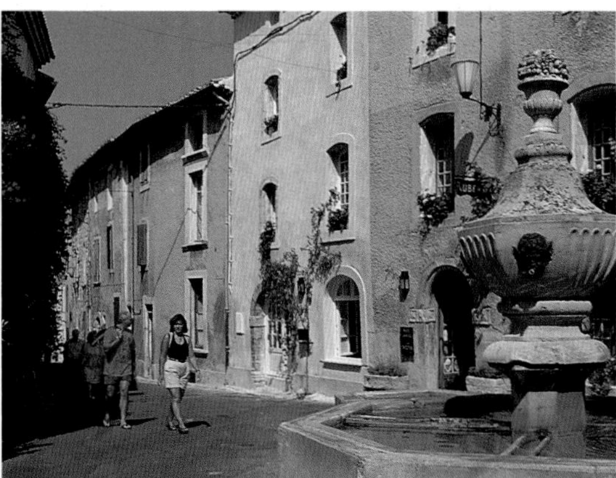

An old fountain in the quiet streets of Venasque

strategic site immediately obvious — in this case, dominating the only route through the mountains between Carpentras and Apt. Occupied since Celtic times, it later became a refuge for the bishops of Carpentras against barbarian invasions. For reasons unknown, this small village gave its name to the entire territory of the Comtat Venaissin.

Alongside this honor, it also possesses one of the oldest religious buildings in France, the **Baptistry▶▶** (open daily, closed Sunday mornings and Wednesday; admission) next to the church. Dating from around the 6th century A.D., it may originally have been a pagan temple dedicated to Diana, Venus, or Mercury. There are many curiosities inside: fragments of a sarcophagus dating from A.D.420, the elegant columns that bear evidence of usage in Roman times, an octagonal font set in the floor, and a strange arrangement of holes bashed in the walls of the north apse, designed to improve the acoustics.

At the opposite end of the village is a huge medieval curtain wall with three turrets, which barred the entrance to this once-formidable stronghold.

Conquering Mont Ventoux
The first recorded ascent of "the Provençal Giant" was by the poet Petrarch, who climbed it in 1336 with his brother. From the 18th century onward there were many scientific expeditions, which led to the building of an observatory in 1882. Later, when a road was built, the steep climb became a proving ground for cars (a de Dion-Bouton made it in 2hrs 15 minutes in 1909) and bicycles (it is one of the most demanding stages of the Tour de France; British cyclist Tommy Simpson died on the way up in 1967).

▶▶▶ **Ventoux, Mont** *45C3*

The highest peak between the Pyrenees and the Alps, with its 6,263 feet summit often in the clouds, Mont Ventoux dominates the Vaucluse plateau and the Rhône valley, marking the northern entrance to Provence.

The summit of Mont Ventoux

From Malaucène D974 winds up past **Notre-Dame du Groseau** (an octagonal chapel which is the only surviving part of a 12th-century monastery) and the **Source du Groseau**, a spring that the Romans channeled in an aqueduct to Vaison. From here on up the views become more and more spectacular, and nearer the summit, the vegetation thins out until only rocks remain. Once at the top, turn your back on the radar towers and radio masts and soak up one of the most astounding views in Provence, extending from the Alps down to the Mediterranean.

Mont Ventoux was once covered in dense forests of oak, cedar, and pine. By the beginning of the 19th century the forest had all but disappeared (cut down to build warships in Toulon), but in the late 1900s a massive reforestation program began, with extensive plantings of Austrian pine and cedar of Lebanon; these now provide a habitat for wild boar, deer, and over 100 bird species including owls and rare eagles. Mont Ventoux is also home to 950 species of plants, both Alpine and Mediterranean.

In 1990 a large part of the mountain was designated a UNESCO Biosphere Reserve and research into its unique flora and fauna continues at the forest ecology laboratory in Malaucène.

Mountain sports
Many sporting activities take place on, and above, the slopes of Mont Ventoux, such as skiing, paragliding, and mountain biking; plus daytime and nighttime walks (you reach the summit at dawn) in the summer from Malaucène tourist office (tel. 90 65 22 59).

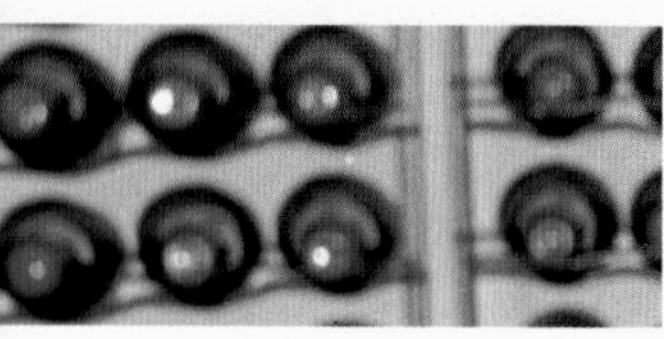

■ **With the exception of a few notable vineyards, wines from Provence used to be sniffed at by connoisseurs but in recent years the quality has improved enormously, adding to the pleasures of the sunny south.....■**

Wine to go
Walk into almost any *cave cooperative* and you can sample local wines and buy them direct by the bottle or case — usually much better value than other outlets. You can also buy your wine *en vrac* (in bulk), which is what most locals do. Simply turn up at the *cave*, pay at the cash desk, and your container is filled from a gas-pump type nozzle from the vats below. You can buy old-fashioned *bonbons* (wicker-covered glass jars) in hardware stores or inexpensive plastic containers which hold up to 33 liters (about 9 gallons) in the *cave* itself.

Although said to have been enjoyed by the kings of France in the 17th and 18th centuries, Provençal wines have not had such a glowing reputation in this century and many have only recently acquired the coveted AOC (*Appellation d'Origine Contrôlée*) status. Hugh Johnson's definitive *World Atlas of Wine*, published at the beginning of the 1970s, is typically dismissive: "An optimistic description of Provence wines always mentions the sun-baked pines, thyme, and lavender and claims that the wine takes its character from them. This is true of some of the best of them...others get by on a pretty colour and a good deal of alcohol. 'Tarpaulin edged with lace' is a realistic summing up of one of the better ones."

However, in the last couple of decades the quality of Provençal wines has improved significantly and this is reflected in Johnson's more recent comments ("rock hills of limestone and shale, and in some cases a cool breeze off the sea, can give considerable distinction to certain *eras*"). You will certainly find plenty of reasonably priced, highly drinkable bottles on your travels through the region.

In addition to the main *appellations* listed below there are numerous wines designated VDQS (*Vin Delimité de Qualité Supérieur*) which, while unlikely to be memorable, are at least good value.

Côtes du Rhône Although not generally considered a Provençal wine, there are several Côtes du Rhône vineyards in the Vaucluse. Most Côtes du Rhône wines are made from a blend of grape varieties, resulting in a robust, full-bodied flavor which develops considerably in depth and subtlety if left to mature (preferably for at least five or six years).

The *appellation* Côtes du Rhône Villages is much more restricted and produces a superior wine, more complex and firmer than the normal AOC. Within the area covered by this guide, the Côtes du Rhône Villages *appellations* come from Beaumes-de-Venise, Cairanne, Rasteau, Roaix, Sablet, Séguret, Valréas, and Visan. In addition, vintage wines (Grand Crus) are produced by Gigondas (rosé and red), Vacqueyras (red, white,

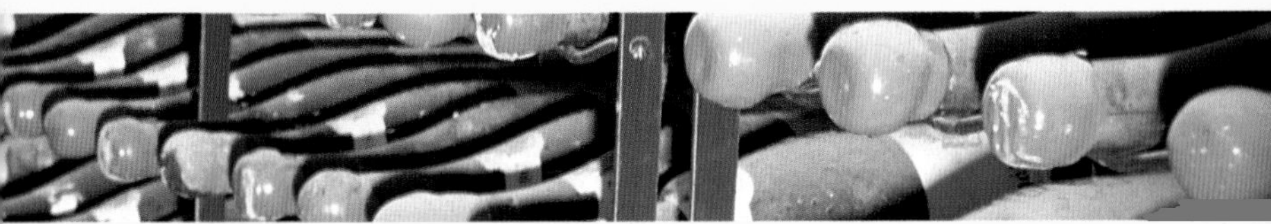

and rosé), Rasteau (Grenache sweet apéritif wine) and Beaumes-de-Venise (Muscat sweet apéritif wine).

The most well-known wine from this area, right in the heart of the Côtes du Rhône district, is that of Châteauneuf-du-Pape (see page 69).

Bandol Covering around 2,000 acres, the territory of the AOC Bandol (one of the earliest in the region, it was designated in 1941) also covers neighboring vineyards in Sanary, la Cadière, le Castellet, and (to a lesser extent) le Beausset, Evenos and Ollioules.

These fine wines owe their unusual characteristics to a high percentage of Mourvèdre grapes (up to 80 per cent in the reds) blended with Grenache and Cinsault varieties. The reds are soft and dark, with undertones of spice, vanilla, and blackberry. They keep exceptionally well — ten to 15 years for the reds.

CHATEAU ROUTAS
GRANDS VINS COTEAUX VAROIS
Dégustation gratuite, visite et vente à la cave, randonnées pédestres et pique-nique.

Cassis The small area of the AOC Cassis wines (covering just 500 acres) means that they can be pricey since output is limited. The calcareous soil around this little seaside port produces a light, dry white with a freshness that seems to come from the sea.

Côtes-de-Provence One of the most recent AOC areas (classified in 1977), Côtes-de-Provence specializes in those dry, fruity rosés that seem to slip down all too easily on a hot summer's day when served well chilled. Seventy-five percent of production is rosé, and just 20 percent red, 5 percent white. With over 100 million bottles produced annually, the *appellation* ranks sixth by volume in the whole of France.

Vineyards in Provence are now producing some highly palatable wines

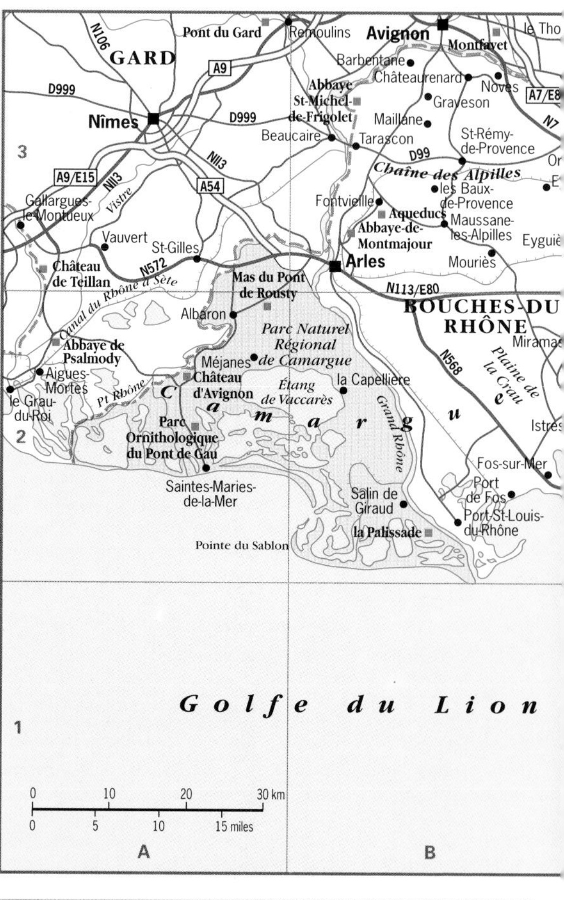

The Espace Van Gogh in Arles, a town that has played a significant role in the story of Provence since the 6th century B.C.

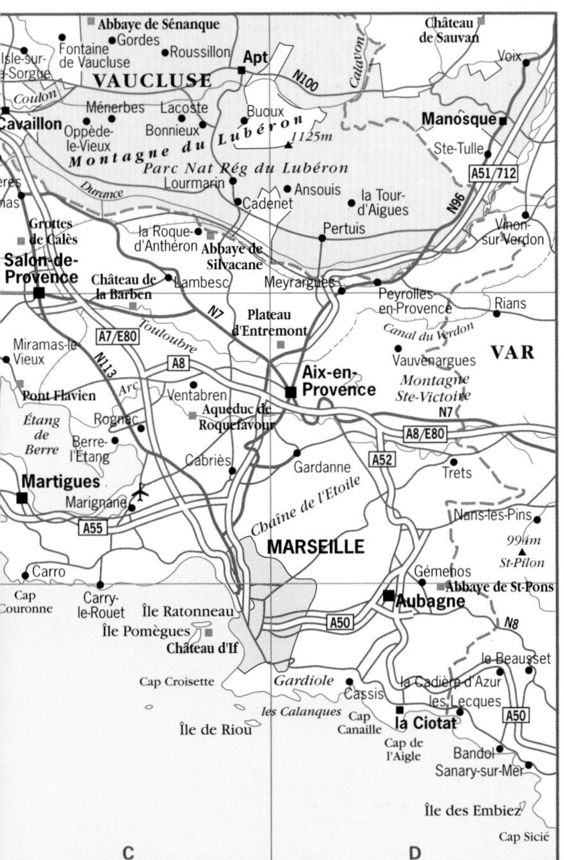

Introduction The Bouches-du-Rhône is one of the oldest inhabited regions in Provence, its roots reaching deep into history and tapping the sources of early civilization. It has some of the best monuments from Roman and medieval times and it was later the cradle of Provençal culture, the home of the troubadours, and the inspiration for great artists such as Cézanne and Van Gogh and writers such as Mistral and Marcel Pagnol.

Bordered by the Durance to the north and the Rhône to the west, the Bouches-du-Rhône is mostly low-lying (below 1,000 feet) although at Cap Canaille it has the highest cliffs in France. It is the most densely populated and heavily industrialized *département* in Provence and yet has more protected areas (covering over 500,000 acres) than any *département* in the whole of France.

Marseille and the east The "capital" of the Bouches-du-Rhône is Marseille, the oldest city in Provence and nowadays almost as well known for organized crime as for its famous fish soup, the *bouillabaisse*.

Marseille's one million inhabitants live at the heart of an industrialized coastline which expands westward around the nearby Étang de Berre, and yet within a short distance in the other direction there is a sublime

coastline of pine-covered cliffs gashed by deep inlets, the famous *calanques*. Nestling beneath the cliffs is the port of Cassis, its streets crowded with gastronomic pilgrims in search of its renowned seafood and delicate white wines.

East of Marseille are the hilliest parts of the Bouches-du-Rhône, with the crest of the Massif de la Ste-Baume marking the boundary with neighboring Var. Beneath the wooded slopes of Ste-Baume, the town of Aubagne is a major ceramics center which produces (among other things) small clay figures known as *santons*, used in Christmas crèches.

Running parallel to the Ste-Baume massif are the limestone ridges of the Montagne Ste-Victoire which dominate the landscapes around Aix-en-Provence.

La Crau At the center of the Bouches-du-Rhône is the vast plain known as la Grande Crau, or just la Crau, divided in two by the jagged peaks of the Chaîne des Alpilles which culminates in a modest summit at la Caume (1,270 feet). To the north of the Alpilles are the fertile plains of the Petite Crau where abundant harvests of soft fruit and vegetables are well protected from the dreaded *mistral* by long rows of cypress and poplar. The man after whom the wind was named was born here in the small village of Maillane, and the legends and customs of the Petite Crau were some of the

primary sources of inspiration for Frédéric Mistral.

Sheltering beneath the northern flank of the Alpilles is the delightful town of St-Rémy-de-Provence, with the ancient ruined city of Glanum on the slopes above it. West of St-Rémy, the Renaissance castle at Tarascon stands guard on the banks of the Rhône, symbol of the centuries-old mistrust between Provence and the Kingdom of France.

On the south face of the Alpilles the windswept heights of les Baux dominate the Grand Crau stretching away down to the Rhône delta. Now drained, the Grand Crau was once swampland with settlements on isolated outcrops: one of these was the former Abbaye-de-Montmajour, whose ruins still dominate the countryside.

Bordering the Grand Crau, the lively town of Arles is, with more than its share of historic monuments, testimony to its role as the Roman capital of Provence. Its neighbour to the west, Nîmes, shares much of the same heritage and is part of a "tourist triangle" (which also includes Arles and Avignon) around Provence, even though it is in Languedoc-Roussillon.

The Camargue Finally, there is the domain of flamingos, white horses, cowboys, and bulls — not to mention mosquitos — down in the Camargue, that marshy triangle that has been created by the joint efforts of man and the mighty River Rhône.

One of the wonders of the Roman world, the Pont du Gard

►► Aigues-Mortes

96A2

The western half of the Camargue is dominated by the imposing fortified walls of Aigues-Mortes. Although it is in the *département* of the Languedoc and not the Bouches-du-Rhône, it is an essential part of the tourist circuit around the delta.

In the 13th century the land around Aigues-Mortes was owned by the monks of the powerful Abbaye de Psalmody nearby, but when Louis IX (St. Louis) began building a port here in 1241 they agreed to exchange their territories for the Château de Villevieille near Sommières. Louis IX was desperate for a French port on the Mediterranean, since the coast on either side was controlled by the Counts of Provence and the Kings of Aragon, and without this base he would have been unable to launch his long-dreamt-of crusades.

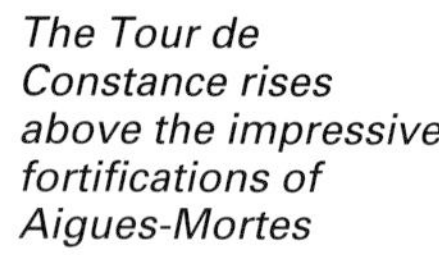

The Tour de Constance rises above the impressive fortifications of Aigues-Mortes

The unappealing name of Aigues-Mortes ("dead waters") was given to the port to distinguish it from the nearby town of Aigues-Vives ("living waters") 12 miles farther north.

By 1248, the port was complete and Louis IX and his 30,000 knights set off in an armada of 1,500 ships to liberate Jersualem. This Seventh Crusade was a disaster for the king, but he survived and came home to prepare for the Eighth Crusade against North Africa. This time,

Aigues-Mortes was to be his last glimpse of French soil, for he died of typhoid at the gates of Tunis in 1270.

Two years after his death his successor Philip III began construction of the town's remarkable ramparts, which took nearly 30 years to complete. The fortifications, which extend for more than a mile around the town, contain no fewer than 15 towers and 10 gates and have been preserved almost entirely intact to this day. The reason for this is that Aigues-Mortes soon went into decline, left high and dry by the retreating waters in the middle of the 14th century.

The most impressive of the towers is the massive **Tour de Constance▶▶▶** (open daily; admission) which, due to its impregnability, was soon put to use as a prison: Philippe le Bel imprisoned 45 Templars here in 1307 but its most notorious period was in the 17th century when hundreds of women, all of them Protestants rounded up in the Cévennes, were incarcerated in the tower in appalling conditions. One of these women, Marie Durand, was kept here for 38 years because she refused to renounce her faith (you can still see where she carved the one word *register* — "resist" in her local dialect — into the stone wall).

From the top of the 170 foot-high tower there is a terrific view across the town and the Camargue, and beneath it you can walk around parts of the ramparts.

Unlike most medieval towns, Aigues-Mortes is laid out in a neat grid pattern with the streets converging on the tidy central square, **place St-Louis**, where there is a statue to Louis IX by Pradier, commissioned in the 19th century to commemorate the Seventh and Eighth Crusades. On the corner with rue Jean-Jaurès is the attractive church of **Notre-Dame-des-Sablons▶** ("Our Lady of the Sands") where sunlight streaming through the stained glass windows colors the simple, airy interior. On the opposite side of the square the former **Cloître des Capucins** now houses the tourist office.

The town has a handful of decent hotels and restaurants, and in the latter you might like to try the local speciality, *taureau à la gardienne*, which is a beef and olive stew.

Salt and wine tours
Aigues-Mortes is an important salt-production center (rivalling the Salin de Giraud at the other extremity of the Camargue) and is famous for its local wine grown entirely in sandy vineyards, the *Vin du Listel*. Tours of both the wine cellars and salt pans are organized every Wednesday and Friday afternoon in July and August by the tourist office (reservations required, tel. 66 53 83 10).

Over half of French salt production comes from the Salins de Midi outside Aigues-Mortes

Above and right: just two of Aix's many fountains

▶▶ Aix-en-Provence *97D2*

Aix owes its origins and even its name to the thermal springs discovered here in pre-Roman times. A Celto-Ligurian tribe, the Salyens, built a fortified camp at Entremont (2 miles north) around the 2nd or 3rd century B.C., but their harassment of the local population led the Greeks of *Massalia* (Marseille) to plead for help from their allies in Rome. In 124B.C. Sextius Calvinus duly razed Entremont, and later set up his own camp. Twenty years later 200,000 Teutoni barbarians arrived — to be defeated by the Roman general Marius. Montagne Ste-Victoire was so named after this great victory.

Under the Romans monuments and aqueducts were built — later destroyed in the Dark Ages. In the 12th century Aix became the capital of the Counts of Provence; the university was founded in 1409; and its golden age came under the reign of Good King René (1434–1480).

After René's death in 1480 Aix endured many centuries of plagues, wars, and religious disputes before blossoming in the 17th century into a wealthy, bourgeois city with political and cultural influence.

The town declined somewhat from 1880 onward, when regional power was transferred to Marseille.

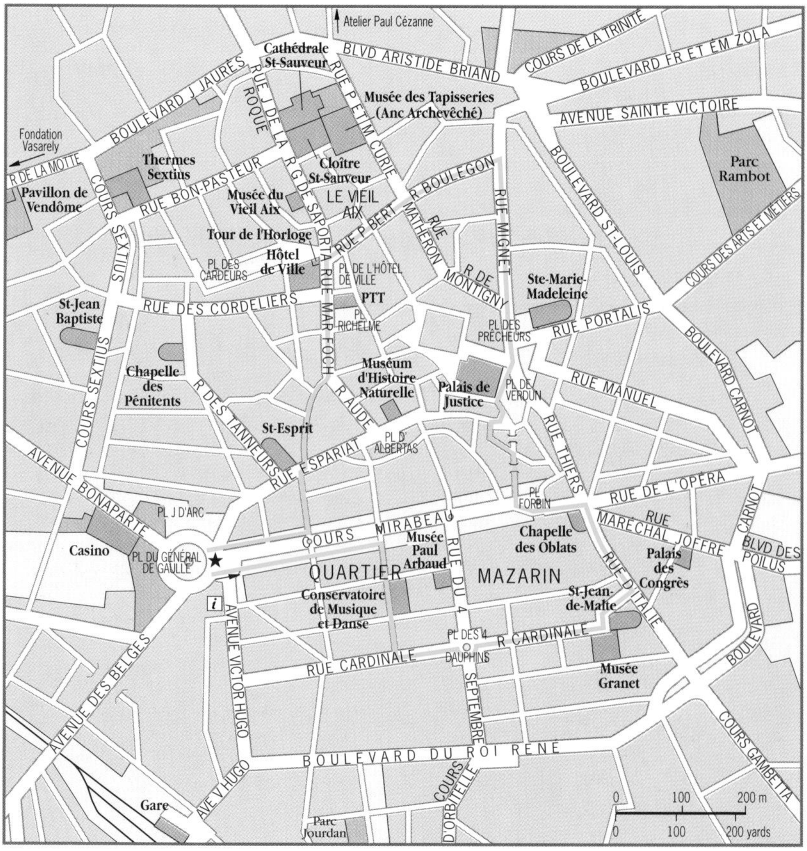

Walk Fountains and fine mansions

This walk covers the best of Aix's fountains and fine mansions, as well as the contrasting areas of the Quartier Mazarin and the old quarter. Allow 2–3 hours. *See map opposite.*

From place Général de Gaulle walk up the right-hand side of the cours Mirabeau.

Turn down rue Joseph Cabassol opposite the Fontaine des 9 canons. On your left farther down is the **Hôtel de Caumont**, designed by the architect of Versailles, now the Conservatoire de Musique et Danse. At the end of the road is the **Lycée Mignet**, once the Collège Bourbon.

Go left down the rue Cardinale to the **place des Quatres Dauphins▶**, with a 17th-century dolphin fountain. Continue on (with a possible detour to the Musée Paul Arbaud in rue du 4-Septembre) to the place St-Jean de Malte for the **Église St-Jean-de-Malte** and the **Musée Granet** (see page 105).

Turn left and left again back to the cours Mirabeau, briefly acknowledging King René before crossing the boulevard to see the old advertisement for the *Chapellerie du Cours Mirabeau* at No. 55, where Cézanne grew up in his father's hat shop.

Follow the small passageway beside the shop through to the place de Verdun, which is dominated by the 18th-century **Palais de Justice**. There is a regular flea market (*marché aux puces*) here and the neighboring **place des Prêcheurs** has a food market on Tuesday, Thursday, and Saturday mornings. Above the square is the **Église Ste-Marie-Madeleine▶** with works by Rubens and Van Loo.

Continue up rue Mignet, which has several fine 18th-century buildings, and the crumbling façade of the ancient Monastère de la Visitation. Turn left down rue Boulegon, continuing on to the **place de l'Hôtel de Ville** (see page 105). From here, either detour northward up rue Gaston de Saporta toward the **Musée du Vieil Aix**, the **Musée des Tapisseries,** and the **Cathédrale St-Sauveur** (see pages 105–106), or return through the **Vieil Aix** back streets to the cours Mirabeau.

Architectural details such as this wood carving enliven Aix's many belle époque *mansions*

Dried flowers make a colorful display in one of Vieil Aix's street markets

What to see To feel the pulse of Aix take a preliminary stroll down the **cours Mirabeau▶▶**, a wide boulevard with a canopy of huge plane trees which shield the passers-by from the sun as they flit from café to café, socializing and checking out everybody else's outfits and partners in what is essentially center stage for chic Aixois society. Locals call it simply *le cours*, as if there were no other of importance. Apart from one or two bookstores the north side is almost entirely cafés, and *patisseries*, with tempting ice creams, cakes and cocktails on offer, inviting you to sit and watch the parade. One of the most elegant cafés (with prices to match) is the *fin-de-siècle* **Les Deux Garçons**, with its interior a riot of gilded mirrors and antique lights. The south side of the boulevard is characterized by splendid 17th- and 18th-century mansions with façades of honey-colored stone ornamented with fine wrought-iron balconies and carved doorways.

Running down the middle of the cours Mirabeau is a series of fountains, including the mossy-covered **Fontaine Chaude** with bubbling hot spring water, and the **Fontaine du Roi René**. At the other end, the roads from Avignon and Marseille meet at the traffic circle in place Général de Gaulle, with its spouting jets from the fountain of **La Rotonde**.

To the south of cours Mirabeau are the orderly streets of the **Quartier Mazarin▶▶**, created in 1646 by Michel Mazarin, archbishop of Aix, specifically for the lawyers and nobles attending parliament. At 2a rue du 4-Septembre is the **Musée Paul Arbaud** (open 2–5, closed Sunday; admission) which houses a fine collection of *faïences* from Moustiers-Ste-Marie and Marseille, works by Puget and Fragonard, sculptures, and an enormous collection of manuscripts, rare editions, and books on Provence. Once the home of collector and bibliophile

Paul Arbaud, the house itself is fairly remarkable, with hand-crafted ceilings and fireplaces, silk wallpaper, and carved wooden doorways.

Also in the *quartier* is the **Musée Granet▶▶** (open daily except Tuesday; admission) devoted to art and archaeology. Upstairs is a disappointing, unimaginatively displayed collection of 18th- and 19th-century paintings. Cézanne is represented by a miserly eight paintings, donated in 1984 by the French government to remedy the total absence of his works in his native city. More interesting are the finds, in the basement, from the ancient oppidum of Entremont. The Celto-Ligurian sculptures (unearthed in the 1940s) rank amongst the oldest known pre-Roman works in France and include some fascinating ritual masks, statues, and torsos.

Next door to the museum is the 13th-century **church of St-Jean-de-Malte** with its elegant fortified Gothic facade.

The harmonious urban planning of the Quartier Mazarin seems a world away once you cross into the chaotic, busy streets of **Vieil Aix▶▶**, on the other side of the cours Mirabeau. This is an area to wander in at a leisurely pace, stopping to admire the many handsome old buildings or fountain-splashed *places* and soaking up the lively atmosphere of people milling around the markets, shops, and restaurants.

At the center of the old town is the **place de l'Hôtel de Ville** which is at its best when filled with the colors and heady scents of the flower market on Thursday and Saturday mornings. The square was built in 1741 to create space in front of the classical Italianate **Hôtel de Ville▶**, which was rebuilt in the late 17th century by Pierre Pavillon. Tacked onto a corner of the town hall is the 16th-century **Tour de l'Horloge▶**, which has an astronomical clock as well as one defining the seasons.

On the south side of the square, the old **Corn Exchange** (now the central Post Office) boasts a massive pediment statue by Chastel. Around the back of the Post Office, the **place Richelme** has a daily fruit and vegetable market and is one of the city's main hangouts for street musicians and students.

Old Aix has a variety of museums, including the **Musée des Tapisseries▶** (closed Tuesday; admission) inside the grand old Archbishop's Palace. Most of the whimsical Beauvais tapestries were collected by archbishops in the 17th and 18th centuries; contemporary textiles are also featured.

Another fine old mansion, the Hôtel Boyer d'Eguilles, now contains the **Muséum d'Histoire Naturelle** (closed Sunday) which has all the usual fossils and bones as well as an astronomy section and a clutch of rare dinosaur eggs.

Tasty Aixois treats
Aix is one of France's biggest exporters of prepared almonds, with which they also make a delectable local speciality, the *calisson*. The almonds are ground into a paste and then mixed with fruit syrup and glazed melons before being trimmed with icing sugar. *Calissons* were first created in Aix in 1473 and they are still made by hand, with around a dozen shops specializing in them. One of the oldest is the Confiserie Bremond at 16 rue d'Italie where you can watch them being made on Friday mornings (by appointment, tel. 42 27 36 25).

The whimsical Tour de l'Horloge, a landmark of Vieil Aix

The Good King René
René d'Anjou (1408–1480) inherited the titles of Duke of Anjou, Duke of Lorraine, Count of Provence, and King of Sicily, Naples, and Jerusalem in 1434. During the first half of his reign he flitted between his various kingdoms, unsuccessfully playing at diplomacy and politics, until he settled in Aix in 1471 and devoted himself to patronage of the arts instead. He was himself a poet, musician, painter, and linguist (he spoke six languages fluently). He introduced Muscat grapes and silkworms to Provence, but it was probably not the general populace who coined the term "Good King René" since he taxed them heavily to pay for his indulgences.

Mirabeau's misfortunes
Later to achieve fame as a political leader during the Revolution, at the age of 23 the penniless Count Mirabeau decided to marry the aristocratic Émilie de Covet Marignane. Although his suit had already been rejected, he sneaked into her house, leaving his carriage outside the door for all to see in the morning. Her virtue compromised, the marriage had to take place but his father-in-law cut off the young couple's allowance. Mirabeau promptly ran up debts all over Aix and was imprisoned in the Château d'If. Once released, he eloped to Amsterdam with another married woman but was summoned back to Aix for the divorce case — which he lost.

Just north of the Tour de l'Horloge in rue Gaston de Saporta you'll find the **Musée du Vieil Aix** (closed Monday; admission) with an assortment of curiosities that includes a set of masks and mechanized marionettes portraying characters in the ancient *Fête-Dieu* ceremonies. This religious festival, once celebrated throughout Provence, was originally initiated in the 13th century by Pope Urban IV; King René revived it in the 15th century and turned it into a massive, popular procession with costumed groups and festivities lasting up to five days. The celebrations were abandoned after the Revolution, but several attempts were made to revive them from the early 19th century onward.

At the top of the same street is the **Cathédrale St-Sauveur▶▶** whose charm largely derives from its curious hodgepodge of styles from different periods. The west face, for example, combines a Romanesque doorway from the 12th century, a flamboyant Gothic facade from the early 16th century, and a belfry from the 15th century. Inside, the 5th-century octagonal **baptistry▶** is one of the oldest in France; the Roman columns supporting a Renaissance cupola above the pool were originally part of a temple to Apollo which stood on this site.

The cathedral is full of art treasures, including a series of 16th-century tapestries originally woven for Canterbury cathedral and Nicolas Froment's *Triptyque du Buisson*.

Just outside the old city center on rue Tava is the **Pavillon de Vendome▶** (open 10–12, 2–5, closed Tuesday; admission). Built in 1665 as a summer house, it was the last work of Pierre Pavillon and now houses a small museum of period furniture.

An elegant door-knocker is just one detail on Pierre Puget's classic Hôtel de Ville

Cézanne in Aix

■ Paul Cézanne was a lonely genius, struggling for most of his life against the incomprehension, and often ridicule, of the public. Driven by an inner conviction, he remained aloof and unsociable, painting feverishly until the very end, intolerant of the bourgeois Aix society into which he was born.....■

Early years Born on January 10, 1839, Paul Cézanne received a classical schooling in Aix. His father, first a hatter and then a successful banker, made him study law, but it soon became clear that the young Cézanne preferred painting.

Parisian sojourn Cézanne went to live in Paris in 1862 at the urging of his friend Zola, and here he fell in with Monet, Sisley, Renoir, Manet, and other young painters. He exhibited with the early Impressionists but their work met with derision and sarcasm.

Return to Aix Rebuffed, Cézanne took no further part in Impressionist exhibitions. He retreated to Aix, painting in solitude in his attic studio in the rue Boulegon or in the Provençal countryside where his work took on a new richness, which went beyond the analytical vision of Impressionism. His mastery of the underlying geometric structure of landscapes grew, and he returned repeatedly to the hilltop village of Gardanne, near Aix, as well as to the Jas de Bouffan and the banks of the Arc river.

Fame at last In the final decade of his life, from 1895 onward, Cézanne completed over 300 paintings — many of which are among his masterpieces. It was only now that he began to achieve some recognition, although it was in Paris, Berlin, and Vienna rather than Aix itself.

Final days When his mother died in 1897 Cézanne built himself a Provençal-style house, Les Lauves, on a hill above the cathedral: he painted in this studio from early morning onward, stopping only for lunch before setting off to work on landscapes in the afternoon. In 1906, aged 67, he was still painting in the open countryside every day despite ill health and fatigue. On October 15 that year he was caught in a rainstorm, collapsed walking home, and died peacefully from pneumonia on October 22.

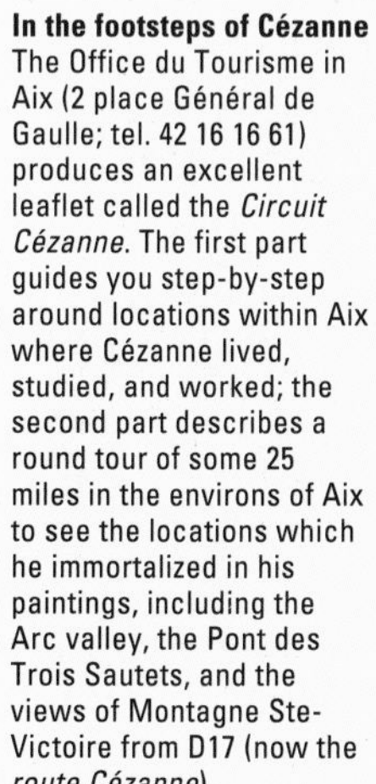

In the footsteps of Cézanne
The Office du Tourisme in Aix (2 place Général de Gaulle; tel. 42 16 16 61) produces an excellent leaflet called the *Circuit Cézanne*. The first part guides you step-by-step around locations within Aix where Cézanne lived, studied, and worked; the second part describes a round tour of some 25 miles in the environs of Aix to see the locations which he immortalized in his paintings, including the Arc valley, the Pont des Trois Sautets, and the views of Montagne Ste-Victoire from D17 (now the *route Cézanne*).

Still life with apples, bottle and chairback, *1900–1906 (pencil and gouache)*

Reliquaries in the Église St-Trophime, Arles

 **Arles** *96B3*

Introduction Once the Roman capital of Provence, then an important religious center in the Middle Ages, Arles later became a focal point for the Provençal renaissance of the 19th century. Today it is the unofficial capital of the Camargue.

First a Celto-Ligurian settlement on the banks of the Rhône, just where the river divides into its Petit and Grand branches, Arles became a major center for trade between the Greeks of *Massalia* (Marseille) and the inland tribes in the 6th century B.C. Its future was assured when the town built a fleet of 12 boats to help Julius Caesar conquer Marseille in 49B.C.

For five centuries Arles thrived at the crossroads of trade routes between Italy and Spain (the Domitian Way) and between the Mediterranean and Northern Gaul, and was a significant center for the early Christian church, and hosted several major synods. Arles went into decline from the 13th century onward — when it was overtaken in political and economic importance by Aix and Marseille.

In the 19th century Arles reemerged as a major focus for Provençal folk traditions, furniture, and crafts. Its women, who still wore the distinctive Provençal costume, inspired Daudet's famous play *L'Arlésienne* (1866), later turned into an opera by Bizet. Mistral thought Arles the embodiment of old Provence and founded his Museon Arlaten here in 1896.

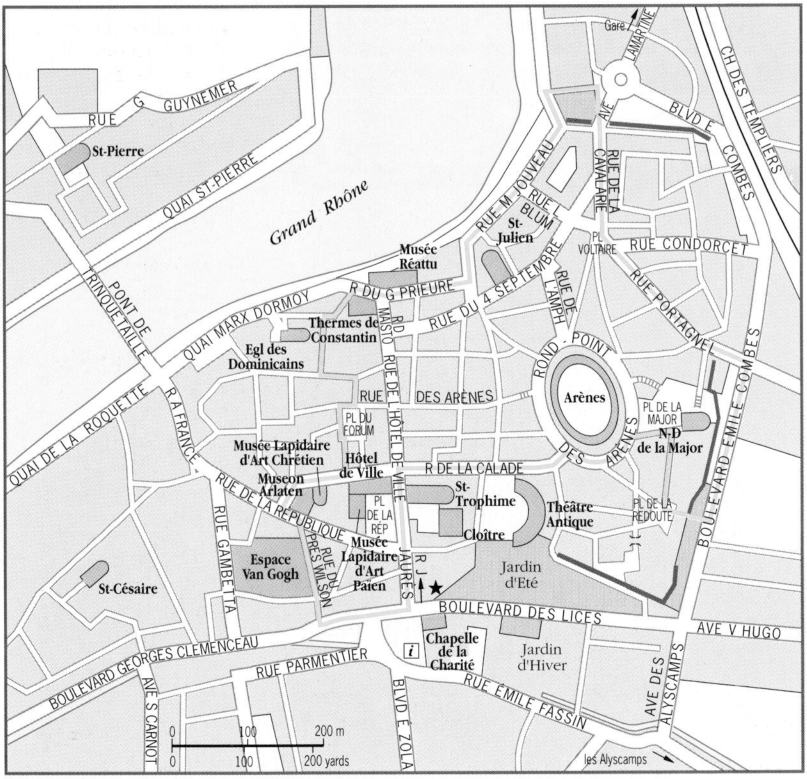

Walk Roman remains and ramparts

This walk will allow you to see most of Arles' major monuments in one circular route, as well as the remains of the Roman and medieval ramparts. Allow 3–4 hours. *See map opposite.*

From the boulevard des Lices head down rue Jean Jaurès to the place de la République. In the far corner, turn right up the rue de la Calade, past the *sous-préfecture* housed in a 17th-century mansion, to reach the **Théâtre Antique** and, just past here, the **Arènes**.

After visiting the arena, climb the steps on the east side to the place de la Major, where there is a viewpoint next to the **Église Notre-Dame de la Major**. Built on the foundations of a paleo-Christian sanctuary (itself built on top of a pagan temple dedicated to Cybele), the church has elements from several different epochs and contains, inside, a wooden statue of St. Georges, patron saint of the *gardians* of the Camargue.

Head down rue Madeleine to place de la Redouté, where two round towers mark the old **Porte de la Redouté** (or Porte d'Auguste) in the Roman ramparts where the Aurelian Way once led into the city.

Follow around the outside of the ramparts, turning in again down rue Portagnel, across place Voltaire and down rue de la Cavalerie to the Porte de la Cavalerie. Walk through the gardens next to the remains of the medieval ramparts to reach the banks of the Rhône. Turn left and walk down the riverbank until you come to the **Musée Réattu** and the **Thermes de Constantin**.

Head up the sinuous rue du Sauvage, at the end of which is the **Hôtel d'Arlaten** and then the **place du Forum**. Continue up to rue de la Calade, turning right past the **Musée Lapidaire d'Art Chrétien**, left around the corner to the **Museon Arlaten**, and then right down rue President Wilson back to the boulevard des Lices.

St-Trophime cloister and tower

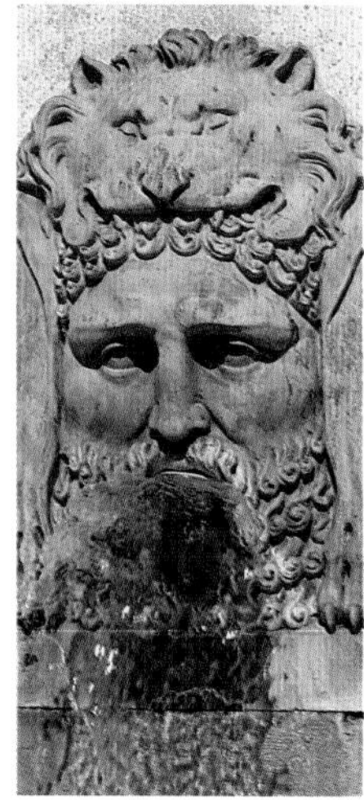

Cooling water flows from a streetside fountain

What to see Most of the sights in Arles are concentrated in a compact area downtown, bordered on one side by the Rhône and on the other by the **boulevard des Lices**, where you will find the main tourist office and numerous cafés in which to sit and watch the world go by (particularly enjoyable on a Saturday, when there is a huge market here).

At the heart of the town is the **place de la République▶** with its unmistakable obelisk (dug up in 1675, it was once part of the Roman forum). Facing the square is the **Église St-Trophime▶▶▶**, one of the most glorious monuments to the Provençal–Romanesque style. Built on the site of a 5th-century church during the 11th and 12th centuries, the most striking aspect of St-Trophime is the great portal, a masterpiece of classical decoration possibly inspired by the triumphal arches of Glanum and Orange. Behind St-Trophime are the equally famous **cloisters▶▶▶** (open daily; admission) which were probably the work of the same master craftsmen who created the façade of the Abbey of St-Gilles.

Opposite St-Trophime on the place de la République is the Musée Lapidaire d'Art Païen (open daily; admission), which houses mosaics and sculptures.

At the end of the square is the baroque **Hôtel de**

Contemporary festivals
Throughout the summer there are contemporary events and exhibitions in Arles, the most important of which are *Festival* in July (with a busy program of dance, drama, music, and opera) and the renowned *Rencontres Internationales de la Photographie* with numerous photographic shows and workshops with top international photographers. Art exhibitions are held in the Espace Van Gogh, a multimedia center installed in the former Hôtel-Dieu where Van Gogh was treated after he cut off part of his own ear.

Al fresco eating is de rigueur *in the lively place du Forum*

Ville▶, whose lobby boasts an unusual flat-vaulted ceiling. Just around the corner you'll find the **Musée Lapidaire d'Art Chrétien▶** (open daily; admission) which has numerous examples of 4th-century paleo-Christian sarcophagi.

The **Museon Arlaten▶▶** (closed Monday in winter; admission), focuses on traditional Provençal life, ranging from costumes to furniture to the *gardians* in the Camargue. It was founded by Mistral in 1896 and, as the great man requested, it is still staffed by attendants wearing traditional Arlesian costumes.

Provençal *santons* are on display in the **Chapelle de la Charité** (open daily; admission) next to the tourist office.

Arles' social hub is the attractive **place du Forum▶** with busy cafés and restaurants presided over by a statue of Mistral. Down toward the river past the place du Forum is the 14th-century priory of the Knights of Malta which now shelters the **Musée Réattu▶** (open daily; admission). The museum houses a collection of 57 ink and crayon drawings by Picasso, which the artist donated in 1972 as a gift to the people of Arles because he had so much enjoyed the bullfights here.

Arles's star attraction is undoubtedly the amphitheater, known as the **Arènes▶▶▶** (open daily; admission) which was probably built around the end of the 1st century A.D. It is only just bigger (by 10 feet) than the amphitheater at Nîmes, although slightly less well preserved — the latter retains its third-story attic. Turned into a fortress during the Saracen invasions, a village was later built inside the arena (which also happened in Nîmes). You can climb up one of the three remaining towers for a view over the arena and the city, with the Rhône behind it.

The **Théâtre Antique▶** (open daily; admission) just to the south, was built during the reign of Augustus, but was pillaged for stone in the 5th century by Christians eager to build churches. Although a mere shadow of its former self, the theater is still a suitably impressive venue for the annual *Fête du Costume* (dance and drama) which takes place in July.

Between the théâtre and the boulevard des Lices is the Jardin d'Été (open daily) with its lovely cedars and a bust of Van Gogh.

Another Roman monument which merely hints at past glories is the **Thermes de la Trouille▶** (or Thermes de Constantin, open daily; admission), near the riverfront. This huge bath house is the largest in Provence and once formed part of Constantine's palace on the waterfront.

The Roman cemetery in Arles was at the **Alyscamps▶** (southeast of town); many of the hundreds of elaborately carved sarcophagi were given away to visiting nobles in the 16th century and the huge necropolis was carved up by train lines and workshop buildings in the 19th century. The 12th-century **Église St-Honorat▶** is the only one left of 19 chapels that once studded the Alyscamps.

Traditional festivals
Arles has a lively calendar of traditional festivals including the *Feria Pascale* in April, which marks the beginning of the bullfight season, the *Fête des Gardians* in May with the Camargue "cowboys" parading on horseback through the streets, and the *Fête d'Arles* in late June, with torchlight processions where everybody wears local costumes. Another festival, revived at the beginning of the 1980s, is the *Fêtes des Prêmices du Riz* which takes place in September to celebrate the rice harvest from the Camargue.

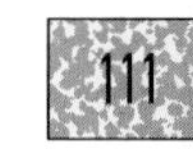

The Hôtel de Ville overlooks Arles's place de la République

Global tickets
If you are planning to visit most of the monuments and museums in Arles buy a global ticket from the tourist office or any participating site. The tourist office organizes various themed walking tours throughout the summer.

■ **Alongside Cézanne (see page 107), Van Gogh is another towering genius whose work will for ever be linked with the light-filled landscapes of Provence and the brilliance of the southern skies.....■**

Arrival in Arles Van Gogh took up painting at the age of 27, having previously been an art dealer, a teacher, and an evangelical preacher. He moved to Paris in 1886 where he fell under the spell of the Impressionists. He moved to Arles in 1888 and, although he wrote that the town had "a worn and sickly look" about it, he nonetheless stayed, captivated by the vivid colors around him. He mostly lived on place Lamartine, where he rented a cheap room opposite the Café de l'Alcazar, which he painted as the *Café de Nuit*. He also painted *La Maison Jaune* and the famous drawbridge of the *Pont de Langlois* (few of the locations he painted remain today).

Self-Portrait with Bandaged Ear, *one of two self-portraits painted by Van Gogh early in 1889 while convalescing in Arles after cutting off a piece of one of his ears*

Confrontation with Gauguin Van Gogh dreamed of setting up an artists' colony in Arles, and implored Gauguin to come down and join him. This Gauguin eventually did, but he hated Arles. Van Gogh's dreams were shattered: he threatened Gauguin with an open razor. Later, in a fit of remorse, Van Gogh went home and cut off part of an ear, which he gave to a prostitute. Gauguin took the first train back to Paris.

Move to St-Rémy Van Gogh was hospitalized in the Hôtel-Dieu but the townspeople petitioned the mayor to get rid of him. He finally left of his own accord in May 1889, checking in as a voluntary patient at the sanatorium of St-Paul-de-Mausole in St-Rémy. While there he worked feverishly, producing over 100 drawings and 150 canvasses including some of his most famous paintings such as *Les Blès Jaunes* and *Les Oliviers*.

Final days A year later Van Gogh left the sanatorium (supposedly "completely cured") and went to stay in Auvers near Paris — he had convinced himself that the southern sunshine was contributing to the agony of his mental illness. Two months later, in July 1890, he shot himself, and died two days later.

▶ Aubagne 97D1

Once a small market town for fruit and vegetables grown in the surrounding Huveaune valley, Aubagne is now in effect a suburb of Marseille, surrounded by *autoroutes* and three industrial zones. Home of the French Foreign Legion, find out what they're about at the **Musée de la Légion Étrangère** (open Tuesday to Saturday in summer; Wednesday, Saturday, and Sunday in winter).

Aubagne is also the birthplace of Marcel Pagnol, who set many of his works in the town and surrounding countryside. Characters from his books have been made into *santons* which are displayed in **Le Petit Monde de Marcel Pagnol** inside the tourist office (open daily).

▶ Barbentane 96B3

Barbentane's main attraction is the classic **Château de Barbentane▶▶** (guided tours daily in summer, open Sunday only, or by appointment, in winter; admission). Started by the Marquis of Barbentane in 1674, finished over a hundred years later, its style owes much to the great châteaux of the Île de France. The house is still occupied by the Barbentane family and its rich furnishings are the result of over 400 years of antique collecting. The interior, which is often used for magazine shoots, is dripping with 18th-century tapestries, Aubusson carpets, porcelain, statues, chandeliers, and priceless furniture. On the outskirts of Barbentane is **Provence Orchidées** (open daily 10–12, 2–5; admission) which has an "exotic garden" with tropical plants, orchids, and butterflies.

Nearby On D35E 3 miles south of Barbentane, the ancient **Abbaye St-Michel-de-Frigolet▶▶** was founded by the monks from Montmajour. Surrounded by hillsides of fragrant herbs, the abbey got its name from the Provençal word for thyme, *ferigoulo*. This is one of the ingredients in the monks' liqueur, *Le Frigolet*, which you can buy in the abbey shop after the guided tour (daily, hours vary; admission). In the 11th-century **chapel of Notre-Dame-du-Bon-Remède** the sumptuous gilt panels were donated by Anne of Austria who came here in 1632 to pray for a son; in 1638 she gave birth to Louis XIV.

Potted history
Aubagne is a major production centre for traditional Provençal ceramics, which have been made here since the 16th century. Local potters specialize in *santons* and beautiful decorative pots, vases, plates, and so on which can be bought from artisans' shops in the old town or during the annual fairs. There are two annual Ceramic Fairs in Aubagne, one from mid-July to the end of August and the other throughout December. There is also the biennial *Argilla* (from the Latin for clay, *argile*) which is now the biggest pottery market in France (due in 1995 and 1997).

Untouched during the Revolution, the Château de Barbentane has been lived in by the Barbentane family for over 300 years

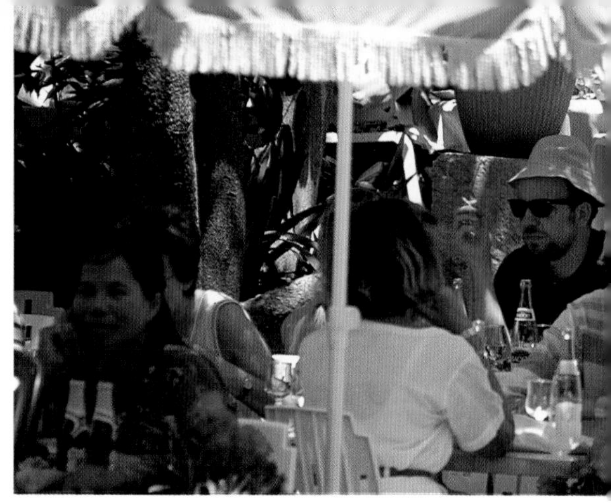

Troubadours
Despite their warring habits, some of the *seigneurs* of Baux were fond of more refined pastimes. In the 13th century their citadel became famous for its court, with troubadours visiting from far and wide to compose passionate odes to the daughters of Baux.

Red "Bauxite" rocks
In 1821, geologists discovered that the red rock from the hills surrounding les Baux could be smelted to create aluminum. They christened it bauxite in honor of the village.

►►► les Baux-de-Provence *96B3*

Les Baux is one of the classic sights of Provence, a powerful evocation of the feudal dynasties which once ruled the country. It is also a classic case of tourist overcrowding with over 1.5 million annual visitors — visit out of season if you can.

Perched on a barren rock plateau jutting out southward from the Alpilles chain, les Baux had been a stronghold since Ligurian times but it first achieved notoriety in the 10th century when it became the power base for the ambitious *seigneurs* of Baux who claimed to be descended from Balthazar of Bethlehem, one of the three kings who attended Christ's Nativity. They adopted the Star of Bethlehem for their coat of arms and waged war incessantly. They gained control over 79 surrounding towns and villages — secure in the knowledge that their eagles' aerie at les Baux was impregnable.

The last of this troubled family was the princess Alix of Baux, and on her death in 1426 les Baux became the property of the Count of Provence, Louis III d'Anjou. Later, King René gave it to his second wife, Jeanne de Laval, and a temporary peace reigned, until les Baux became a Protestant stronghold under the Manville family and more troubles beset the fiefdom during the Wars of Religion. They then made the fatal mistake of siding with the Duc d'Orleans in a rebellion in 1632 against Louis XIII, who retaliated by besieging the citadel.

Tired of their bothersome overlords (and partly prompted by Cardinal Richelieu), the inhabitants of les Baux asked Louis XIII to demolish the citadel, and the castle and ramparts were pulled down in 1633.

For nearly two centuries les Baux became a ghost town, until the 1940s when Raymond Thuilier opened his famous hostelry, L'Oustaù de Baumanière, which attracted celebrities and politicians. Gradually the forgotten village was restored and the tourist trickle turned into a torrent, engulfing les Baux in souvenir shops, *crêperies*, art galleries, ice-cream parlors, and boutiques.

If you can stand this overload there are some interesting places to visit within the village, such as the 16th-century **Hôtel de Manville►** which now houses the town hall and a small **musée►** (open daily in summer; admission) tracing the history of les Baux.

On the other side of the village, on place l'Église, is the

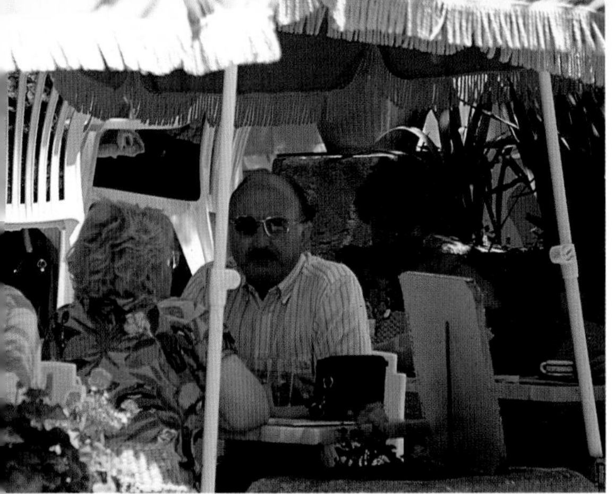

The cafés and souvenir shops in this once-deserted village are, in the high season, packed with tourists

Église St-Vincent►, which was partly hewn out of the rock in the 12th century. On Christmas Eve the famous pastoral festival (see panel) takes place here. Across the square is the old **Chapelle des Penitents Blancs**, decorated by Yves Brayer in 1974.

Rue du Château leads up through the middle of the village to the entrance to the **Citadel►►►** (open daily; admission) where there is a small **musée►** inside the Maison de la Tour du Brau. Strewn across the arid plateau there are about a dozen buildings still standing.

Explanatory signboards here are poor if not non-existent, but this may change as the whole site is being redeveloped with excavations planned to last through until 2010. In 1993, the discovery of ceramics proved that les Baux was occupied as long ago as the Bronze Age.

To the north of les Baux is a valley, leading into the Alpilles, known as the **Val d'Enfer** (the Valley of Hell) whose tortured-looking rock formations, eroded gullies, and caves were supposedly the inspiration for Dante's *Inferno*. Jean Cocteau shot scenes from *Orphée* in the deserted quarries here in 1950 and one of these huge underground caverns has now been converted into the extraordinary **Cathédrale d'Images►►**. Thirty-five projectors beam powerful, enveloping images across the ceilings, walls, and even the floor of the vast space within the enclosed quarry. Projection is continuous with the show lasting 30 minutes (open daily, closed mid-November to mid-February; admission).

Christmas festivities

In a chapel on the right-hand side of theÉglise St-Vincent is the *charette de l'agneau* (lamb's cart) which plays a key role in the *fête du pastrage* on Christmas Eve, in a tradition dating back to the 16th century. During midnight mass, an angel hidden behind the altar announces the Nativity to shepherds at the back of the church. The shepherds come forward, dancing and singing traditional Christmas songs, accompanied by shepherdesses with flowers and fruits strung about them. They are followed by the chariot bearing a newborn lamb.

Les Baux is perched romantically on a rocky outcrop

A duck trap
Duck hunting is big business in the Camargue and many of the large estates have flooded huge areas to create freshwater marshes. The ducks are shot as they move every morning and evening between the saltwater marshes in the reserve (where they rest in the daytime) and the private freshwater marshes (where they feed at night). The reserve is therefore unwittingly acting as a gigantic duck trap. This is causing problems because of excessive hunting (between 100,000 and 150,000 are shot annually) but also because the shot used is killing other aquatic birds through lead poisoning.

▶▶▶ The Camargue *96B2*

Approaching the Camargue from Marseille, the road skirts the Étang de Berre and passes through the industrial nightmare of the Port de Fos complex, a wasteland of oil terminals, cranes, and chimneys crisscrossed by a web of roads, train lines, and electricity pylons.

But then all of a sudden, once you have crossed the Rhône on the Bac de Barcarin ferry, a transformation takes place: here are groups of pink flamingos elegantly picking their way through the shallow lagoons in search of food, while birds of prey stand sentinel on the fence posts by the roadside. The space around you seems infinite as the horizons of the marshes, lagoons, and the sea stretch away into the distance. The silence is almost total apart from the honking of geese as they migrate in ever-changing, fluttering ribbons across the open sky.

All the more extraordinary for its proximity to industrial civilization, the Camargue is a rich tapestry of many different ecosystems, a haven for wildlife and a joy for anyone seeking tranquillity or long, wild walks amid its watery landscapes.

The Camargue is a vast delta formed by the two branches of the Rhône (the Grand Rhône to the east and the Petit Rhône to the west) where they meet the sea. In the Middle Ages communities of monks settled on the edge of this swamp to collect valuable salt and reclaim the land, but by the 17th century they had been replaced by ranchers whose primary purpose was the raising of

The neat little cabanes *that dot the Camargue were the traditional homes of the* gardians

the famous white horses and the black, longhorn bulls which thrive on the saline pastures. Sheep were also grazed here in the winter, before being moved up to Alpine pastures during the annual *transhumance*. It may appear to be a wilderness but in fact it is an environment

An avenue of plane trees shades a quiet Camargue back road

shaped by human activities with several overlapping zones. The conflict between different users of the Camargue is graphically illustrated by the problem of duck hunting (see panel).

The whole of the delta is part of the *Parc Naturel Régional la Camargue*, created in 1970, which covers 210,000 acres and aims to achieve a balance between traditional activities, the interests of local inhabitants, and nature conservation. At the core of the park the most sensitive areas have been classified as nature reserves; the most important is the *Réserve Nationale Zoologique et Botanique de Camargue* (first protected in 1928) covering 33,360 acres around the Étang de Vaccarès.

On average, visitors spend less than half-a-day in the Camargue and in this time you can only see the "postcard Camargue" — the bulls, horses, and flamingos. To appreciate it fully, you have to put in some effort — walk, rent a bike, ride a horse, or go on safari to get the most from this wonderful region.

Flooded
The vulnerability of the Camargue was highlighted in 1993 when the Rhône burst its banks and flooded over 30,000 acres of the delta; over 5,000 bulls, horses, and sheep were evacuated by helicopter and truck while frantic efforts were made to fill the breaches in the dike. Over 4.5 billion cubic feet of fresh water flooded into the system, altering the salinity of the lagoons and marshes dramatically. Undoubtedly many mammals will have died, and although floods have occurred previously (principally in 1960 and 1978) they have never caused such a sudden change in salinity which may have a brutal effect on the entire ecosystem.

The hardy horses of the Camargue are well adapted to the salty marshlands

Rosy pink flamingos
The most spectacular and photogenic of the delta's residents are the flamingos, one of the three "icons" of the Camargue (bulls and horses are the other two). These beautiful birds are easily seen at any time of year, although the greatest numbers (up to 50,000) are present during the spring and summer. Most migrate to Africa or Spain for the winter, but around 5,000–6,000 stay on. During March and April their pink plumage is shown off to best effect in spectacular courtship displays. Flamingos feed mostly on small invertebrates, and have been known to live for up to 34 years.

Do's and Don'ts
Not all wildlife in the Camargue is as charming as the flamingos: the mosquitos, for instance, are voracious and ever-present — they breed prolifically in the marshes. Never venture out without adequate protection, except perhaps on windy days in winter when you should be all right. The wind (specifically the all-powerful *mistral*) can also be a hazard if you are biking or walking long distances. Lastly, don't go marching off down the beaches or the *Digue-à-la-Mer* without adequate supplies of water.

What to see Apart from **Arles** (see page 108), which is within easy reach of the Camargue, the main accommodation and tourist centers are at **les Saintes-Maries-de-la-Mer** (see page 141) and **Aigues-Mortes** (see page 100). From les Saintes-Maries you can hike part or all of the way along the *Digue-à-la-Mer*, a sea wall that divides the unspoiled beaches and lagoons around the southern perimeter of the Étang de Vaccarès. The reserve of the Étang de Vaccarès itself is open only to visitors with a special permit but you can still find many vantage points on the surrounding roads (principally D37) from which you can watch birdlife.

The headquarters for the reserve is on the eastern side of the Étang de Vaccarès at **la Capellière▶▶** (closed Sunday; donation) which has one of the best and most up-to-date displays on the Camargue. There are two observatories within a minute or two of the Center (open sunrise to sunset) and a 1 mile walking trail.

Continuing on past la Capellière, you will arrive at **Salin de Giraud**, a quaint town that was created at the turn of the century by a Belgian company to house factory workers: hence the neat streets, shaded by plane trees and acacias, which are laid out in a strict grid pattern. Most of the employment now is with the *Salins du Midi* who manufacture salt in the massive lagoons south of town: after the "harvest" in late summer the huge salt mounds are a startling sight, gleaming in the sun and lining the edge of the lagoons in long, serried ranks. There is a viewpoint just off D36D south of Salin de Giraud for an overview of this rather unusual production process.

Farther down the same road is **la Palissade▶** (open daily, closed Saturday and Sunday from September to mid-June; admission). This former private hunting estate was bought by a private conservation group in 1976 and is unusual in that it is one of the few areas in the Camargue not controlled by dikes, with the waters of the Rhône mixing with seawater in the lagoons, giving rise to fauna and flora typical of the lower Camargue before it was altered. Inside la Palissade there are audiovisual displays, a herbarium, and an aquarium. Several walking trails crisscross the 1,735 acre estate, with guided tours available on request.

Back on the west side of the Étang de Vaccarès there are two more observation points on the edge of the reserve. The **Centre d'Information de Ginès** (closed Friday), 2.5 miles north of les **Saintes-Maries-de-la-Mer**, has displays, including a 15-minute video (admission), and huge plate glass viewing windows. To get in close to the birdlife, go to the **Parc Ornithologique du Pont de Gau▶▶**, a few yards away (open daily; admission), which has well-marked trails around the Étang de Pont de Gau (a half-hour walk), or the more extensive Étang de Ginès sanctuary,where bulls graze in the summer. Large aviaries near the entrance to the park house predators such as buzzards, black kites, Egyptian vultures, and eagle owls (the bird park looks after injured predators sent here from all over Europe).

If you've overdosed on avian antics, you might like to visit the **Château d'Avignon▶** (open daily April to September; admission) 8 miles north of les Saintes-Maries, which is an 18th-century mansion converted into a luxurious hunting lodge by the Marseille industrialist Louis Prat-Noilly in the last century. The interior contains some fine Gobelins and Aubusson tapestries as well as paintings and carved woodwork.

Dotted about the countryside you will see many vast farmhouses (or *mas*), often surrounded by trees and nearly always built with their backs to the biting north-westerly *mistral*. Many of the *mas* were originally owned by wealthy Arlesians and managed on their behalf by the *bayle* (steward), while the *gardians* had their own traditional homes, little *cabanes* with thatched roofs that you can also see by the roadsides.

The *gardians* were at the heart of the romantic image of the Camargue conjured up by Mistral and the Félibrige, and they still play a major part in the Provençal tradition of the *cocardes* — (see page 132), traveling from village to village throughout the summer with their bulls and horses.

A good introduction to the traditions of the Camargue is the inspirational **Musée de la Camargue▶▶** (open daily; closed Tuesday, October to March; admission), in an old barn at the Mas du Pont de Rousty, which was until recently a working sheep and cattle ranch. As well as exhibits on the geology and history of the Camargue there are sections on the *gardians* and farmhouse life in the last century. The 2 mile walking trail crosses pastures and the swamps of the Marais de la Grand Mar.

To see the *gardians* in action you can head down to the **Domaine de Méjanes▶** which is owned by the *pastis* magnate Paul Ricard. In typical Ricard style he has turned this huge estate into a popular entertainment center with bullfights and *ferrades* (Sunday and public holidays between Easter and mid-July) in the stadium, horserides, and even a *petit train* which does a 20-minute circuit of the marshes (daily but Sunday and Saturday afternoons only in December, January, and February; admission).

Jeep safaris of the Camargue and boat tours of the canals operate from les Saintes-Maries-de-la-Mer, or you can rent mountain bikes or go horseback riding.

Saved by tourism
You still sometimes see old graffiti that proclaim "*tourisme — mort au Camargue*" ("tourism — death to the Camargue") but it is now recognized not only that tourism brings economic benefits but that the birdlife is almost completely unaffected. In fact, park managers say the ducks have learned that landing near a tourist bus is the safest option. Those ducks that don't learn this very fast are likely to be shot dead by hunters outside the reserve.

Looking towards the Camargue from the bell tower of the church in the center of les Saintes-Maries-de-la-Mer

■ **The mass of marshes, canals, and lagoons that make up the Camargue delta provide a wide diversity of habitats for an enormous number of wildlife species, including the greatest variety of aquatic birds — some 400 different species — found in one place in the Mediterranean.....■**

Threatened dunes
The beaches and sand dunes are one of the most threatened areas in the Camargue, partly due to rising sea levels and partly because the Rhône has too many dams on it and no longer carries enough silt downstream to replenish the delta. Dikes and sea groins have had to be built to protect the beach, and wooden fencing erected to stop the dunes from disappearing.

Salty zones Starting at the coast, the first and most obvious ecosystem encompasses the beaches and sand dunes. In the winter months, rainwater accumulates beneath the surface of the dunes and nourishes spring plants such as perfumed *Helichrysum* and sea wormwood, elegant sand lilies, and delicate sea rocket and sea stock. Once the supply of water is exhausted other species appear which are better adapted to survive the summer heat, such as sea holly and sea spurge.

Also on the coast are the salt pans, center of a vast salt-production industry since the 19th century. Seawater is pumped across a series of lagoons between April and September, gradually increasing in density until it finally reaches the settling beds completely saturated with salt. Between August and October the salt starts to crystallize and it is then raked up into giant mounds (known as *camelles*) over 60 feet high before being washed, dried, and crushed.

The constant water levels of the salt pans throughout the summer months, as well as the wealth of

Eagle owl nestlings — rarely seen but part of the prolific birdlife here

invertebrates living there, make them very attractive to colonies of flamingos, terns and black-headed gulls, as well as solitary species such as the oystercatcher, shelduck, or redshank.

The third type of habitat in the lower half of the Camargue is the *sansouire*, huge flat expanses of salt-

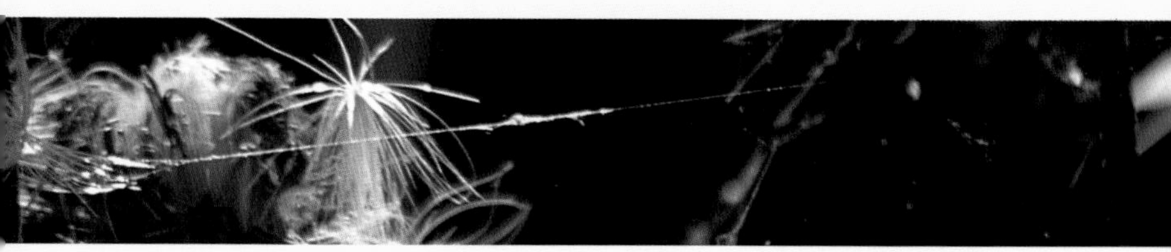

marsh between the sea and the lagoons covered in scrubby vegetation: flooded in winter, they become mudflats in the spring and autumn and a salty desert in the summer. These wide open spaces are typical of the Camargue, their role changing with the seasons. On the higher ground of the *sansouire*, where only sea lavender and glasswort can survive the changing water levels, skylarks thrive all year round. When it is flooded in winter, tens of thousands of duck use the *sansouire* as a daytime resting place. From February onward the water level drops and thousands of waders stop here on their long journey from northern Europe down to Africa.

In the summer months, herds of cattle and horses, no longer free to roam, graze behind the endless barbed wire fences.

Freshwater zones The freshwater marshes, with their extensive reed beds, provide ideal conditions for many species of bird which you can easily see from the roadside, such as herons, moorhens, coot, mallards, and egrets.

Another inhabitant of the freshwater marshes which you are likely to see is the enchanting coypu, which makes a curious burbling noise as it swims across the surface in search of aquatic plants (it is particularly fond of bulrushes) to nibble on. The coypu is often mistaken for a beaver, but it is an entirely different family (it was introduced from South America); there are beavers, mostly along the banks of the Rhône, but they are nocturnal and rarely spotted.

On slightly higher ground are the remains of the grasslands, which provide a vital habitat for the colorful bee-eater as well as rollers and hoopoes; the grasslands are a particularly beautiful sight in the spring, when they are covered in white daisies, and again in the autumn, when they are a mass of purple sea lavender.

Agriculture has also taken its toll on the woodlands, remnants of the riverine forest which used to cover most of the north part of the delta. The predominant species are white poplar, willow, ash, and elm, and there are still narrow belts along the banks of the Rhône which provide nesting sites for owls, woodpeckers, tits, and starlings. Herons and egrets also nest here, feeding in the daytime in the freshwater marshes.

Rice paddies
Cattle and horses once used to graze on the richer pastures of the grasslands, along with sheep, but huge areas of this productive ground were converted to rice paddies in the 1950s. In the 1960s the Camargue was growing nearly a third of France's rice requirements but since 1970 production has dropped dramatically and only a third of the former paddies are now in use for growing rice. Instead, other crops such as fruit and vegetables have taken over, thanks to the fact that the paddies cleaned the soil of salt.

Wading birds such as storks find rich feeding grounds in the Camargue marshes

The attractive port of Cassis was a favorite of the turn-of-the-century Fauve artists

►►► Cassis 97D1

Squeezed into a little bay between the cliffs of the Gardiole (which conceal the famous *calanques*) to the west and Cap Canaille to the east, this photogenic fishing port has long been popular with visitors. It is also a great favorite with the Marseillais, who flock here throughout the year to eat a huge seafood meal, washed down with copious quantities of the excellent local *vin blanc*, in one of the many restaurants that line the dockside.

Presiding over the port is a rambling château built by the *seigneurs des Baux* at the beginning of the 13th century, now privately owned by the Michelin tire family. In the center of town is the small **Musée Municipal** (open daily except Sundays and holidays) with local paintings, amphoras, coins, and other relics.

Apart from seafood restaurants the main attraction of Cassis is its proximity to the magnificent **calanques►►►**, which are long, narrow inlets (like small fjords) eroded from the limestone cliffs of the Gardiole. There are several ways to see them: by passenger boat (regular departures from the quayside, with tour lengths which vary according to how many *calanques* you want to visit); you can also rent kayaks, small motorboats, and windsurfers; alternatively, you can set out on foot (see Calanques walk, page 124).

Hemmed in as it is on all sides by high hills, there isn't much space around Cassis for vineyards and so the annual production from its 500 acres of vines is highly prized: the light, fruity whites go admirably with local seafoods and *bouillabaisse*. If you want to take some home, some of the best *caves* are the Clos Ste-Magdeleine (tel. 42 01 70 28), the Domaine Caillol (tel. 42 01 05 35), the Domaine de Paternel (tel. 42 01 76 50), and the Clos Val Bruyère (tel. 42 01 73 36).

Lumière Brothers
By inventing the simple technique of piercing the edge of a roll of film with holes and running it through a toothed mechanism attached to a projector, Auguste and Louis Lumière gave birth to modern cinema. In 1895, they showed the first ever moving picture images to a private audience in la Ciotat. Three months later these same films were shown to a public audience in Paris, where spectators almost jumped out of their seats as a train approached them on the screen in *L'Entrée du train à la Ciotat*. The film festival (now encompassing photography and art exhibitions) takes place in the second half of July.

► la Ciotat 97D1

Entering la Ciotat from any direction you can't miss the industrial architecture that symbolizes its maritime past — the massive, gaunt gantries, now immobilized, which dominate the small harbor at the center of the town. La

Ciotat has been a port since the 4th century, when the Greeks from Marseille set up an anchorage here, and in the 17th century the local mariners invented a system (called *la caravanne*) to get the most from their ships by never sailing empty from one port to the next — today, every modern shipping line operates a similar back-to-back cargo system.

The first boats were built here in 1836 and the first dry dock opened in 1936, but the dockyards were finally shut down in April 1990. Exhibitions on the town's maritime history are housed in the **Musée Ciotaden** opposite the tourist office (open Monday, Wednesday, and Saturday afternoon and Sunday morning).

With the derricks now standing idle above the fishing boats and pleasure craft in the harbor, la Ciotat has turned to tourism for its survival, with glossy brochures extolling the virtues of the beaches of the "*Golfe d'Amour*" and the "*Ville des Lumières*": the appropriately named Lumière brothers gave the first ever public showing of motion pictures here (see panel). Capitalizing on this connection, there has been an annual film festival since 1981 and, more recently, an annual jazz festival as well.

Behind the dockyards to the west of town, in the shadow of the Bec de l'Aigle (eagle's beak) promontory, rearing 229 feet high, is a small wilderness area now protected as the **Parc Naturel du Mugel▶▶** (open daily). Pathways lead through typically Mediterranean vegetation to a viewpoint beneath the Cap. In the park the Atelier Bleu du Cap de l'Aigle (tel. 42 08 07 67) runs courses on the ecology of the reserve. There is an underwater nature trail in the Calanque du Petit Muguel.

The Cosquer cave
In 1991 a local diver, Henri Cosquer, discovered an underwater fissure in one of the *calanques* which led to a cave containing hundreds of wall paintings, similar to the famous Lascaux paintings, depicting bison, horses, and over 50 human hands in charcoal. However, there are doubts about the paintings' authenticity and since few paleolithic experts have the skills to dive to 120 feet., no one yet knows whether they are an elaborate hoax or not.

The Route des Crêtes
One of the wildest coastal roads in Provence is the 11-mile-long Route des Crêtes between la Ciotat and Cassis. Take avenue Camusso out of la Ciotat and follow the twisting road as it dips and plunges along the clifftops, with spectacular views from the many stopping places *en route*. From the heights of Cap Soubeyran and Cap Canaille you can peer over the edge of the highest cliffs in France, with the sea pounding the rocks nearly 1,300 feet below. The hillsides behind the cliffs, devastated by fire several years ago, now sprout neatly curving rows of replanted pines.

Fishing boats tied up at the Cassis quayside, their catches by now being prepared in the waterfront restaurants

Walk The Calanques

From the Calanque de Port-Miou just outside Cassis harbor to the Calanque de Callelongue at les Goudes, south of Marseille, the 12 mile-long coastline is crisscrossed with walking trails. This walk, from Cassis, is one of the easiest and takes around three hours.

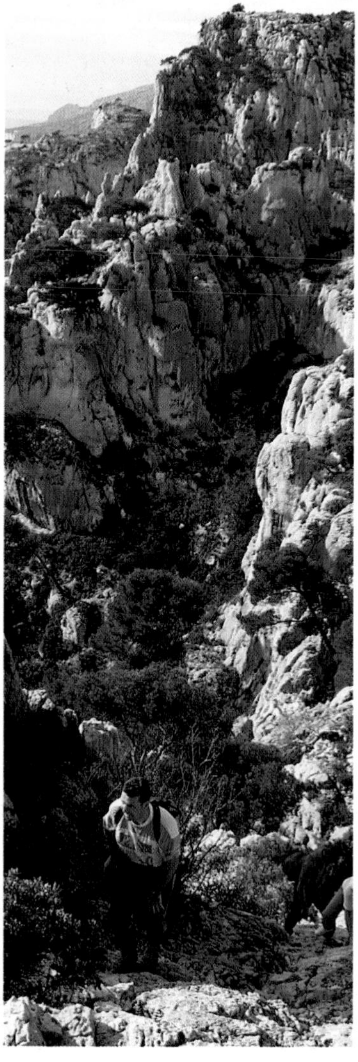

From Cassis, follow the signs for les Calanques and park at the end of the road. Walk along the length of the Calanque de Port-Miou through the old quarry. Untypically Port-Miou's entire length is taken up with yacht berths.

Climb up the terraces over a low ridge to reach the **Calanque de Port-Pin▶**, named after the *pins d'Alep* which once covered the Domaine de la Fontasse behind the inlet but which were mostly burnt down in 1990. The small shingle beach gets very crowded since this *calanque* is the easiest to reach from Cassis, whether on foot or by water.

Continue up a narrow gully and climb up to the Plateau de Cadeiron. From here, there are wonderful views back to the magnificent cliffs of the Montagne de la Canaille rearing up above Cassis bay. In front of you, the ground starts to fall away until you reach a viewpoint over the **Calanque d'En-Vau▶▶**, one of the most spectacular of all the *calanques*. Beneath the dramatic, chalk-white cliffs and needle-like rocks, there is a small sandy beach, with rocky steps leading down — if you've warmed up enough for a swim.

Beyond En-Vau you can see the Riou archipelago (comprising the islands of Jarre, Jarron, Calseraigne, and Riou itself).

The cliffs continue down into the limpid depths, sheltering a rich profusion of marine life which make their steep underwater slopes as much a favorite with local scuba divers.

From here, you can either continue along the GR98 all the way to les Goudes (at least a full day's walk), or turn back along En-Vau out toward the pinnacle known as *Doigt de Dieu* ("God's finger"), and then around the headland back to Port-au-Pin and Cassis. Note that in the summer months (June 15 to September 15) it is forbidden to stray off the GR98 because of the fire risk.

Hikers in the Calanques

► Gémenos 97D2

This village outside Aubagne is worth a detour for the nearby **Abbaye de St-Pons** (see page 166), or if you are passing through on the way to Ste-Baume stop in the main square and look inside the courtyard of the unusual **Granges du Marquis d'Albertas**, a huge building designed to house agricultural workers which was built in the second half of the 18th century. Bacchus astride a barrel over one of the four doorways (three are now closed off) attests to the function of what was essentially a huge barn with accommodation above. Most of the hundreds of rooms are now empty, the cobbles in the courtyard long gone, but the original circular fountain in the middle still remains.

Graveson 96B3

Once surrounded by swamps, Graveson is part of the fertile Petite Crau. Just outside Graveson is the **Musée des Aromes et du Parfum▶▶** (open daily; admission) founded by aromatherapist Nelly Grosjean. Fragrant aromas permeate the whole of this converted farmhouse and barn, which houses a number of huge copper alembics (stills) as well as other traditional distilling equipment — some still in use. Essential oils, soaps, and perfumes made from the local herbs are on sale; Nelly Grosjean also holds one-day aromatherapy courses (tel. 90 95 81 72 for details).

► Maillane 96B3

In the 14th century the village of Maillane was almost wiped out by the plague. Among those who repopulated it was a man from Tarascon called Mermet Mistral: several centuries later, Maillane was the birthplace of Frédéric Mistral (see pages 60–61), Provence's most famous literary figure. Mistral was brought up in the *Mas du Juge* (no visits) just outside Maillane, but on the death of his father in 1855 he moved with his mother into *Au Lezard*, a house in the middle of the village (opposite the *tabac*). In an alleyway alongside is the house Mistral moved into 20 years later when he married, and where he lived until his death in 1914. The latter is now the recently refurbished **Museon Mistral▶▶** (closed Monday morning; admission).

Gastronomy in Gémenos
Every November the tourist office in Gémenos organizes a gastronomic festival which brings together some of the excellent local restaurants and vineyards around themes such as "Wine in Provençal Cuisine." As well as a two-day wine and food fair there are special menus in participating restaurants (for details, tel. 42 32 18 44). *L'Avenir du Vin* (tel. 42 32 11 45) organizes courses which cover the alliance of wine and food — so if you want to know what to drink with your *bouillabaisse*, they will teach you.

Gleaming copper stills at the Musée des Aromes et du Parfum in Graveson

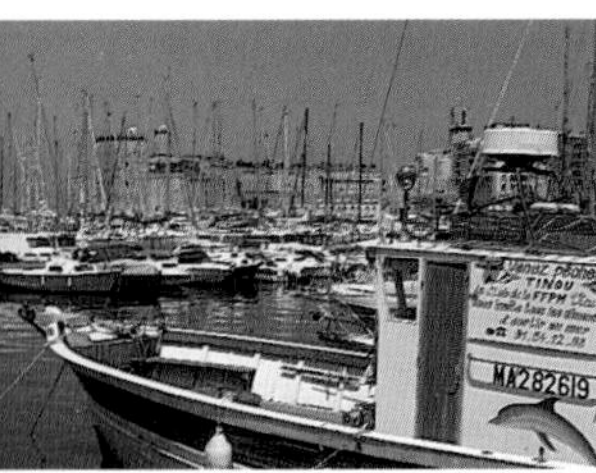

Speedboats, yachts, and fishing boats rub shoulders in Marseille harbor

Laid out in the 17th century, la Canebière is Marseille's main thoroughfare

Marseille 97D2

Introduction Compared to the glittering resorts of the Côte d'Azur or the historically rich inland cities of Provence, Marseille has never been a prime tourist destination and its image is one of work not play. However, as France's second biggest city (after Paris) and the Mediterranean's largest port, it has tremendous vitality and a cosmopolitan atmosphere which you cannot help but admire, even if you are unlikely to fall in love with the place.

Opening out to the sea from its niche between mountains and towering cliffs, Marseille's reputation precedes it, attracting all the worst labels — "the gangster capital of France," a "fascist hotbed," "a dirty, vulgar, and noisy city" — and yet to the casual visitor none of this is necessarily apparent. Like any major city, there are areas to be avoided at night — but then both Nice and Avignon have much higher crime rates per head of population than Marseille.

Marseille boasts over a dozen theaters, four times that many galleries and art exhibition centers, numerous music venues with everything from world music to chamber music, and of course the renowned Marseille opera. It also has a carnival every March which celebrates the story of Protis and Gyptis and the founding of the city by the Greeks (see panel on page 130).

The settlement — which they named *Massalia* — prospered rapidly. As a maritime people, the Massalians established a series of trading posts along the coast (notably at Nice, Hyères, and Antibes) and their explorers ventured as far afield as Senegal in Africa and the Baltic.

For protection from the Celto-Ligurian tribes, it allied itself with Rome but *Massalia*'s standing as a free city was irrevocably damaged when Caesar sacked the city in 49B.C. for remaining neutral (ie not taking his side in his war against Pompey). Despite this *Massalia* remained a stronghold of Hellenic civilization. Its port declined in importance until the crusades, when it profited hugely by providing transport to the wars.

In 1720 a single ship, the *Grand Saint-Antoine*, slipped through the quarantine net around the port and unleashed the plague that was to devastate much of Provence; in Marseille alone, half the population died. But the town bounced back, benefiting particularly from the opening of the Suez Canal in 1869.

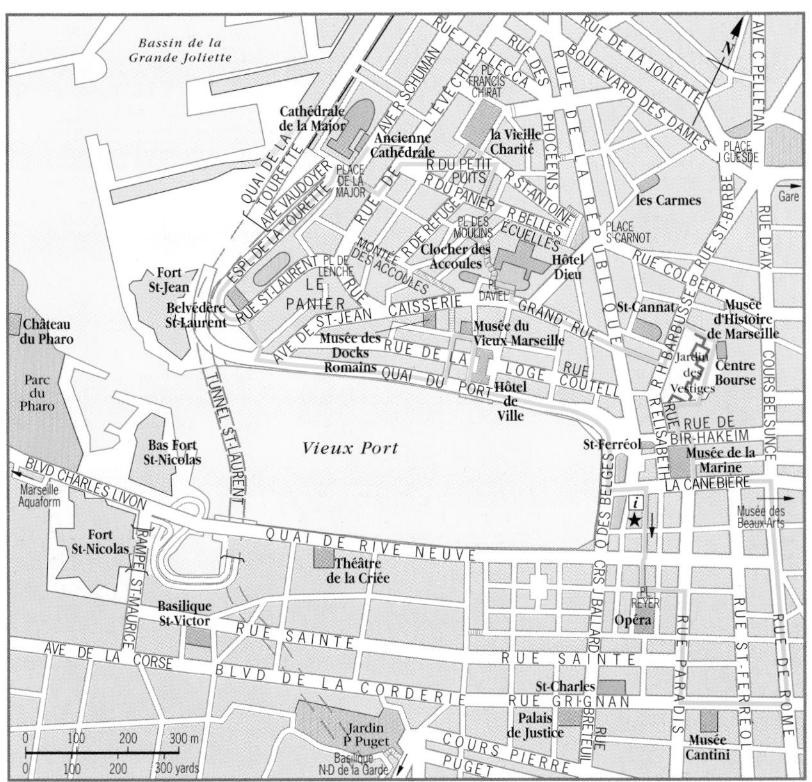

Walk Marseille's history

This walk takes in many of the best museums of Marseille, as well as the interesting old quarter of Le Panier. Allow 3–4 hours.

Start at the tourist office on the quai des Belges. Take rue Beauvau down to place Reyer for the **Opéra**▶▶ — the wonderful art deco interior dates from 1924. From here, head northeast for the pedestrianized rue Paradis. Turn south, and in Rue Grignan on your left is the **Musée Cantini**. Continue to the rue de Rome and turn left: keep going until you reach La Canebière.

Go through the Bourse shopping center (entrance to the **Musée d'Histoire**). Exit through the **Jardin des Vestiges** and follow the Grand Rue across rue de la République to the place Daviel. Take the steps past **Clocher des Accoules** (all that remains of one of the city's older churches; parts date back to the 7th century) and follow the signs for the route through the old quarter of Le Panier to la Vieille Charité. Continue down rue du Petits Puits, take the steps in the place des Treize Cantons to reach the **Cathédrale de la Major**. Esplanade de la Tourette leads you to a belvedere, with a superb view over the old port. Go down the steps to the quay, and follow it along until place Jules Verne, for the Musée des Docks Romains and the remarkable Maison Diamantée, which houses the **Musée du Vieux Marseille**. Rejoin the quai du Port and walk back round to the quai des Belges.

Towering above the city, Notre-Dame de la Garde was used as a Nazi headquarters during World War II — bullet marks are still visible on the walls

The big blue
First it was Richard Rogers in Nîmes and now another British architect, Will Alsop, has joined the ranks of those who have designed controversial and prestigious buildings in Provence. Alsop's daring new departmental headquarters (L'Hôtel du Département) in Marseille is unmistakable, a sculpted statement in bright blue which expresses the essence of post-high-tech architecture. Partially raised on stilts, it echoes one of the most famous architectural experiments in social housing — Le Corbusier's Unite d'Habitation, which still stands on the outskirts of Marseille.

With the loss of France's colonies in the 1950s the importance of trade again declined but Marseille was left with the legacy of thousands of immigrants who had flocked here from North Africa in the 1960s (the population grew from 660,000 in 1955 to 960,000 in 1975); none of this was new to Marseille, which had welcomed refugees over the centuries. But, combined with unemployment, racial tensions have now been fueled by the rise of Jean-Marie Le Pen's *Front National*, whose supporters still command a third of the vote in the city.

What to see At the heart of the city is the **Vieux Port▶▶**, where a bronze plaque on the quai des Belges marks the spot where Protis first stepped ashore. Fishing boats still pull in here every morning to unload their catches which are sold straight to waiting customers. Alongside are the tourist boats for trips out to the **Frioul Archipelago** and the **Île d'If** (see page 131).

Leading up from the Vieux Port is the broad boulevard of la Canebière, Marseille's most famous street — though now full of dreary banks and airline offices. North is an area of steep streets and narrow alleyways known as **le Panier▶**, Marseille's oldest district. Before World War II it housed fisherfolk and many Italian and Corsican refugees, and later gave shelter to hundreds of Jews hoping to escape the Nazis by catching a ship to America. In January 1943 the Nazis gave all 20,000 inhabitants one day's notice to quit and blew the whole lot up, rounding up 3,500 victims for the concentration camps in the process. The only buildings not destroyed were the Maison Diamantée and the 17th-century Hôtel de Ville on the quayside.

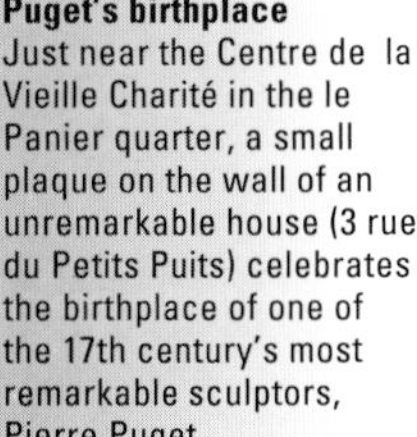

Puget's birthplace
Just near the Centre de la Vieille Charité in the le Panier quarter, a small plaque on the wall of an unremarkable house (3 rue du Petits Puits) celebrates the birthplace of one of the 17th century's most remarkable sculptors, Pierre Puget.

On the south of the Vieux Port the quai de Rive Neuve houses ship-chandlers' shops and the new Théâtre National de Marseille de la Criée, with the **Basilique St-Victor** (see page 131) behind. From here, the road continues around the walls of the Fort St-Nicolas to the **Château de Pharo**, built by Napoleon III as a gift for the Empress Éugenie.

Past the headland, the Corniche President John Kennedy (with views over the offshore islands) leads to several artifical beaches, a small yachting basin, and the new **Marseille Aquaform▶▶** (open daily; admission). This enlightening aquarium and research center houses many rare and fascinating species from tropical and Mediterranean waters.

Museums Marseille has numerous museums and it pays to be selective — or you will get exhibition fatigue. Starting on the north side of la Canebière, just across from the tourist office is the **Musée de la Marine et de l'Economie de Marseille** (closed Tuesday) housed inside the Palais de la Bourse — France's first stock exchange. Displays trace the maritime history of Marseille from the 16th century onward, with models of old trading ships, paintings, and engravings.

Just behind is the Bourse shopping center, with the **Musée d'Histoire de Marseille▶▶** (Monday–Saturday 12–7; admission) on the first floor. Here is the wreck of an ancient Roman merchant vessel, discovered in 1974, which sank in one corner of the Roman port (now unearthed in the **Jardin des Vestiges▶** outside the museum). Audiovisual displays explore the Greek heritage of *Massalia*.

The Tricolore *flies over the entrance to the 17th-century Hôtel de Ville*

Protis and Gyptis
In 600B.C. a shipload of Greek colonists from Ionia landed in what seemed like an ideal spot, the Lacydon inlet, and went to seek permission from Nann, the local king, to start a settlement. The king was throwing a banquet that day during which, according to custom, his daughter Gyptis would choose her future husband. She went for Protis, the good-looking leader of the onian delegation, and as their wedding gift the king bequeathed them Lacydon (now the *vieux port*) where they founded a colony.

Inside the unusual **Maison Diamantée▶** on rue de la Prison is the **Musée du Vieux Marseille▶▶** (closed Tuesday and Wednesday A.M.; admission) with an eclectic selection of curiosities ranging from traditional Provençal *santons* and Arlesian furniture to gory paintings of the 1720 plague and a fine display on the manufacture of playing cards (once an important local industry), which includes the famous Marseille tarot cards.

Across the place Jules Verne is the **Musée des Docks Romains▶** (closed Monday), built over the site where all the artifacts were recovered. Huge storage jars for oil, grains, and wine sit on the 1st-century Roman quay.

Farther north in the Le Panier quarter is the **Centre de la Vieille Charité▶▶▶**, a wonderful building which was designed by Pierre Puget. Built out of rose-colored stone, the courtyard is surrounded by three floors with arcades of different heights, with a curious elliptical baroque chapel as the central focus. The hospice became a barracks earlier this century; fell into disrepair; then was thoroughly renovated in the 1980s as a multimedia art and culture center. It also houses the excellent **Musée d'Archéologie Méditerranéenne▶▶** (Monday–Friday 10–7, Saturday, Sunday 12–7; admission) which features a number of revolving exhibits from around the Mediterranean basin.

Marseille's oldest art museum is the **Musée des Beaux-Arts▶** (closed Tuesday and Wednesday A.M.; admission) in a wing of the Palais Longchamp in the eastern quarter of the city. Much more centrally located is the **Musée Cantini▶▶▶** (closed Monday; admission), the main focus for 20th-century art, with a collection of over 400 contemporary works of which only a small fraction are ever on display. Artists represented include Dufy, Bacon, Balthus, César, Max Ernst, and Miró.

Churches and cathedrals

The most prominent church in Marseille is **Notre-Dame de la Garde▶▶**, which stands sentinel on an

The gilded Madonna atop Notre-Dame de la Garde is the largest in France

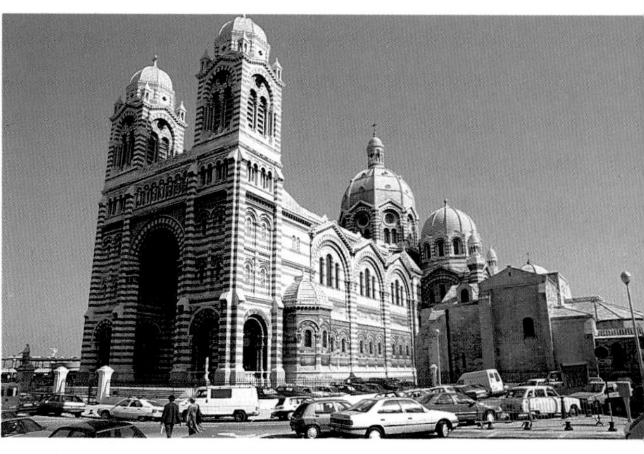

The massive Cathédrale de la Major

outcrop 530 feet above the city. This Romano-Byzantine monster is surmounted by a 33 foot-high gilded Madonna and was built in the latter part of the 19th century. It is worth making the trek up here (or taking bus No. 60) for the fabulous view of Marseille spread out beneath you.

Built in a similar neo-Byzantine style, the **Cathédrale de la Major►►** overlooks the modern docks on the north side of the *vieille ville*. With its 229 foot-high basilica and 444 marble columns supporting the roof, it is the largest church built in France since the Middle Ages. Despite its grandeur, it is not as interesting as the **Ancienne Cathédrale de la Major►►►** which it replaced, and which sits alongside in its shadow. Although partially destroyed to make way for the new cathedral in the 19th century, what remains is a superb example of 11th-century Provençal Romanesque (both closed Monday).

Across on the other side of the harbor is the **Basilique St-Victor►►►**, originally part of a powerful abbey which spawned over 300 monasteries and priories throughout Provence and overseas. Founded in the 5th century, the abbey was damaged by the Saracens and later rebuilt with added fortifications — its walls are 10 feet thick. Inside, you can descend into the **crypt►** (closed Sunday morning; admission) which has a series of sarcophagi hidden away in its ancient passageways. In the Chapelle Notre-Dame de Confession there is a black wooden statue of the Virgin which is venerated in an ancient Candlemas ceremony (see panel).

Candlemas at St-Victor On Candlemas Day (February 2) a large procession gathers at the Basilique St-Victor where the Archbishop blesses green candles in front of the black statue of the Virgin. The faithful then take their candles back home, where they are lit to celebrate regeneration and rebirth. On the same day, small loaves are baked in the shape of boats, called *navettes*, to commemorate the arrival on Provençal shores of St Lazarus and Saints Mary Magdalene and Martha in les Saintes-Maries-de-la-Mer.

The Islands No visit to Marseille is complete without a visit to the infamous **Château d'If►►**, perched on the rocky islet of the Île d'If (boats from quai des Belges; travel time 15min., throughout the day, except in bad weather; admission). François I decided to build a fort here after visiting the island in 1516, and it was completed in 1531. However, it was soon turned into a prison and in the 17th century hundreds of Protestant prisoners perished inside its gloomy walls. Novelist Alexandre Dumas used it as the setting for his book *The Count of Monte Cristo*.

The other islands in the Frioul archipelago are **Île Pomègues** and **Île Ratonneau**, where Julius Caesar anchored his fleet in preparation for the siege of Marseille in 49B.C. In the 17th century the Île Ratonneau became a quarantine center for plague victims, with the ruins of the old **Hospital Caroline** on a hilltop attesting to the belief that the sea winds would sweep the germs away. These barren-looking islands, alive with wild plants and flowers, can be visited on a round trip which also encompasses the Île d'If.

On the Roman quay

Provençal bullfights

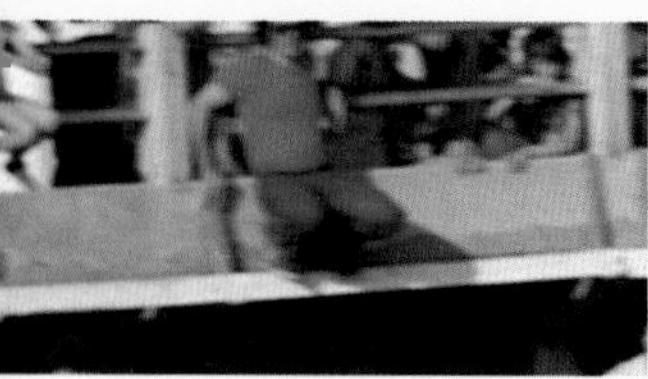

■ Summer is the season of bullfights in the Bouches-du-Rhône, with posters plastered on trees and billboards everywhere advertising Cours de Taureau in the nearest town with an *arène* worthy of the name. Unlike Spanish bullfights, the bulls are not put to death.....■

Rami
One well-known bull, Rami, who belonged to *manadier* Marcel Mailhan, died a natural death at 24 years old — a record longevity which is celebrated by a monument over his tomb in the Camargue!

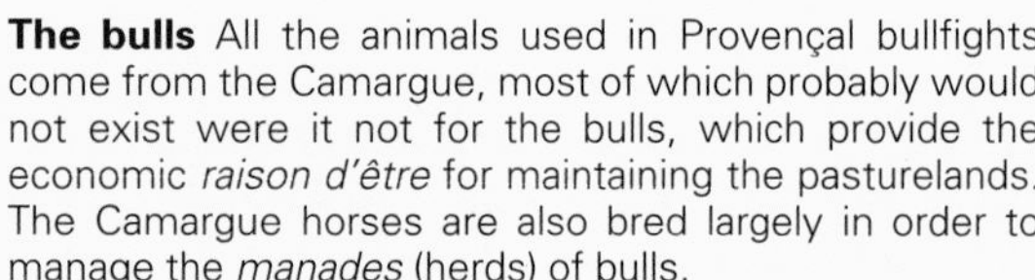

The bulls All the animals used in Provençal bullfights come from the Camargue, most of which probably would not exist were it not for the bulls, which provide the economic *raison d'être* for maintaining the pasturelands. The Camargue horses are also bred largely in order to manage the *manades* (herds) of bulls.

The Camarguais bull, lighter than its Spanish counterpart (some of which are also reared here), is a vigorous, agile, and intelligent breed. It is not suited to agricultural work and were it not for the *cours* it would probably exist only in zoos. The animals suffer no great hardship: each bull spends a maximum of 15 minutes in the ring, appearing perhaps a dozen times in a year. At the end of its career, it retires to graze in the Camargue.

The game The *Cours Camarguais* (also known as the *Cours à la Cocarde*) is more of a game than a fight, a contest of agility, courage, and skill between the bulls and the participants. Dressed in white, the *razeteur* has a long hook (the *razet*) with which he has to snatch a *cocarde* (rosette) from between the horns of the bull. He is helped by a *tourneur*, whose role it is to distract the bull. He has to accomplish this within a 15-minute time limit, and if he does, gains a prize. He risks being chased out of the ring by the bull, or forced to leap over the barricades

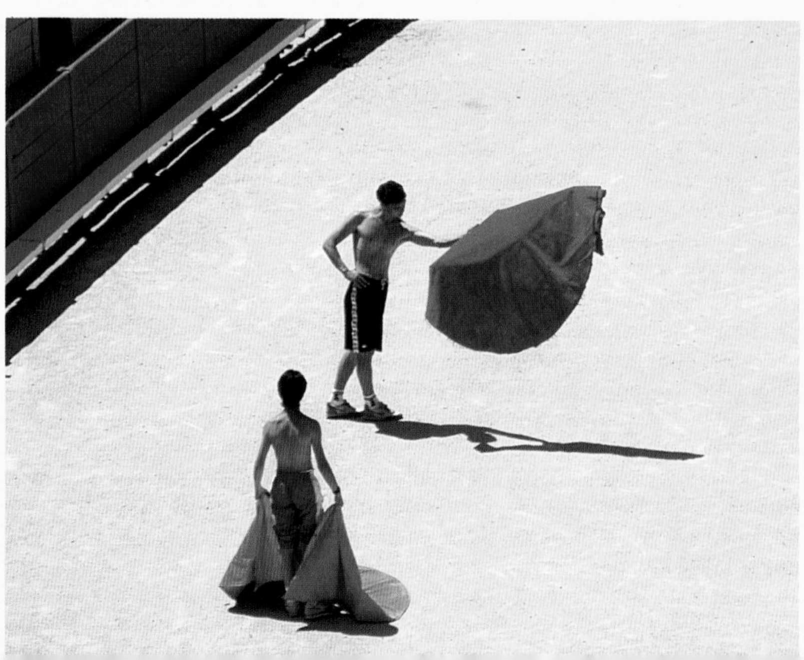

Young tourneurs *in the making?*

The Roman arena at Arles, packed to capacity

— and he hopes he doesn't fall back on to the bull's horns beneath him.

The roundup A tradition with more practical origins is that of the *ferrade*. At one year old, the young bulls are separated from the herd, chased on horseback, and then grappled to the ground by the *manadier* (herdsman) in order to be branded. This too has evolved into a spectator sport, as has the *abrivado*, during which the bulls are driven through the streets on their way to the arena, chasing or being chased by the crowds.

Anyone can try Although nowadays the *Cours Camarguais* is organized on a professional basis (it became an official French sport in 1975) and the *razeteurs* train rigorously, most of the fun for the hundreds of people who flock down to their local ring on a Friday or Saturday night is in the *Cours à la Vachette*. The local youth — and sometimes even children — leap into the ring to be chased by the *vachette* (which has capped horns) and to try and tempt it to jump after them into a shallow pool in the middle. Cash prizes are the reward for this risky-looking game!

In the arena The most spectacular settings for local bullfights are in the old Roman arenas such as at Arles, where at least 30 *cours* are held each year. However, if you find Spanish-style *corridas* (where the bulls are put to the death) distasteful, avoid the arena at Nîmes, which still clings to old traditions, dating back to Roman times when the Nîmes arena had a reputation for bloodthirsty games.

Origins
The first recorded bullfights were held in honor of King Louis and Queen Yolands in Arles in 1405. The birth of the *Cours Camarguais* as it is today dates back to 1793, when a Commissaire called Fréron was welcomed into Arles with a spectacle that involved the now characteristic *cocarde* in which the winner was awarded a prize. It was the Marquis de Baroncelli who stimulated the revival of this colorful tradition in the last century.

Comic capers
The *vachette* often vaults over the inner barrier around the ring and as it chases round the outside everybody leaps to safety *inside* the ring — just like a comedy cartoon, the bull's progress can be measured by the escaping bodies popping one by one back over the barrier. When it gets halfway round, the *vachette* is sent back in the ring again.

The serene cloisters of the Abbaye-de-Montmajour

▶ Martigues 97C2

Martigues is a pleasant base for exploring the Étang de Berre or for stopping over *en route* for the Camargue, not least because of the picturesque canals that run through its center between its three separate "villages."

On the southern side of the main canal is Jonquières, the busiest village if you are looking for a meal or a drink. In the middle is L'Isle, which has several restored 17th- and 18th-century houses as well as the splendid **Église de la Madeleine▶** which recently had a much-needed facelift. From the bridge next to the church is a celebrated view known as the **Miroir des Oiseaux▶** (the birds' mirror). This little cameo of fishing boats moored in a curve of the canal at the *quai Brescon* was painted by Corot, Ziem, and several other turn-of-the-century artists. Works by Ziem and others are on display in the **Musée Ziem** (closed Tuesday) on the boulevard du 14 Juillet in the third village of Martigues, Ferrières.

The much-photographed and painted Miroir des Oiseaux, Martigues

▶ Maussane-les-Alpilles 96B3

Situated at the foot of the Alpilles with the fertile Plaine de la Crau stretching away to the south, Maussane-les-Alpilles is a prosperous village that made its fortunes from olive oil: at the beginning of the century it had over a dozen olive mills but today only one survives, which still presses olives in the traditional way (open daily except Sundays: follow the signs for the *cooperative oleicole* down rue Charlour Rien on the north side of the main road).

▶ Miramas-le-Vieux 97C2

Miramas-le-Vieux has recently been restored (and the streets recobbled) to create the kind of medieval *village perché* that you are more likely to expect in the Vaucluse. The manicured ruins of the old château are the setting for music concerts on summer evenings.

Keep going on D10 and you will reach **St-Chamas**, a former fishing village currently reorienting itself toward yachting and tourism. In the town center the **Église▶▶**

has an impressive baroque façade attributed to the 17th-century Aixois architect Pierre Pavillon. Just outside is a well-preserved Roman bridge, the **Pont Flavien▶**. Built in the 1st century A.D., it is framed by two triumphal arches.

▶▶ Montmajour, Abbaye-de- *96B3*

Set on a hillock 3 miles north of Arles, Montmajour was one of the most powerful monasteries of medieval Provence and even in ruins is still an impressive sight.

Montmajour owes its origins to one of the early Christian saints, St. Trophimus, who fled here from Arles to hide in a cave in the hillside. Later, a group of hermits took up residence to safeguard the site, which led to the founding of the monastery in the 10th century. Under Benedictine rule the abbey went from strength to strength, establishing numerous priories and starting on the Herculean task of reclaiming the surrounding marshlands. Thanks to these landholdings, the abbey became very wealthy — and decadent. In 1639 a group of reformed monks was sent in to sort it out but those already in residence, reluctant to leave a fat sinecure, sacked the abbey in revenge.

In the 18th century Montmajour was partly rebuilt but Louis XVI disbanded the abbey in 1786. Restoration began in 1907.

The **upper church▶**, 12th-century but never completed, is an impressive, austere structure. On the right of the nave is an interesting crypt, part-built into the side of the hill, with fine Romanesque vaulting. The **cloister▶▶▶** ranks among the most important in Provence, with finely detailed carvings of demons and beasts on the bases and capitals of the cloister's colonnades.

From the 86 foot-high **keep**, a mighty fortified structure built in 1369, there are panoramic views across to the Alpilles, Arles, and the Plaine de la Crau. From the keep, go down the side of the hill to the wonderful little **chapelle St-Pierre▶▶**, half-carved out of the hillside in the caves where St. Trophimus sought refuge. The chapel is sometimes closed, but the abbey is open daily except Tuesday (admission).

Fresh fish

Until big industry moved into the nearby Fos complex, the village of Martigues relied almost entirely on fishing and there are still plenty of working boats moored up on the canal sides. In July and August the abundant sardine catch is distributed free every evening, freshly grilled, in an old custom known as the *sardinades*.

Montmajour was one of the most important medieval monasteries in Provence

Olive festival
The annual harvest of green olives from Mouriès' 80,000 trees is around 1,300 tons. If you want to try out their famous olives (as well as a multitude of other olive products) the best time to come is in the middle of September, when there is an annual, two-day festival, which also features bullfights and Provençal dances.

► Mouriès *96B3*

Mouriès is well known for its peppery oils — so if you are an olive oil aficionado this is the place to come. Mouriès is about 4 miles southeast of Maussane-les-Alpilles. Olive oil mills have been part of the landscape here for over 100 years. There were 18 mills in 1882, now there are only two (the *moulin cooperatif* and the *moulin moderne*) but they still produce 200,000 liters (about 50,000 gallons) of olive oil between them each year.

►►► Nîmes *96A3*

Although situated 15 miles west of the Rhône and well outside the borders of present-day Provence, Nîmes shares much of the Provençal heritage — in particular, a glorious past as a Gallo-Roman city.

Nîmes first rose to prominence as the capital of the Celtic tribe of the Volcae-Arecomici, when it was known as *Nemansus* after a sacred and prolific spring that the Celts revered. The settlement was also strategically positioned on the main Spanish–Italian trade routes, and when the Romans forged through in the 1st century A.D. the inhabitants were quick to embrace their new overlords. *Nemansus* became *Colonia Nemausensis.*

Augustus reciprocated the Celtic welcome by heaping privileges on the town and encircling it with a monumental, 5 mile-long wall; soon after, a large amphitheater was added, as well as the celebrated Maison Carrée and the aqueduct of the Pont du Gard, which brought water to the city's baths and fountains.

After the decline of Rome, Nîmes fell into the hands of the Visigoths, followed by the Franks. In the 16th century the town sided with the Protestant Huguenots, which led to considerable bloodshed, but peace was restored with the Edict of Nantes in 1598. The 17th century saw further conflict

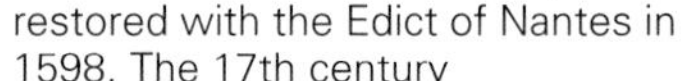

One of the best-preserved Roman temples in Europe, the Maison Carrée in Nîmes was built in the 1st century B.C.

but after the troubles Nîmes concentrated on building up its textile industry and by the 18th century over 10,000 people and 300 looms were churning out silk fabric and serge for export. One of its best-selling lines was a hard-wearing blue serge which became known simply as de Nîmes ("from Nîmes"), and when some of this fabric found its way to California in 1848 Levi Strauss adopted it to create his famous denim jeans.

Nîmes has had little success since; to quote an early guidebook: "20th century Nîmes has stagnated...and it has been supplanted by Montpellier." Enter, in 1983, the dynamic Jean Bousquet, former head of the locally based fashion empire of Cacherel, elected mayor on a ticket of turning Nîmes's fortunes around.

By pouring money into arts and culture, and in particular by commissioning world-class architects to embellish the city with buildings and monuments, Bousquet has sought to regain the crown from rival Montpellier and rejuvenate the city. Some resent his high-handed approach, but his ambitions have put Nîmes firmly back on the map.

What to see Most of the sites are within easy walking distance of each other in the center of Nîmes. First stop — the spectacular **Arènes▶▶▶** (open daily; admission), one of the best-preserved Roman amphitheaters in existence. Dating from the turn of the 1st century A.D., its mellow, honey-colored sandstone exterior is now completely black from exhaust fumes and pollution.

A lapidary Cupid in the Jardin de la Fontaine

The Arena Village
After gladiator fights were banned in the 6th century under the influence of Christianity, the Nîmes arena was turned into a fortress by the Visigoths. Later, people started to move in and build houses inside it (a fate that also befell the arena at Arles and the theater at Orange); by the 18th century this had grown into an entire village, with 2,000 people, 200 houses, and even a couple of churches. It took over 30 years to clear the whole lot away in the early 19th century.

The place aux Herbes is the focal point of Nîmes's old quarter

Despite this, the arena is in remarkable condition and on the upper stories you can still see the sockets for the posts which held the *velum*, an adjustable awning that sheltered spectators. Now the arena has the 20th-century equivalent, a massive inflatable canopy weighing over 9 tons which is put up in the winter months: it takes a team of engineers over three weeks to erect (the canopy goes up in October and comes down in April; during these months visits to the arena are by guided tour only for safety reasons).

The other "must" in Nîmes is the **Maison Carrée▶▶▶**, a delightful temple also in exceptional condition. Built in the 1st century A.D. and modeled on the Temple of Apollo in Rome, it was dedicated to Augustus' grandsons, Caius and Lucius. Surrounded by elegant Corinthian columns, it remains almost perfectly intact despite having been used for (among other things) a stable in the Middle Ages.

Facing the Maison Carrée on the place du Forum is a high-profile reminder of Bousquet's commitment to modern architecture, the **Carre d'Art▶▶** which opened in 1993. Its name — "art edge" — playfully echoing the "square house" opposite, this beautifully designed Norman Foster building takes up the purity of line of the ancient temple and translates it into 20th-century idiom. Inside, light pours down a huge central well to the library on the basement floors; the upper levels house a **Musée d'Art Contemporain ▶▶** (open daily; admission). There is a café beneath the roof canopy with great views of Nîmes and the Maison Carrée beneath.

Just north of the Carre d'Art is another Bousquet-inspired project, the **place d'Assas▶**. Designed in 1989 by Martial Raysse, water flows across the square between two figures representing Nemausa — deity of the original spring — and Nemausus.

Water also plays a central role in the wonderful **Jardin de la Fontaine▶▶** nearby. Created in the late 18th century the gardens channel the waters of the Nemausus spring through a series of Roman-style pools beneath a maze of balustrades and statuary. On the left of the lower promenade are the remains of the **Temple of Diana**.

Follow the gardens uphill for the **Tour Magne▶** (open daily; admission) at the top of Mont Cavalier. This 100 foot-high tower was once part of the city walls built by Augustus; steps lead to a viewing platform at the top.

Detail of one of the many statues in Nîmes's delightful Jardin de la Fontaine

The heart of the city, old Nîmes, is almost entirely pedestrianized and is a pleasure to wander around. In the middle of the old quarter is the place aux Herbes, dominated by the **Cathédral Notre-Dame-et-St-Castor▶** which has been rebuilt many times over the centuries. Its west front (facing the square) is ornamented with a classical frieze illustrating Old Testament stories. In a corner by the cathedral is the **Musée de Vieux Nîmes▶▶** (open daily; admission) which has a well-presented collection of Renaissance furniture, and historical documents.

On the eastern side of the old quarter, the **Musée d'Histoire Naturelle et de Préhistoire▶** (open daily; admission) is worth a look for its extensive collection of sculpted *menhirs* (dolmens) and Gallo-Roman bits and pieces such as jewelry, pots, oil lamps, and household items. A model shows the full extent of Augustus' amazing wall that once encircled the city.

South of the Arènes, the **Musée des Beaux Arts▶** (open daily; admission) has some significant Roman mosaics as well as paintings and other works spanning the 15th to the 20th centuries.

Nearby Nîmes is inevitably associated with the nearby **Pont du Gard▶▶▶** and it is well worth a detour to see what has always been considered "one of the wonders of the Ancient World."

The Pont du Gard owes its existence to the almost insatiable thirst for water of the average Roman city — not just for domestic use but for the many fountains and public baths — and their desire for totally pure water. When the spring of Nemansus was deemed no longer sufficient, the city engineers did not hesitate to carve out an aqueduct from the Source d'Eure near Uzès, nearly 30 miles away. Faced with the impetuous River Gard in their path, the Romans — or rather their slaves — erected this stunning masterpiece built of masonry blocks weighing up to 6 tons each. Its three tiers of arches span the valley for 900 feet and reach a height of 157 feet above the river.

Despite the huge numbers of people who come to visit the aqueduct, the area immediately surrounding it has thankfully been kept free of intrusive buildings (shops, cafés, and so on are located well away from the bridge) so you are left to gaze in awe at this grand gesture to Roman public hygiene.

Blood games

In Roman times the Nîmes arena had a reputation for particularly bloodthirsty games, and people would travel from far and wide across the country to witness gladiators fight it out to the death, either with each other or with wild animals. Blood-lust continues even now, although it is nearly always the animals that die in the Spanish-style *corridas* (which here they call *Ferias*). The main *Ferias* are during the Carnival in February, the *Feria de Pentêcote* (Pentecost), and the *Feria des Vendanges* (September).

The fountains of Nîmes are a constant reminder that the town owes its origins to the waters of the spring of Nemansus

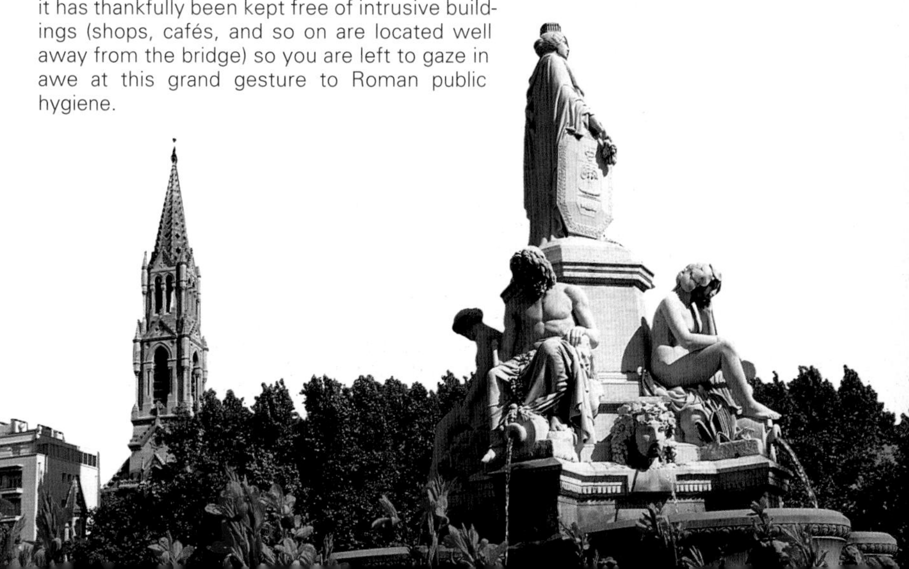

Van Gogh's landscapes There is a walking trail around some of the scenes which Van Gogh painted near St-Rémy (the tourist office can supply a detailed leaflet, *Promenade sur les lieux peints par van Gogh*) with placards showing which works were done where, along with Van Gogh's own comments.

Glanum's Mausoleum: inside there are statues of Caesar and Augustus

▶▶▶ St-Rémy-de-Provence *96B3*

Despite nowadays being heavily dependent on tourism, St-Rémy is still undoubtedly one of the most delightful towns in all Provence. Encircled by a boulevard of plane trees, the center of the town is a warren of fine old buildings, pretty squares, plant-filled alleyways, and cooling fountains. Its charms inspired Provençal poets such as Joseph Roumanille, Marie Mauron, and Marcel Bonnet, as well as novelist Gertrude Stein.

On the edge of the circular boulevard is the **place de la République**, with outdoor cafés and a lively market on Wednesday mornings. Facing the square is the neoclassical **Collegiale St-Martin▶** with its famous organ: built in 1983, it is said to be one of the finest contemporary organs in Europe. Regular recitals take place on Saturday evenings between July and September.

Behind St Martin in place Favier the 16th-century **Hôtel Mistral de Mondragon▶** houses the **Musée des Alpilles▶** (open daily, closed January, February and March; admission) with exhibits on local folklore, geology, ethnography, and Nostradamus (see panel, page 145). Next door in another fine Renaissance palace, the **Hôtel de Sade▶**, is the **Musée Archéologique▶▶** (same hours as above), devoted to finds from Glanum, including some well-preserved temple decorations, statues of the gods, and everyday Roman items such as jewelry and jars. Another old mansion, the **Hôtel Estrine**, contains the **Centre d'Art Presence Van Gogh▶** (closed Monday; admission), with audiovisual displays and documentation on Van Gogh, and exhibitions of contemporary works.

Nearby Within walking distance down D5 (a half-mile outside St-Rémy) are the ruins of **Glanum▶▶▶** and the remarkable Roman monuments known as **les Antiques▶▶▶**, consisting of a well-preserved mausoleum and a triumphal arch by the side of the road. The 60 foot-high mausoleum, with elaborate bas-reliefs on the podium was erected in around A.D.30. The triumphal arch, dating from around the same time, was one of the first of its kind in Provence.

Opposite the Antiques is the entrance to the site of **Glanum** itself (open daily; admission) where excavations since 1921 have uncovered many different layers of habitation from the Celto-Ligurian period through to its sacking in A.D.270. There is an enormous amount to see, including the Forum, the *thermae* (baths), a sacred well from the Gallo-Greek period, several large private houses, and the remains of various

temples. One of these has recently been partially reconstructed, with the moldings, columns, and elaborate capitals faithfully copied (using ancient tools and techniques) from the originals kept in the Musée Archéologique.

Just below the site is the former monastery of **St-Paul-de-Mausole▶**, where Van Gogh was hospitalized (see page 112). It is still a private sanitorium but you can walk down the main driveway and visit the church and the 12th-century cloisters.

The entrance to the Musée des Alpilles, housed in a 16th-century building

▶▶ les Saintes-Maries-de-la-Mer *96A2*

This seaside resort is a popular base for visiting the Camargue and has plenty of things to do, including horse-riding, biking, sailing, windsurfing, and swimming.

The resort is at its busiest during the annual *Pèlerinage des Gitanes*, a gypsy pilgrimage which takes place on the last weekend in May each year to honor Sarah, the black Egyptian slave who was washed ashore along with the three Marys (see panel). Sarah's remains are interred in a reliquary in the crypt of the **Église▶▶** in the center of the old town. This stately Romanesque church, strengthened during the 12th century after a series of Saracen raids on the town, is one of the best examples of fortified churches in Provence; from its bell tower (open daily April to mid-November) there is a panorama of the vast, open spaces of the Camargue.

Just near the church is the **Musée Baroncelli** (closed Tuesday; admission) with displays on local wildlife, Arlesian costumes, and furniture, and a few mementos of Baroncelli's life, including signed photographs from his Native American friends (see panel, page 59).

Baroncelli's **tomb** is down on the waterfront next to the *arènes*, and although (strangely) unmarked, it is unmistakable because it incorporates carvings of his two main passions, a horse and a bull.

The legend of Sarah
According to legend, Sarah arrived here with Mary Magdalene, Mary Salome, Mary Jacobe, and several disciples after they had been cast adrift from the Holy Land. Once they reached the Camargue in the "boat of Bethany," the disciples dispersed, the elderly Mary Salome, Mary Jacobe, and Sarah stayed and were eventually buried in the oratory which they had built here. Their tombs soon attracted pilgrims, particularly gypsies from all over Europe who had adopted Sarah as their patron saint. At the end of May effigies of the saints are carried down to the sea to be blessed during the annual *Pèlerinage des Gitanes*.

Drive The Alpilles

An extension of the Lubéron range, the Alpilles are one of the prime landmarks in the middle of the Crau plain. This tour goes through the heart of the range and encompasses interesting places around the base of the Alpilles (about half-a-day); you could also extend it to include les Baux (allow a full day).

From St-Rémy take D99 eastward, turning right down D74A across the Canal des Alpilles toward **Eygalières**►►, a charming little town with a long history. In the streets are many fine old houses; there are the remains of the 12th-century castle keep of the old château; below the ruins on the north side of the hill the 17th-century **Chapelle des Penitents Blancs** has been converted into the small **Musée**► (open Sunday afternoon or by calling the caretaker, M. Pezet, tel: 90 95 92 51) which has a wonderfully haphazard collection of local ethnography.

Follow D24B east toward Orgon, to see the charmingly simple, 12th-century **Chapelle de St-Sixte**►► on a hillock to the right of the road. There is an annual pilgrimage from Eygalières at Easter (it is not otherwise open). Return via Eygalières and turn left down D24, a lovely scenic road which winds through the heart of the Alpilles, surrounded on either side by pine forests and vineyards. Turn right at the hamlet of le Destet toward Maussane on D78, which snakes around the south face of the Alpilles along an ancient route once

The remains of a Roman aqueduct at Barbegal

used for the annual *transhumance*.

At **Maussane** (see page 134) you can either detour back up to **les Baux** (see pages 114–115) or continue on D17 toward Paradou, where outside the village a huge hangar houses **La Petite Provence du Paradou**► (open daily; admission). This "Provence-in-miniature" features over 200 figures — shepherds, gypsies, farmers, fishermen and so on — integrated into a vast, three-dimensional tableau with working windmills and other careful touches. Turn off down D78E until you see the

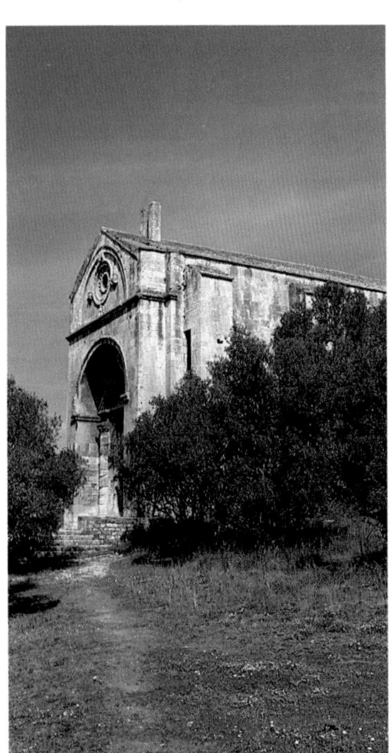

The impressive 12th-century Chapelle St-Gabriel and (top) the Italianate rose window on its facade

Aqueduct de Barbegal►►. Park near the remains of the aqueduct and follow it between a cutting in the rocks to the edge of a small escarpment: beneath you, the slope of the hill is covered with a series of ruins — one of the few surviving examples of a Roman flour mill. This interesting structure — the only one of its kind powered by hydraulics — consisted of no fewer than 16 mills, linked up with two parallel series of paddle-wheels in the middle. Turn right down D33 toward **Fontvieille**►. This attractive town largely owes its reputation to the link with novelist Alphonse Daudet. An avenue lined with pines to the south of town leads to the **Moulin de Daudet**►► (Daudet's windmill; open daily, closed January; admission) set on a hillock with views across to the Alpilles and the Tarascon plain. Just outside the windmill there is a small museum containing first editions of his writings, portraits, manuscripts, and other memorabilia.

From Daudet's windmill a path leads back to Fontvieille, past two other windmills, to the **Château de Montauban**► (open daily; admission) where Daudet actually stayed while in Fontvieille; it now houses an exhibition – "Bonjour Monsieur Daudet" – which focuses on Daudet's personal life.

Take D33 out of Fontvieille until you come to the lovely **Chapelle St-Gabriel**►► just before N570. This is nearly all that remains of a once-thriving Gallo-Roman settlement, *Ernaginum,* which was a port for rafts which plied the surrounding marshes. The drying up of the marshes signaled the death knell for the town. From here, return to St-Rémy on D32 and D99.

► Salon-de-Provence 97C2

Salon's fortunes were founded on soapmaking and olive oil but its present-day prosperity is largely due to the French Air Force flying school just outside of town.

The medieval seer Nostradamus moved here during the last years of his life (from 1547 to 1566), and his house in the old quarter is now a modern museum, **La Maison de Nostradamus** (open daily; admission). A series of fairly unconvincing *tableaux* depict scenes from his life, with a rambling commentary on portable CD players. Unfortunately the overall effect is greatly disappointing.

Just near Nostradamus' house the lovely old **Porte de l'Horloge►** was built of honey-colored stone between 1626 and 1664. Opposite the gateway in place Crousillat is the beautiful 18th-century **Grand Fontaine►** which has become so encrusted in moss that it looks like a huge green mushroom cloud.

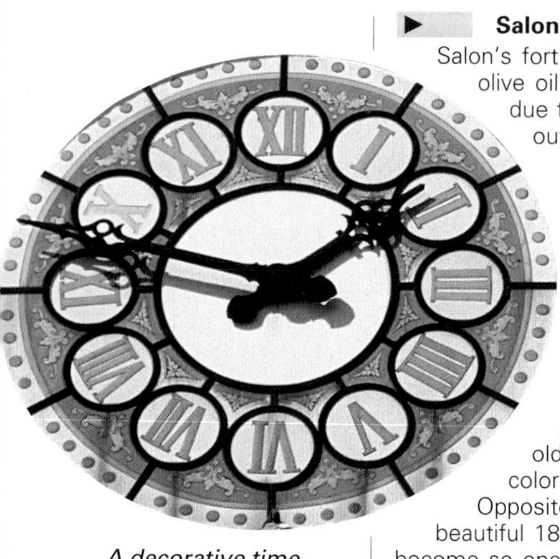

A decorative timepiece on the clocktower, Salon

The Tarasque monster
After arriving in the "boat of Bethany," at les Saintes-Maries-de-la-Mer, Ste Marthe came to Tarascon only to find the town terrorized by an amphibious monster that devoured local children and cattle alike. Ste Marthe tamed the beast by showing it her crucifix, after which it was captured and led away on a lead. To celebrate this miracle, in 1474 the Good King René organized an annual carnival — which still takes place on the last Sunday in June — with a ferocious, dragonlike Tarasque led through the streets snapping his mighty jaws at onlookers; bonfires, fireworks, bullfights, and dances precede the parade of the captive monster.

Waxwork figures are also the main ingredient in the nearby **Musée Grevin de la Provence►** (open daily; admission), which somehow manages to convey more spirit in its displays depicting key events in the history of Provence.

Within the "old" town center, the 13th-century **Église St-Michel►** has a noteworthy part-Gothic and part-Romanesque façade, which has just been restored. At the top of the hideous new square in the old town is the **Château de l'Emperi►►**, a massive fortress dating back to the 10th century; it now houses the **Musée d'Art et d'Histoire Militaire►** (closed Tuesday; admission). The collection of over 10,000 items includes arms, uniforms, waxwork figures, and flags, spanning the period from Louis XIV to World War I.

Just to the north of the town center is the **Église St-Laurent,** which houses the tomb of Nostradamus.

►► Silvacane, Abbaye de 97C3

Set amid fertile fields on the south banks of the Durance, the Abbaye de Silvacane (open daily except Tuesday; admission) was the last to be built of the three great Cistercian abbeys in Provence (the other two being Sénanque and le Thoronet). Its name comes from *silva cana* ("forest of rushes"), which was all that was here before the monks set about draining the marshes to create farmland. Founded in the 12th century, the abbey prospered until pillaging and disastrous crops in the 14th century ruined it. It was turned into farm buildings before restoration began in the 19th century. As with its sister abbeys, the uncompromising austerity of Silvacane's architecture reflects the chaste lives of the Cistercians. The stark beauty of the clean-lined, pale stone church is echoed in a charming cloister with an old fountain.

VILLE DE TARASCON
MAISON de TARTARIN
RECETTE MUNICIPALE
Tarif normal
N° 01413
A présenter à toute réquisition

►► Tarascon 96B3

A former port on the banks of the Rhône, Tarascon is famous for its

The 16th-century sage looks down over the ages — the Nostradamus mural, Salon-de-Provence

fabulous castle and the equally fantastic legends woven into its history — principally the story of Ste Marthe and the Tarasque (see panel).

King René spent the last ten years of his life surrounded by troubadours and artists in the fairytale **Château▶▶▶** (guided tours daily, closed Tuesday, holidays; admission) overlooking the Rhône. The building of the castle was initiated by Louis II of Anjou in 1400 and finished off by his son René in 1449. It was used as a prison from 1800 right up until 1926.

Considered to be one of the finest fortified medieval châteaux in the whole of France, its massive walls and crenellated towers contrast markedly with the graceful and elegant interior architecture, particularly the flamboyant *cour d'honneur* where the royal apartments are linked by a spiral staircase.

Ste Marthe's remains, conveniently discovered in 1187, lie in the **Collegial Ste-Marthe▶▶** just opposite the château. The church has suffered many indignities over the centuries, having lost its best sculptures during the Revolution and been bombed in World War II.

Tarascon has another claim to fame in the contemporary legend of Tartarin, a comic figure invented by the novelist Alphonse Daudet in 1872, who bumbles through life bragging about his improbable adventures. After shunning Daudet for many years because the ridiculous Tartarin made them into a laughing stock, the people of Tarascon eventually forgave him to cash in on the fat man's fictional life in the **Maison de Tartarin** (closed Sunday; admission) on the boulevard Item.

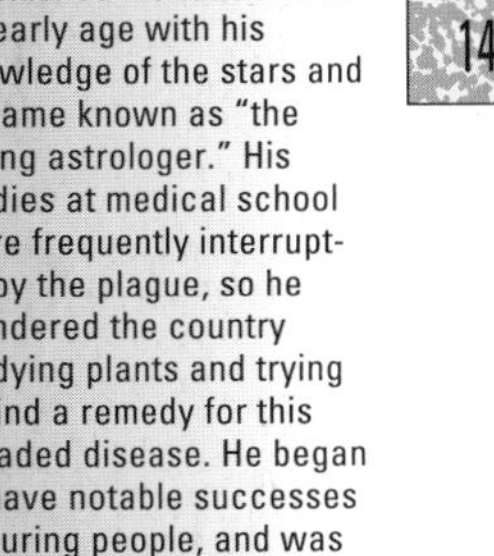

The Provençal seer
Born in 1503 in St-Rémy, Michel de Nostradamus astonished his teachers at an early age with his knowledge of the stars and became known as "the young astrologer." His studies at medical school were frequently interrupted by the plague, so he wandered the country studying plants and trying to find a remedy for this dreaded disease. He began to have notable successes in curing people, and was called upon from far and wide. He moved to Salon in 1547, and published the first of his astrological -predictions in 1555. They were an immediate sellout, and he was summoned to Paris to predict the futures of Henri II's four sons. Nostradamus died peacefully in 1566, but his *Centuries* (predictions) are still widely read today.

A country calendar

■ **Despite modernization and the presence of missile sites, country life in Provence continues according to the cycle of the seasons, a calendar which alternates periods of intense work with equally intense festivities to celebrate the fruits of the earth.....■**

Spring blossom (top) and autumn vines

Spring Spring unfolds quickly in Provence, and by February or March almonds and mimosa are starting to bloom, soon followed by carpets of wild flowers. Olives and vines (if they have not been seen to in November) must be pruned, and cereal crops sown.

By April plums, peaches, apples, apricots, pears, and quinces are in blossom, and fires are lit in the orchards to stop frost from killing the delicate buds. The sheep are sheared, and Easter celebrated with the first spring lamb. The first nightingales and swallows appear. In Arles, Pain de St. George is baked to celebrate the feast day of the patron saint of the Camargue on April 23.

Summer May 1 is considered the beginning of summer in Provence. *Primeurs* (early fruit and vegetables) brighten up market stalls, with asparagus, cherries, peas, apricots, melons, and strawberries from the truck gardens heralding a taste of sunshine. The flocks are shepherded back to the hill pastures, following the ancient traditions of the *transhumance*.

The autumn sowing of wheat is ready for harvesting in June, with migrant workers in their thousands descending from the mountains to cut the ripe sheaths. On the summer solstice, St. John's Day (June 24), bonfires are lit on hilltops to celebrate the end of the harvest. Other harvest festivals celebrate St. Eloi or St. Roch, and nearly all involve a great deal of wine and merriment, music and dancing, and huge banquets in village squares with grand *aïolis*.

As the summer progresses Spanish broom scents the *garrigue*, the lavender fields are resplendent with color, and thyme, rosemary, marjoram, and sage can be culled from the wild. Melons, peaches, and almonds are in abundance, and August is the perfect time for *ratatouille*, with zucchini, tomatoes, eggplant, garlic, onions, and peppers overflowing in the markets. Honeysuckle, clematis, and myrtle blossom on trellises and sunny walls.

Van Gogh on summer
"I keep remembering what I have seen of Cézanne, because he has exactly caught the harsh side of Provence. It has become very different from what it was in spring, and yet I certainly have no less love for this countryside burnt up as it begins to be from now on. Everywhere is old gold, bronze — copper, one might say — and this with the green azure of the sky blanched with heat: a delicious color, extraordinarily harmonious, with the blended tones of Delacroix." Van Gogh, in a letter to his brother, Theo.

Autumn September is dominated by the grape harvest, the *vendange*, a time when friends, neighbors, and families

get together to pick grapes and spend long evenings quaffing jugs of wine and laughing after the day's arduous labor. The countryside is a patchwork of red, gold, and rust-colored tones as the leaves turn in the vineyards and forests. Mushrooms, particularly the much sought after *cèpes*, begin to spring up in woodlands and everybody is out on weekends with collecting bags and sticks for turning over leaves to seek them out. Figs are in season, and the rice harvest is in full swing in the Camargue.

The *vendange* continues through into October (depending on the region), and chestnuts are collected in the woods. A less peaceful harvest also gets underway as the hunting season opens, and shotguns obliterate the sound of birdsong on every hillside. Wild boar and walnuts appear in the markets.

Winter The last major harvest of the year, picking olives, starts in November (in his twilight years Mistral named his last work *les Olivades* since he knew, too, that his season was over). The first bottles of heady young wines go on sale. The encroaching cold weather signals the *transhumance* of sheep back down from the mountains and hunting begins in earnest for the black diamonds known in Provençal as *rabasse* (truffles). While hardy souls are out hunting or truffling in the forests, the countryside seems to hibernate and many people only venture forth to warm themselves with hearty, nourishing soups and stews in the local tavern. Christmas is a major celebration in the depths of winter.

Pope-Hennessy on spring
"An April landscape, discovered at dawn from a moving train: Then, as I watched, the sun rose, and with it the whole panorama ceased looking like an underexposed photograph and came literally to light – the cabin roofs shone orange, the fields turned out to be scattered with poppies the colour of new blood, the long green grass was streaked with yellow flowers and cobalt flowers and round scabious flowers that were a hard, firm mauve. Over the distant crimson hills the sky was already blue, and the few people in the fields were a very dark walnut brown. Nothing I had expected of Provence equalled the harsh and yet mysterious quality of this flying landscape." James Pope-Hennessy, *Aspects of Provence*

A summer harvest

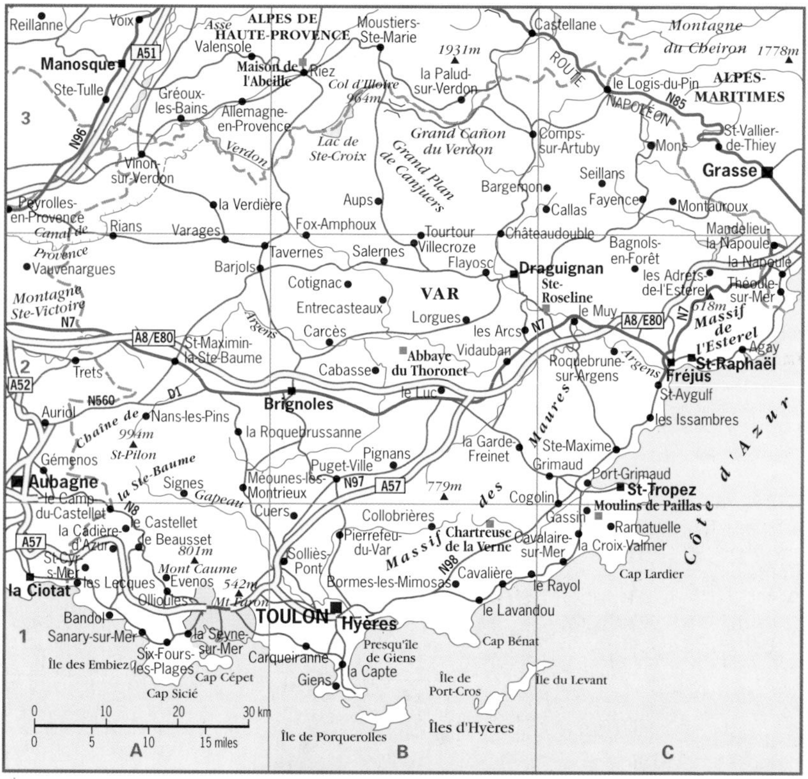

Right: the gardens of the Villa Ste-Claire in Hyères
Far right: a fountain in Cotignac

VAR

Introduction Bordered by the hinterland of Marseille to the west and the Riviera to the east, the Var coastline stretches for 265 miles along the shores of the Mediterranean. It is, quite simply, the most affordable and accessible coastline in Provence. Affordable because you are not paying the overinflated hotel and restaurant prices of the Riviera, and because it has more than twice as many campsites than any other *département* (nearly 300 in total). Accessible because it has over 90 miles of beaches, most of which are free, and because 105 miles of the coastline is open to the public thanks to the *Sentier du Littoral* (coastal path). The Var is also blessed with two unusual wilderness areas, the Massif des Maures and the Massif de l'Esterel.

The coast Tourism in the Var is oriented toward the sea, with plenty of opportunities for scuba diving, windsurfing (notably L'Almanarre beach at Hyères and "Brutal" beach at Six-Fours), or brushing up on your port and starboard. The Var has 65 ports and marinas (twice as many as the Côte d'Azur) and although some of the new marinas tend to be huge and characterless there are other, smaller ports which are perfectly charming.

And then there are the resorts: laid-back and friendly ports such as Sanary-sur-Mer or Bandol; simple beach resorts such as les Lecques or Cavalière; stylish spots such as le Lavandou or St-Raphaël; and of course not forgetting flashy St-Tropez (usually considered part of the Côte d'Azur, although in fact part of the Var).

Inland With three fourths of the population living in coastal areas (and 80 percent of tourists spending their time there too), the inland expanses of the Var are sparsely populated and well worth exploring. From the coastal *massifs* the plains roll northward, covered in a patchwork of vineyards (producing the renowned Côtes-de-Provence wines) and a smattering of villages and larger towns such as Draguignan and Brignoles. North of Draguignan, in the Haut Var, olives, truffles, and honey still provide the mainstay of many small communities.

The historic sites The Var is not without its share of historic monuments, from the brooding mass of the Chartreuse de la Verne high up in the Massif des Maures to the Romanesque purity of the Abbaye du Thoronet in the valley of the Argens; other outstanding sights include the Collégiale Ste-Pierre at Six-Fours and the Cité Episcopal of Fréjus. One of the oldest pilgrimage sites is the cave where Mary Magdalene reputedly spent the last years of her life, in the mountains of Ste-Baume on the western edges of the Var.

With all this, as well as plenty of appealing villages with welcoming bistros beside sun-dappled squares, it is perhaps not surprising that the tourism statistics show that on average people spend longer on vacation in the Var than they do in any other *département* of Provence.

Originally a watch-tower, Aups' Tour de l'Horloge now has a fine belfry

▶ les Arcs 148B2

Les Arcs is an attractive medieval village in the Argens valley between Draguignan and Fréjus. The old quarter, known as le Parage, culminates in the ruins of a 13th-century castle from where there is a view over the Massif des Maures and the surrounding vineyards which today provide les Arcs with its main source of income. Inside the **Église St-Jean-Baptiste** there is a large Provençal pastoral tableau (crèche) depicting le Parage as it once was, and a 15th-century polyptych by Jean de Troyes.

In the opposite direction (2.5 miles northeast on the D91) the **Chapelle Ste-Roseline▶** is worth a small detour. Originally part of the 11th-century Abbaye de la Celle-Roubaud, this Romanesque chapel was restored in 1970 and contains a bronze relief by Giacometti, stained glass windows by Ubac, and a mosaic by Chagall (open 3:30–6 and all day Saturday in summer, 2:30–5 Wednesday and Sunday in winter, closed January and February).

► **Aups** *148B3*

This small town in the middle of the woodlands of the Haut Var, dominated to the northeast by the Montagne des Espiguières, is famous for its honey and truffles (the truffle market is held every Thursday morning from November to February). Although still mainly an agricultural town it is becoming an increasingly popular base from which to tour the Haut Var or visit the Grand Cañon du Verdon (14 miles to the north; see page 190).

As well as the remains of its medieval ramparts, several fountains and a 16th-century tower with a fine wrought-iron belfry, Aups has an attractive Gothic church, the **Église St-Pancrace►**, with a recently restored Renaissance doorway.

►► **Bandol** *148A1*

Bandol is one of the busiest resorts west of the Côte d'Azur, with a pleasant, tree-lined promenade running the length of the port. It has all the trappings of the Riviera — discos, nightclubs, watersports, and a casino — without the usual sky-high prices, which makes it a popular family resort.

Bandol has three beaches, the best of which is the Anse de Renecros sheltered behind the headland on the west side of town. There is a lively Provençal market every morning in the place de la Liberté in the center of town. The hills behind Bandol have been completely disfigured by a series of ugly, low-rise apartment blocks, but down in the town you can ignore them and concentrate instead on the yachts bobbing in the harbor and the palm trees along the port.

A hundred years ago Bandol was better known for the cultivation of immortelle flower bulbs (which were exported as far afield as Russia and America) and for its tuna fisheries. As the flower trade gradually died off at the beginning of the century literature flourished in its place; Katherine Mansfield, Aldous Huxley, and D. H. Lawrence were among the illustrious literati who descended on Bandol at the time.

The tuna fisheries are also long gone, and today the quayside is lined with boats offering deep-sea fishing, scuba diving, or simply *promenades en mer*. A frequent ferry service links the port with the offshore island of **Île de Bendor►**, which has three hotels, diving and windsurfing schools, an exhibition center, an "artisans village," and the *Exposition des Vins et Spiriteux►* (open daily in summer except Wednesday). Housed in a huge hall decorated with art students' frescoes, the museum contains over 8,000 bottles of wine and liqueurs culled from over 50 countries worldwide.

Just near Bandol on D559B toward le Beausset is the **Jardin Exotique et Zoo►** (open daily except Sunday morning; admission). The greenhouses and rock gardens display thousands of rare varieties of succulents, cacti, and other tropical plants; in the small zoo there are parrots, toucans, flamingos, gibbon, and gazelles.

Farther up the same turn off the main road is the newly opened **Musée de l'Automobile Sportif►** (closed Monday; admission). More than 60 pristine racing cars and roadsters from France, the United States, England, Germany, and Italy are displayed in a purpose-built hall.

Winetasting

In the Argens valley the local wines can be sampled at the *Maison des Vins des Côtes-de-Provence* (open daily in summer), about 2 miles south of les Arcs, where there is an exhibition on the history of Provençal wines and a restaurant specializing in regional food.

Bandol is one of Provence's best-known areas for wine, particularly the reds. Head inland and you will pass several vineyards where you can stop for tastings, or else check out the selection available at the *Maison des Vins du Bandol* on the allées Vivien in Bandol.

Boats in the resort of Bandol, tied up alongside the promenade

A statue adorns the old palace which now houses Brignoles's Musée du Pays Brignolais

Flight-seeing
In the middle of the Circuit Paul Ricard at le Camp du Castellet is the Aérodrome du Castellet from where you can take a flight in a plane over the coast for a bird's-eye view of the *calanques* at Cassis or other areas: with the cost shared between three people, these spectacular flights are relatively inexpensive. Contact the Aéro-Club du Soleil (tel: 94 90 70 50).

► le Beausset *148A1*

Although the suburbs of le Beausset have expanded considerably in recent years, the old town center retains much of the atmosphere of a typical Provençal town. Napoleon stayed in a house on the rue Pasteur for a month in 1793, but le Beausset's most recent claim to fame is being the home town of a gang that carried out one of the most successful bank robberies in French history in Toulon in the late 1980s. Of the 20 or so gang members only one has so far been caught.

In the town square there is a lovely old fountain dating from 1832 with three sculpted dolphins in the middle — although the dolphins are entirely hidden beneath a mass of mossy vegetation. On the outskirts of the village the Cave des Maîtres Vignerons du Beausset (tel. 94 98 70 17) sells *vin du pays*, Côtes-de-Provence AOC, and Bandol wines.

On a hillside 1,300 feet above le Beausset is the Romanesque **Chapelle Notre-Dame du Beausset-Vieux►►** (open Saturday all day, every day 2–6 in summer). Built on the site of a Celto-Ligurian settlement in 1164, the chapel was at the center of the original settlement of le Beausset before the inhabitants moved down the hillside to the present location in 1506. Inside the chapel there is a gilded statue of the Virgin from the workshops of Pierre Puget and, on the right-hand side of the nave, an 18th-century wooden statue of Christ which once stood outside the chapel, where it was miraculously untouched by a fire in 1936 — apart from the right hand, which is missing.

Alongside the chapel there is a gallery with an interesting collection of around 80 *ex-votos* including an unusual olive-wood group dating from the 15th century. An outbuilding houses a typical Provençal crèche.

From the tower atop the chapel there are sweeping views across to the Bay of Ciotat (Baie de la Ciotat), Toulon and Ste-Baume.

►► Bormes-les-Mimosas *148B1*

Bormes would probably be just another *village perché* were it not for the bright yellow, vanilla-scented mimosas that it has adopted for its own and which flower throughout the village during the springtime; in summer the streets are filled with bougainvillea, huge pots of geraniums, and colorful windowboxes. As the most celebrated "floral village" in Provence, there are no fewer than three flower festivals (February, April and June).

Bormes-les-Mimosas has been "carefully" restored by artists and second-home owners and there is the usual plethora of potteries and galleries as well as the **Musée Arts et Histoire** (open daily Wednesday to Sunday in summer, Wednesday and Sunday mornings in winter), which traces the history of Bormes. The museum also holds regular exhibitions of contemporary works.

There are lovely views of the coast from the courtyard of the medieval château.

▶ Brignoles *148B2*

A large and lively town midway between the Haut Var and the Côte d'Azur, Brignoles has an extensive and very attractive medieval quarter and is a good stopping point for a night or two if you are touring in the area. The heart of old Brignoles is best explored on foot (the tourist office provide a comprehensive leaflet, *Visite de la Vieille Ville*). The star attraction, not to be missed, is the fascinating **Musée du Pays Brignolais▶▶** (open daily Wednesday to Sunday; admission) housed in the 13th-century summer palace of the Counts of Provence.

The museum was started by a local doctor in 1947 and since then has expanded to include two floors' worth of curiosities, an enormous 13th-century wine press, the world's first reinforced concrete boat, designed by local inventor Joseph Louis Lambot in 1849, and the Gayole sarcophagus, dating from the 1st century A.D. Discovered about 5 miles west of Brignoles, its incredibly well-preserved bas-reliefs depict both pagan and Christian figures.

The second floor is less compelling, but among some dire local paintings there is an outstanding collection of 18th- and 19th-century *ex-votos* and an automated Provençal crèche.

Ex-votos
Provence has some splendid collections of *ex-votos* — offerings (usually paintings) giving thanks for having been saved from some personal tragedy. Originating in Italy, they first appeared in Provence in the 17th century and reached their peak of popularity in the mid-1800s. *Ex-votos* display an intriguing compendium of the hazards of preindustrial life, with people shooting themselves accidentally, being squashed under carts, falling out of windows, sawing their hands off, and so on. The paintings are usually crude and naive and always combine images of the terrestrial (the sickbed, the accident, etc.) with the divine (the saints intervening from heaven).

Bormes's château is surrounded by pantiled houses

The old church and adjoining château overlook the cobbled streets of le Castellet

Sweet chestnuts
Collobrières was once an important center for cork-making but now it is sweet chestnuts from the surrounding forests that provide the economic mainstay: if you have a sweet tooth then you should visit the *Confiserie Azurienne* where there is a shop selling everything imaginable made from chestnuts, from ice cream to nougat to *marrons glacés.*

▶ la Cadière d'Azur *148A1*

Not as picturesque as neighboring le Castellet across the valley, Cadière has many fewer tourists and is a much quieter, more genuine *village perché.* Three portals lead up into the old part of the village, where the 12th-century **Église St-André** has a fine marble altarpiece. At the top of the village is the old **Chapelle Ste-Madeleine** built by the Pénitents Gris (now a private house) and, farther down, the Chapelle-Notre-Dame-de-la-Miséricorde built by the Pénitents Noirs and now used for jazz concerts and other events in summer. On D266 just outside the village, olive oil and other regional specialties can be bought at the excellent *Moulin de St-Come* (tel. 94 90 11 51).

▶▶ le Castellet *148A1*

Surrounded by the terraced vineyards of Côte-de-Provence wines, le Castellet was one of the first *village perchés* to be rejuvenated by artisans who were encouraged to settle here in the 1950s. It now has a well-established mix of craft shops, art galleries, potteries, and cafés and restaurants.

The delightful flower-filled streets lead up to the parish church (parts of which date from the 12th century) with the old château (rebuilt in the 15th century) which now houses the *mairie* (town hall) next door. To the left of the *mairie* is the so-called *Trou de Madame,* a gateway that leads onto a small balcony with magnificent views northwards across the vineyards in the valley and the foothills leading up to Ste-Baume.

The place de la Mairie in the peaceful Haut Var village of Cotignac

▶ Cogolin *148C2*

On the edge of the Massif des Maures about 4 miles inland from Port Grimaud, Cogolin does have some ruins, but most people come here for shopping rather than sightseeing since it has a lively crafts-based tradition.

First and foremost are Cogolin's famous pipes, which are made at two workshops on the main street (*Fabrique de Pipes Courrieu* and *Pipes Roux*). Even if you are not a

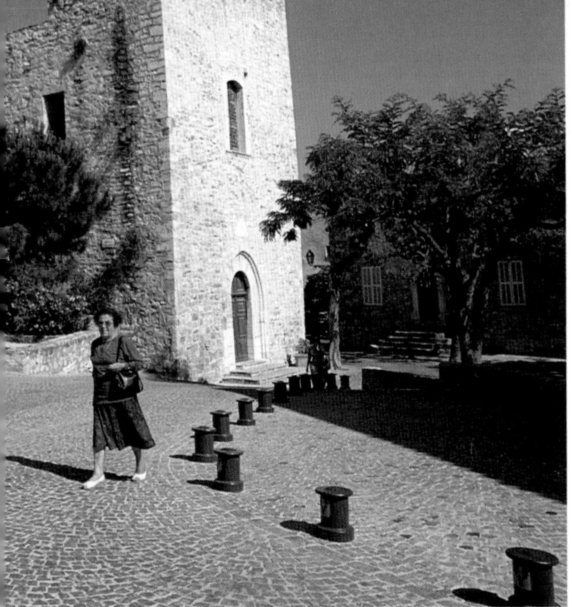

pipe-smoker it is worth glancing in their windows just to see the amazing variety of pipes made here: pipes with lids, pipes with faces, pipes with frills, inlaid, carved, long-stemmed, short-stemmed, even some with two bowls.

Cogolin is also famous for its carpets, an industry that started up in the 1920s with the arrival of Armenian immigrants who brought with them a tradition of hand-knotted ancestral rugs; you can see *Tapis de Cogolin* being made in the workshops in boulevard Louis Blanc (open weekdays). Other craftsmen in the village specialize in pottery, ironwork, corks for the wine trade, cane furniture, and top-quality reeds for wind instruments.

Movie set
Le Castellet's photogenic medieval streets have been used more than once for film sets, most notably by Marcel Pagnol who shot *La Femme du Boulanger* here in the 1930s and returned more than 50 years later to film scenes from *Manon des Sources*. But the village's cinematic associations go back farther, since it was here that the Lumière Brothers bought a house (now the Castel Lumière hotel) to use as a pre-production studio in 1895 for the production of France's first moving picture (see la Ciotat, page 122).

► Collobrières *148B1*

Time seems to have passed by this large village in the heart of the Massif des Maures where there are few concessions to modernity apart from a factory on the outskirts which turns out chestnut products by the truckload.

Otherwise, Collobrierès is a rest stop on the long and winding road up to the **Chartreuse de la Verne►►** (open daily except Tuesday) isolated amongst the forests of the Maures. Founded in 1170, this Carthusian monastery has been ransacked and rebuilt many times and is still undergoing restoration. The rambling complex of cloisters, chapels, and monks' cells (each of which has its own garden) is built from a combination of dark red schist and green-colored serpentine, a local Maures stone.

The high walls that surround the monastery give it a dark, brooding presence but it has uninterrupted views of the forested hills and the Gulf of St-Tropez beyond.

►► Cotignac *148B2*

This dreamy Haut Var village is dominated by two ruined towers on top of a 260-foot cliff which is riddled with caves and grottos. Behind the Romanesque parish church (with a facade rebuilt in the 19th century) is an enchanting *Théâtre de Verdure* where concerts are held in the summer. Wine, honey, and olive oil are the village's main products.

Twin bells atop the medieval parish church in le Castellet

■ Provençal cuisine is at its best when bursting with the aromatic, sun-drenched flavours of the Mediterranean. The essential ingredients — peppery olive oil, piquant garlic, the ubiquitous tomato, and herbs such as thyme, rosemary, and basil — are combined in many colorful dishes usually described as à la Provençale. An added bonus is that the Provençal style of cooking is good for your health!....■

Apéritifs
The locals like their *pastis* before a meal. Pastis is an amber-colored liquor distilled with anis and other herbs which goes cloudy when water is added. It is an acquired taste but hugely popular in Provence — perhaps due to its potency (at 90 proof, its effects are quickly felt in the southern sun!). Pastis is usually accompanied by a dish of black or green olives or canapés spread with a savory paste called *tapènade*, an appetizing purée of capers, olives, and anchovies.

Created in Provence, pastis *was once illegal — if you have one too many, you'll probably find out why!*

Soups *Soupe au pistou* (essentially a thick minestrone, heavily flavored with basil and garlic) is usually made in summer, but Provence's famous fish soups can be enjoyed year round: the most substantial of these is *bouillabaisse*, which is more of a stew than a soup and usually served as a meal in its own right. Originating in Marseille, *bouillabaisse* can include a myriad number of fish such as the hideous-looking *rascasse* (spiny hog fish), *loup* (sea bass), *rouget* (red mullet), eels, crabs, and anything else that the fishermen have pulled out of the sea that morning. The fish are cooked together very quickly in a *bouillon* (stock) containing saffron, garlic, herbs, and fennel and served up separately from the liquid at the table, accompanied by a spicy red paste called *rouille*: you spread the *rouille* on croûtons, sprinkle them with cheese and dunk them in your soup, accompanied by bits of fish.

You will also find *rouille* being served with the less expensive (although no less tasty) *soupe de poissons*, while another classic fish soup, *bourride*, is more properly accompanied by *aïoli*.

Aïoli Aïoli is a thick mayonnaise made with plenty of garlic and rich olive oil served alongside raw vegetables (*crudités*) as an hors d'oeuvres, or as an *aïoli garni*, with freshly cooked cod, potatoes, and hard-boiled eggs which are dipped into it.

Salads and vegetables The wonderfully full-flavored, sun-ripened local tomatoes appear in many dishes: sliced with onions, sprinkled with olive oil and basil, in a simple, appetizing *salade de tomates*, or stuffed with rice, eggplant, breadcrumbs, parsley, and garlic and baked as *tomates farcies*. They are an essential ingredient in *salade niçoise* alongside salad leaves, black olives, tuna, hard-boiled eggs, and green beans. No two *salades niçoises* are ever the same and the ingredients vary, as they do in the classic *ratatouille*, a vegetable stew of tomatoes, eggplant, onions, peppers, and zucchini braised with olive oil, garlic, and herbs.

Meat The most common dish is lamb, usually grilled with savory herbs or served stuffed with sausage, garlic, and herbs and cooked in a sauce *à la Provençale*. The best and tastiest lamb is the lean, spicy *agneau de Sisteron,* which has grazed on mountain pastures. Beef often comes braised in red wine and vegetables as a succulent *daube de boeuf*, or in the Camarguais version as

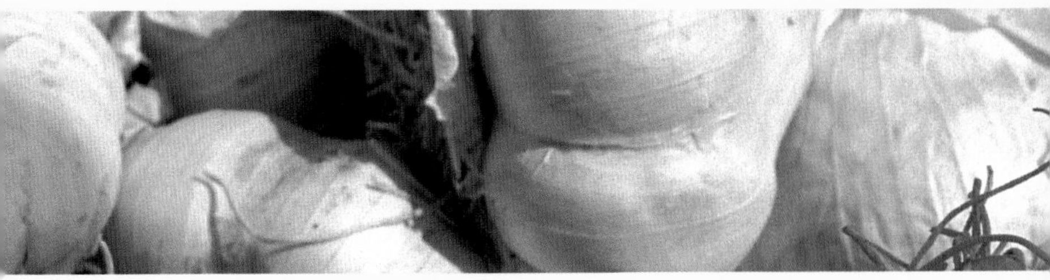

boeuf à la gardianne. Rabbit and hare are also simmered in wine and herbs.

Fish Naturally enough fish features heavily on menus in coastal restaurants, with some of the best being *loup de mer* (sea bass) grilled with fennel or vine shoots, *rouget* (red mullet) served whole, *pageot* (sea bream), sardines, or *merlan* (hake). Up in the hills *truite* (trout) often has a very short trip from a mountain stream to your table. The shellfish is usually excellent, and includes everything from *moules* (mussels) to *gambas* (giant shrimp), *palourdes* (clams), *oursins* (sea urchins), and crabs and lobsters.

Cheeses Local cheeses are usually made from the milk of goats (*chèvres*) or ewes (*brebis)*. In any market you can find an enormous selection of goat's cheese, which is usually either very creamy and fresh (with a fairly mild flavor) or has been left to dry out, in which case it has a much stronger, sharper taste. *Petits chèvres* are small roundels of goat's cheese, often flavored with bay, thyme, and other herbs. *Poivre d'âne* is a goat's cheese with a particularly peppery flavor, while *Banon* is a creamy sheep's cheese.

Desserts and fruit Desserts are always served after the cheese in France and the range of tempting flans, pastries, and fruit tarts is enough to melt your resolutions about a light meal. However, you can always salve your conscience with some fresh fruit — and there is plenty to choose from in the appropriate season, including strawberries, cherries, figs, peaches, nectarines, apricots, pears, and dessert grapes.

Snacks
Apart from *baguette* sandwiches, pizza slices, and the ubiquitous *frites* (french fries), a popular option is the *pan bagnat*, a monster bread roll spread with olive oil and filled with *a salade niçoise*-type mix. *Croque monsieurs* (toasted cheese and ham sandwiches) are not particularly Provençal, but *pissaladière* (a delicious onion, olive, and anchovy flan, best eaten cold or just warm) is very much local. In Nice the specialty is a slice of the extremely filling *socca*, a highly palatable pancake made from chickpea flour. Another Provençal specialty is the *fougasse*, a baked slice containing olives, sausage, cheese, and other ingredients.

A salade niçoise — no two versions are the same

Market day in Draguignan, the Var's biggest inland town

▶ Draguignan 148B2

Descending from the isolated villages and sparsely populated countryside of the Haut Var, Draguignan comes as something of a shock. Spreading over the entire valley, the outskirts of the town are an unattractive conglomeration of commercial centers, hypermarkets and second-hand car lots. And yet, hidden away like a pearl inside this ugly outer shell, Draguignan has an extremely well preserved *vieille ville* and, as an extra bonus, one of the best ethnographic museums in the whole of Provence. The absorbing **Musée des Arts et Traditions Populaires▶▶▶** (closed Monday and Sunday mornings; admission) displays the culture and heritage of the Var through a series of imaginative reconstructions, full of detail and authentic props, of country life. Olive-oil pressing, silk culture, winemaking, agriculture, cork manufacturing, beekeeping, hide-tanning, and tile-making are all faithfully covered. There are also Provençal costumes, musical instruments, religious art, and temporary exhibitions on a variety of topics.

Above the old town stands the **Tour de l'Horloge▶**, on the site of the first settlement here. Built in 1663, it replaced an earlier keep which was part of the medieval

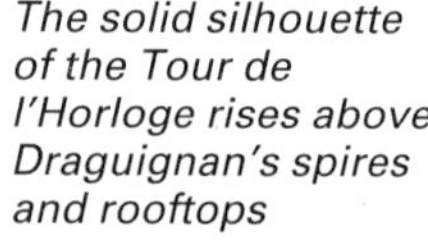
The solid silhouette of the Tour de l'Horloge rises above Draguignan's spires and rooftops

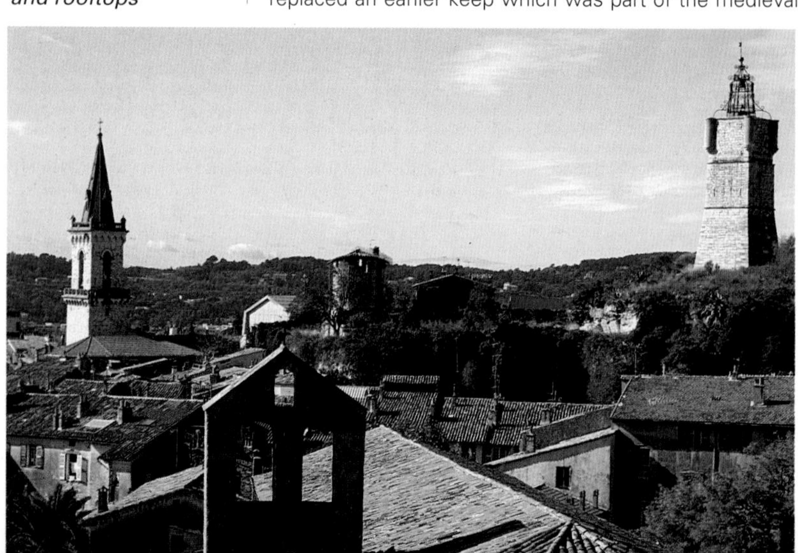

fortifications. Between the tower and the crumbling 13th-century **Chapelle de St-Sauveur▶** just below it on the hillside is the recently built, absolutely charming **Théâtre de Verdure▶**, an open-air theater artfully created with rocks, lawns, and olive trees in perfect proportion. Contact the tourist office for details of concert performances in this lovely setting (tel. 94 68 63 30)

▶ Embiez, Île des *148A1*

Like Bendor, the Île des Embiez is owned by Paul Ricard. Apart from a couple of small beaches, the main attraction for visitors is the **Institut Océanographique Paul Ricard** (open daily, closed Wednesday mornings in winter; admission) where there are several small aquarium tanks with around 100 species of Mediterranean fish and displays on marine ecology and local shipwrecks.

Ferries cross from le Brusc at regular intervals. The islands also have their own underwater seabus, the *Aquascope*, which tours the marine world around the coast (tel. 94 74 63 74).

▶ Entrecasteaux *148B2*

This small village is dominated by the 17th-century **Château▶** (open daily; admission) which was restored in the 1970s by an eccentric Scots painter, Ian McGarvie-Munn. The interior is rather bizarre, since parts are furnished in contemporary style (and decorated with McGarvie-Munn's own paintings) while others display period furnishings. Photographic and art exhibitions are also held inside the château, and there is a charming semi-formal garden, designed by le Notre.

▶▶▶ Esterel, Massif de l' *148C2*

Romantic travel posters in the past used to depict SNCF trains emerging from the tunnels in the Esterel *massif* to landscapes of brilliant red cliffs and bright blue seas: it is still so, but if you restrict yourself to the train or even the *Corniche d'Or* (N98) alongside the train line you will be missing one of the great splendors of Provence, an evocative wilderness hidden away behind the coast.

The Esterel (see page 171) is one of the Var's best-kept secrets. Most of the range (over 11,000 acres out of a total of 15,000 acres) is only accessible on foot or by mountain-bike. There are numerous tracks throughout the Esterel (some of which may be closed off in summer due to the fire risk), for which the best source of information is a map produced by the Office National des Forêts (National Forests Office), available from the tourist offices in St-Raphaël or Fréjus. There are also 23 miles of maintained roads, offering fabulous drives through parts of the *massif*.

▶ Evenos *148A1*

High above the Gorges d'Ollioules, the sombre walls of Evenos' 12th-century castle create a spooky atmosphere. It is worth the drive up the twisting road to walk around the outside of the walls (the interior is closed off). Huddled around the castle and a 13th-century church the tiny village itself is actually quite cheerful, with plenty of the crumbling houses having been restored. There is just one *auberge*, called, simply enough *On Mange, On Boit* ("One Eats, One Drinks").

Strange sights
A square at the entrance to Evenos is dedicated to the Provençal writer Marie Mauron, who graphically describes the castle as "black and torn apart, standing tragically against the open sky," adding that "the approaching silhouette, the ruins of dark basalt, wring your heart." It is indeed a strange place, as is the Grès de Ste-Anne outside the village of Ste-Anne d'Evenos below the château. This weird moonscape of sandstone formations (reached via a path on the right of the road just to the south of Ste-Anne) has many hidden grottos and startling formations and is at the base of the nearby Gros Cervau (the "big brain") range.

The sixties meet the 16th century in Entrecasteaux's château

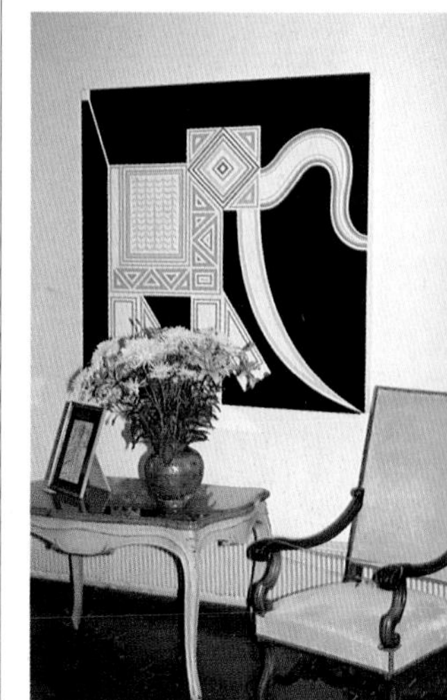

The Saracens
Apart from generally pillaging the surrounding countryside (until finally expelled by Count William in A.D.973), the Saracens did also introduce the tambourine, flat roof tiles, and the art of cork-making to Provence; the latter was to become the economic mainstay of la Garde-Freinet until the 19th century.

▶ Fréjus *148C2*

Fréjus and its neighbor, St-Raphaël, lie at the mouth of the Argens river between the Massif des Maures and Massif de l' Esterel. Now merged together into a somewhat characterless holiday conglomeration, Fréjus does have several relics which are worth investigating.

Founded by the Romans, Fréjus never recovered from Saracen attacks in the 10th century, nor the silting up of its harbor, leaving the port 2 miles inland. The sandy delta created by the Argens river is now Fréjus-Plage — crowded but handy for nearby children's attractions such as the water theme park Aquatica off RN98 or the Zoo-Safari Park next to the A8 autoroute.

Compared with others in Provence, the **arènes** is not particularly impressive, although some of the upper tiers have recently been rebuilt (open daily; admission). Most of the other **Roman remains** — the theater and remnants of the aqueduct and harbor wall — are somewhat scattered, so hopping on the town's *petit train* is a good idea on a hot day.

Fréjus' real treasure is the complex of episcopal buildings at the center of the old town. Begun in the 10th century, the **cathedral▶▶** boasts a magnificent set of carved walnut doors from the Renaissance. Protected by a set of shutters for the last 200 years, they are only opened on a guided tour (daily in summer, closed Tuesday in winter: guided tour also includes the baptistry, museum, and

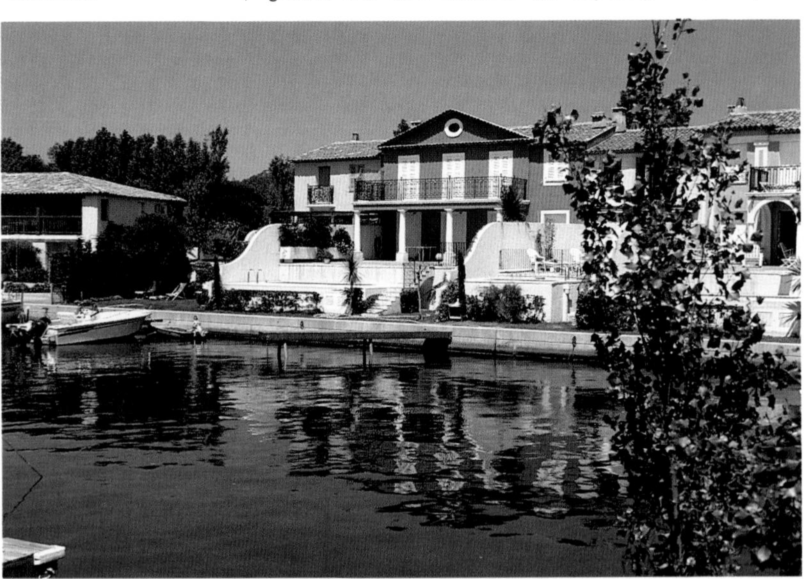

A palatial quayside residence in Port Grimaud

cloister; admission). The octagonal **baptistry▶▶▶** dates from the 4th or 5th century and is one of the best preserved of its era in France.

The final part of the cathedral complex is the charming **cloister▶▶▶**, with its slender columns and fantastic panoply of wood carvings on the ceiling — only 400 remain of the 1,200 panels. The remarkable **archaeological museum▶** contains finds from *Forum Julii* (see panel) including the famous double-headed bust of Hermes,

Boats are the only way to get around in Port Grimaud

discovered in 1970. This is in fact a copy; the priceless Hellenistic original never emerges from secure storage.

▶ la Garde-Freinet *148B2*

Straddling a pass across the rolling hills of the Massif des Maures, this now peaceful village was one of the last Saracen strongholds in Provence during the 10th century. Visit the **Maison de la Garde-Freinet et Pays des Maures** (housed in the old chapel St-Eloi to the south of the village) for information on the region and crafts products, or take a hike or drive up to the **Fort Freinet▶** to the west, from where there are extensive views back across to the le Luc plain and the foothills beyond.

▶▶ Grimaud *148C2*

A picture-perfect *village perché* on the eastern flanks of the Massif des Maures, Grimaud is named after the Grimaldi family who owned it from the 10th century onward. The rue des Templiers, with its arcades and Gothic doorways, leads up to the Hospice of the Knights Templars and the Romanesque **Église St-Michel▶**. Overlooking the village are the ruins of the Grimaldi **château▶**, with views down to the Gulf of St-Tropez and inland across the Maures.

Down on the coast is **Port Grimaud▶▶**. With its hundreds of pastel-shaded villas lining over 5 miles of quayside along the canals, it was designed by architect François Spoerry in the 1960s as a community of seafarers where everyone could have their boats parked outside their own front doors. Inevitably this pastiche of a fishing village has become a big tourist attraction in its own right, with most yacht-owning residents simply jetting in for their summer vacations.

It is worth a look just once, if you are passing by, although restaurants and cafés are absurdly overpriced and the compulsory parking outside the gates is expensive. View the whole *ensemble* from the top of the church tower — and boats leave regularly from beside the main square for trips around the canals.

The Roman port

The port of Fréjus, or *Forum Julii,* was founded in 49B.C. by Julius Caesar as a staging post on the coastal road which later became known as the Aurelian Way. It was the first Roman town in Gaul, and was soon turned into a major naval base by Octavian (later to become the Emperor Augustus) who used it to build a fleet of fast, light galleys with which he defeated Antony and Cleopatra in the Battle of Actium.

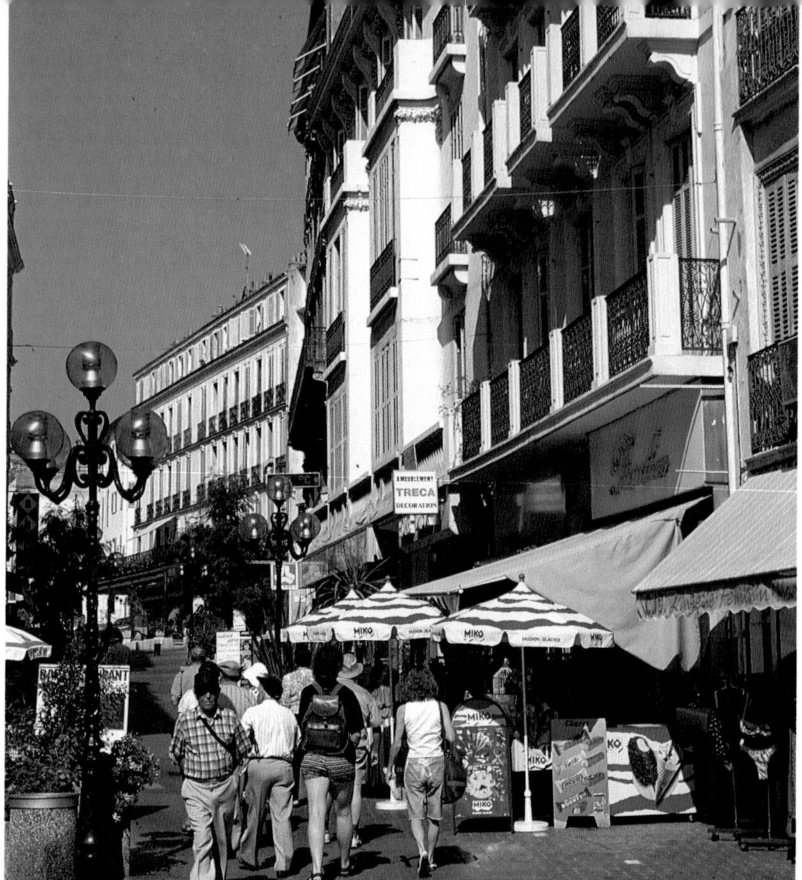

Once a fashionable resort, Hyères thrives on local horticulture

Mad about palm trees
Palm trees were originally introduced to France from the Canary Islands in 1864 by an amateur horticulturalist, the Comte Vigier. He planted the first three trees in Nice in 1865, and in 1867 the first seeds found their way to Hyères. Hyères very quickly became the "palm tree capital" of the Riviera, sending 300,000 trees a year all over Europe. Some 12,000 majestic palms currently grace the streets of Hyères les Palmiers and there is even an association, the *Fous des Palmiers* ("mad about palms"), for enthusiasts to swap seeds, knowledge and growing tips.

▶▶ Hyères *148B1*

The cultivation of fruit, flowers, and vegetables has long been an economic mainstay in Hyères, and today the sale of flowers alone (principally roses, marigolds, irises, tulips, and gladioli) brings in around 400 million francs annually and accounts for around 20 percent of France's total production.

Hyères is also well known for its palm tree nurseries (see panel), hence the recent change of name to the more exotic Hyères les Palmiers. This embraces Vieux Hyères, the modern town, and the Port d'Hyères down on the seafront.

From the place Clemenceau in the center of town the 14th-century **Porte Massillon** leads through into the old town, where all streets eventually converge on the spacious place Massillon, site of the daily market. At the top of the square is the half-rounded **Tour St-Blaise▶**, built by the Knights Templar in the 12th century. Behind the square is the **Collégiale St-Paul▶**, which houses over four hundred *ex-votos* (dating from 1613 right up to 1985) and a huge Provençal *crèche* (tableau) re-creating the Hyères of yesteryear.

To the right of the church a huge archway leads beneath a Renaissance house up to the **Parc St-Bernard▶** which culminates in the **Villa de Noialles** (no visits) at the top of the hill. Now a private arts center, the Cubist-inspired villa was designed by the architect Robert Mallet-Stevens for the arts patron Charles de Noialles in 1924.

The park itself (open daily) displays a wide variety of Mediterranean flowers and shrubs, with the pathways opening up into delightful vistas where you least expect them. Follow the old walls westward from the park for an insignificant-looking gateway which leads into the **Villa Ste-Claire▶** (open daily) where the gardens of similar style, although far more extensive, have a glorious profusion of Mediterranean flowering plants under the management of the Botanic Conservatory of Porquerolles.

Back down in the main town, the **Musée Municipal** (closed Tuesday) contains antiquities from the ancient port of Hyères, as well as two engraved menhirs found nearby. More flowers, plants and exotic trees (as well as a small zoo and a tropical greenhouse) can be found in the 17 acre **Jardin Olbius Riquier▶** (open daily) on avenue Gambetta.

▶▶▶ Hyères, Îles d' *148B1*

The three islands off the coast of Hyères have been known since the 17th century as the *Îles d'Or* thanks to the golden glint of the mica shale in their southernmost cliffs. They are scattered about with forts and the French military still maintains bases on two of them, but their wild natural landscapes have been partially protected since the 1960s.

The islands are covered in dense vegetation — pine, eucalyptus, lavender, heather, and rosemary scent the sea-swept air; spring is the best time to come, when migrating birds pass through. The underwater flora is also protected, and spear-fishing prohibited. The entire archipelago is currently being upgraded to the Parc National des Îles d'Hyères.

The islands can be reached by ferry from most nearby ports, including Toulon, la Tour-Fondue, Hyères-Plage, and le Lavandou.

The most easily accessible is **Porquerolles▶▶▶**, the largest of the three and the only one permanently inhabited. The village (also called Porquerolles) has cafés, restaurants, and one or two hotels, as well as bike rentals. You can bike or walk as far as the lighthouse and the cliffs on the south coast, or visit the gentle sandy beach of Notre-Dame at the northeastern tip of the island.

Port-Cros▶▶ is the hilliest of the three, and its wealth of flora and fauna has been protected since 1963. France's smallest national park, it has marked walking trails (which you are forbidden to wander off) around the island or across the middle to the Vallon de la Solitude or the Vallon de la Fausse-Monnaie.

The third island, the **Île du Levant**, is mostly occupied by the military. What hasn't been claimed by them has been taken over by a nudist colony set up in the 1930s in the village of Heliopolis.

Birth of the "Azure Coast"

A wealthy vineyard owner from Dijon, Stephen Liegeard, decided one day in 1887 to leave the rain and fog of the north behind and take a vacation in the South of France. Stopping at Hyères, he alighted on the beach to behold the luminous skies and translucent blue waters of the Mediterranean — at which point, so it is said, Liegeard cried "Côte d'Azur!" When Liegeard returned to Paris he published an illustrated book, *La Côte d'Azur 1888*, extolling the virtues of this wonderful coastline. Thus was coined what is possibly one of the most successful tourism marketing slogans in history.

The Tour St-Blaise is all that remains of a Knights Templar lodge

Forests and fires

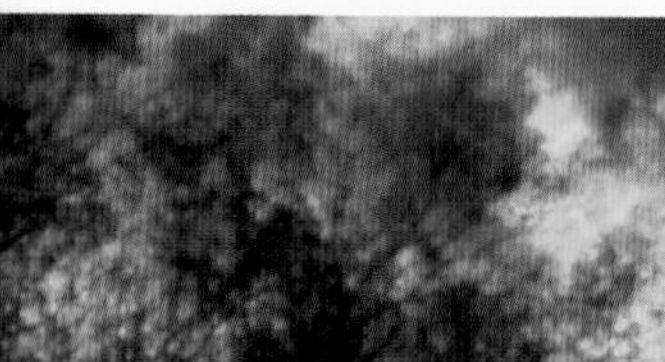

Hot, dry summers mean that fire is an ever-present menace in Provence and yet, contrary to popular belief, fires cause much less damage than they used to. In addition, tree-planting programs mean that there is now a far greater area of woodland than there was a century ago.....

Re-afforestation
The Foundation for the Protection of Mediterranean Forests replants an average of 60,000 trees every year. Just as you may see many burned-out areas in Provence, you will also see many others where signs proclaim "this area has been replanted by the schoolchildren of the village — please respect their work." With schemes such as these and natural regeneration, the forests of Provence have crept back up from 1.5 million acres just over a century ago to more than 2.5 million acres today. All is not yet lost for the woodland heritage of Provence.

The forests The forests in Provence are dominated by conifers such as the maritime, umbrella, and Aleppo pines, as well as cedars. Around 60 percent of existing woodland is coniferous, the rest comprising mostly deciduous trees such as chestnut, or evergreens, such as cork oaks and holm oaks. The majority of the forests are in the Var (840,000 acres), with the Alpes-Maritime, Vaucluse, and Hautes-Alpes all with less than half this amount of forest and the Bouches-du-Rhône with just 240,00 acres.

Setting the forest on fire The Provençal forests are particularly susceptible to fires due to summer droughts and strong winds. During the long, hot summer months the dried-up forest floor, littered with leaves, twigs, and resinous pine needles, can easily catch fire. If there is any wind — or, worse still, a *mistral* — the flames can be quickly fanned into an inferno, creating a wall of fire up to 100 feet high which consumes all in its path.

Today the major causes of fire are carelessness on the part of hikers and picnickers — and the vandalistic acts of arsonists. The worst fires since records have been kept were in 1764 (when the whole of the Esterel burned down), 1864 (when 26,000 acres of the Maures were destroyed), and in 1899 and 1964.

Devastation You don't have to drive far in Provence to witness blackened hillsides and stark slopes, littered with

The aftermath of a forest fire, an all too common sight

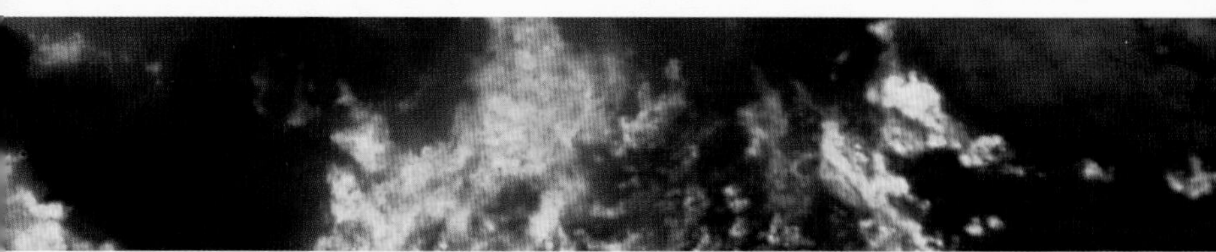

the charred skeletons of trees, where fire has passed. The unprotected slopes are prone to erosion and a new flora soon takes over, that of the *maquis*, a sparse, low-lying cover of thistles, gorse, stunted downy oaks, and hardy lavender, thyme, and rosemary. Without help, the ancient forest cover seldom regenerates in this impoverished soil.

Prevention Since 1963, the various *départements* in Provence have coordinated their fire prevention and fire-fighting efforts and this was strengthened in 1989 with the creation of the Fondation pour la Forêt Méditerranéene (Foundation for the Mediterranean Forests).

Through research, public education, and experiments with fire-prevention techniques, they have had considerable success in reducing forest fires. New laws require undergrowth to be cleared around houses and along roads in high-risk areas, and a vast network of cisterns (over 700 in the Var alone) has been installed in the forests to give fire-fighters access to water.

Whole areas of forest are now closed off during the summer in periods of drought, and if you try and venture past the barriers you will soon find there is a forest patrol warning you away.

Aerial attack Sunning yourself on a Riviera beach during the summer, it is quite likely you will witness the extraordinary sight of a plane descending to the sea, skimming the surface as it scoops up millions of gallons of water, before taking off again and heading inland. You have just seen a Canadair, one of the main weapons in the fight against fire. There is now a fleet of 11 of these *Bombardiers d'Eau* (water bombers), based in Marignane airport at Marseille. They are guided and assisted by 12 tracker aircraft, which constantly patrol and monitor the hinterland. In 1986, the first helicopter water bombers (HBE) made their appearance, and 13 of these are also now on permanent stand-by during the summer.

Thanks to better coordination and more "water bombers," in recent years 95 percent of fires have been extinguished before they covered 12 acres. In 1992, just 32,000 acres in Provence were lost — a third of the previous annual average.

"Shoot the arsonists"
Arsonists are usually considered a latter-day phenomenon but this is not so, as evidenced by a letter from Napoleon to the Prefect of the Var, written on August 21, 1809: "I have learned that several fires have broken out in the Department which I have entrusted to you," he wrote, "and I order you to shoot on the spot anyone convicted of the crime of having set them on fire. If these fires break out again I shall be forced to replace you."

High risk areas are now closed off during the summer

Drive and country walk Ste-Baume

The Ste-Baume massif is only 7 miles long, but it shelters one of the most unusual forests in Provence and also a shrine sacred to Mary Magdalene. This drive encircles the whole of the massif, and includes two walks, a short one up to a beautiful abbey and a longer one up to the sacred grotto itself. Allow 4–5 hours from Gémenos.

Take D2 out of Gémenos until you see the signs for the **Parc de St-Pons►►** on the right. From the bridge, a delightful woodland path leads up through a valley shaded by beech and ash, with the waters of the Frauge constantly bubbling over cascades and rocks. After 15 minutes, you will reach the **Abbaye de St-Pons►**, one of the best-preserved Cistercian convents in Provence. Established in 1205, it was a popular retreat for ladies of nobility. Just behind the abbey, the source itself gushes out of a small fissure in a rockface.

Continue on up D2, which curves around the rock circle of the Pic de

The summit of Ste-Baume

Bretagne before climbing up to the pass at the Col de l'Espigoulier. Here the view southward suddenly opens out in front of you, with Marseille and the Chaîne de l'Etoile in the distance behind the Aubagne plain. Keep going through Plan d'Aups until you reach the Hôtellerie de la Ste-Baume. From here, follow signs for the Grotte de Ste-Baume. There are two paths up to the sanctuary. On the left is the Chemin des Rois (chosen by the kings of France — hence the name — who made pilgrimages here in the Middle Ages). The oratories were built in 1516 by Monseigneur Jean Ferrier, archbishop of Arles and Aix. The right-hand path, the Chemin des Canapés, follows broken-down, moss-covered stone steps. It is easier to take the former on the way up, and the latter back down.

Both paths meander through a 320-acre forest of ash, beech, aspen, holly, maple, and ancient yew trees. On the forest floor lichens, moss and wild mushrooms flourish. This fantastic forest, one of few locally where Northern European tree species grow, is the last remnant of the woodlands that once covered Provence in the Tertiary Period. Its survival is thanks to the shade created by the towering cliff faces above it. Always considered a sacred forest, it is now a Biological Reserve.

The two paths meet at the Carrefour de l'Oratoire (the oratory cross-roads). Follow a flight of steps on the right up to the terrace where there is a good view.

Behind you is the **Grotte de Ste-Baume▶▶**, where Mary Magdalene is supposed to have spent the last years of her life. The cave is enormous, with stained glass windows set in the rock, several statues of Mary Magdalene and an altar with Bossan's *Rock of Penitence* behind it. Water drips constantly from the walls, and there is also a spring at the back of the sanctuary. Open every day, there are services at Pentecost, on July 21 (Mary Magdalene's saint day), and midnight mass on Christmas Eve.

Return to the oratory crossroads and, if you are feeling energetic, take GR9 zigzagging up to the **Col de St-Pilon▶** half-an-hour farther on. From nearly 3,300 feet, the 360-degree view encompasses Mont Ventoux, the Massif des Maures and the Alpilles. The small chapel at the summit stands on the site of the column (hence "St Pilon") which once stood here.

Back down at the parking lot, follow D95 to Mazaugues, continuing on to la Roquebrussanne. Turn down D5, bearing right at Méounes-lès-Montrieux (with several fountains) toward Signes with more fountains and a 16th-century Gothic church.

Continue parallel to the southern slopes of Ste-Baume to reach the escarpment overlooking the Plan du Castellet and turn right on N8 toward Gémenos.

In the lee of the cliffs, Ste-Baume's forest is now designated a biological reserve

► le Lavandou 148B1

At the start of the smarter part of the coast, yachts now outnumber fishing boats in le Lavandou's harbor, and the prices in the numerous restaurants, boutiques, and cafés in the pedestrianized streets behind the port are beginning to tip toward those on the Riviera. Le Lavandou's main attraction is a good selection of beaches. The town's own wide, sandy beach curves around the bay toward the west and there are several smaller and more secluded retreats hidden away nearby.

Around 2 miles to the east, **la Fossette** is a small horseshoe shaped beach with just one café-restaurant, while past here **Aiguebelle** has three beaches: the one on the seafront can be crowded, but about 500 yards farther on a steep path leads down to a wonderful double bay, which is far less crowded. The east half is a nudist beach, as is the next beach along, the well-known **le Layet**, where *textiles* (i.e. people with clothes on, as French nudists call them) will be frowned upon. Finally, there is a superb beach at the pleasant little resort of **Cavalière**► (not to be confused with the hideously built-up Cavalaire-sur-Mer farther on). Le Lavandou is a good base for exploring the Massif des Maures, whose wooded slopes come almost down to the sea behind the coast road (the *Corniche des Maures*).

An imposing town hall dominates the main square in Ollioules

Coastal walk
At the eastern end of the Baie des Lecques is la Madrague from where a coastal path leads around the headlands to Bandol. The *Sentier du Littoral* winds around the unspoiled coastline for about 5 miles, but it is an easy half-hour walk — scented with heathers, pine and sweet-smelling *salsepareille* (sarsaparilla)— out to the Pointe Grenier, where the Tour de Vigie (partially restored in 1993 under the auspices of APARE — see page 74) sits atop a headland with lovely views back down the coast to la Ciotat and along the cliffs eastward.

► les Lecques 148A1

The seaside suburb of the nearby town of St-Cyr, les Lecques is a popular family resort largely because of its safe, sandy, gently shelving beach. The family appeal is further enhanced by a massive water theme park, **Aqualand**, just outside St-Cyr.

Les Lecques claims to be the site of the ancient Greek settlement of *Tauroentum*, although only Roman remains have been found so far. These are on display in the **Musée Tauroentum** (open daily except Tueday in summer, weekend afternoons in winter; admission) with mosaics, frescoes, vases, and household utensils.

Cork oak in the Massif des Maures

▶▶▶ Maures, Massif des *148B1*

Around 37 miles from end-to-end and 20 miles wide, the Massif des Maures stretches from Fréjus to Hyères, dipping down to the sea to form wide bays at Cavalière, Pampelonne (near St-Tropez) and Bormes. The glittering mica cliffs of the Îles d'Hyères are an extension of the chain out into the sea.

The hills of the Maures, up to 2,487 feet high, are thickly forested with chestnuts, cork oaks, and Aleppo and umbrella pines. The forest's shaded depths gave rise to its name, which comes from *mauram*— Provençal for "dark". In contrast to the wooded slopes, vineyards spread across sunlit valleys where there are signs of human habitation. Much of the forest is impenetrable — except by forest fires, which have taken their toll here as elsewhere.

In the Dark Ages the Maures was ruled by the Saracens, who built their strongholds (*fraxinets*) on the hilltops and plundered the surrounding countryside for more than 100 years before Count Guillaume drove them out in A.D.972. There are still very few settlements in the heart of the Maures, the main ones being Collobrières (see page 155) and la Garde-Freinet (see page 161).

Drives and walks
One of the most rewarding tours through the Maures is the 44-mile *Routes des Crêtes*, which starts in la Garde-Freinet and circles around via Collobrières and D14 to Grimaud. You can also make a slightly longer tour (around 68 miles) from le Lavandou, via Bormes-les-Mimosas, Collobrières, Grimaud, and Cogolin.

For hikers, the GR9 from la Garde-Freinet skirts the highest points of the *massif* through the Forêt Domaniale des Mayons toward Pignans on N97, while the GR51 takes a much longer, more southerly route from near Port Grimaud all the way to Pierrefeu-du-Var on D12.

▶ Ollioules *148A1*

The southern outskirts of Ollioules, with their ever-multiplying superstores, have become practically a suburb of Toulon, but, within the town itself, strict speed limits, recobbling of streets, and facelifts for many buildings have created an entirely different atmosphere.

Behind the church, the picturesque streets lead up to the ruined 11th-century **château▶** (open daily in summer) which was once a stronghold ruled over by the Seigneurs de Signe et d'Evenos. A lone window punctuates the sole remaining full-height wall of the castle; since 1992, volunteers have been slowly restoring the remaining rooms and doorways.

Ollioules has an active crafts community, an arts exhibition center, and a small amphitheater with summer dance and drama.

The neo-Byzantine Église Notre-Dame de la Victoire rises up behind the Grand Casino in St-Raphaël

Bikini cover-up
Even in the summer heat-wave of 1993, the Mayor of St-Raphaël decided he had had enough of the bare flesh of tourists in the shops and streets of the resort. Dredging up an obscure municipal decree which forbids anyone to walk around the town in bathing suits he sent out the *gendarmes* to lay down the law, warning people wearing bikinis and swim-suits that they were not on the beach and had better cover up. The only other place where this might happen is Ste-Maxime, where there is a fine of 75 francs for anyone caught wearing less than a T-shirt.

►► Ramatuelle *148C1*

In the heart of the St-Tropez peninsula, Ramatuelle is a typical Provençal village with a typical influx of second-home owners. The vineyards surrounding Ramatuelle produce much sought-after Côtes-de-Provence wines, with the best place to sample them being the cellars of *Les Maîtres Vignerons de la Presqu'Île de St-Tropez* just outside Cogolin.

Nearby On D89 heading out above Ramatuelle are three ancient windmills, **Les Moulins de Paillas►**, perched on a hillside with fabulous views across the Presqu'Île de St-Tropez and the Îles d'Hyères. There are also spectacular panoramas from the small village of **Gassin►►** farther up the same road. Gassin was built as a lookout point during the time of the Saracen invasions and several restaurants now enjoy the same views — although you may well feel plundered yourself when presented with the check.

► St-Raphaël *148C2*

St-Raphaël is a popular family resort with a big sandy beach curving around the bay between its marinas. It was popularized in the mid-19th century by the writer Alphonse Karr, who lured Maupassant, Alexander Dumas, and Berlioz down for their winter holidays. Unfortunately all the grand hotels and *belle époque* villas were destroyed during World War II, although there are still remnants of the medieval village surrounding the Romanesque **Église St-Pierre** on the other side of the train line that runs through the center of town.

Just beside the church, the **Musée Archéologique►** (closed Tuesday in summer, Sunday in winter; admission) has some interesting displays on underwater archaeology (as well as local terrestrial finds) including an enormous number of amphoras dating from the 1st century B.C. onward discovered in wrecks off the coast.

The town plays host to a lively International New Orleans Jazz Competition during July, with outdoor performances along the promenade.

The Esterel Massif

■ The heart of the Esterel is one of the most captivating areas on the whole of the Riviera coastline, as unexpected and as wild as the Massif des Maures, yet more beautiful, more precious, more astonishing for its proximity to the built-up areas and its serenity and total lack of habitation.....■

The massif Like the neighboring Massif des Maures, the Esterel is much older than the limestone that predominates in most of Provence, and presents a series of jagged profiles, rust-red canyons and dramatic rock formations. The vivid red porphyry (volcanic rock) has solidified in ridges and peaks that plunge into the sea, indented by small bays and inlets, creating a striking contrast with the deep blue of the Mediterranean. Elsewhere, the rocks have been mined for their blue tints, much favored by the Romans for temple columns.

Flora and fauna The Esterel was originally heavily wooded with cork oaks and holm oaks, but forest fires have taken their toll: over 120 fires have ravaged the hills and valleys since 1828, four of which (in 1838, 1918, 1943, and 1964) have hit practically the whole of the *massif*.

The predominant vegetation is *maquis* (scrub), a dense covering of heathers, gorse, mimosas, lavender, and other shrubs. Spring is one of the best times to be here, when wild flowers color the landscape and scent the pure air.

The Esterel is home to wild boar, hares, partridge, pheasant, rabbit, and a huge variety of birds. Deer, introduced here in 1988, are so far doing well.

Protection and access Since 1984 the Esterel has been a protected area under the management of the National Forests Office, which maintains 70 miles of fire-roads through the *massif*. In addition two special areas have been designated Biological Reserves, the Ravin du Mal-Infernet and the Ravin du Perthus. Both these gorges have cold, humid conditions which have produced an exceptional flora unknown elsewhere on the Mediterranean coast. They are both spectacular, and easily reached from the road.

Dying pines
Thousands of acres of the Esterel were once covered in maritime pines, but since 1958 the pines have succumbed to a plague of toxic, parasitic insects (*Matsucoccus feytaudi*). Considerable reforestation has been taking place, but whether or not the new trees prove to be resistant to the insects or regenerate themselves has yet to be seen.

Rust-red rocks meet the sea on the Esterel's craggy coast

People-watching is the main pastime in "St-Trop"

Pavement art in the old port

 **St-Tropez** *148C2*

For many years a byword for all that was *chic* on the Riviera, St-Tropez is a summertime honeypot whose charms are not at all evident if you are stuck in a traffic jam trying to drive in, or being jostled in the streets by all the other tourists (around 100,000 every year) who have come here to find out what it's all about. Come by boat (from St-Raphaël or Ste-Maxime) or, better still, come in the spring or the autumn if you don't want to end up as red-faced and hot-tempered as St-Tropez's traffic police.

The huge reputation of this surprisingly small resort (which has only 6,000 inhabitants) started with Roger Vadim's film *Et Dieu Créa La Femme* (*And God Created Woman*) in 1956, starring the then-unknown Brigitte Bardot. The bandwagon of celebrity fun, fashion, and sex has rolled on since then, with every *poseur* with a yacht worthy of the name wanting to be seen dining in exhibitionist elegance, stern to the quay, for all to see.

The French have always known it as "St-Trop" (St Too Much) and as long as you are expecting just that (too much on the bills, too much posing, too much trash and pollution...) then it can be fun for a day. The town boogies until the small hours and sleeps late. In the early morning hours, when no one else is around, the port is pretty as a picture, recalling the works of the Fauvist artists who were so inspired by St-Tropez at the beginning of the century.

St-Tropez was founded by the Greeks from Marseille, when it was known as Athenopolis. Later destroyed by the Saracens, it was rebuilt by settlers from Genoa in the 15th century who were granted indemnity from taxes by Good King René on condition that they defended the coastline from attack, which they did most notably when they fended off 22 Spanish galleons in 1637.

The first celebrity to breeze into St-Tropez was Guy de Maupassant, who arrived in the harbor in the 1880s on board his yacht. He set the scene to come for another century or so by his eccentric behavior (in his case, it was due to pre-syphilitic insanity). A decade or so later the Impressionist painter Paul Signac was forced into port by bad weather and liked St-Tropez so much he built a house here and invited all his friends down to take advantage of the wonderful southern light. Matisse was one of the first, followed by Dufy, Bonnard, Van Dongen, Vlaminck, Derain, and others.

By the beginning of World War I St-Tropez had already established itself as *the* artists' colony in Provence. Between the wars it received an influx of literary talent with the arrival of writers such as Colette and Anaïs Nin, and became a home-from-home for the in-crowd from St-Germain-des-Prés. Then, in the 1950s, it was the turn of movie stars, starting with Vadim and Bardot.

What to see At the heart of St-Tropez is the *vieux port*, chockablock with sleek yachts, bad sidewalk artists, ostentatious fashion victims, and trendy bars such as *Café Sénéquier*. All is redeemed, however, by the superb **Musée de l'Annonciade▶▶** (closed Tuesday and November; admission) housed in the former chapel of the Annunciation on the south side of the port. The collection of paintings and sculptures features representative works by Paul Signac's circle and most of the other post-Impressionist and Fauvist artists who worked here at the turn of the century.

Still a fishing port, despite the razzmatazz

On the other side of the port, you can watch the boats coming back into harbor at dusk from the embankment of the Mole Jean Réveille. From behind the quai Jean-Jaurès the old streets lead up past the town hall, a massive tower (built by William I in A.D.990) and the Italian–baroque church to the old **citadelle▶**. There are views back over the rooftops of the town and across the Gulf from this 16th-century fortress, which also houses a small **naval museum** (closed Thursday and mid-November to mid-December).

Apart from the port, St-Tropez's other main focal point is the enormous **place Carnot** (often called by its old name, place des Lices). Surrounded by cafés, there is nearly always a game of *pétanque* taking place here — except on Tuesday and Saturday, when the whole square is taken over by the local market. Between place Carnot and the port endless designer-label shop windows display the latest items to tempt those with money to burn.

The St-Tropez *bravades*
Every year the residents of St-Tropez celebrate two *bravades* (literally, acts of bravado), the first of which coincides with the *fête* of their patron saint, St. Tropez on May 16. In this colorful, noisy 400-year-old tradition the townspeople parade in historical costumes, armed with breech-loaded muskets, through the streets to the town hall and the church. St. Tropez is then paraded through the streets, with much noise and smoke from fusillades of muskets. The second *bravade* takes place on June 15 to commemorate the successful defense of the town against a Spanish fleet in 1637.

Beaches The beaches of St-Tropez are around the headland to the south of the port, and if you do not have your own speedboat then it is best to take the regular mini-bus from place Carnot, since parking charges are high.

In fact the "beaches" are mostly private concessions (each with their own restaurants, bars, parasols, and luxury beachchairs) along one huge, sandy beach in the Baie de Pampelonne. Some parts of the beach are free, but otherwise you will have to pay dearly for almost everything. In the summer months some 450 people work on these beaches, which generate an annual income of around 80 million francs — Pampelonne has come a long way since the first bamboo-and-thatch beach hut was built here in 1952.

That first beach bar was at **Tahiti-Plage**, at the start of the bay, and stars like Errol Flynn, Lana Turner, and Clark Gable would come here to relax after visiting the Cannes film festival. Tahiti is still considered the "movie stars' beach," although nowadays the neighboring **Voile Rouge** attracts American celebrities such as De Niro, Eastwood, Stallone, and Don Johnson. The Voile Rouge was also the first beach where women ever dared to go topless, doing for St-Tropez in the 1970s what one-piece bathing suits did for Juan-les-Pins in the 1930s.

Next to the Voile Rouge is **Moorea**, frequented by actor Alain Delon and best known for having launched the Gypsy Kings to stardom when they played in the bar. Following the South Pacific theme, other beaches on the northern section include **Bora Bora** (seafood a speciality) and **Pago Pago** (watersports and delicious chocolate profiteroles). Farther down, **Club 55** is popular with Parisians, politicos, and heads of state (Gorbachev, King Hussein, and King Leopold of Belgium have all dropped by for lunch), whereas the **Aquaclub** is preferred by models (Linda Evangelista) and is a well-known gay rendezvous. **Tropezina** is more sporty, with a young crowd, whereas at **Le Blouch** or **Le Liberty** you won't even need to wear the minimum "string" to go and have an ice cream. Just your wallet will do.

Nearby On the north shore of the Golfe de St-Tropez is **Ste-Maxime**, with none of the glitz of its hyped-up neigh-

Not as chic as St-Tropez, Ste-Maxime is just across the bay

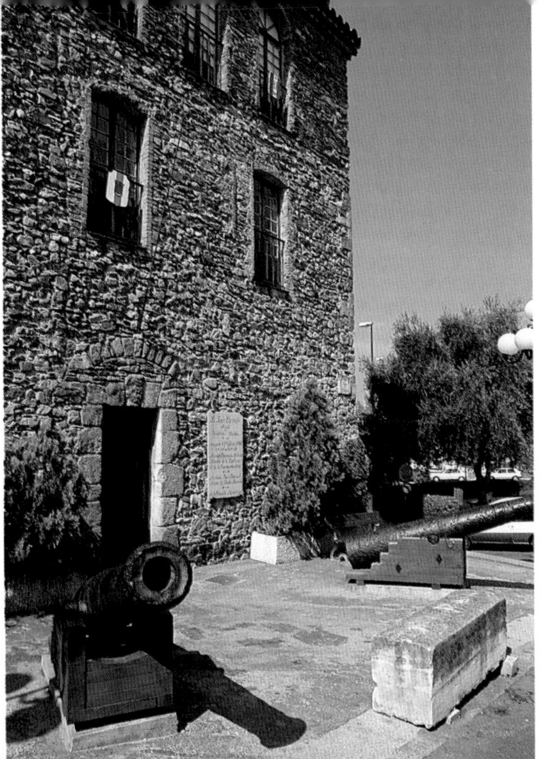

The Musée des Traditions Locales in Ste-Maxime

The headless saint
St-Tropez's name comes from the legend of a Roman soldier named Torpes, who was beheaded by Nero for his Christian beliefs. His decapitated body was put in a boat, along with a cockerel and a dog, and set adrift in the Mediterranean. The animals were meant to eat the body but didn't, and the boat eventually drifted on to the shore here. A sanctuary was erected for the brave soldier, and in the 4th century the town adopted St. Torpe's name.

Maritime trading in the 18th century is reflected in this statue of sea captain, Pierre André de Suffren de St-Tropez

bor and happy enough in its role as a sedate family resort — with a casino thrown in for a bit of excitement. In front of the palm tree-lined promenade there is a big sandy beach with plenty of watersports (windsurfing, jet-skis, and water skiing) and seductive beachside bars.

Ste-Maxime has several colorful markets, including a daily food and flower market, crafts on Thursday and bric-a-brac on Friday. In the 16th-century **Tour Carrée▶** on the seafront there is a small **Musée des Traditions Locales** (closed Tuesday), which focuses on the history of the Golfe de St-Tropez. Far more compelling is the unusual **Musée du Phonographe et de la Musique Méchanique▶** (open Easter to mid-October; admission) which is 6 miles north of town on the road to le Muy. Treasures in this collection include one of Edison's phonographs from 1878, the first ever recording machines, a language-teaching machine (the "pathegraphe") from 1913, and an extraordinary assemblage of barrel organs, musical boxes, pianolas, and the like.

►► Sanary-sur-Mer *148A1*

Sheltered from the *mistral* by wooded hills to the north, Sanary is a charming resort with a small harbor surrounded by palm trees and pastel-colored buildings. Although fishing has never been of huge importance here, there is a small fleet (including several *pointus,* old-style boats with high curved prows) and every morning you can buy fresh fish, *oursin* (black spiny sea urchins), lobster, and whatever else is in season from the quayside.

The discovery nearby of amphoras for exporting wine, as well as ovens dating from the 2nd century, proves the antiquity of the port. Like many Provençal towns, Sanary has gone through numerous name changes since antiquity: originally called St-Nazaire after its patron saint, during the Revolution it became Sanary, then St-Nazaire again from 1809 until 1890, then Sanary once more, finally settling on Sanary-sur-Mer in 1924.

A 17th-century representation of Pentecost in the Collégiale St-Pierre-aux-Liens

Six-Fours-les-Plages *148A1*

The town of Six-Fours is a drab ribbon development stretching almost from la Seyne to Six-Fours-les-Plages across the neck of the Cap Sicié peninsula. Six-Fours itself is of limited interest but nearby are two churches worth navigating your way around the suburban streets to find. The old village of Six-Fours once topped a small hill inland from the present-day town but was totally demolished to make way for the Fort (still in use, no visits).

Beneath the walls of the fort is the **Collégiale St-Pierre-aux-Liens**►►► (closed Tuesday afternoon and

The Gothic-style nave of the Collégiale St-Pierre-aux-Liens adjoins a much older chapel

The sheltered little port at Sanary-sur-Mer

Wednesday and Thursday morning), which is unusual in that it has two naves, one (5th-century) from the original Romanesque chapel and another, larger Gothic-style nave added at right angles to the first in the 17th century.

The older chapel has one or two curious features, the most striking of which is a niche on the right-hand side of the massive stone altar, which was known as the *reliquaire des morts*. Here, local people used to hang up coats, hats, or the clothing of dead friends or relatives so that they could come and pray to them. This unique custom dates back to pagan times and, incredibly, was still being practiced up to World War I (an old photo in the chapel shows the archway hung about with these reliquaries in 1909). Another niche inside the chapel contains beads and coins found during excavations of the 4th-century baptistry, fragments of a stained glass window, and a relic of St. Philomene.

At the other end of the Romanesque chapel (or at the back of the Gothic nave, depending on which way you look at it) there is a polyptych by Louis Bréa which features popular local saints; also look for the marble statue of the Virgin and the Assumption attributed to Puget, which is in the Chapelle des Carmes on the right-hand side of the main church.

Also near Six-Fours is the **Chapelle Notre-Dame de Pépiole▶** (open afternoons) which claims to be one of the oldest chapels in France, although little is known about it. It probably dates from the 3rd century (with a 10th-century nave added) and was restored from the 1950s onward by a Belgian priest, M. Charlier. It contains two massive paleo-Christian altar stones and "stained glass" windows which, as the *gardien* will explain, were made from old bottles because they had no money for the real thing. M. Charlier is buried outside the walls of this little old chapel to which he devoted his life.

The chapel can be hard to find: the easiest route is to take D63 from Six-Fours toward la Seyne and turn left at the *Garage du Midi*, where there is a sign.

The Targo

A plaque opposite the Six-Fours fort commemorates the founding on October 20, 1880 of the *Escolo de Targo* (the Targo School), to promote the Provençal language — the school still functions today. The *targo* is an old Provençal game similar to jousting, with teams of eight using boats instead of horses. The aim is to knock your opponents off the prow of their boat with a long wooden "lance." The player who knocks three of his opponents off without getting a drenching himself wins a prize. *Targo* games are usually held in ports such as Toulon, Marseille, la Ciotat, or Martigues.

The cloisters in the Abbaye du Thoronet, echoing the clarity of its pure Romanesque style

►►► Thoronet, Abbaye du *148B2*

Hidden away in the forest of la Daboussière to the south of Entrecasteaux, the Abbaye du Thoronet (closed Tuesday; admission) is one of the most remarkable monasteries in Provence. It is the purest of the three great Cistercian monasteries (the other two are Sénanque and Silvacane) of the 12th century, and the first to be established. By the 14th century it had gone into decline; during the Wars of Religion the monks were chased out of the property; and it was finally abandoned in 1791. Restoration began in the 1850s.

The architecture of the complex (church, cloisters, and chapterhouse) is in the purest Romanesque style, stripped of all decoration in accordance with the austere principles of the Cistercian order. The cloister is unusual in that it has been built on different levels and is one of very few to have a fountainhouse in the middle, which fills the cloister with the gentle sound of running water. In the cellars there is a display documenting the restoration of the abbey over the last 150 years — and indeed, some of the outbuildings are still propped up with massive beams to counter the damage from subsidence caused by bauxite mining in the surrounding hills.

►► Toulon *148B1*

France's second largest naval port, Toulon is often bypassed in favor of more glamorous locations farther to the east — one guidebook dismisses it as "a sprawling commercial and industrial city with many ugly buildings, dirty side streets, and much of the sordid underworld which grows up around a large port." Grounds enough to keep going, you might think. However, given the port's enviable surroundings (a huge natural harbor, backed by a ring of high hills) and its lively character, Toulon is worth a visit

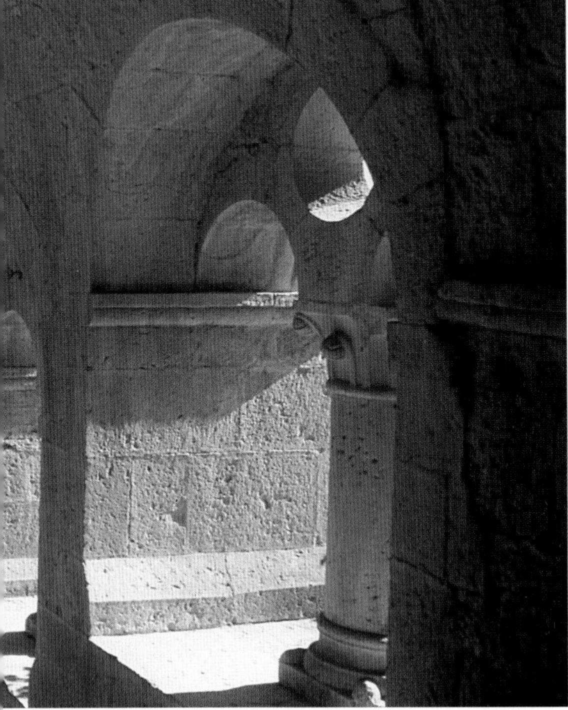

The siege of Toulon
Fiercely Royalist, Toulon accepted an offer of help from the English during the Revolution and welcomed their fleet into the bay in the summer of 1793. The British had built a seemingly impregnable fortress (on the site of the present Fort Napoléon) which they were so sure of they christened it "little Gibraltar." In the Siege of Toulon that followed, the Republicans set up a battery opposite the fort and it was here that the young Napoléon Bonaparte (then aged 24) distinguished himself as an artillery commander in the Republican forces.

if you are nearby. In fact for many years people driving along the coast have not had much choice about stopping here, since the streets of the town center have been the only link between the *autoroutes* A50 and A57 on either side of Toulon. Fortunately a tunnel is now being built to take the *autoroute* beneath the town.

Toulon's image as little more than a sleazy port is also fast disappearing as the city embarks on an imaginative transformation of the old parts of town. In what is possibly one of the largest architectural redevelopment programs of its kind in Europe, over 50 acres of the town center will emerge from behind the scaffolding in 1997. Over 600 million francs is being invested in the restoration of old houses and shops and the creation of gardens, fountains, and pedestrian areas. Some of the work is already complete, adding significantly to the already extensive pedestrian streets in the heart of the town.

Most of the current rebuilding is happening in the lower town, which was Toulon's traditional red light district. The redevelopment has been boosted by the building of a huge new Law Faculty and an Electronics Institute as well as the gleaming Centre Mayol just near the port, with conference centers and a stylish, two-story shopping mall with over a hundred stores, boutiques, and restaurants.

Toulon became a naval base soon after Provence became part of France in 1481, with Louis XII building the first fortifications here. Under Louis XIV Toulon was elevated to the strategic center for the Mediterranean fleet, a role that still maintains today. The town was partially destroyed by Allied bombings in World War II and the Germans blew most of the rest up before surrendering on August 26, 1944. The story of the Allied victories in the South of France is recounted in a museum at the top of Mont Faron (see page 181).

One of sculptor Pierre Puget's famous Atlantes *propping up Toulon's old town hall doorway*

St-Exupéry's wreck
Antoine de St-Exupéry, author of *Le petit prince*, died in a plane crash while on a reconnaissance mission to survey German positions just before the Allied invasion of Provence in August 1944. Eyewitnesses reported seeing his Lightning P-38 go down in the Baie des Anges in Nice, but underwater soundings in 1992 found no wreckage. The search (led by those who discovered the *Titanic*) moved farther west in 1993 after further witnesses reported seeing his plane crash offshore from Toulon. What appears to be St-Exupéry's Lightning has now been found encased in sand in the Baie de Carquieranne.

What to see In the postwar reconstruction of Toulon some fairly hideous buildings were put up, most notably the Soviet-style apartment blocks which now form a windswept wall along the back of the aptly named quai Stalingrad, the main waterfront promenade. However, beneath these monstrosities are the famous **Atlantes▶** by Pierre Puget on either side of the old town hall doorway; these powerful figures were one of Puget's first sculptures, their straining faces modeled on stevedores Puget had seen unloading ships in his native Marseille.

The quai Stalingrad is the embarkation point for trips around Toulon's **harbor▶** and although modern catamarans have now replaced the old-style tourist boats, the boatmen's patter hasn't changed one wit: "*depart en quelques minutes*" still means they will leave when there are enough passengers, which could be anything up to an hour away. So — choose a boat and relax in a quayside café until it really does look like it is going to leave.

The majority of trips around the bay circle the inner roads (*la petite rade*) and the ship-building yards of neighboring la Seyne. A lively commentary fills you in on the details of the warships, aircraft carriers, and submarines of the Mediterranean fleet as well as any visiting warships which happen to be in port.

Toulon's maritime history is well documented in the **Musée de la Marine▶▶** (closed Tuesday; admission) near the entrance to the Arsenal. The excellent **Musée de Toulon▶▶** (open daily) has an extensive collection of over 500 Provençal paintings from the 17th century onward, as well as the second most important collection of French contemporary art in the country, starting from the 1960s. On the other side of the building is the **Musée d'Histoire Naturelle▶** (open daily) which has an interesting room devoted to crystals and minerals and an embarrassingly large collection of stuffed animals.

Sandwiched between storefronts on the cours Lafayette is the **Musée du Vieux Toulon** (open after-

Toulon's town center is a maze of pedestrian streets and well-shaded cafés

noons, closed Sunday) with various historic documents and memorabilia. The cours Lafayette itself is the setting every morning (except Monday in winter) for Toulon's well-known market, a huge spread of the best and cheapest produce that Provence has to offer.

Within the network of pedestrian streets in the town center, look for the **Fontaine des Trois Dauphins▶** in place Puget. Toulon has no fewer than 17 fountains (probably more than Aix, although they would not boast about it) but this is one of the best, with the three dolphins in the center (sculpted in 1782) now completely obscured by a mini-jungle of fig trees, oleanders, ferns, and ivy. Just nearby is the **Opéra▶**, which has a beautifully decorated interior inspired by Charles Garnier.

Guided walking tours of the town depart from the tourist office at 8 ave Colbert (tel. 94 93 51 51) every Wednesday morning at 9:30.

Nearby The limestone *massif* of **Mont Faron▶▶** rises 1,774 feet above the town and bay of Toulon, with wonderful views from the top which are well worth the hair-raising, 5.5-mile drive to get there. A quicker way is via the *téléphérique* (funicular railway) which whisks you up in about ten minutes from the terminus in blvd Amiral Vence (closed Monday and windy days; admission).

Once at the top, you find a Sherman tank at the entrance to the old Fort de la Tour Beaumont which is now the **Musée Memorial du Débarquement▶** (open daily except Monday; admission); it commemorates the Allied landings of August 1944 in Provence. From the rooftop of the museum there is a panorama over the whole of the bay, with views which on a clear day reach as far down the coast as the Bec l'Aigle at la Ciotat. In the surrounding wooded park there are a couple of restaurants and a **Zoo** (open daily in summer, afternoons in winter; admission) which specializes in monkeys and big cats (it also breeds wolves and snow leopards).

Navigating or lost?
At the western end of the quai Stalingard is a statue by Daumas, "the Genius of Navigation." Local wags have it that the real story behind this is that the figure, naked except for a trailing loincloth, is in fact a drunken sailor emerging from the red light district (which he has his back to) in the early hours of the morning, having lost his all. His pointing finger has nothing to do with navigation at all — the poor sailor is in fact desperately pointing in the direction of his ship, which is departing over the horizon.

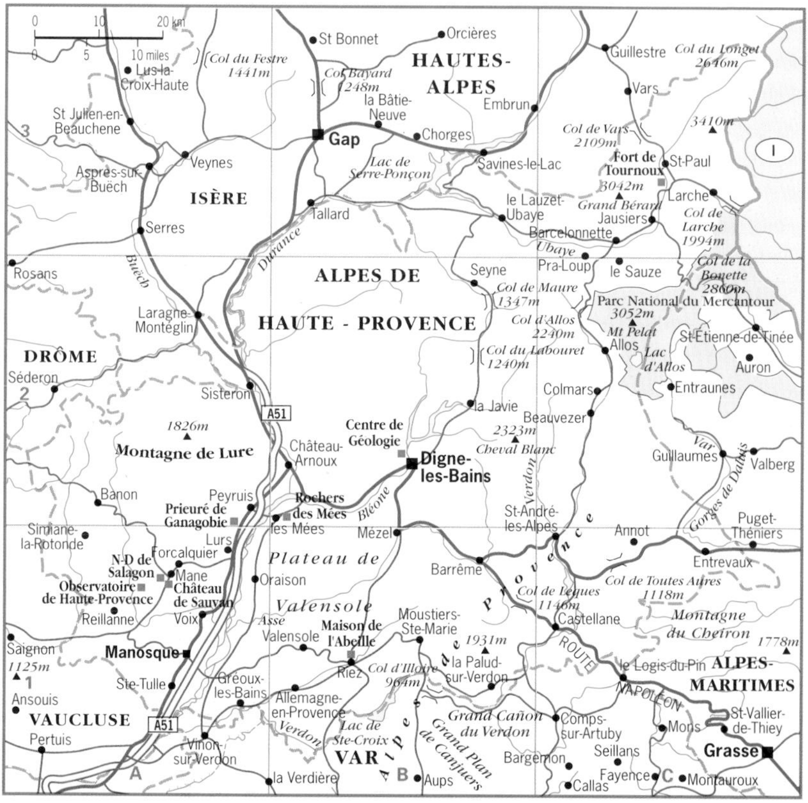

The 14th-century Porte Saunerie leads into rue Grande in the heart of Manosque, one of the largest towns in the Alpes de Haute-Provence

ALPES DE HAUTE-PROVENCE

Introduction The northernmost *département* in Provence, the Alpes de Haute-Provence is a land of wild open spaces and clear skies, of captivating mountain peaks, deep ravines and rushing rivers, of tiny hamlets and twisting mountain roads. If you are looking for action in the discos, this is the wrong place — most of the action here is in the great outdoors, racing down rugged hillsides on a mountainbike, hang-gliding above deserted valleys, sailing on massive lakes, or simply walking peacefully amid the Alpine landscapes.

Covering nearly 270,000 square miles, the Alpes de Haute-Provence is the most sparsely populated region in Provence: its 130,000 inhabitants would fit into a city the size of Avignon with room to spare. It is also the least well-known area among tourists, with just 175,000 annual visitors (compared with over 2.5 million on the Côte d'Azur). Significantly, the average length of stay here is just as long as it is on the coast — those who have discovered the Alpes de Haute-Provence know a good thing when they see it and are prepared to take the time to unwind, to explore its hidden corners, and to relax in the pure mountain air.

Although temperatures can drop below freezing in winter, the climate in summer is a serendipitous balance between Provençal sunshine and cool Alpine weather. It is the perfect antidote to the insufferable summer heatwaves that sometimes grip the rest of Provence.

Natural assets It is a region of great natural beauty, ranging from the superb Lac d'Allos (just one of 140 mountain lakes) to spectacular mountain passes (such as the Col d'Allos and the phenomenal Col de la Bonette) and the Grand Cañon du Verdon itself. This natural heritage is valued and protected, whether in the Réserve Géologique (the largest in Europe) around Digne, the Parc National du Mercantour (which is shared with the Alpes-Maritimes on the eastern boundaries of the *département*) or the innovative Conservatoire du Patrimoine Ethnologique de la Haute-Provence at the Prieuré de Notre-Dame Salagon near Mane.

This is a country where farmsteads hang out signs proclaiming *miel des mes ruches* ("honey from my hives") and where spring and autumn are eagerly awaited for their harvest

The Fort de France guards the mountain passes above Colmars in the Haut Verdon Valley

of *cèpes*, morels, and other prize mushrooms, as well as truffles. This is the home of the delectable *agneau de Sisteron*, tender lamb cooked in herbs and garlic, as well as the renowned goats' cheeses of Banon and honey-and-almond nougat for the sweet-toothed.

This is an area where picturesque mountain villages (such as Lurs or Simiane-la-Rotonde) have not yet been overrun with banal souvenirs — even though many are becoming increasingly popular as *résidences secondaires* with city folk from Paris or Marseille.

This corner of the Alps has not always been so peaceful. The many wars that have been fought here have left a legacy of fortified towns and mountain strongholds which are visible everywhere from the 14th-century walls of Colmars to the 17th-century citadel of Entrevaux and the 20th-century pillboxes of the Maginot Line in the Vallée de l'Ubaye above Barcelonnette.

The Alpes de Haute-Provence is full of surprises: the unusual history of Barcelonnette, for instance, from where many impoverished inhabitants left for Mexico in the early 19th century and returned decades later to build themselves grand villas around the town, having made their fortunes. Another exotic connection is that of Alexandra David-Néel, who journeyed for decades in Tibet before settling in Digne, where her house is now a shrine to Buddhism and the spirit of adventure.

The great outdoors But above all it is a part of Provence where the rewards are to be found in the wilderness — in the air, there are five gliding centers and nine schools for hang-gliding, parascending, and motorized ultralights (ULM). On the water, there are catamarans, windsurfing, rowing, and sailing on half-a-dozen major lakes. On the rapids, you can raft, kayak, or whitewater swim all the way down the Ubaye and the Verdon. On horseback, you can choose from 300 miles of bridlepaths and a dozen or more riding centers. On two wheels, there are over a hundred different mountain-biking routes, some of which take several days to explore. On two feet, routes range from one to ten days (guided or on your own) along 3,000 miles of marked paths. And, of course, on two skis you can choose any one of 11 winter ski resorts.

The lie of the land The northwest of the Alpes de Haute-Provence is dominated by the Montagne de Lure, whose peaks have traditionally marked the gateway to this part of Provence from the north. Wedged into a narrow gap protecting these approaches is the old town of Sisteron, whose citadel stands high above the Durance river as it flows southward.

This turbulent river, once the scourge of low-lying villages, has been tamed by a complex system of dams and now irrigates fertile agricultural land in the valley. To the west of the Durance and the Marseille–Grenoble *autoroute,* which runs alongside it, is the Pays de Forcalquier, a rugged area of valleys and plateaux with a patchwork of forests and pasturelands.

To the east of the Durance the central section of the *département* starts to rise into the pre-Alps, with the dignified spa town of Digne-les-Bains at its heart. To the south, the Plateau de Valensole is one of the main lavender-growing areas in Provence, with the old lavender-distilling center of Riez now starting to re-orient itself toward tourism and reclaim its architectural heritage in the quiet backstreets.

Below Riez, the magnificent Grand Cañon du Verdon is the biggest tourist attraction in the *département*, and one which is best visited out of the peak season. At either end of the Cañon, Moustiers-Ste-Marie and Castellane are often swamped by traffic but provide numerous facilities for exploring Europe's longest and deepest limestone rift.

Following the Verdon back to its source brings you to the dramatic Alpine landscapes of the Parc National du Mercantour and, high up in the Vallée de l'Ubaye, the charming town of Barcelonnette, surrounded by towering peaks, which is the northernmost town in the whole of Provence.

Place Manuel, at the center of Barcelonnette, a town with an unexpected past

Vacation chalets dot the countryside around Allos

The "Mexicans" from Barcelonnette
In 1821, the three Arnaud brothers emigrated to Mexico (see text). In 1830 they were joined by two of their compatriots, Eugene Caire and Alphonse Jauffred. It was these two who opened the floodgates when they returned to Barcelonnette 15 years later with 250,000 francs apiece — a large fortune in those times — and precipitated a mass emigration that lasted for over a century as hundreds of people from the valley (and eventually the surrounding valleys as well) left to seek their fortunes — some thrived in commerce; others simply managed to survive; many ended their days in poverty.

► Allos *182C2*

Where sheep once grazed on the pastures surrounding Allos the slopes of the valley are now a patchwork of ski chalets and summer vacation homes in this remote spot in the Haute Vallée du Verdon (Haut Verdon Valley).

One of the main attractions in the vicinity is the dramatic **Lac d'Allos►►** (9 miles east along D226) which is the largest high-altitude mountain lake in Europe. The road twists and turns as it climbs 2,600 feet above Allos, stopping around a half-mile short of the lake itself: a 30–40 minute walk brings you to an immense amphitheater encircling the lake. Covering around 150 acres, the Lac d'Allos is so cold that nothing grows in it. Its wonderful, pure color reflects the surrounding peaks like a giant mirror.

The mountains around the lake are part of the Parc National du Mercantour (see page 236), and following the 2 mile-long path around the edge of the lake you can see ibex, chamois, and other wildlife high up on the scree, with birds of prey circling overhead. Just outside Allos there is a large leisure park and, to the north, the ski resort of la Foux d'Allos. From Foux d'Allos D908 leads up to the spectacular **Col d'Allos►** (7,332 feet) with views toward the Vallée de l'Ubaye and Barcelonnette.

►►► Barcelonnette *182C3*

High up in the Vallée de l'Ubaye in the most northerly corner of the Alpes de Haute-Provence, Barcelonnette is a graceful, welcoming town. During the summer months it is a good base for exploring the Parc National du Mercantour (see page 236), whose northernmost boundaries extend into the valley. The *Maison du Parc* (tel. 92 81 21 31) near the center of town has details on guided tours, walks, and the park's wildlife. From the Col du Longet at the head of the valley the river Ubaye flows for

56 miles down to the Lac de Serre-Ponçon and downstream from Barcelonnette there are activity centers offering kayaking, canoeing, and rafting. During the winter, when snow blankets the valley for up to five months, ski resorts (such as Pra-Loup, le Sauze/Super-Sauze, and Ste-Anne-la-Condamine) come into their own.

Founded in 1231 by Count Raymond Berenger V, Barcelonnette ("little Barcelona") was named for the Catalan city where the count's family originated. But a more intriguing connection with the distant world outside the valley began in 1821 when three local men, the Arnaud brothers, emigrated to Mexico, via Amsterdam and New Orleans, to look for work (see panel). By the turn of the century, around 4,000–5,000 people from the region had emigrated and there may be around 40,000–50,000 of their descendants living in Mexico.

The Arnaud brothers never returned, but many others came back to build huge, sumptuous villas on the outskirts of town, mainly along the avenue des Trois Frères Arnaud and the avenue de la Libération.

This far-flung connection is presented in imaginative displays in the **Musée de la Vallée▶▶** (open 2–7 daily; admission) on ave de la Libération; here too is a small ethnographic section and a room devoted to the fantastic travels of writer Émile Chabrand, who went from Barcelonnette to Mexico via the Far East in the 1880s. There is also a **Maison du Mexique** (open daily) which is more commercially oriented.

TARIF NORMAL
Nº 034242
MUSÉE DE LA VALLÉE
LA SAPINIÈRE
04400 BARCELONNETTE
ALPES DE HAUTE-PROVENCE
TÉL. 92.81.27.15
MUSÉE MUNICIPAL CONTRÔLÉ PAR L'ÉTAT

Alpine peaks rise up above the streets of Barcelonnette

Valley fortifications
Near Barcelonnette there is a series of remarkable fortresses spanning several centuries of military architecture. One of the most impressive is the Fort de Tournoux, built in 1843, on D900 east of town; on the other side of the valley is the Fort de Roche-lá-Croix, one of the most powerful batteries in the Maginot Line; farther up the valley, the Fort de Haut de St-Ours was part of the same defensive scheme. These and several other forts in the area can be visited on regular guided tours organized by the *Maison de la vallée de l'Ubaye* (tel. 92 81 03 68).

Digne's geological reserve Digne is at the center of the largest geological reserve in Europe, the Réserve Géologique de Haute-Provence, which covers 375,000 acres. Fossils and imprints from the Mesozoic era some 200 million years ago are numerous, and include the skeleton of a large sea reptile. The Reserve is administered from the Center de Géologie, 2 miles north of Digne along D900A, which has a research center, library, and exhibitions (open daily except Saturday in summer, closed November to April; admission). The Center has leaflets on sites open to the public, and organizes guided tours (tel. 92 31 51 31).

► Castellane — 182C1

Advertising itself as the gateway to the Cañon du Verdon, Castellane is inevitably overrun during the summer season with foreign cars and languages. Although it has no great attractions of its own, it is a useful place for stocking up on supplies (with plenty of camping and outdoor shops) or for arranging activities such as rafting, climbing, hiking or mountain biking in the gorges. There are around a dozen hotels in town and no fewer than 14 campsites within a 2 mile radius.

The most striking aspect of the town is the sheer pinnacle rising up behind it, which is topped off by the **Chapelle Notre-Dame du Roc**. If you are feeling energetic you can climb up to the chapel via a path to the left of the church (it takes around 30 minutes to reach the top).

►► Colmars — 182C2

Just down the Haut Verdon Valley from Allos (see page 186) is Colmars, a lovely old fortified town in a picturesque position amid the surrounding woodlands and peaks. It acquired its first defenses in the late 14th century, and remained an important frontier town until 1713.

At the end of the 17th century two forts were added to protect the town from constant attacks by the Savoyards, each fort guarding a bridge at either end of the village. To the south is the **Fort de France**, with the much larger and more imposing **Fort de Savoie►** to the north. Inside the Fort de Savoie exhibitions are held in the summer in the *Centre Culturel de Colmars-les-Alpes*.

► Digne-les-Bains — 182B2

Digne is a placid, genteel town that has built its reputation on the seven springs to the south of town which supply

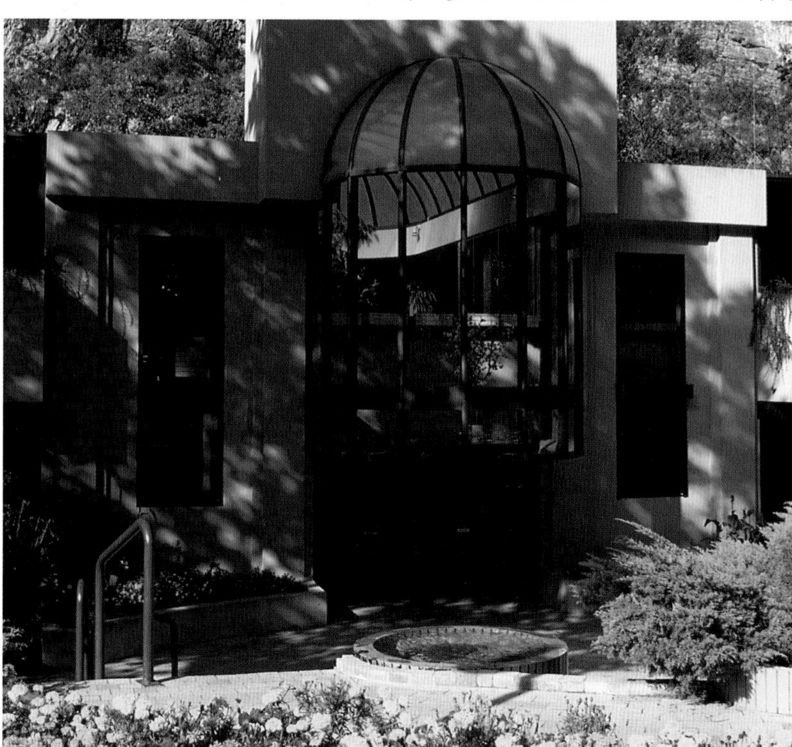

The modernized thermal baths in Digne offer all sorts of different cures

It is a steep climb up to the Chapelle Notre-Dame du Roc, which dominates the skyline above Castellane

its renowned spa — where *"les cures anti-stress"* are now offered alongside the more traditional rheumatism treatments. It is also the main center for lavender production in the mountains of Haute Provence, which it celebrates with the *Grande Foir Expo de la Lavande*, running for four days during late August.

The town center is bisected by the boulevard Gassendi. At the eastern end is the place du Général-de-Gaulle where the Wednesday and Saturday markets are good value if you are looking for *miel de lavander* (lavender-blossom honey) or other lavender products. On the south side is the old town with the crumbling **Cathédrale St-Jérôme**. Farther up the boulevard is the **Musée Municipal▶** (open daily in summer, afternoons in winter; closed Monday; admission) with various archaeological finds and 19th-century Provençal paintings, as well as an extensive collection of 19th-century scientific instruments and a model for the first Channel tunnel, conceived by local engineer Alex du Breton in 1880. To the north the **Cathédrale Notre-Dame du Bourg▶** is a good — if neglected — example of the Provençal Romanesque.

Digne's star attraction is the **Fondation Alexandra David-Néel▶▶** (open daily, guided tours only; donation). In 1928 David-Néel (see panel) bought this house, which she called *Samten Dzong* ("the castle of meditation") although then it was in the countryside and not next to a busy main road. It houses a fascinating collection of Buddhas, prayer wheels, other Tibetan mementos, and many of David-Néel's personal effects. The foundation (20 minutes' walk from the town center, 27 avenue Maréchal Juin) also houses a meditation center and a Tibetan shop.

An intrepid traveler
Born in Paris in 1868, Alexandra David-Néel studied Oriental languages at the Sorbonne and then spent many years in Tibet, traveling across the country on foot and living in the forbidden city of Lhasa in disguise. On her return she published several books, becoming one of the top Tibetan scholars in the West. At the age of 69, a decade after moving to Digne, she spent nine more years in Central Asia. In 1968, aged over 100, she renewed her passport because she wanted to visit China. She died in Digne on September 8, 1969, having just started to write another four books.

The first explorers
The first inhabitants of the Verdon gorges were the Ligurians; several centuries later, shepherds fleeing the Saracens converted caves near the Circque de l'Escales into farmhouses and haylofts. In the Middle Ages the gorges were reputed to be the home of "wild men" and other assorted devils. The first scientific expedition was carried out in August 1905 by the speleologist E. A. Martel and several companions equipped with ropes, cameras, and collapsible canoes. It took them three-and-a-half days to get from one end of the canyon to the other.

Carving on the Chapelle Notre-Dame-de-Provence, Forcalquier

►► **Entrevaux** *182C1*

Approaching Entrevaux from either direction along the Var Valley it is easy to see why it was such an important town in the 17th century. The gorges here narrow to just a few hundred yards across — plug this, and you block a major route between what was France and Savoy to the northeast.

On the west bank of the Var a jagged curtain of rock makes the hillside impassable. On the east bank, this natural barrier is reflected in the grand **fortifications►** (open daily, closed November to February; admission), built by Vauban, Louis XIV's military adviser, which zigzag up to the citadel perched 450 feet above the town.

The main access to the town is via a fortified **bridge►,** another of Vauban's works. Entrevaux had drifted in the doldrums, but with a steady trickle of visitors drawn by Vauban's handiwork there are signs of life again in the old medieval streets. Some restoration is underway and there are concerts and festivals in the summer.

► **Forcalquier** *182A1*

From a simple village on the Domitian Way in Roman times, Forcalquier rose to become an independent state in the 12th century. The Counts of Forcalquier held sway over Sisteron, Apt, and Gap from their citadel, and the town became the center of cultural and commercial life in Haute Provence.

Only the ruins of one tower remain of the Counts' château on the **citadel** above the town. However, it is worth the walk for the view over the surrounding Pays de Forcalquier, and the 19th-century **Chapelle Notre-Dame-de-Provence.**

The spacious place du Bourguet is dominated by the austere, Gothic façade of the **Cathédrale Notre-Dame du Marché.** On Mondays, the *place* and the surrounding streets are transformed into a vast market, overflowing with local produce. South of the cathedral are the narrow streets of the **vieille ville►,** with many 13th- and 15th-century houses (guided tours start at the tourist office on Wednesday and Saturday mornings at 10A.M.). You can skip the stuffy old **municipal museum,** but the **Couvent des Cordeliers►►** is worth visiting (guided tours several times daily in summer, closed Tuesday; admission). Founded in the 13th century, it is one of the oldest Franciscan monasteries in France.

►►► **Grand Cañon du Verdon** *182B1*

Rising just above la Foux d'Allos in the Mont des Trois Evêchés, the Verdon river flows south before looping west just above Castellane to carve its way through the limestone plateau of Haute Provence on its journey towards the Durance.

Between Castellane and Moustiers-Ste-Mairie the river has hewn a deep crevice in the plateau — the spectacular, 13

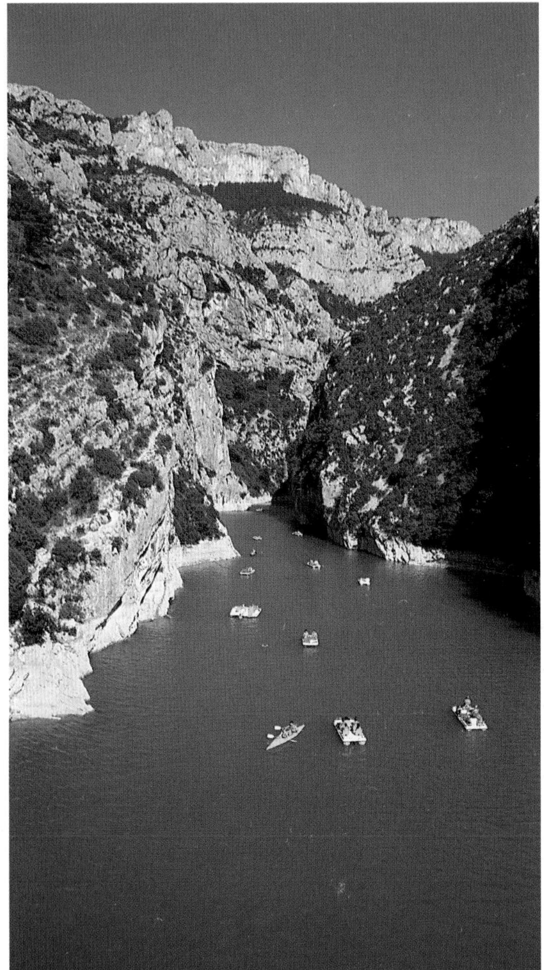

Taking to the water through the Grand Cañon

The Haute-Provence Observatory
After considerable research to find the location with the clearest atmosphere in Provence, the Observatoire de Haute-Provence was eventually built on a plateau just to the south-west of Forcalquier in 1936 near the village of St-Michel-l'Observatoire. Its 14 domes house a number of telescopes but their usefulness has diminished in recent years due to increased pollution. Tours of the observatory take place on Wednesday afternoons and the first Sunday mornings of the month in summer (admission), but since they take place in daytime are not particularly enlightening.

mile-long Grand Cañon (or Canyon) du Verdon. From sheer cliffs some 2,300 feet above the rushing torrent there are panoramic views down the length of this corridor, with the emerald green waters of the river (which was named for its unusual color) sparkling in the sunshine below.

The first survey of the canyon was not carried out until 1905, when the eminent speleologist E. A. Martel charted its course. His report that it was "a marvel without parallel in Europe" prompted the Touring Club de France to build the first tracks and belvederes in 1928. In 1947 the first road (the *Corniche Sublime*) was built on the southern side of the canyon, and the northern half opened up in 1973 with the *Route des Crêtes (crests)*.

Since then traffic volumes have been inexorably increasing — in high season you are likely to find yourself in a slow-moving convoy of cars and campers.

The Grand Cañon was due to become a *Parc Naturel Régional* in 1994, but this has been postponed until 1996 or 1997.

Walking the canyon
The canyon is best appreciated on foot. On the right bank the *Sentier Martel* runs from Mayreste to Rougon following the GR4, but this takes about two days: a section of this route, from la Maline to Point Sublime, can be accomplished in about 7–8 hours. The *Sentier Imbut* follows the GR99 for part of the way on the left bank, crossing over at the Passerelle de l'Estellié to reach the refuge at la Maline (around 2.5 hours one-way). Always take a flashlight, sweater, water, and provisions, and beware of surges in water levels due to upstream power stations. A detailed color booklet of the routes, *Canyon du Verdon*, is widely available (in several languages) in Moustiers or Castellane.

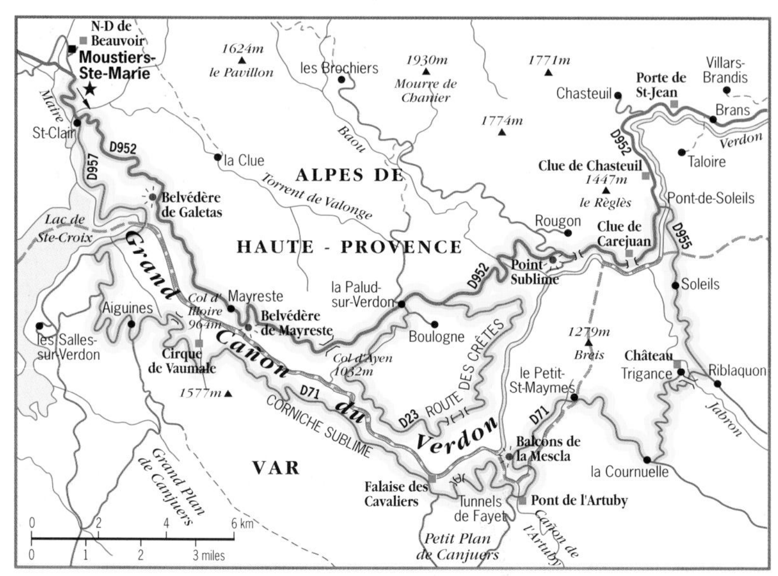

Drive Grand Cañon du Verdon

One of the classic tourist routes in Provence — and best undertaken outside the peak months of July and August. Allow at least the whole day for the entire circuit, departing from and returning to Moustiers.

From Moustiers take D952 to the Belvédère de Galetas, the first of many viewpoints. Here, the view is of the impressive canyon mouth where the river pours out into the vast Lac de Ste-Croix.

From here, the road starts to climb upward and shortly you arrive at the Mayreste Belvédère, which involves a 10-minute scramble over the rocks to the cliff edge from where there is the first overall view of the canyon upstream. After passing through the Col d'Ayen, the road temporarily leaves the gorge and descends to the plateau of la-Palud-sur-Verdon, now a major center for mountain-biking, climbing, pony trekking, canoeing, and rafting.

Just after la Palud take a right turn down D23, signposted *Route des Crêtes*. This loop returns after a nerveracking 15 miles to la Palud. It passes by several dramatic viewpoints, most notably the Trescaïre Belvédère, the Escales Belvédère (the view rendered even more dramatic by the climbers usually seen clinging to the cliff-face — this is an internationally renowned rock-climbing site), the Baou Pass Belvédère (with a drop of 2,340 feet into the canyon), the Tilleul Belvédère (fabulous panorama back across the Plan de Canjuers) and the Imbut Belvédère.

Back in la Palud, continue on D952 toward Castellane. After about 4 miles you will come to a large car parking area for the Point Sublime. Walk up to the viewpoint, to see the meeting of the Verdon and the Baou rivers and the openings into the Couloir Samson and the Grand Cañon itself.

The route follows the Verdon through the Clue de Carejuan until it reaches the Pont-de-Soleils, the crossover point between the right and left banks. Take D955 on the other side of the bridge and then turn right into the village of Trigance. Turn right again onto D71 and you soon reach the Balcons de la Mescla, a series of impressive belvederes almost directly opposite the *Route des Crêtes* on the north bank. Several hundred yards below the Verdon meets the equally turbulent Artuby river in the middle of the bend.

From the Balcons de Mescla you cross the Artuby canyon on the impressive, single-span Pont de l'Artuby before arriving at the Tunnels de Fayet; between the tunnels, there are views of the Falaise des Cavaliers. The road follows these cliffs and then continues on the edge of the precipice past the Falaise de Baucher and the Imbut Pass before leaving the canyon and climbing up to the Cirque de Vaumale; from here, views extend over to the north bank and downstream to the opening into the lake.

At the Col d'Illoire the road finally leaves the gorges behind — stop at the belvedere for a last look back before continuing to the village of Aiguines. From here, a series of hair-pin bends downhill gives lovely views across the whole Valensole plateau and the Lac de Ste-Croix. Cross the Pont du Galetas (with a panorama of the lake on one side and the entrance to the gorges on the other) before joining D952 into Moustiers.

The Grand Cañon is one of the natural wonders of Provence

► Gréoux-les-Bains 182A1

Dominated by the ruins of a 12th-century castle built by the Knights Templars, Gréoux has relied since antiquity on making a living from the warm, sulphurous springs which rise just to the south of this small town. In the 2nd century A.D. the Romans built the first spa here, but the baths then fell into disuse for many centuries until being re-opened in the 17th century. They became fashionable at the beginning of the 19th century when Napoléon's sister Pauline Borghese visited for a couple of curative immersions, but once again fell out of favor until being taken over in 1962 and entirely rebuilt. They are now doing a roaring trade with *curistes* from all over the country, and pump out around 800,000 gallons a day at an average temperature of 97°F.

If you are not here for a "*mini cure*" then Gréoux is a good place to stock up on picnic supplies with plenty of excellent food shops along the length of its Grande Rue.

A ruined Knights Templar castle stands guard over the town of Gréoux

►► Lurs 182A1

From its position high above the west bank of the Durance, Lurs commands a wonderful view across the surrounding countryside. The neatly kept streets and attractive houses amply justify the sobriquet of *village de caractère*, and the whole village is now classified as a historical site.

During the Middle Ages Lurs thrived when the Bishops of Sisteron had their summer residence here, but the population fell to zero earlier this century when it was abandoned due to the lack of electricity and running water. The village was saved from oblivion by a group of graphic artists and printers (led by the typographer Maximilien Vox) who moved in after World War II.

Lurs now plays host every year to the prestigious *Rencontres Internationales de Lurs* which brings together graphic artists, photographers, designers, and printers during the last week in August.

Nearby Narrow D30 north of Lurs leads to the **Prieuré de Ganagobie►►** (guided tours daily during summer; admission), a Benedictine monastery founded in the 10th century. The 12th-century church has an unusual decorative doorway and an even more striking set of mosaics composed solely of white, black, and red tiles: restored in the 1960s, the mosaics combine geometric motifs with wonderful representations of fantasy beasts and animals.

▶ Mane 182A1

This small village 2.5 miles south of Forcalquier has a well-preserved old quarter, a château (private property), and a 16th-century church — but the chief attraction in the vicinity is the **Prieuré Notre-Dame de Salagon▶▶** just outside Mane on N100. Established at the end of the 11th century by Benedictine monks from Villeneuve-lès-Avignon, the priory complex includes a 12th-century Romanesque church, a small lodging house for the Abbot (added in the 15th century) and barns and farm buildings which date from the time the priory was deconsecrated after the Revolution.

Since 1981 Salagon has been home to the *Conservatoire du Patrimoine Ethnologique de la Haute Provence*, a conservation organization actively involved in local heritage issues. As well as a museum dedicated to ethnography of the region, there are also revolving exhibitions on aspects of the traditional lifestyle. The center (open every afternoon from April to September, weekends in winter; admission) also has an excellent bookstore with titles on regional culture. Outside, there are two small gardens, a re-created medieval monastery garden, and a medicinal herb garden.

Further down the same road you will find the 18th-century **Château de Sauvan▶** (guided tours afternoons in summer, closed Saturday; admission). The architecture of this classical mansion echoes that of the Petit Trianon and is all the more surprising for being found in Haute Provence, especially since it overlooks extensive lawns and a lake with geese. The interior style matches the palatial ambitions of the château's facade.

▶ Manosque 182A1

"Certain towns can show you their proud cathedrals, their medieval ramparts, or the guts of martyrs but Manosque has only its beauty." Thus wrote Jean Giono, who lived nearly all his life in Manosque and wrote evocative poems and stories about the surrounding countryside of Haute Provence and its inhabitants. His myopia can perhaps be forgiven but he certainly would not have appreciated the sprawling, ugly industrial suburbs that surround Manosque today, nor the Cadarache Nuclear Research Center on the banks of the Durance.

Once you have penetrated the core of the old town via the 14th-century **Porte Saunerie**, Manosque takes on a more pleasing aspect. The pedestrianized **rue Grande** is the central axis of the old town, lined with stores (a plaque above a shoe shop at No. 13 marks Giono's birthplace) and leads to the lively **place Hôtel-de-Ville**. Market days in the rue Grande are Monday, Wednesday, Friday, and Saturday.

Manosque may have no cathedrals, but it has two churches: the **Église St-Sauveur** combines a Gothic doorway with a Romanesque nave and an intricate wrought-iron belfry from the 18th century; on place Hôtel-de-Ville, **Notre-Dame-de-Romigier** has a finely carved Renaissance doorway and a 12th-century blackwood Virgin.

Flowers and plants to go, in the old town of Manosque

Modern-day faïences *for sale in Moustiers*

Moustiers faïences
According to local tradition, it was an Italian monk who passed the secret of the glaze on to local potter Pierre Clérissy in 1668; his luminous blue designs on a brilliant white background became hugely popular during the reign of Louis XIV. Multicolored designs were introduced around 1740, and by the end of the century there were a dozen or more workshops in the village. The potteries thrived until the Revolution but with many of their clients lost to the guillotine the industry declined, and the last kiln closed down in 1874.

►► Moustiers-Ste-Marie *182B1*

The western gateway to the Grand Cañon du Verdon, Moustiers suffers badly in the summer months from traffic jams and overcrowding, and like the Grand Cañon itself, the village is best visited out of season. The old, tile-hung houses of the village cling precariously to the banks on either side of the Rioul, a torrent which descends from the craggy cliffs above Moustiers. Suspended across the gorge is a 720 foot-long chain with the famous star of Moustiers (see panel) hanging down in the middle.

As well as being one of the principal access points for the Grand Cañon, the village is famous for its glazed ceramics (*faïences*), examples of which can be seen in numerous museums throughout Provence. This centuries-old tradition (see panel) died out in the 1870s but was revived by Marcel Provence in 1927 and there are now around 15 studios in the village doing a thriving trade. However, do not expect any bargains (prices range from around 80 francs for the smallest butter dish up to around 8,000 francs for a large, decorative wall-plate) and there is a lot of overpriced junk on display.

If you want to see what the classic designs should look like you can visit the **Musée de la Faïence**►► (open daily from April to October except Tuesday; admission), which

was founded by Marcel Provence in 1929. The museum has a superb collection of faïences by the master potters (such as Clérissy, Olérys, Laugier, Ferrat, and others) who made Moustiers' reputation in the 17th and 18th centuries.

Opposite the museum the 12th-century **Église▶** is dominated by a three-tiered Romanesque bell tower; inside you can watch the rushing waters of the torrent beneath through a glass panel in the floor.

Moustiers was settled in A.D.433 by monks from the Îles de Lérins, who moved into the caves high up in the rock face above the village and founded a monastery: in the 12th century the **Chapelle Notre-Dame De Beauvoir▶** was built on this site. The 20-minute walk up to the chapel, via a winding path lined with oratories, is a popular way of escaping the pottery shops. The chapel was rebuilt in the 16th century and has an unusual Romanesque porch with carved wooden doors.

A pilgrimage to the chapel takes place on the first weekend after Easter, when villagers wearing 18th-century costumes climb the path for mass. There is also a procession to the chapel during the *Fête de la Nativité de la Vierge* on September 8.

An ancient bell tower looms above the tiled roofs of Moustiers

The chaine de l'Étoile
The chain with its five-pointed star that hangs high above Moustiers was originally placed here in the 12th century by a seigneur of the Blacas family: imprisoned during the Crusades, he vowed to make an offering to Notre-Dame de Beauvoir if he was released. The star on the chain was originally made from silver, but it was supposedly stolen during the Wars of Religion. It was replaced with a metal chain and star, although the chain is in such an exposed, windy position that it has frequently fallen down — the current one has been there since 1957.

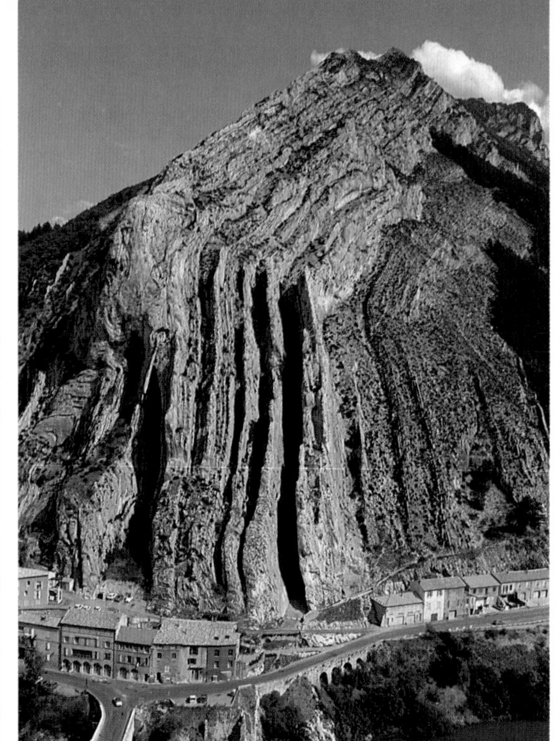

The Rocher de la Baume, with its all-but vertical strata, faces Sisteron's equally impressive citadel across the Durance

Music in the round
The circular tower in Simiane-la-Rotonde has very pure acoustics and concerts have been staged since 1986 under the patronage of the Simiane Festival. Recently the summer season has been renamed *Les Riches Heures Musicales de la Rotonde,* and although this tiny venue can seat only 150 people it has attracted musicians of considerable calibre. As befits the setting, the repertoire is mostly medieval music. Concerts take place from mid-July to mid-August (for details, tel. 92 75 90 47).

▶ Riez *182B1*

Riez is at the center of the **Plateau de Valensole,** which covers 300 square miles to the northwest of the Lac de Ste-Croix and the Verdon. This huge plateau, bisected by the river Asse and punctuated by wooded ravines, is a patchwork of wheat fields and lavender — it is one of the largest lavender growing areas in Provence, and if you want to capture the endless rows of vivid plants on camera the time to come here is in July when they flower.

As well as being a center for traditonal lavender-distilling, Riez has a long history as a market town on the crossroads of the Roman route through Provence from Fréjus to Aix. From the Roman era all that remains are four Corinthian **columns▶**, once part of a temple dedicated to Apollo which overlooked the road to Aix. Standing in splendid isolation in the middle of a field on the western edge of present-day Riez, they are soon to become the centerpiece of an urban park.

In the 5th century Riez became a bishopric and a **baptistry▶** was erected over the ruins of the Roman baths (just near the Roman columns — ask at the tourist office for a key). It is one of only a handful from the Merovingian era (A.D.476–751) still surviving in France, although the dome dates from a much later period. Inside, there is a small museum with bits of sculpture, inscriptions, and other archaeological finds.

At the heart of the old town the **Grand Rue** has preserved several fine Renaissance houses and in the streets and alleyways off to either side are a number of craft workshops, *santonniers,* and potteries. Local crafts also feature in exhibitions at the **Musée d'Histoire Naturelle en Provence** (open daily except Tuesday; admission) alongside the usual fossils and mounted birds.

Nearby On D953 toward Digne, just outside Riez, the intriguing **Maison de l'Abeille▶** (House of the Bee) presents displays on the old-fashioned production of honey, the life cycle of the bee and other aspects of apiculture. There is an insect museum (open daily) and a shop.

▶▶ Simiane-la-Rotonde *182A1*

Spiraling around a hillock on the edge of the plateau that marks the boundary between Haute Provence and the Vaucluse, Simiane-la-Rotonde is a charming *village de caractère* surrounded by farmland and lavender fields.

At the summit of the village is the **Rotonde▶▶** from which it gets its name. Built in the 12th century, this curious, truncated structure is one of the few remaining examples of nonreligious Romanesque architecture in Provence. The main feature of the Rotonde (open daily in summer except Tuesday, closed November to May; admission) is the extraordinary domed ceiling with a series of finely detailed carved masks and figures on the columns supporting the cupola. Most of the buildings around the Rotonde have long since gone, except for part of the seigneurial manor linked to it on the south side.

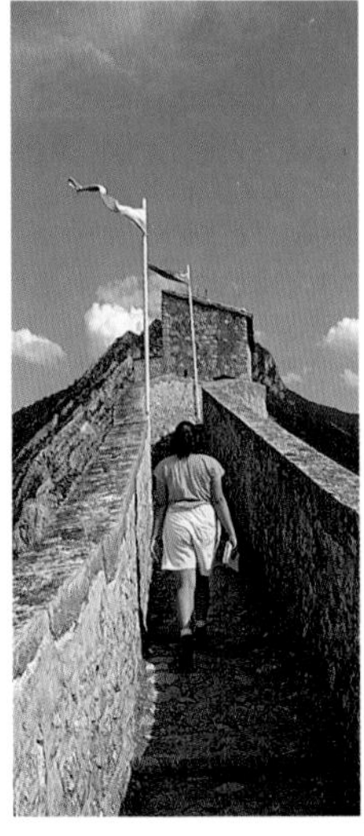

Ramparts in Sisteron's old citadel

▶▶ Sisteron *182A2*

Strategically situated where the Durance valley narrows down to about half a mile wide, Sisteron guards the mountain gateway between Provence and Dauphiné.

This ancient fortified site is capped by a **citadel▶** (open mid-March to mid-November; admission) standing 1,650 feet above the waters of the Durance, which has a 12th-century keep. The citadel was badly damaged (like much of the town) during Allied bombing raids in August 1944.

At the center of town is the place de la République, with three huge towers (remnants from the medieval ramparts) and the **Cathedrale Notre-Dame▶** to the east. Behind here is the **vieille ville▶▶**, a maze of steps and alleyways between tall houses linked by covered archways (known locally as *andrones*). A signposted route leads past some fine houses in the old quarter, ending up in the place de l'Horloge on the north side, where a lively market is held on Wednesday and Saturday mornings.

Closeup of the scant remains of Roman Riez

COTE D'AZUR AND ALPES-MARITIMES

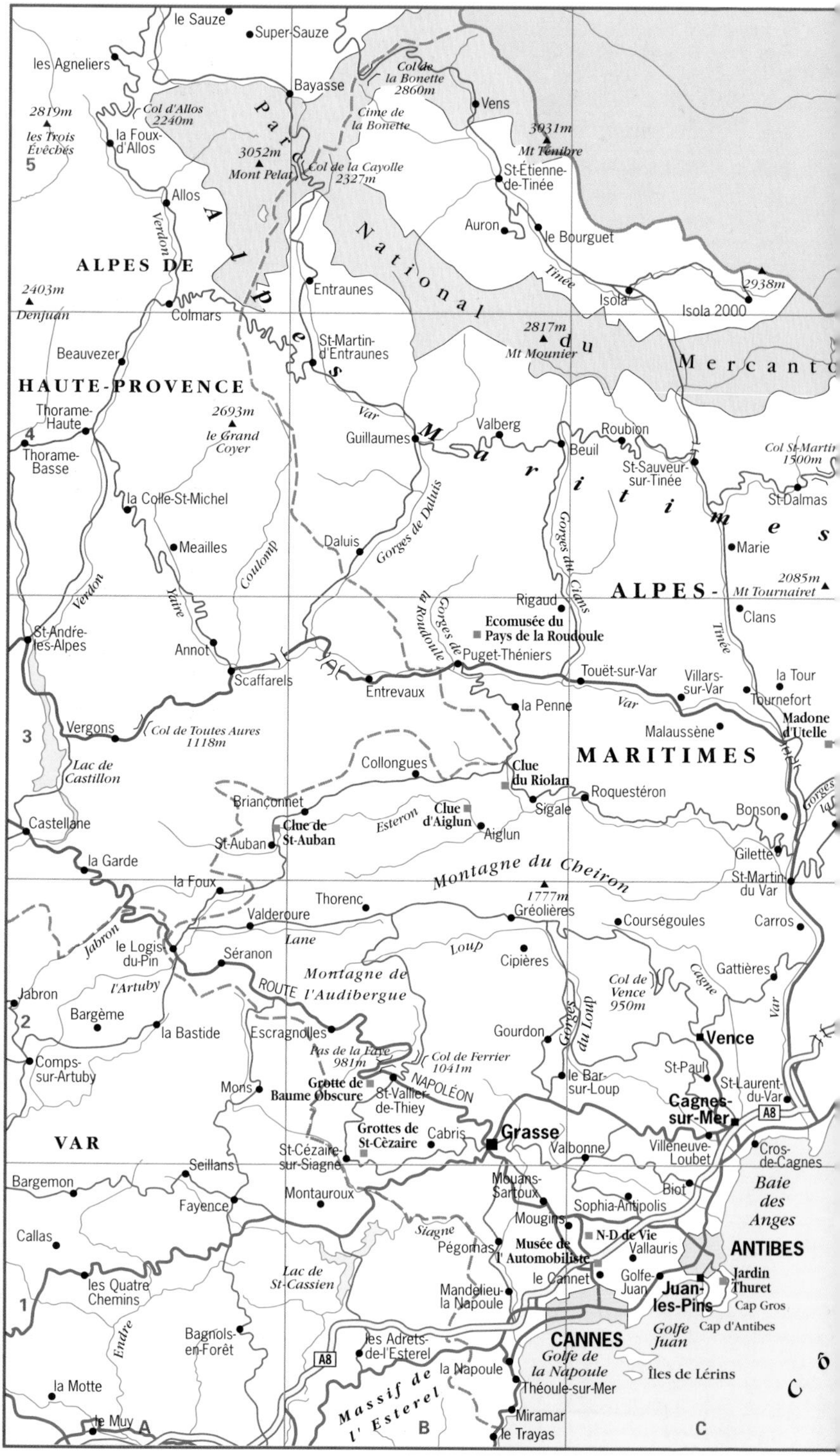

COTE D'AZUR AND ALPES-MARITIMES

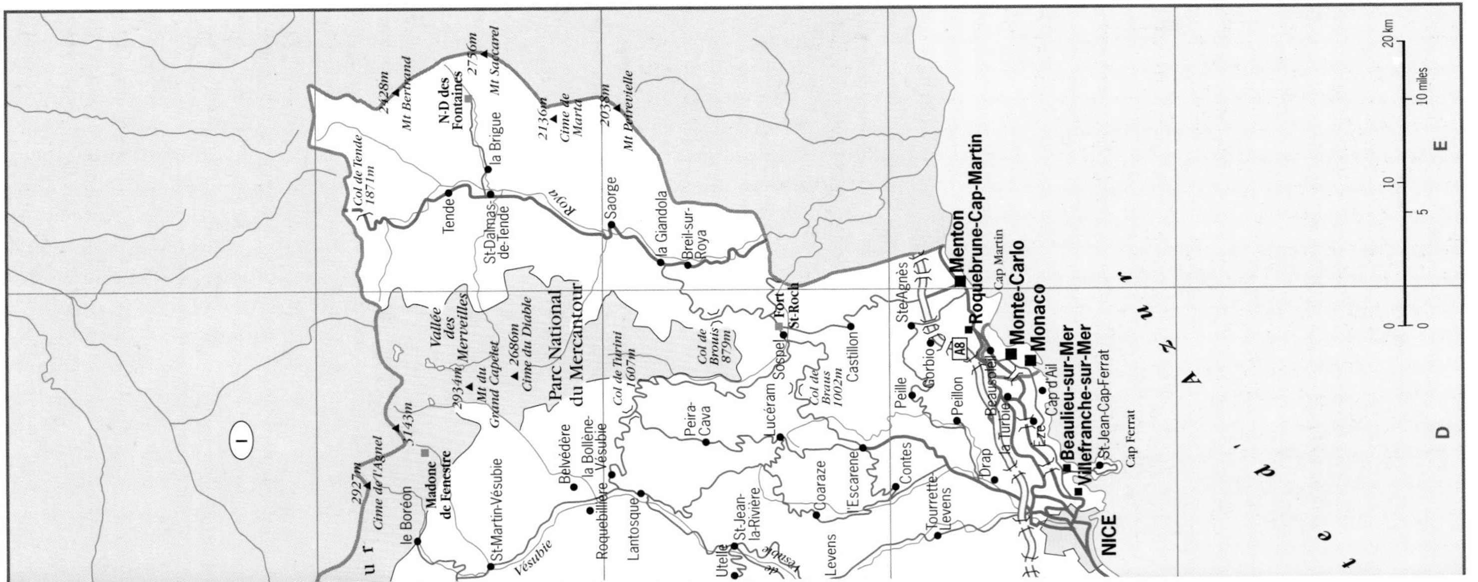

I
2927m
Cime de l'Agnel
3143m
le Boréon
Madone de Fenestre
2934m
Mt du Grand Capelet
Vallée des Merveilles
2686m
Cime du Diable
St-Martin-Vésubie
Vésubie
Parc National du Mercantour
Belvédère
la Bollène-Vésubie
Roquebillière
Lantosque
Col de Turini 1607m
Col de Tende 1871m
2428m
Mt Bertrand
Tende
N-D des Fontaines
2756m
Mt Saccarel
St-Dalmas-de-Tende
la Brigue
2136m
Cime de Marta
Roya
Saorge
2038m
Mt Peirevielle
la Giandola
Breil-sur-Roya
Peira-Cava
Col de Brouis 879m
Utelle
St-Jean-la-Rivière
Lucéram
Sospel
Fort St-Roch
Coaraze
Col de Braus 1002m
Castillon
Levens
l'Escarene
Contes
Peille
Ste-Agnès
Gorbio
Tourrette-Levens
Peillon
A8
Menton
Roquebrune-Cap-Martin
Drap
Beausoleil
Cap Martin
la Turbie
Monte-Carlo
Eze
Monaco
Cap d'Ail
Beaulieu-sur-Mer
Villefranche-sur-Mer
NICE
St-Jean-Cap-Ferrat
Cap Ferrat
Côte d'Azur
0 10 20 km
0 5 10 miles
D
E

A year-round reminder of Cannes' international film festival

Introduction The most famous corner of Provence, the southeastern coastline know as the Côte d'Azur, often seems like part of another country giving rise to the idea of Provence as the California of Europe, a wealthy golden state where high-tech business parks will be the future motor for the economy.

But today marinas rather than microchips still symbolize the real wealth here: in over 30 marinas from Menton to la Napoule, 15,000 yachts generate 1.5 billion francs in annual income. They seem to encapsulate the image of this glamorous playground: conspicuous riches, the jet-set lifestyle, and the joys of a sensual break next to the warm, blue Mediterranean.

The pleasures promised by the hyperbole surrounding the Riviera, as this 42 mile-long stretch of coastline is also called, can seem like a distant dream when you are stuck in a traffic jam along one of the corniches, contemplating a beach down below packed to overflowing, with the sea a mass of pedal boats, bobbing bodies, jet-skis, and sailboards. And the glories of the *belle époque* hotels on the seafront have been eclipsed in many places by a contagious rash of houses and apartment blocks spreading up every available sea-facing hillside.

Inland peaks Fortunately, the real Provence is never far away, with the mountains of the Alpes-Maritimes forming a splendid backdrop to the glittering coastline. Just an hour or so from the beach the *arrières-pays* (the back-country) shelters dramatic hill villages, linked by twisting mountain roads where signs warn of multiple *lacets* (hairpin bends).

Some of the more well-known of these *villages perchés* (such as Èze or St-Paul) are horribly overcommercialized, but there are still plenty of others (such as Peille, Peillon, Coaraze, or Gorbio) where the narrow streets retain more of an authentic flavor.

Behind Cannes the rolling hills culminate in the pre-Alps of Grasse. Behind Nice the narrow river valleys lead up to the wilderness of the Parc National du Mercantour. Further east, the remote Roya valley displays characteristic Italianate architecture and many fine works of art in the old border towns of Tende, Sospel, Saorge, and Breil.

In the summer you can hike and mountain bike beneath the snow-clad peaks of the Alpes-Maritimes, while in winter the ski resorts come into their own. For the budget-conscious it can make sense to stay in the *arrière-pays*, where hotel prices are more reasonable, descending to the coast for a taste of the high life when the bright lights call.

The Riviera resorts Nice is the capital of the *département* of the Alpes-Maritimes and France's fifth largest city, with more than 450,000 inhabitants. Around a third of all tourists who visit the Riviera come to Nice, drawn partly by its lovely setting on the big, blue *Baie des Anges* (the Bay of Angels). Nice has a well-preserved *vieille ville*, as has the charming port of Antibes, which houses the remarkable Picasso museum — just one of an extraordinary number of first-class modern art museums along the coast, a legacy of the contemporary artists who settled here from the end of the 19th century onward. The beaches at Antibes are mostly shingle and those on the neighboring Cap d'Antibes largely private, but neighboring Juan-les-Pins has a fine sandy beach.

Cannes is perhaps the most snobby of the Riviera resorts, a place to see-and-be-seen — but avoid during the Film Festival! It is, though, the jumping-off point for the lovely, unspoiled Îles de Lérins — the only islands on this part of the coast.

East of Nice, the picturesque port of Villefranche and the old resort of Menton, with its sedate charms, both have their devotees. In between is the independent principality of Monaco, where the harbor with its massive yachts moored below the famous Monte Carlo casino has to be seen at least once.

The "perched village" of Gourdon, with its bird's-eye view into the gorge of the river Loup

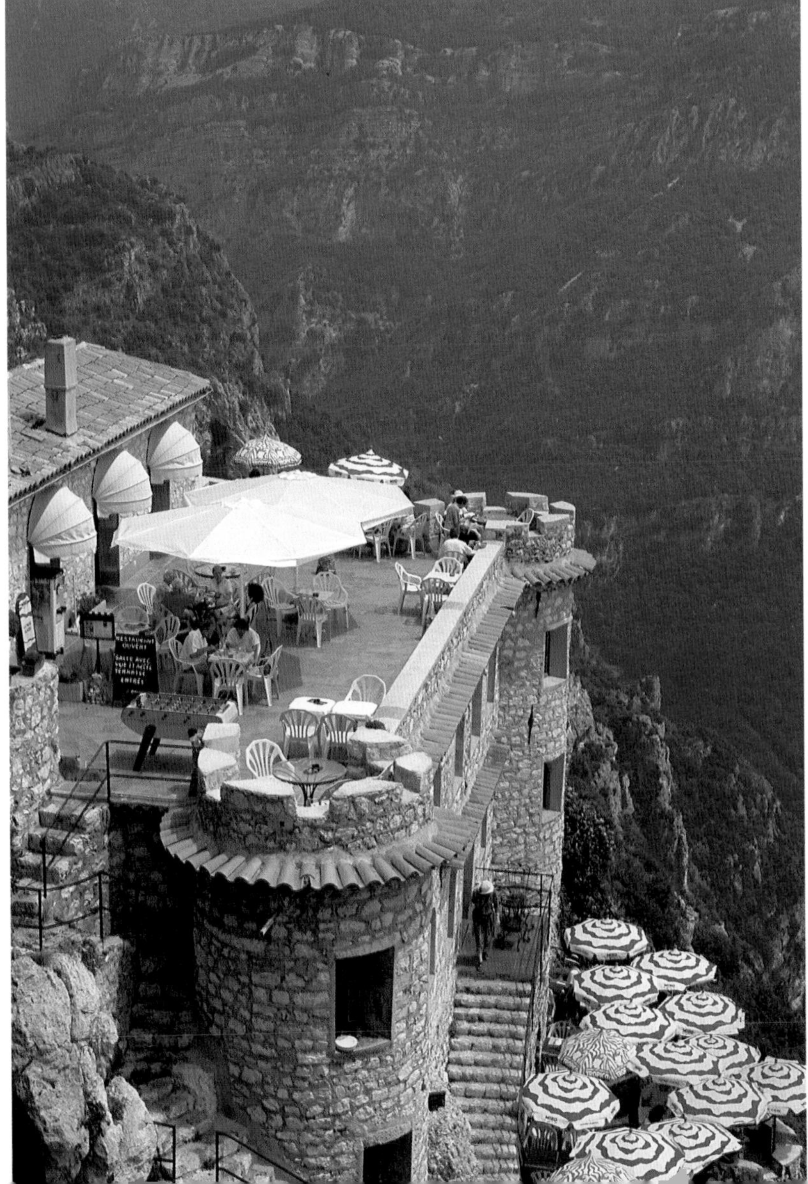

From forts to flowers
Like so many ports along the coast, Antibes started out as a Greek trading post and was known as *Antipolis* — "the city opposite," referring to Nice. The town was destroyed by the Saracens but took on a new role as a frontier outpost when Nice became part of Savoy in 1388. Over the centuries the fortifications were improved on, culminating in the solid ramparts built by Vauban in the 17th century. When Nice became reunited with France in 1860 Antibes lost its military functions and, strangely enough, turned to growing flowers instead.

►► Antibes

200C1

For Riviera regulars, Antibes holds a special place — not just because of its setting but for the *ambiance* of a lively town which does not rely solely on tourism for a living.

Across the Baie des Anges from Nice, the old town of Antibes is protected from the sea by stout ramparts. Inside the ramparts the narrow, bustling streets evoke another world — but step through an old gateway and you are immediately on a quay alongside the multimillion-dollar yachts of movie moguls and megastars. Antibes has its share of ugly modern apartments on the outskirts; Graham Greene lived in one until his death in 1991.

Antibes is the largest horticultural center in the Alpes-Maritimes *département* and is well known for its roses (which are exported worldwide), tulips, and carnations.

Flowers brighten the produce market (daily except Monday) in the cobbled **cours Masséna►**, the main street of the old town. Barrels of herb-flavored olives, little roundels of goat's cheese, melons, asparagus, figs, and Provençal *primeurs* (early vegetables) offer a treat for the eyes and nose.

Wander southward from the cours Masséna between the tall 17th- and 18th-century houses ("climbing on top of each other for a view of the sea," as one writer put it) until you come to the **Château Grimaldi►** at a strategic point overlooking the ramparts. Converted into a museum of local history in the 1920s, the château was in a fairly run-down state in the 1940s when the curator offered Picasso (then living in a cramped flat in Juan-les-Pins) the use of it as a studio. When Picasso moved to Vallauris, in thanks he left behind the majority of the work which he had done on permanent loan. This *oeuvre* now forms the core of the **Musée Picasso►►►** (open daily, closed Tuesday and November to mid-December; admission).

Alongside the astonishing Picasso collection are works by Nicolas de Staël, Léger, Modigliani, Max Ernst, and many others, as well as photographs of Picasso by Bill Brandt and Man Ray.

Porte de l'Olivette, a small bay on the Cap d'Antibes

Interior of the Chapelle Notre-Dame-du-Bon Port

Housed in the Bastion St-André to the south of the Grimaldi château, the **Musée d'Histoire et d'Archéologie** (same hours as above; admission) draws together Etruscan, Greek, Roman, and medieval finds from the vicinity, as well as *objets trouvés* from shipwrecks. Just next to the château the old cathedral, the **Église de l'Immaculée Conception**, is worth a look inside for the 16th-century altarpiece, the *retable du Rosaire*, attributed to Louis Bréa.

To the east of the huge marina are boat-building yards and a stadium, behind which stands the massive **Fort Carré►** (open in July and August). This impressive, geometric structure was started in the 16th century and finished by the great military architect Vauban.

Children will enjoy **Marineland** and **Aquasplash** on the road toward Biot.

Picasso in Antibes
During the six months from July to December 1946 that Picasso was in Antibes his work achieved new heights of creative genius, an outpouring of Mediterranean exuberance and fantasy. Picasso was in high spirits: the war was over, and he had a new lover, Françoise Gillet. His pleasure at life's prospects (despite a post-war shortage of materials which meant he sometimes had to use boat paint instead of oils) is reflected in the uncomplicated geniality of the still lifes, the aptly titled *Joie de vivre* or the mythologically inspired *faunes musiciens* or *Ulysse et les Sirènes.*

► Antibes, Cap d' *200C1*

Between Antibes and Juan-les-Pins the **Cap d'Antibes** is dotted with sumptuous villas and private beaches; on the eastern side of the peninsula there is a huge sandy public beach, la Salis, and farther round the Plage de la Garoupe and the Plage Joseph are also both free. From Plage Joseph a coastal path meanders for 2 miles around the shoreline to Cap Gros.

Most of the Cap d'Antibes is cordoned off into private estates and you can but glimpse some of the palatial houses behind their massive gates and electric fences. However, you can visit the **Chapelle Notre-Dame-du-Bon Port** at the top of the Garoupe plateau, where there is an extensive collection of sailors' *ex-votos.*

Just beneath the Garoupe plateau, the **Jardin Thuret►** (open daily except weekends) covers 10 acres with collections of rare exotic and tropical plants. Plant lovers can also visit the world-famous **Roseraies Meilland** (by appointment, tel. 93 61 30 30) on boulevard Cap d'Antibes.

At the westernmost point of Cap d'Antibes there is the **Musée Naval et Napoléonien** (open daily, closed Tuesday and November to mid-December; admission). As well as model ships and cannons there are all sorts of items relating to Napoleon's return from exile in Elba and his connections with Antibes.

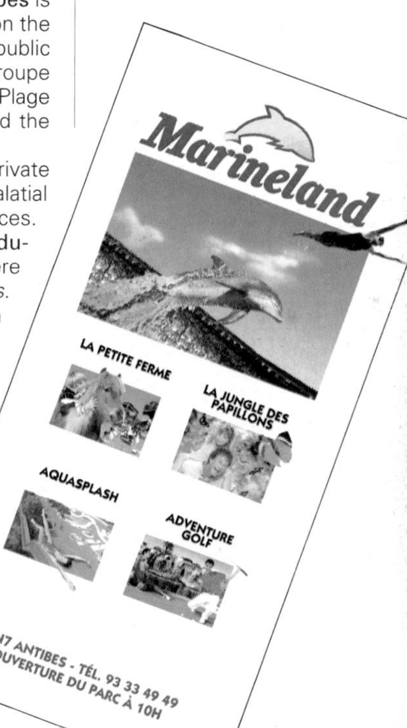

The macabre dance
The *Danse Macabre* is a mysterious 15th-century tableau, which some say is an invocation against the plague, whilst others claim it is a sort of collective exorcism. The most likely explanation is that it illustrates the legend of the Count of Bar, who insisted on throwing a grand ball in his château during Lent: several of the "sinners" who took part died as a result, and the painting shows the dancing couples being struck by Death's arrows and dragged off down to hell.

▶ le Bar-sur-Loup *200B2*

High above the river, le Bar-sur-Loup has been a military encampment under the Celts, the Gauloise, the Ligurians, and the Romans. From the Roman period the only traces that remain are two tombstones (one set in the base of the church clocktower) and, from medieval times, the château's cylindrical towers in the town center. In the main square is the château's dungeon, once seven stories tall, reduced to just a single story during the Revolution.

The **Église St-Jacques▶** has a fine Renaissance doorway with carved wooden panels, but the strangest sight in the village is the curious painting of the *Danse Macabre* (see panel) at the back of the church.

▶ Beaulieu-sur-Mer *201D2*

Like nearby Menton, Beaulieu has an exceptionally mild climate (they claim a mere four nights of frost per year, and even bananas are grown here) and was a fashionable retreat during the late 19th century. The town's name is due to a visit made here by Napoleon, who, not at his most eloquent, exclaimed in Corsican *O qual bel luogo*! ("Oh what a lovely place").

In contrast to the sedate, palm-fringed seafront on the Baie des Fourmis, fantasy takes over completely in the extraordinary **Villa Kerylos▶▶** past the casino on the northern headland. Designed in 1908 by archaeologist Theodore Reinach, it is a faithful reproduction of an Athenian villa which was built using lavish amounts of Carrara marble, alabaster and rare woods. Decorated with reproduction frescoes, furniture, vases, and bronze statues, the only concessions that Reinach made to the 20th century were modern plumbing, glass windows, and a hidden piano. For the last 20 years of his life Reinach lived here in emulation of Greek society, exercising and bathing with his male friends — women were banished to separate suites. The villa is now a museum (open afternoons, closed Monday and November; admission).

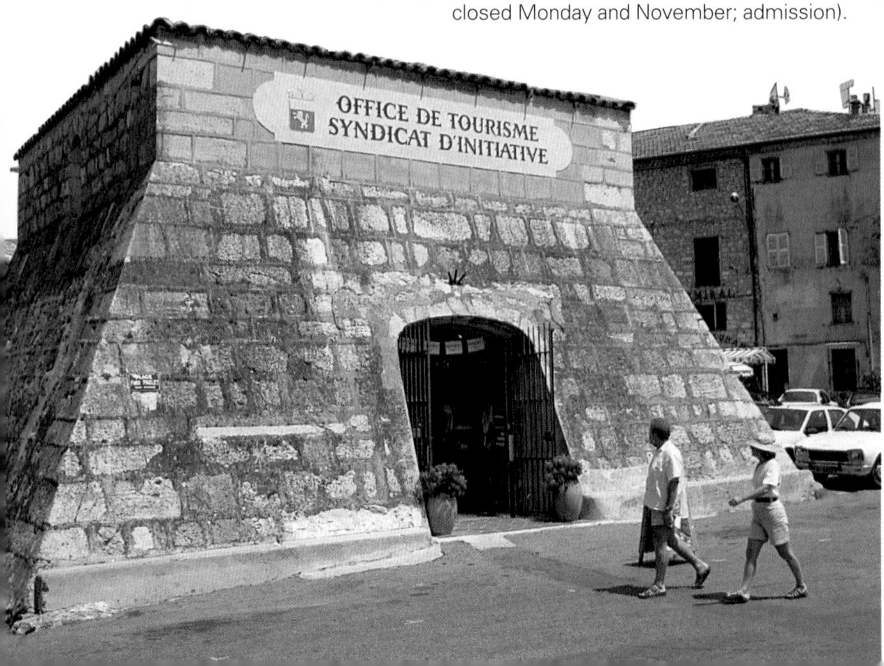

The old dungeon of le Bar-sur-Loup's château, now a tourist information center

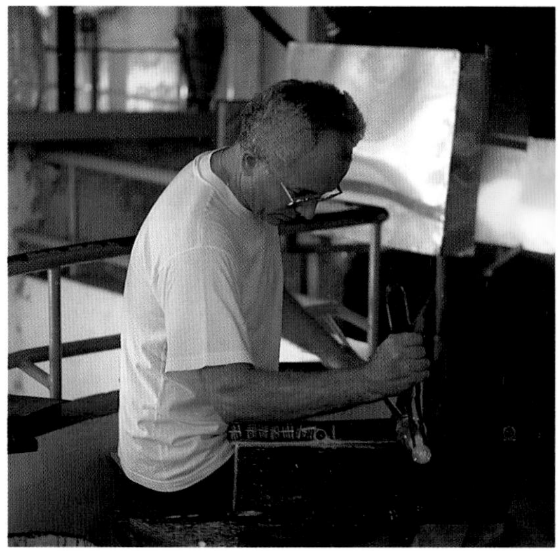

A glassblower at work in one of the many glass workshops in Biot

▶▶ Biot *200C1*

As you approach Biot there is little doubt as to the village's main industry, with signboards at every corner of the road announcing *verrerie* — glassware. Biot started out in Roman times producing huge clay storage jars but this trade ended in the 19th century. Biot's conversion to glass and ceramics is largely due to the brief sojourn here of artist and sculptor Fernand Léger, who bought a plot of land to build a ceramics museum in 1955. Sadly he died soon afterwards, but his inspiration led to the opening of the Biot Glassworks, and in 1960 the **Musée Fernand Léger▶▶** (closed Tuesday; admission).

The museum was later expanded to include nearly 400 of his works including ceramics, tapestries, stained glass, and mosaics. On the façade is a monumental mosaic designed for the entrance of the Olympic stadium in Hanover, while the galleries trace Léger's artistic development through Cubism (he was a fellow pioneer alongside Picasso) to his obsession with machinery to the bright, geometric tableaux that became his trademark.

On the outskirts of the village the **Verrerie de Biot▶▶** (closed public holidays) has grown into a mini-commercial center with several galleries, shops, the glass works itself (where you can watch the local speciality of *verres à bulles* being blown), and a museum (now fashionably relabeled as the *Eco-Musée du Verre*), and an exhibition center with extraordinary and imaginative glass art exhibits.

Biot itself is a delight, especially the unusual **place des Arcades▶** at the heart of the village. At the south end of place des Arcades is the tiny place l'Église, where a doorway in a crumbling belltower leads into a surprisingly capacious **church** hidden away behind the houses. On the left as you enter is a red-and-gold altarpiece, the 16th-century *Retable de Rosaire*, from the Bréa school; on the right, *Christ aux Plaies*, also 16th-century, attributed to Canavesio.

In the **Musée d'Histoire Locale▶** (open afternoons, closed Monday and Tuesday; admission) are photographs, documents and *objets trouvés* from Biot's past.

Fernand Léger's mosaics embellish the exterior of a museum in Biot devoted to his works

La Brigue's situation, well off the beaten track, belies its remarkable artistic heritage

Kayaking on the Roya
By the time it reaches Breil the Roya has broadened out enough after its sinuous passage through the gorges to justify a hydroelectric station and to provide enough open water for kayaking. This can be arranged (as can pony trekking and mountain-biking in the surrounding hills) through a small agency in the village, Roya Evasion (tel. 93 04 91 46).

►► Breil-sur-Roya *201E3*

The first major town you meet traveling up the Roya valley from the border with Italy, Breil straddles the Roya river with the old quarter on the eastern bank. At the center of the narrow streets in the *vieille ville* is the 18th-century church of **Sancta-Maria-in-Albis**, with an altarpiece by Bréa hidden away somewhere inside its gloomy baroque interior. Far more cheerful are the two belltowers with their jolly caps of colorful Niçois tiles. Next door, the pastel-colored, Renaissance **Chapelle Ste-Catherine** is literally falling apart.

Just outside Breil, the quaint **Ecomusée du Haut Pays** (open Saturday and Sunday and Wednesday, Thursday and Friday afternoons in summer) has been set up inside three old railroad cars in the station sidings. On display are the flora and fauna, agricultural activities, and history of the valley.

►►► la Brigue *201E4*

La Brigue is an attractive and welcoming village set amidst the lovely landscapes of the Levenza valley, 4 miles southeast of Tende. The Levenza babbles past the main square in the village, from where the snowcapped peak of Mont Bégo is visible to the west. The old houses of the village are built from the local gray-green schist, as is the Romanesque **Église St-Martin►►** which contains an astonishing collection of primitive paintings by Louis Bréa and his followers from the Niçois school of the late 15th and early 16th century. There is a notable contrast between the nobility of Bréa's wonderful nativity altarpiece and his gruesome painting of St. Elmo having his intestines pulled out with a rope, which shows a degree of cruel realism unusual for Bréa.

But the most macabre paintings are the truly remarkable frescoes in the **Chapelle Notre-Dame des Fontaines►►►**, 2.5 miles up the valley to the east. Any hotel or bar in the village will give you a key to the chapel (in exchange for your passport), which is reached via a winding road passing a pretty zigzag bridge, the Pont du Coq, which dates back to the 15th century.

Perched above a mountain stream in the middle of a woodland valley, the chapel is all the more extraordinary for being in such a remote location. The 15th-century frescoes, painted by Giovanni Baleison and Giovanni Canavesio, depict the life of Christ in a series of 38 episodes culminating in a grisly Last Judgment on the back wall, where the tortures of the damned are shown in gory, violent detail.

▶▶ Cagnes-sur-Mer *200C2*

The seaside section of Cagnes (known as Cros-de-Cagnes) is the sort of place you want to leave as quickly as possible but there are two compelling reasons to slow down and turn inland. The first of these, in Cagnes-Ville, is the **Musée Renoir▶▶** (closed Tuesday and mid-October to mid-November; admission) in the Domaine des Collettes. The museum and gardens contain several works by Renoir (including bronzes and sculptures in the gardens) as well as portraits and sketches by friends and visitors such as Bonnard, Dufy, and Albert André.

The medieval streets of **Haut-de-Cagnes▶▶**, with their vaulted passageways and steep steps, are crowned by a crenellated castle built by Rainier Grimaldi in 1309 and which now houses the **Château-Musée▶** (closed Tuesday and mid-October to mid-November; admission). Spanning several centuries of culture, the château not only houses an olive museum on the first floor but also a display of over 40 paintings of the cabaret star Suzy Solidor by well-known names such as Dufy, Cocteau, Van Dongen, Otto Friesz, and others. In one section is the **Musée d'Art Méditerranéen Moderne,** which embraces a wide assortment of painters including Chagall, Matisse, Brayer, and many more who have worked on the coast. In the summer, the château hosts the prestigious *Festival Internationale de la Peinture*.

The Genoese who worked on the château also created the frescoes in the **Chapelle Notre-Dame-de-Protection** (open afternoons, closed Tuesday, Friday; admission) just behind the château.

A mural in la Brigue

Renoir in Cagnes
Renoir moved to Cagnes in 1908 in the hopes that the warm weather would alleviate his arthritis. He built the Domaine des Collettes amid luxuriant gardens which also included a grove of 100-year-old olive trees. His talent flourished in this setting, despite the crippling disease which forced him to strap paintbrushes to his fingers in order to work. His north-facing studio has been preserved just the way Renoir left it, with his palette, easel and wheelchair in place. He died here in 1919.

The vieille ville *of la Brigue*

The rich and famous

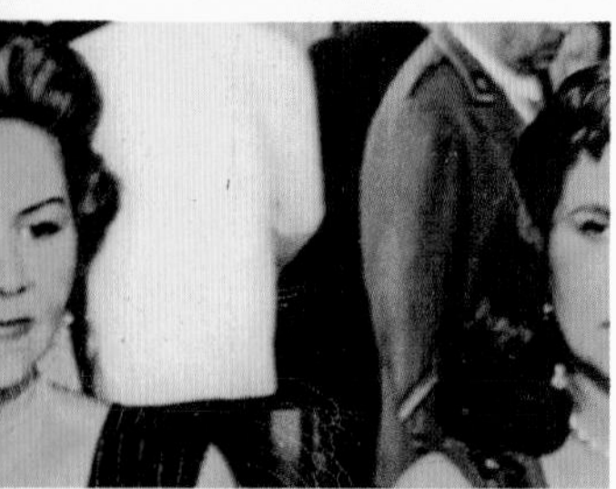

■ The Côte d'Azur has always been one of the glitziest holiday destinations in Europe, and curiosity about the lifestyles of the rich and famous has no doubt contributed considerably to its popularity in the past. Today, however, superstars and the ultrarich are more likely to be ensconced behind the security fences of private villas than spotted speeding along the corniche in an open-top roadster....■

Above: The Monte Carlo Story

Bardot's woes
Once the icon of St-Tropez, Brigitte Bardot is never long out of the headlines, however hard she tries. Having turned her back on the limelight and sold all her jewels to set up an animal sanctuary, she caused a furore by marrying right-wing politician Bernard d'Ormale in 1992, celebrating the wedding on the yacht of *Front National* leader Jean-Marie Le Pen. Since then she has criticized Muslim ritual slaughter and been accused of being a fascist — millions of francs in donations have been withheld from her animal foundation. "I would have been better off falling in love with a shoe salesman," said Bardot.

Bardot burst upon the scene in 1957

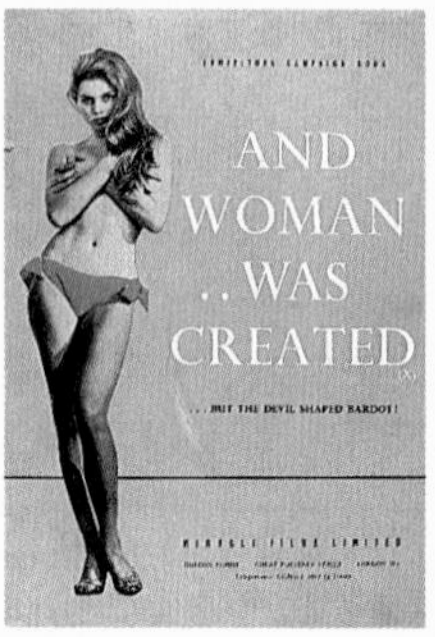

Early decadence In the early days of tourism the Côte d'Azur was principally a sedate winter resort for the English and Russian nobility, but the pace changed in the late 1800s when the first casino was opened in Monte-Carlo, and the Riviera first acquired its racy image. Stories of the *fin-de-siècle* decadence that followed abound: a Russian princess, for instance, was celebrating a big casino win in a rented villa one night but when the owners decided that the revelry had gone on too long; she simply bought the house rather than stop the party.

The first yachts had already begun to frequent the coastal ports, with the writer Guy de Maupassant putting in to St-Tropez in the 1880s, followed by the painter Paul Signac in 1892, who stepped ashore and liked the place so much he bought a house and started the first wave of contemporary artists to settle there.

The American influx After World War I the Riviera got back into the swing again with a new wave of clients, mostly wealthy Americans and stage and opera stars. Jazz clubs sprang up everywhere and Zelda and F. Scott Fitzgerald arrived to document the shenanigans (Gertrude Stein and Cole Porter were among the guests who stayed at the Antibes villa of rich Bostonians Sara and Gerald Murphy — a couple who served as role models for Dick and Nicole Diver in Fitzgerald's novel, *Tender is the Night*).

Noel Coward, Ernest Hemingway, Katherine Mansfield (who adored Menton, and now has a street named after her there), and Colette (who preferred St-Tropez) were among those descending for the season — which had now become a summer rather than a winter phenomenon, prompted by Coco Chanel, who made suntans fashionable in the late 1920s. The American dancer Isadora Duncan came to a tragic end in Cannes in 1927 when her scarf caught in a wheel of her Bugatti and strangled her.

The American influx came to an abrupt end with the stock market crash of 1929, although royalty (the Prince of Wales and King Faisal of Saudi Arabia) and the rich (such as the Aga Khan) remained faithful to the Riviera up until World War II.

Star turns The first Cannes Film Festival was planned for 1939, although it did not take off properly until 1947 (which was also the year that Picasso moved into his

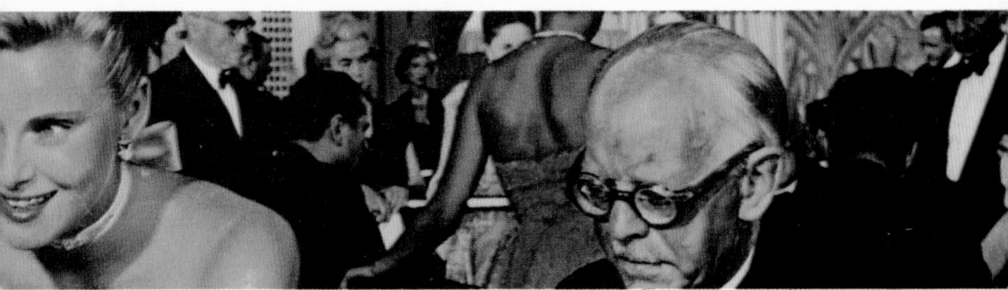

studio in Antibes). The Festival soon became a compulsory stop on the itinerary of international movie stars, and by the 1950s the likes of Clarke Gable, Errol Flynn, Lana Turner, and Kirk Douglas were to be seen taking a post-Festival break on the beaches of St-Tropez. It was at the Cannes Festival in 1955 that Prince Rainier fell in love with the American movie star Grace Kelly, whom he later married.

In 1957 the Riviera took on a whole new dimension when Roger Vadim filmed Brigitte Bardot in St-Tropez in the film *Et Dieu Créa la Femme* (*And God Created Woman*). The coast again became a byword for all that was chic and sexy. More recently, celebrities such as Mick Jagger and Elton John, plus the Onassis family and the composer Herbert von Karajan, have all owned houses in St-Tropez.

The beaches of St-Tropez continue to attract megastars (see page 174) and although you might see the occasional television celebrity shopping in Monaco or lunching in Mougins, today's beautiful people are keeping a much lower profile — and not necessarily staying on the coast.

Where are they now?
St-Rémy-de-Provence in the Bouches-du-Rhône is one of the latest haunts of the rich and famous — Princess Caroline of Monaco moved there in 1990 to recover from the loss of her husband, Stefano Casiraghi. She set the tone for a more discreet lifestyle, renting an old *mas* (farmhouse) and sending her children to the local school.

Now the Parisian *beau monde* and wealthy American and English families have followed, happy with the quiet, rural life.

Luxury yachts line the Riviera's many marinas

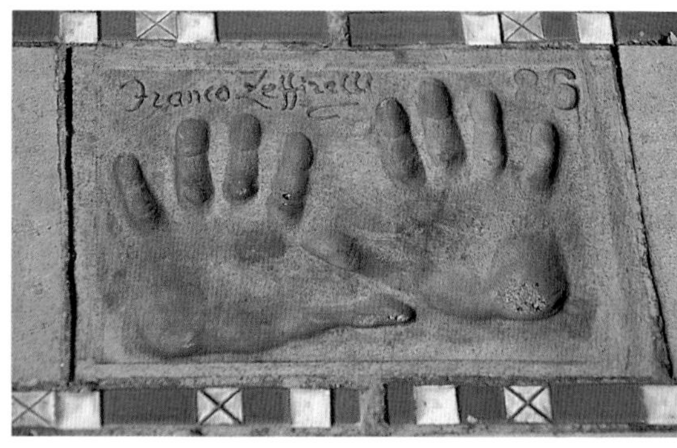

Franco Zeffirelli is one of many show-biz talents to have left his mark on la Croisette at Cannes

The Film Festival
It will come as no surprise to discover that Cannes is twinned with Beverly Hills, and even if the outrageous cost of hotel rooms does not give you a clue then the snobbery and hype associated with the International Film Festival certainly will. More than 12,000 movie moguls, directors, and celebrities, a press contingent of around 3,000 journalists, hundreds of movies screened around the clock, wheeler-dealers wining and dining with fat checkbooks at the ready, aspiring starlets posing on the beach for the photographers — yes, the best place to be in May is...somewhere else.

▶ Cannes *200C1*

"Closed for the summer" — a signboard on Cannes' casino long ago, when winter holidays on the Riviera were all the rage — would not be tolerated today during the high season, with visitors arriving in their thousands to catch a glimpse of the glitter and glamour for which Cannes is now famous. That glitzy reputation is, of course, largely due to the International Film Festival (see panel) held in May each year, when thousands of agents, producers, distributors, and stars descend for a two-week expense-account binge of celluloid consumption.

It was in December 1834 that the Lord Chancellor of England, Lord Brougham, arrived here by accident — *en route* to Italy, but prevented from going further due to an outbreak of cholera. Cannes then was a sleepy fishing village of some 4,000 souls. Brougham slept so well in the one and only auberge that he decided to stay, and built a house — the Château Eleonore behind ave du Docteur Picaud — where he spent the next 34 winters up until his death. Many of the mansions built by the English (and the Russian nobility) have been demolished, but you can seek out those which still stand with the help of a booklet, *Ces Belles Demeures qui on fait Cannes* ("These lovely homes which made Cannes"), available free from the tourist office.

The seafront promenade, **la Croisette▶**, is bordered by elegant hotels with big reputations, such as the Carlton, the Martinez, and the Majestic. The beach itself is divided up into the color-coded concessions where you will not have to budge from your beach chair for a cocktail or a snack. The only free section is in front of the hideous, orange-colored **Palais des Festivals** where all the real work goes on during the film festival: known as "The Bunker" to regulars, its basement screenings represent the real *marché du film* (film market) where options change hands at astronomical prices.

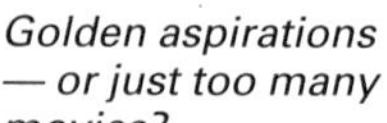

Golden aspirations — or just too many movies?

Behind la Croisette the streets around rue d'Antibes have window displays that look like color spreads for glossy magazines, but for mere mortals the shops in rue Meynadier two blocks further back might be more useful, with excellent *charcuteries*, pasta shops, *patisseries,* and cheeseshops. At the western end of rue Meynadier there is a great food market in the Forville covered market (daily except Monday).

On a small hill above the port is Cannes' oldest quarter, **le Suquet**. In the 11th century it belonged to the monks from the Îles de Lérins (see below) who fled here after Saracen raids on their island retreat. The monks built a watchtower to warn of coastal raids, and fortifications, remnants of which are behind the Gothic **Notre-Dame de l'Espérance** on the hilltop. The monks' fortified priory now houses the **Musée de la Castre▶** (open daily, closed Monday, Tuesday, and November to mid-December; admission) which has an eclectic archaeological and ethnographic collection covering five continents. Admission to the museum includes the **Tour du Suquet**, the monks' watchtower — the platform at the top has views down the coast and out to the Îles de Lérins.

As an antidote to the traffic and crowds in Cannes there can be no better place than the **Îles de Lérins▶▶**, just 15 minutes away on a ferry from the *gare maritime* in the port (up to a dozen departures daily in summer, five daily in winter).

The smaller of the two, **St-Honorat▶▶**, is completely unspoiled and has been the property of monks since the 4th century, when Honoratus first landed here. Today it is Cistercian monks who cultivate the vineyards, olive groves, and lavender fields around the abbey, which was rebuilt in the 19th century. Apart from visiting the remains of a fortified 11th-century abbey on the clifftops, there is little to do except wander among the eucalyptus and pine trees and enjoy the peaceful atmosphere of this little haven.

Ste-Marguerite▶▶ is nearly twice as big (although it still only takes two hours to walk around), has some good beaches on the southern shores and walking trails through the woods. The **Fort Royal** was built by Richelieu and reinforced by Vauban (open daily); the Man in the Iron Mask (see panel) is supposed to have been held prisoner here. On the ground floor is the **Musée de la Mer** (open daily) with archaeology exhibits and finds from shipwrecks.

"The Man in the Iron Mask"
In 1687, a prisoner was brought to one of the cells in the Fort Royal on Ste-Marguerite who was later immortalized by Alexander Dumas as "he Man in the Iron Mask." He was held here for over ten years, but the question of his identity has never been fully resolved. Was he the illegitimate brother (or the twin) of Louis XIV? Or a loose-mouthed relative of the doctor who performed an autopsy on Louis XIII? That autopsy showed that the King was incapable of fathering children — and when the doctor's son-in-law inherited his papers he couldn't keep this secret to himself.

The monks' watch-tower rises high above Cannes harbor

Sunny ceramics
The sunshine theme in Coaraze — the *village du Soleil* — inspired a clutch of artists to create a series of massive and colorful ceramic sundials throughout the village in the 1960s: those by Henri Goetz and Ponce de Léon are in the place Félix Giordan in front of the church, while others by Cocteau, Mona-Christie, Douking, and Valentin are less happily placed on the pink façade of the town hall/post office building.

▶▶ **Clues de Haute-Provence** *200B3*

As the Var river changes course in Haute-Provence and heads down toward the sea it encircles a sparsely populated region cut through with rifts known as *clues*. Forged by torrential streams, the valleys traverse limestone mountains where small, isolated villages hang onto a precarious existence. In the middle of this region is the 5,817 foot-high Montagne du Cheiron, to which skiers from the Riviera resorts flock in the winter months.

At the center of the *clues* on the northern slopes of the mountain is **Roquestéron**, a fortified village that is separated in two by the Esteron river (prior to 1860 this river formed the frontier between France and Savoy, so each half of the village was in a different country). Leaving the village westward on D17 the **Clue du Riolan▶** opens up on your right; further past here on D10 is the **Clue d'Aiglun▶**, which is perhaps the most spectacular of these narrow gorges, with a vertical torrent pouring down from the mountains above. Farther west, the village of St-Auban perches on a hillside at the opening to the **Clue de St-Auban▶**, where the steep sides are riddled with grottos and caves.

▶▶ **Coaraze** *201D3*

This little circular village perched atop a peak in the hills behind Nice has a sunny reputation — signboards proclaiming *Village du Soleil* mark the entrances to Coaraze — although why it should get more solar rays than anywhere else is not easily explained.

The village has its fair share of cobbled stairways and vaulted passageways, as well as a handful of *artisans d'art* and second homes for Niçois trendies.

On the outskirts of the village the **Chapelle Notre-Dame des Sept Douleurs▶** (Our Lady of the Seven Sorrows) took on a much more cheerful character and a new name, the Blue Chapel, when Ponce de Léon redecorated the interior in 1965 with bright murals and a vivid green stained glass window. To reach the chapel, take the small road beside the *Bar Tabac Les Arts* either by car or on foot (20 minutes round trip walking).

A curious fountain in the village square, Èze

Contes *201D2*

This old town is full of legends, which may possibly account for its name, *conte* meaning story. The most famous fable is that of the caterpillar plague (see panel) and there are several others revolving around appearances by the devil, who has his tail glued down by villagers and is forced to shed it and flee. Contes' myths are far more colorful than the village itself, which is now surrounded in the Paillon valley by numerous suburbs, factories, and a huge cement works.

▶▶ **Èze** *201D2*

Halfway along the *Moyenne Corniche* between Nice and Monte-Carlo, the dramatic location of Èze — 1,407 feet above the sea, making it the highest

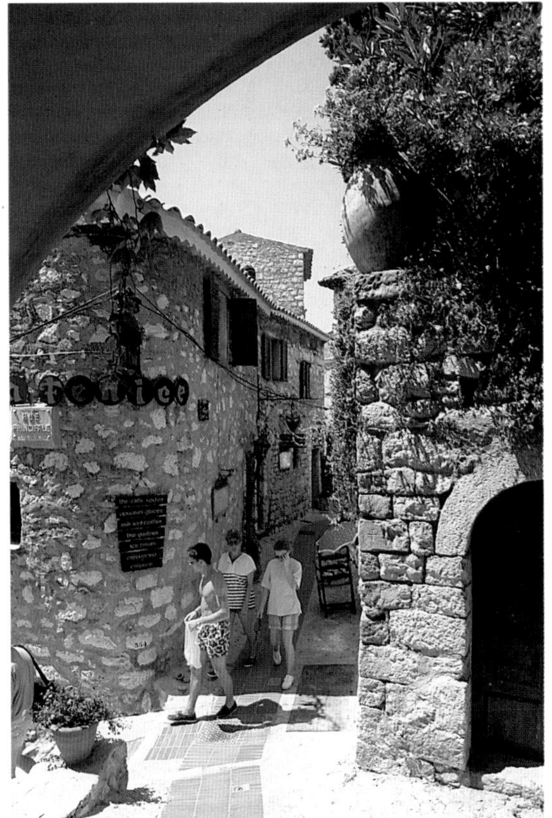

A quiet day in picturesque Èze

Nietzsche's path
An old mule path that wends its way down to the seaside at Èze-sur-Mer from just outside the village of Èze is now known as the Sentier Frédéric-Nietzsche. This is in recognition of the fact that Nietzsche is supposed to have conceived the third part of *Thus Spake Zarathustra* while walking through the countryside here.

perched village you will find anywhere in Provence — has contributed to its popularity, with amateur snappers keen to capture the extraordinary sight of this settlement clinging to a cone of rock.

Entering the village through a crenellated 14th-century gateway, you find yourself in a maze of narrow streets and stepped alleys, a labyrinth designed for easy defense. The *bijou* flower-filled passageways are now chockablock with boutiques, antique dealers, and artisans; in the summer, the crowds can be insufferable.

Some respite can be found in either the **Chapelle des Pénitents Blancs** (which has an unusual 13th-century Catalan crucifix with Christ smiling down from the cross) or in the **Jardin Exotique** (open daily; admission) surrounding the ruins of the château at the top of the village; the château itself was dismantled in 1706 at the order of Louis XIV.

Golfe-Juan *200C1*

This rather bland resort does at least have the merit of a long sandy beach, sheltered by the headlands of Cap d'Antibes and the Pointe de la Croisette on either side. Unless you are stopping for a swim, though, it has little else to detain you except for a glance at the mosaic on the **quai du Port** marking the spot where Napoleon stepped ashore on March 1, 1815 after escaping from Elba.

Plagues of caterpillars
In 1508 Contes was inundated by hordes of large caterpillars, nasty little beasts that defoliated the woods by munching their way through massive amounts of pine needles, secreting a poison that causes painful rashes and allergies in humans. The villagers were so desperate they called in the Bishop of Nice, who performed an exorcism to banish the creatures. Faced with a similar dilemma in 1993, the municipality of Villefranche — evidently with more faith in germ warfare than prayer — brought in helicopters to spray the district with bacteria which, when eaten by the caterpillars, causes their intestines to burst.

▶ Gorbio 201D2

An attractive *village perché* 10km northwest of Menton, remarkable for being practically a souvenir-free zone, Gorbio is often swept by clouds and mists, which has led to the locals being nicknamed *les nebuleux* ("the cloudy ones"). Although it has at least half-a-dozen chapels and churches in or near the village, the most arresting spectacle in Gorbio is the annual *Procession dai limaca* (see panel), which takes place during the *Fête Dieu* (Corpus Christi) in mid-June.

Magical procession
The *Procession dai limaca* is a pagan ritual giving thanks for the previous winter's olive harvest and exorcising any demons that might damage the next crop: the whole village of Gorbio is illuminated by little flickering lamps made from snail shells (*limaca* in Provençal; snails are also a pagan symbol of renewal) set in beds of sand and filled with olive oil. Dabs of plaster fix the shells on walls, doorways, window sills and on the pavements; a nighttime procession makes its way from the church through the magically lit streets for the blessing.

▶▶ Gourdon 200B2

Situated in a remarkable position some 1,650 feet above the river Loup, Gourdon merits the description *nid d'aigles* (eagles' nest) with its stunning views, embracing 50 miles of the coastline on a clear day. A fort was built on this dizzying site in the 9th century to watch out for Saracen invaders; the vast rectangular **château▶▶** which stands at the heart of the village today dates from between 1607 and 1654, when it was entirely rebuilt by the Lombard family.

This immaculately preserved building contains a pair of museums, the better of which is the **Musée Historique▶▶▶** (open daily in summer, afternoons except Tuesday in winter; admission includes guided tour). A veritable treasure house on the first floor of the château, the museum houses a large collection of antique armaments and suits of armor, 16th- and 17th-century furnishings (including Marie-Antoinette's writing desk and an Aubusson tapestry), and religious works of art in the chapel (including a rare sculpture of St. Sebastian by Greco).

Upstairs, the **Musée de Peinture Naïve** (same hours) is less compelling, although among the 150 works on display there is a self-portrait by Douanier-Rousseau. Outside the château the curved stone balconies of the lovely Le Notre-designed gardens jut out over the hillside, where you can admire the view while waiting for the next guided tour.

Apart from the château, Gourdon has several fountains and the usual clutch of stores with Provençal souvenirs such as olive-wood carvings, honey, nougat, and scented soap.

Santons — *Provençal dolls — on sale in Gourdon*

Demonstrating the art of perfumery in Grasse

The salt seat
One of the curiosities in the château at Gourdon is a small *fauteuil à sel (salt armchair),* which dates from the time when there were heavy taxes on salt: the family's salt supplies were hidden under the seat and granny promptly sat down on top when the taxmen called — a crafty solution, since it was also forbidden to force old people to stand up!

Heady blooms
In the valleys surrounding Grasse lavender, jasmine, mimosa, roses, and other sweet-scented plants are cultivated before being harvested (always at dawn, when the dew is still upon them) to undergo the alchemical process of extracting their essences: it takes 900,000 rose buds or eight million jasmine blooms to render just one kilo (2.2lb.) of the heady elixir, which is the essence of the flower.

▶▶▶ Grasse 200B2

On a still day the scent on the air as you enter Grasse is probably a lot more appealing than first impressions of the town itself, which sprawls unattractively across the lower slopes of the Provençal Alps and down across the valley. But apart from the famous *parfumeries* which are the main lure for tourists, Grasse has a quaint old quarter and several sights worth seeking out once you have done the obligatory tour of the perfume factories.

Grasse started out in the Middle Ages by specializing in the less-than-fragrant industry of tanning sheep skins from Alpine pastures and hides imported from Spain and Sicily. In the middle of the 17th century many of the tanneries abruptly switched over to glove-making to meet demand from Parisian society for perfumed gloves, which had become a hot fashion item since being adopted by Italian aristocracy during the Renaissance. The Grassois became *gantiers parfumeurs* (perfumed glovemakers) until gloves ceased to be a status symbol after the Revolution, at which point they became simple *parfumeurs.*

With the rise of the big perfume companies in Paris at the beginning of the 19th century the Grassois abandoned making the finished product and decided to specialize instead on what they did best, the distillation of raw materials into concentrated fragrances for perfume-making. The ancient techniques of *enfleurage* (whereby flowers are placed in trays of fat, which are then washed in ethyl alcohol to extract the scent) and *maceration* (whereby hot fat is saturated with blooms) and subsequent distillation will all be explained if you take a factory tour at one of the *parfumeries.*

Up to 300 different essences may go into a single fragrance

The main *parfumeries* in the center of town are Galimard (73 route de Cannes), Molinard (60 blvd Victor Hugo) or Fragonard (20 blvd Fragonard). Tours in English and French are free, and naturally enough end up in the factory store (although there is no pressure to buy).

The Fragonard *parfumerie* also has an enchanting **musée▶▶** (open daily) in the same building which covers over 5,000 years of perfume making and has a beautiful collection of more than 3,000 rare perfumery objects, with many exquisite antique *flacons* (flasks) from Egypt, the Orient, Rome, and Greece. Unfortunately the **Musée International de la Parfumerie** (open daily, closed November and Monday and Tuesday in winter; admission) just nearby cannot compete with the Fragonard collection and is a bit of a disappointment.

Grasse's *vieille ville* (old town) was at the core of the city when it declared itself an independent republic in the Middle Ages, allying itself with Pisa and Genoa, and the influence of Grasse's trading partners is evident in the Italianate architecture of the old town (Stendhal, visiting in the 19th century, declared it to be "completely Genoese in character"). The old quarter has the friendly atmosphere of a working community.

At the center of the old town is the **place aux Aires▶▶**, which is best seen in the early mornings when there is a colorful fruit and vegetable market; by late morning, the square has been taken over by tables from the cafés and restaurants underneath the surrounding arcades. Above the arcades are the old mansions of the 18th-century tanning magnates, including in one corner the grand Hotel Isnard with a typical Provençal balcony with wrought-iron work.

On the south side of the old quarter is the **Cathédrale Notre-Dame-du-Puy▶**, whose spartan, 12th-century interior contains several interesting works including three early paintings by Rubens, a rare religious painting by Fragonard, and an altarpiece from the Bréa school. Note also the splendid 18th-century carved wooden doors at the entrance.

Finally, the **Villa-Musée Fragonard** (closed Monday and Tuesday; admission) has works by this famous scion of a local family. The **Musée d'Art et d'Histoire de Provence▶** (open same as above), housed in an Italianate mansion that once belonged to Count Mirabeau's sister, displays Mirabeau's death-mask, as well as a good cross-section of Provençal decorative arts and furniture.

The smell of success
There are currently around 30 *parfumeries* surrounding Grasse, each of which employs a head perfumer known as *le nez* (the nose). He has his own laboratory where he performs a sort of olfactory orchestration to select and blend different essences to create a fragrance. He has around 3,000 different essences to choose from, and may include anything up to 300 of these in a single fragrance. There are only 300 "noses" worldwide with a good enough olfactory memory of the raw materials to be able to do this, 150 of whom work in France, and 50 of whom work in Grasse.

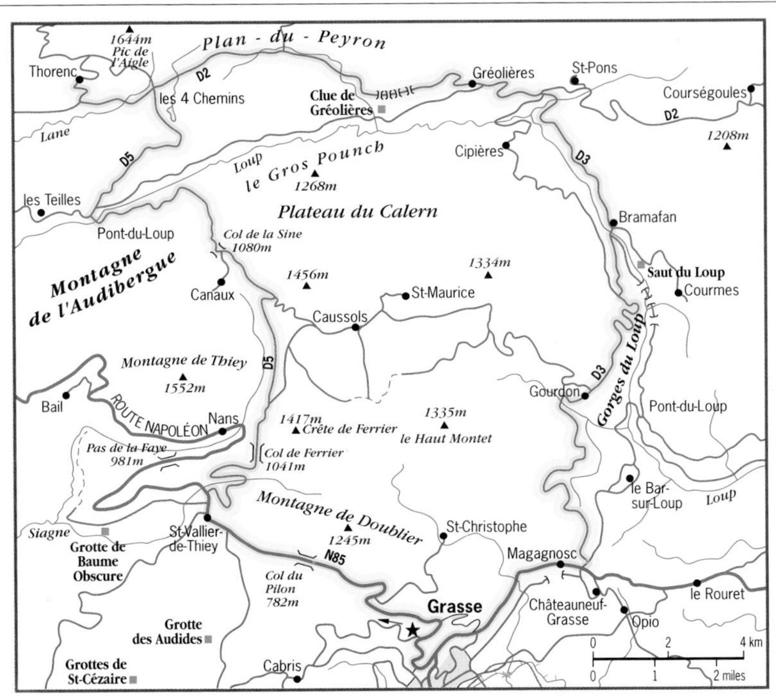

Drive Gorges du Loup

The River Loup, on its short journey from its source on Montagne de l'Audibergue down to the sea, cuts a spectacular path through the mountains. Allow 3–4 hours for this round trip from Grasse.

Take N85 northwest out of Grasse, which climbs up to the Col du Pilon. In St-Vallier-de-Thiey (see pages 240–241) turn right along scenic D5, which soon climbs up to the Col de Ferrier at 3,408 feet. Beyond the Col de la Sine, follow the road down into the valley and across the Pont-du-Loup.

At the les 4 Chemins crossroads, turn right toward Gréolières, crossing the Plan-du-Peyron, bordered by pine forests and pastureland. The road starts to descend down the Clue de Gréolières, and, as the rift opens out, there is a series of tunnels through the rock face and a belvedere for a view of the river a dizzying 1,300 feet below you.

After crossing a small stone bridge outside Gréolières the road divides: the eastern, left-hand fork, D2, ends up in Vence (see page 247); the western side of the gorge is just as spectacular, ending up in Gourdon (see page 216). Continue through Gourdon to return to Grasse.

PERFUMERY MUSEUM

▶ Guillaumes 200B4

Dominated by the ruins of a château and perched some 2,600 feet above the confluence of the Var and the Tuébi, Guillaumes is one of the largest villages in the Upper Var valley. At its entrance is the chapel of **Notre-Dame-du-Buyei**▶, which houses a remarkable painting showing the village in flames during the terrible fire of 1682.

From Guillaumes D2202 leads southward through the spectacular **Gorges de Daluis**▶▶ (named after the village of Daluis) which cut through the red schist down toward Entrevaux. Dramatic views of the Var below can be had from the serpentine road on the west bank.

Isola 2000 200C5

A popular ski resort due to its proximity to Nice (1½ hrs away), Isola 2000 was designed and built in the 1970s. Its unimaginative name derives from the altitude (at 2,000m/ 6,547 feet it is the highest ski resort in the Sud-Alpes) and the old village of **Isola** 11 miles away back down the valley.

▶▶ Juan-les-Pins 200C1

Protected by the headland of Cap d'Antibes on one side and la Croisette on the other, Juan-les-Pins has a fine sandy beach in front of what used to be a magnificent pine forest.

Although a resort had been established amid the pines as early as 1881 (by the Duke of Albany, Queen Victoria's son, who coined its name), it did not really take off until the 1920s when a restaurateur from Nice, M. Baudoin, bought up the old wooden casino and opened a cabaret restaurant. On honeymoon nearby with his third wife, American railroad heir Frank Jay Gould (who already owned two hotels on the coast) decided to go into partnership with Baudoin, and together they launched the

Enjoying the sun, sea, and silvery sands on the beach at Juan-les-Pins

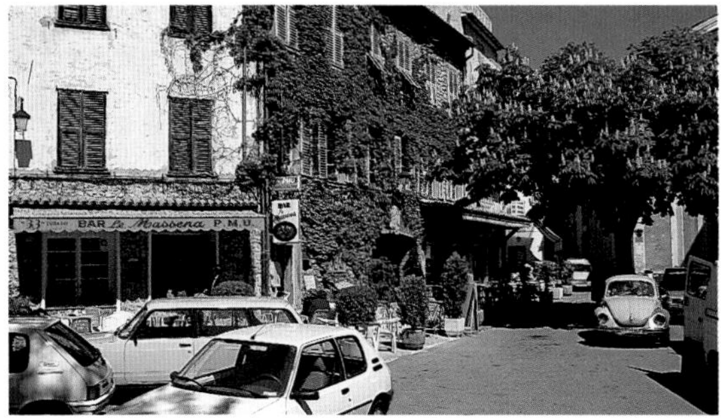

Place de la République in Levens, at the mouth of the Gorges de la Vésubie

first summer season on the Riviera — at the time, it was still only a winter tourist destination.

By the 1930s Juan-les-Pins had become a huge success, helped along by scandalized publicity — here was the first beach in France where young women dared to swim in one-piece bathing suits.

Outside the jazz festival (see panel), Juan-les-Pins' reputation for nightlife remains undiminished, with live bands competing on decibel levels in cafés, bars, and discos. Not a place to stay, unless you have a pair of earplugs, but tons of fun to visit late at night and people-watch over an exotic cocktail in a plush, streetside bar.

Jazz nights
The popularity of Juan-les-Pins was boosted in the 1950s with the arrival of singers and jazz musicians such as Edith Piaf, Eddie Constantine, and Sidney Bechet (who was married here and has a square named after him). Jazz is still going strong, with the famous International Jazz Festival taking place in the second two weeks of July every year. Each evening of the festival is devoted to just one group or musician, with outdoor performances taking place in a pine grove (*les pinedes*) against the romantic backdrop of the Esterel and the Mediterranean. Tel. 92 90 53 00.

► **Lantosque** *201D3*

There can be few other villages in Provence that have suffered quite so many landslides and earthquakes as Lantosque, with almost the entire village having been sent hurtling down into the ravine below numerous times during the 15th, 16th, and 17th centuries. It was rebuilt so many times because Lantosque was an important staging post on the *route du sel* (the salt route), which was followed by caravans of pack animals carrying this precious commodity from the *salines* of Hyères up to the Sud-Alpes and beyond into Piedmont.

Lantosque still looks as if it is about to slide down the hillside from its perch on a rocky spur overlooking the Vésubie valley, but beyond here the valley itself opens out into richer greener pastures. When covered in snow, these slopes are much appreciated by skiers from the coast who flock here in winter to the small but trendy ski resort of **la Bollène-Vésubie**, northeast of Lantosque along D70.

► **Levens** *200C3*

This large village (unusual because it once had two rows of encircling medieval ramparts) dominates the plains at the mouth of the **Gorges de la Vésubie►►** leading back up into the Vésubie valley. From Levens, D19 on the east bank and D2565 on the west bank snake round the scenic gorges before meeting up at **St-Jean-la-Rivière**. A hair-raising, 4-mile detour from here leads up to one of the most isolated sanctuaries in the mountains, the **Madone d'Utelle►►**. The panorama down toward the sea from the peak just past the chapel is outstanding; the chapel itself is still an active pilgrimage center, with processions on Easter Monday, the Monday after Pentecost, August 15, and September 8.

Dying for a vacation
As early as 1861 Menton was put on the map of international tourism thanks to a book written by an English doctor, J. Henry Bennett, that lauded the virtues of its climate for invalids. By 1870 Menton had become a *chic* seaside resort with sumptuous villas and luxury hotels financed by aristocratic English, German, and Russian tourists. Many more people came in the hopes that Menton's warmth and sunshine would alleviate the symptoms of consumption (tuberculosis): among the better known, whose graves can be found in the hilltop cemetery, were Katherine Mansfield, Aubrey Beardsley, and the Spanish writer Blasco Ibáñez.

►►► Menton *201E2*

Hemmed in by a chain of mountains behind the bay which protect it from the cold north winds, Menton is known for its unusually warm climate. No doubt this is what prompted the first ever visitors to the Riviera to settle here: the 30,000-year-old skull of "Menton man," discovered nearby in 1884, is one of the oldest paleolithic relics in France.

The name Menton was first mentioned in the 13th century, and the town was acquired by Charles Grimaldi of Monaco in 1346. In 1793 it became part of France, then reverted to the Grimaldi family in 1814 under the Treaty of Paris. In 1848 Menton revolted against the high taxes demanded by Monaco and opted for independence under the protection of Sardinia. In 1860 they decided to rejoin France, when Napoléon III bought Menton and its neighbor, Roquebrune, from Charles III of Monaco for four million gold francs.

Today Menton is a charming resort that tries hard to counter its image as a retirement haven with a lively program of arts, culture, and festivals. The most celebrated event is the 60-year-old Fête du Citron (Menton has been famous for its lemons for more than 500 years), which lasts for ten days from Shrove Tuesday onward. Now equally as well known is the Chamber Music Festival in August, which is held in the attractive setting of the **Parvis St-Michel** overlooking the harbor. There is also a biennial Art Exhibition.

The most important museum in Menton is the excellent **Musée Cocteau►►** (closed Monday and Tuesday; admission) housed in a quaint truncated watchtower on the seafront. The museum contains mosaics and tapestries and his portrayal of love affairs in the *Inamorati* series as well as photographs, poems and ceramics. Another must is the Cocteau-decorated **Salle des Mariages►** (daily except Saturday and Sunday) on the right-hand side of the town hall in the main square. The skull of "Menton man" can be found in the **Musée Municipal** (closed Monday and Tuesday) which also houses rock carvings from the Vallée des Merveilles (see page 246) and thousands of prehistoric exhibits.

Menton, a resort that enjoys a particularly favorable climate

Olives

■ Rare is the Provençal market without at least one stall groaning under the weight of colorful vats or baskets of olives, with as many different herb flavorings as there are days in the month.....■

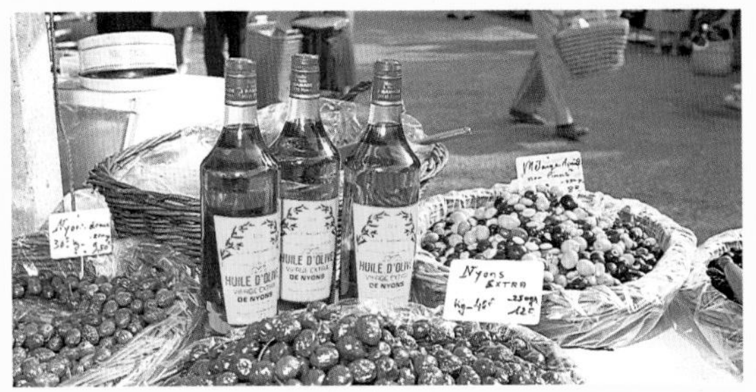

Top: olive trees are planted with enough space between them for a mechanical harvester to operate
Left: a scene typical of any Provençal market

All thanks to the Greeks Wild olive trees grow naturally in Provence but their fruit is sour and produces very little oil. The cultivation of more productive varieties (and the art of grafting) was introduced by the Greeks some time around 600B.C.

Olives grow equally well in limestone or sandy soil and, provided their roots do not get too wet, they can live for hundreds of years. What *will* kill them is a late, hard frost — such as the one in 1956 that destroyed hundreds of olive groves.

A young tree starts to bear fruit in its fifth or sixth year and attains its full yield when around 25 to 30 years old. Wild trees can reach heights of 50 to 70 feet, but modern varieties are pruned, making them easier to harvest.

The harvest Olives are usually harvested from the beginning of November through to January. At first the olives are green, but they ripen on the tree, turning brown and then black.

Harvesting is traditionally a family affair, with friends and neighbors joining in. The old method was for someone to climb up the tree and shake the fruit loose on to mats spread on the ground beneath, although green olives have to be picked by hand because they do not dislodge so easily. Nowadays mechanical harvesters do the work by grasping the tree trunk and shaking it until the olives tumble down.

Olive oil A mature tree can produce up to 65 pounds of olives, yielding between 5 and 6 quarts of oil. Even if you only have one or two trees in your garden, the nearest *moulin à huile* (olive mill) will process your olives to give the appropriate amount of oil.

The first pressing produces the best olive oil, sold as *premier pression à froide vierge extra*, or simply *vierge extra* (extra virgin). The residue (the *grignon*, or pulp) is pressed again with more cold water added, and labeled *fine* or *extra fine*. The third pressing, with warm water, produces an oil that is used commercially.

Cracked olives
Raw olives are inedible unless properly cured, and one of the most popular ways of doing this at home is to make *olives cassées*, or cracked olives. The recipe is simple: the olives are broken with a mallet and then mixed with water and equal amounts of wood ash (preferably olive or vine wood). This mixture is left for two days (with frequent stirrings) and the olives are then rinsed in cold water and left to soak for another week. Finally, they are covered in brine flavored with coriander, fennel, and orange peel, and put into storage jars.

Scourtins
Before the advent of modern hydraulic presses, the olive paste was spread on flat, densely woven mats called *scourtins* before the oil was squeezed out in a hand mill. The first *scourtins* were made from straw, but later sisal or coconut fiber was used instead. *Scourtins* are still produced in Provence, and you can sometimes find them in souvenir stores.

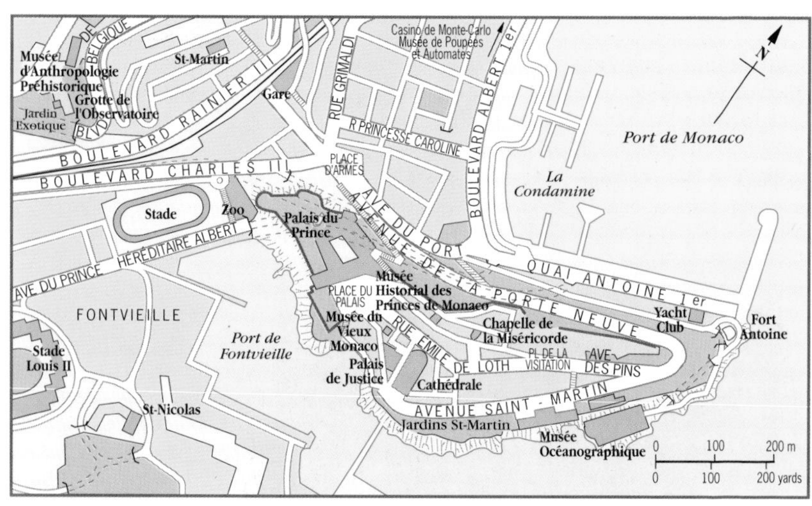

224

Safe on the streets
Monaco likes to portray an image of stability and safety, and is said to have more remote-controlled cameras and police on the streets than practically anywhere else in Europe (yes, you can walk around wearing jewelry at night). Crime (apart from the white-collar variety) and delinquency are virtually nonexistent: it is said that if it were not for a steady stream of divorce cases, the Law Courts could have shut up shop long ago.

The view from old Monaco down to a new marina

▶▶ Monaco and Monte Carlo *201D2*

Monaco conjures up images of glamour and wealth, of high-rollers winning or losing fortunes in the casino, high-octane Formula One racing cars screeching through the streets during the annual Grand Prix, high society cavorting in nightclubs until dawn. Yet Monaco is a surprisingly sedate place: in the lobby of the Hôtel de Paris you are more likely to see bored-looking businessmen hammering out deals. In the gaming room built on the side of the Café de Paris, gambling has been reduced to the unglamorous level of ranks of one-armed bandits. The sanitized streets of the old town hold about as much allure as a tawdry souvenir shop — of which it also has plenty.

But Monaco is still worth visiting for the day, if only to gaze at the wonderful *belle époque* casino and the lavish hotel lobbies — and to marvel at the justly famed Musée Océanographique, probably one of the best in Europe, which alone justifies the trip.

The principality of Monaco covers a mere 482 acres (about 0.75 square mile, much of which has been reclaimed from the sea), making it Europe's second smallest independent state after the Vatican.

After they had seized Monaco, the Grimaldis (see panel) continued to expand along the coast, eventually taking control of Menton, Roquebrune, Antibes, and Grimaud. In 1848 Menton and Roquebrune declared themselves independent republics, fed up with the high taxes imposed by the Grimaldis on their lemons and olives. Facing bankruptcy, Charles III decided to take advantage of his independence from France and open a casino, since gambling was still illegal in France at the time. But the venture failed, and it was not until 1863 when he called in François Blanc, director of the hugely successful casino in Bad Homburg, that it began to take off. The royal coffers were so flush that Charles decided to abolish all taxes, a situation that still holds today.

His successor Albert I lavished money on the arts and sciences and commissioned Charles Garnier (architect of the Paris Opéra) to rebuild the Casino, incorporating an opera house, which became the home of Diaghilev's Ballet Russe. He initiated the first Monte Carlo rally in 1911, but spent most of his vast inherited wealth roaming the oceans on a series of fabulous yachts collecting scientific data for his beloved Oceanographic Institute.

These halcyon days came to an abrupt end in 1933 when France legitimized gambling, and by the time Rainier III came to the throne in 1949 Monaco was relatively down on its luck. However, this tax-free zone still attracted offshore finance and Rainier has tried to build on this as well as encourage business tourism, conferences (a brand-new convention center is due to open in 1996/7) and diversify into light industry. Even though Monte Carlo now has four casinos, gambling today only brings in 4 percent of revenues — compared to 95 percent in the golden days at the turn of the century.

The principality continues to attract numerous anonymous tax exiles, not to mention more well-known faces such as Boris Becker, Claudia Schiffer, Karl Lagerfield, and (until his death in 1993) the writer Anthony Burgess.

Guarding the Grimaldi home, the Palais du Prince, in Old Monaco

François the Spiteful

In the 12th century Monaco became the property of the Genoese, who were split between the Guelfs (allied to the Pope) and the Ghibellines (allied to the German emperor). Legend has it that in 1297 the chief of the Guelf faction, a Grimaldi known as François the Spiteful, disguised himself and his men as monks and knocked on the door of the Ghibelline garrison in Monaco asking for help. Having been admitted, they pulled out their swords and massacred the garrison. This is the origin of the two monks brandishing swords on the crest of the Grimaldi family, who have (apart from a couple of hiccups) ruled Monaco ever since.

The Jardin Exotique, overlooking the sea

Monaco-ville▶▶ On the northwest corner of the rock on which the old town was built is the **Palais du Prince▶** (guided tours daily from mid-June to September; admission), with its Court of Honor, Hercules Gallery (with 17th-century frescoes), Throne Room, and various plushly decorated state apartments. The ornate facade of the palace overlooks the **place du Palais▶**, where the rows of cannons (a donation from Louis XIV) are complemented by neatly stacked piles of cannon balls: the Toytown impression is further reinforced by the daily changing of the guard which takes place at 11.55A.M. sharp every day.

The **old town** stretches south from the palace; immaculately kept but about as stimulating as the endless Prince Rainier mugs, dishtowels, and ashtrays on sale in just about every shop. The **Musée Historial des Princes de Monaco** (open daily; admission), which promises 40 "bigger than life" waxworks tracing the history of the Grimaldi family, is equally dull.

At the heart of the old town is the **cathédrale**, a neo-Romanesque structure inside which is one of Louis Bréa's masterpieces, the **retable de St-Nicolas**, as well as his *Pietà de curé Teste*. Here too are the tombs of all the Grimaldi, including that of Princess Grace, which is often smothered in bouquets from admirers.

The highlight of the old town is undoubtedly the splendid **Musée Océanographique▶▶▶** (open daily; admission) on the headland. Founded in 1910 by Prince Albert I, this huge edifice was built into the cliff-face to hold the specimens he collected on his many voyages and to house marine research laboratories (under the direction of Jacques Cousteau 1957–1988). The excellent aquarium features the weirdest and most wonderful fish from the world's oceans, including the spectacular giant groupers and jacks, piranha, and black-tipped sharks swarming over a small, sunken boat. There are also beautifully lit displays of living corals. Don't come on a Sunday (particularly a wet one) when the crowds will be three or four deep around every tank.

The upper floor has a bit of everything, from natural history to displays on the atmosphere and deep sea trenches. It also has the world's first submarine (powered by pedals, it was built in 1774 and used by the U.S. Navy against English ships during the Revolutionary War) and models of all the magnificent ships which Albert had built for his voyages.

If the museum prompts your curiosity about the underwater world you can take a ride on the **Seabus** (tel. 93 30 64 15) which does a 1 hour tour departing from the quai des États-Unis in the port.

Fontvieille Just off the **Moyenne Corniche** above Fontvieille is the **Jardin Exotique▶** (open daily; admission), which has an extensive collection of some 7,000 succulents and cacti. Guided tours of the **Grotte de l'Observatoire**, an ancient cave, once inhabited, are included in the ticket.

Monte Carlo▶▶▶ No visit here is complete without a look (let alone a flutter) inside the **Casino de Monte-Carlo▶▶**, for many years the chief income-earner of the principality and still its main showpiece. You have to be over 21 (with passport as proof) to enter the American Room, where slot machines line the walls around the crap, roulette, and blackjack tables — and the gilded rococo ceilings have to be seen. The stakes get higher and the decor more extravagant once you reach the European rooms, which you will have to pay to enter.

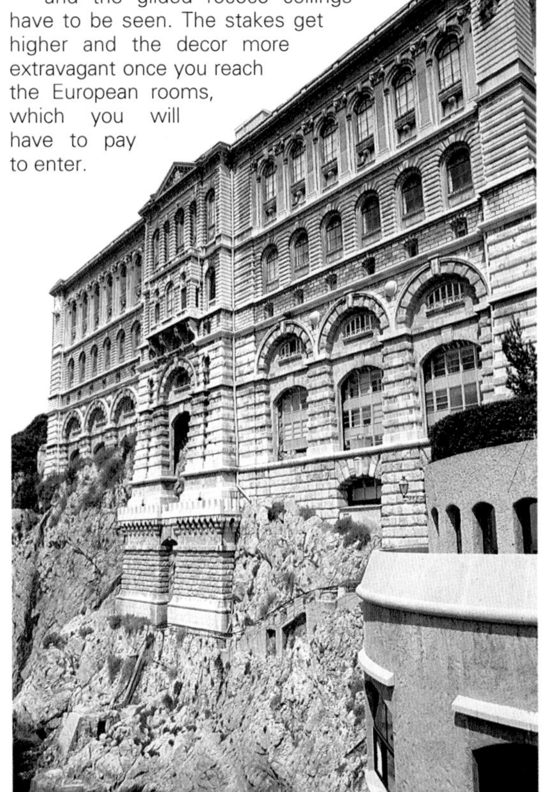

"The Man Who Broke The Bank"
When Garnier's casino first opened in 1878 the clientele were almost entirely wealthy, visiting several times a week from the other resorts for a bit of fun. But the passion for gambling spread and people began to believe they could make their fortunes — partly inspired by Charles Deville Wells, who turned $400 into $40,000 in a three-day gambling spree in 1891 later immortalized in the song *The Man Who Broke The Bank At Monte Carlo*. Other gamblers were not so lucky, and the growing number of suicides was covered up by the casino for fear of bad publicity.

Founded in 1910, the Musée Océanographique is one of France's most popular museums

Faites vos jeux — *Monaco's famous Casino*

Flanking the casino on either side are the **Café de Paris** and the **Hôtel de Paris**, both worth a look-in: the Café de Paris for the clientele and the Hôtel de Paris for its sumptuous lobby.

The only museum in Monte-Carlo is the **Musée National des Poupées et Automates►** (open daily; admission) with a collection of over 400 dolls, automated toys, and miniature doll's houses from the 18th and 19th centuries.

On the other side of Monte Carlo are the artifical beaches and Olympic-size pools of the Larvotto beaches (admission).

You will also have to pay for sidewalk-space during the annual Monte-Carlo Grand Prix (May); the Monte-Carlo rally takes place in January. The best time to visit the old town is during the annual carnival and fireworks display (September).

Sky-high gastronomy
Although there are "only" half-a-dozen restaurants in the village, Mougins' gastronomic reputation has extended far and wide largely due to the presence of Roger Vergé, one of France's most celebrated and charismatic chefs, who owns two of the restaurants and also runs an expensive gourmet food shop. Critics say that the exorbitant prices —up to 800 francs ($160) per person in some restaurants — are not matched by the quality of the food and that it is all just hype: nonetheless, Mougins continues to be popular, although anyone on a tight budget will have a hard time finding an affordable meal.

►► Mougins *200C1*

It makes a change to find a *village perché* behind the coast that has not been overrun with souvenir shops – but then such downscale commercialism probably would not be allowed to spoil the tasteful medieval streets of Mougins, where the much more serious art of gastronomy holds sway (see panel).

If you are not here to eat, Mougins is still worth a visit, if only to wander around the immaculate streets with their carefully restored houses. There is also an interesting **Musée de la Photographie►** (open 1–7P.M. Wednesday and Sunday, 2–11P.M. daily during July and August, closed Tuesday and November; admission) just next to the Porte Sarrasine. Art exhibitions are also held in the old wash house, **la Lavoir**, on the picturesque place de le Mairie.

Just outside Mougins (1.2 miles southeast on D3) is the charming **Chapelle de Notre-Dame de Vie►►** on a hilltop flanked by ancient cypress trees. This 12th-century retreat was largely rebuilt in 1646 and used to be a popular place of pilgrimage: stillborn babies were brought here and it was believed that they came back to life during Mass just long enough to be baptized. Picasso spent the last years of his life in a villa hidden away behind the trees just opposite the chapel.

Back down toward Cannes at the *Aire des Breguières* exit from *autoroute* A8 is the huge **Musée de l'Automobiliste►►** (open daily except mid-November–mid-December; admission), which has a vast collection of vehicles, from vintage Bugattis to racing cars and armored cars.

► la Napoule *200B1*

At the western end of the Golfe de Napoule opposite Cannes, la Napoule marks the start of the Riviera. On the road above the marina is the extraordinary **château►**, a folly rebuilt on the site of a medieval castle in 1918 by the American sculptor and millionaire Henry Clews. The gateway is ornamented with a series of mythical beasts, grotesque monkeys, toads, serpents, and fish, a theme that is carried through in the interior (guided tours daily from 3–5P.M. in summer, closed Monday and November; admission). The château also houses the Napoule Art Foundation.

Boules

■ As Provençal as *pastis*, the outdoor game of *boules* is a familiar sight in every town and village during daylight hours — sometimes even at night too, if there is a floodlit *boules* court.....■

The game *Boules* looks like a fairly easy game; certainly anyone can take part and enjoy it from the first throw. However, for serious players there is a great deal of gamesmanship involved — not to mention plenty of noisy Gallic exclamations and dramatic gesticulation.

The game starts with a small wooden ball, the *cochonnet*, being thrown some distance up the court, which is usually a reasonably flat, hard area of gravel or sand — or even an asphalt parking lot or road. Each player has three steel balls (they were once made from wood, studded with tacks), usually etched with different patterns or colors for identification. The winner is the person who throws their ball closest to the *cochonnet*.

Tactics Although it sounds straightforward enough, the skill (and the fun) of *boules* is in choosing the right tactic to get your ball next to the marker. For instance, you can simply roll your ball along the ground until it gently comes to rest (you hope) next to the *cochonnet*. But your opponent (who becomes the *tireur*) can "fire" his ball at yours, knocking it out of the way. Or he can "fire" at the *cochonnet*, knocking it toward his other balls on the court — a tactic called *faire le carreau*. At the conclusion of the round, there will be much careful scrutiny of the positioning of the balls to see who has won, often involving a tape measure to check distances to the millimeter.

Pétanque The original game of *boules* was known as *la longue* — that is, over a long distance (usually 30–65 feet) — in which players would make three short hops from a marker before throwing their balls. Nowadays, *la longue* has been overtaken in popularity by *pétanque*, a variation which originated in la Ciotat. The game starts off *pieds tanques* ("feet together") and the balls are thrown over a shorter distance, usually 23–33 feet.

Social boules
Glance at the window of any rural café and you often see a handwritten notice announcing "*Boules Tournament— Vendredi 6pm.*" For many little villages this is the social event of the week, with much discussion as to who is going to be on which team, and plenty of *pastis* to lubricate play. Championships are often held between different villages, with prizes for the winners. Competitions are usually between teams of three (*triplettes*) or four (*quadrettes*), with points awarded for each of the team's balls closest to the *cochonnet*.

Boules *is part of the fabric of life in Provence*

Up and down the hill
Around 1000 B.C. the Ligurians built two forts here, one near the mouth of the Paillon river and the other further up the valley. The Phocaeans set up a small trading post, Nikaia, from the 6th century B.C. Plagued by Ligurian pirates, they asked the Romans for help, who arrived in 200 B.C., founding a town near the old *oppidum*, which they named *Cemenelum* (now the district of Cimiez). Cemenelum became the capital of the Roman Alpes-Maritime, with 20,000 inhabitants by the 3rd century A.D. It was destroyed during the barbarian invasions, and the inhabitants moved down to the more easily defended site of Nikaia in the bay.

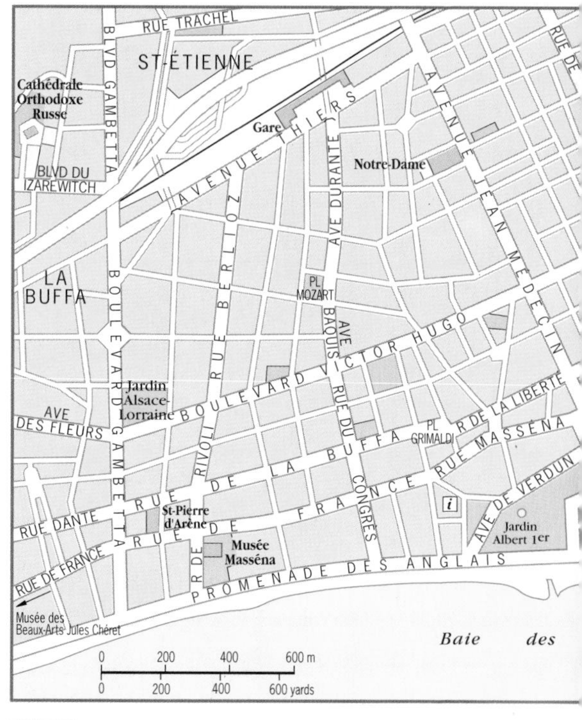

▶▶▶ Nice *201D2*

Like the bubbling fountains in the place Masséna, Nice sparkles by day and night, confident of its position as Queen of the Riviera. It might not attract celebrities in the way Monaco or St-Tropez do, but it is far more interesting for that — a lively, energetic city with an independent character that is not at all swayed by tourism.

After the fall of the Roman town of *Cemenelum* the port of Nikaia was the main medieval settlement. The city prospered under the Counts of Provence but in the 14th century it passed into the hands of the Counts of Savoy, and mostly remained under Italian control for the next 400 years. In 1860 Napoleon III signed a secret treaty with the House of Savoy in which Nice would revert to France in return for helping Vittore Emanuele II of Savoy drive the Austrians out of northern Italy.

By this time the first tourists had begun to arrive, and in 1864 the building of the train station sealed Nice's future as a Riviera resort. By 1827 around 600 visitors were descending on Nice for the winter season and by the end of the century this had risen to 20,000. Construction began of the many *belle époque* mansions and follies so beloved of the aristocracy. Queen Victoria and other titled heads of state added to the allure of the resort, and by the start of World War I there were 150,000 visitors per year. With the advent of the "summer vacation" in the 1920s, Nice switched seasons. Now the emphasis is on year-round tourism, with the development of such facilities as the Acropolis convention center.

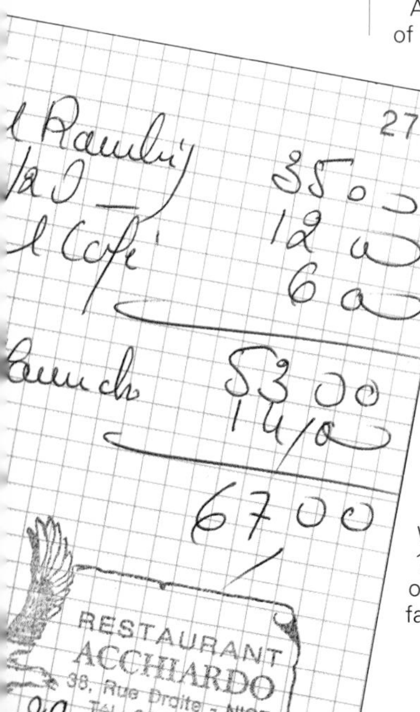

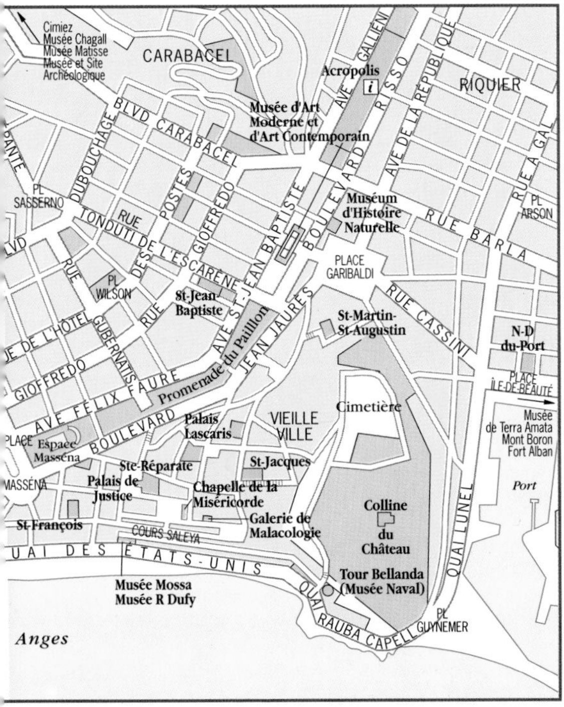

Seafront and town centre▶▶ The **Promenade des Anglais▶▶** (see panel, page 234) has been widened many times since the 1820s and has since been extended right out to the Nice–Côte d'Azur airport, becoming fairly traffic-clogged as a result. About midway along the promenade the **Hôtel Negresco** still stands facing the Mediterranean in all its domed splendor. Behind the Negresco is the **Musée Masséna** (open daily, closed Monday and November); it does contain a couple of fine 15th-century paintings by Jacques Durandi and a Bréa polyptych but the rest is all-to-predictable Napoleonic souvenirs and dusty First Empire mementos.

West of the Musée Masséna is the **Musée des Beaux-Arts Jules Chéret** (open daily, closed Monday and November), with 17th-century Italian works right through to the Impressionists and contemporary works, with all sorts of oddities such as Kees Van Dongen's entertaining paintings of bejeweled and/or completely naked *belles dames* of the roaring twenties.

It is worth the trek north up blvd Gambetta to the **Cathédrale Orthodoxe Russe▶▶** (open daily except Sunday; admission) beyond the overpass and railway tracks: this colorful, elaborate cathedral (which is still in use) was financed by Tsar Nicolas I in memory of his son Nicolas, who died of consumption in Nice.

At its eastern end, the Promenade des Anglais stops at the Jardin Albert 1er, where there is a small *Théâtre de Verdure* (it offers a program of concerts in the summer months). Behind here is the **place Masséna▶** with its gardens, fountains, and *belle époque* façades, such as that of the Hôtel Plaza Concorde.

The Riviera corniches
The three famous *corniches* ("cliff roads") of the Riviera run between Menton and Nice along a dizzying stretch of coastline overlooking the resorts and beaches. The most spectacular views are from the Grande Corniche (D2564), built by Napoleon along the route of the old Via Julia Augustus; the route passes through la Turbie (see page 243) and some of the most sweeping panoramas are found above Èze. The Moyenne Corniche (N7) also has good views and is the only way to reach Èze itself (see page 214) by car. The lowest of the three is the Corniche Inférieure (N98), which gives access to all the coastal resorts and is the most prone to traffic jams during summer. The top two *corniches* are notoriously accident-prone so if you are in a hurry it is better to take the A8 *autoroute*, which carves its way through the mountains behind the three coast roads from Nice as far as the Italian border.

Crowds enjoying the Mardi Gras in Nice

From the place Masséna a broad concourse runs northeast, following the course of the river Paillon, now buried underground. This boulevard was the site chosen for Jacques Médecin's grand civic projects such as the enormous **Musée d'Art Moderne et d'Art Contemporain▶▶**, known as MAMAC; four octagonal marble towers linked by glassed-in walkways. The museum (open daily 11A.M.–6P.M. except Monday, until 10P.M. on Friday) concentrates on the Second Nice School, with Pop Art and New Realist works, as well as other influential figures from the 1960s and 1970s such as Lichtenstein, Warhol and Niki de St-Phalle. Most of the displays were conceived as a send-up of not just consumer society but the whole art world. Next to it is a huge conference center: cunningly disguised as a gigantic air-conditioning vent, the **Acropolis** could not be more inappropriately named.

West of the Paillon is the central district of Nice, bisected by the main high street, the avenue Jean Médecin, busy with cafés, movie theaters, banks, department stores, and the large Nice–Etoile shopping center.

Cimiez▶▶▶ Beyond the train line to the north the streets start to climb up to the smart district of Cimiez, at the beginning of which is the intriguing **Musée National Message Biblique Marc Chagall▶▶▶** (open daily, closed Tuesday), dedicated to Chagall's canvasses on Old Testament themes. Chagall also contributed the stained glass windows.

Farther up the hill is the **Musée Matisse▶▶▶** (open daily except Tuesday) recently reopened after a major renovation. Matisse came to live in Nice in 1917, and the museum contains a good cross-section of his works from the early experiments with Fauvism through to the cutout compositions done just before he died here in 1954, aged 85. The museum holds the world's largest collection of his drawings

(238), etchings (218), and nearly all the bronze sculptures he ever made. Next to the museum is the **Musée et Site Archéologique▶** (open daily, closed Sunday mornings, Monday and November), which stands on the site of the Roman town of *Cemenelum*.

Vieille ville▶▶▶ The *vieille ville* is beneath the Colline du Château at the eastern end of the Baie des Anges. You might once have risked losing your wallet in these alleyways, but since the 1980s massive redevelopment has turned it into one of the trendiest areas in the city — an admirable mix of bistros and boutiques alongside shops serving residents' needs and no-nonsense cafés.

In the backstreets you will come across the 17th-century **Cathédrale de Ste-Réparate▶**, a baroque extravaganza topped by a roof of colorful Niçois tiles. One block north is the Genoese-style **Palais Lascaris▶**, which houses a museum (open daily, closed Monday and November) with sumptuous 17th- and 18th-century paintings, furnishings, and tapestries. On one corner of the **cours Saleya▶▶**, site of the daily market, is the **Chapelle de la Miséricorde▶**, with a distinctive baroque façade. Next to it is the tiny **Galerie de Malacologie** (open daily in summer except Sunday and Monday) with a collection of 1,500 shells from around the world.

On the south side of the cours Saleya a double row of low buildings, known as les Ponchettes, house a number of seafood restaurants while on the seaward side there are a pair of quirky museums: the **Galerie-Musée Mossa▶** (closed Sunday mornings and Monday) houses the Symbolist works of Gustav-Adolf Mossa, whose morbid watercolors revolve around the themes of love, sex, and death. A few doors along the **Musée Raoul Dufy▶** (same hours as the above) shows a revolving selection of much more lighthearted fare from the extensive collection of Dufy's works held by the Musée des Beaux-Arts.

The Nice Carnival
Nice's famous carnival during the two weeks before Lent dates back to the 13th century. It fizzled out around 1850, but was revived in 1873 by Alexis Mossa (the curator of the Musée des Beaux-Arts) and his son Gustave-Adolfe, who created a burlesque parade that escorted a float bearing the figure of King Carnival (*Sa Majesté Carnaval*) through the town. During the festivities — which involve dancing, battles of flowers, and confetti, and cavalcades of *grosses têtes* (figures with huge papier-mâché heads) — the King sits enthroned in the place Masséna until he is taken down to the seafront and ceremoniously burned amidst a gigantic fireworks display on Mardi Gras night.

One of many processions during the famous Nice Carnival

The Promenade
One of the first celebrities to visit Nice was the English writer Tobias Smollett, who lived here for ten months in 1763. He was soon followed by a bevy of English milords and ladies attracted by the climate and the casino. In the 1820s they clubbed together to build a promenade (later named the Promenade des Anglais) so they could stroll along the shoreline: and also supposedly for the altruistic motive of helping the local unemployed through the harsh winters of 1820 and 1821, but in reality because they were fed up with being bothered by beggars on the streets.

Eastern hills and the port► Above the *vieille ville* is the **Colline du Château►**, where from the belvedere an artificial cascade draws the eye down to the rooftops of Vieux Nice. On the other side of the hill is the **port►►**. Nice's first "port" was simply an anchorage on the other side of the Colline du Château; the present harbor was excavated in the late 18th century and named Port Lympnia and enlarged a hundred years later.

At the back of the port is the **Musée de Terra Amata►** (closed Monday), which occupies the first floor of an apartment block. The explanation for this rather bizarre location is that when excavators started to build the flats they discovered traces of the very first settlements in the area, dating back 400,000 years: these now form the core of the museum.

The road continues beyond the port up to the wooded slopes of **Mont Boron►**. The 150-acre Mount Boron forest was planted in the 1860s and now has about 7 miles of hiking trails around the hilltop. The best of the several forts around the hill is **Fort Alban►**, a rare example of 16th-century French military architecture. Its four turrets, adorned with glazed Niçois tiles, give it a sort of Playland look, but as a watchtower its position is superb.

A wedding ceremony in Nice's cathedral

■ Ever since *The French Connection* hit movie screens, Marseille's reputation as an international drug-trafficking center has been well known, and the local papers are never short of copy on shootouts between members of the local mafia (known as the *milieu*) or arrests of leading gang members involved in vice rings and protection rackets. But that's Marseille, and the Riviera is a different matter...or is it?.....■

'Azur Dimanch

assins du ministre
rchés sur la Côte

r Hugues Chevallier
t Tomas Maréchal

u 'Yann d'Arc' comme tout le monde

mais parce qu'il ne mar
d'aller à Montpelier à la
types qui ressemble à la
les témoins.'

Grahame Greene's *bête noire!* Nice likes to portray an image of the *grande dame* of the Riviera but beneath the surface the murky currents of civic corruption run deep. As long ago as 1982 the late Graham Greene published a booklet entitled *J'Accuse: The Dark Side of Nice*, which pilloried the city's mayor, Jacques Médecin, for his links with the *milieu* and for siphoning off public money for his private use. The Médecin dynasty had been in power in Nice since 1928: Jacques, who took over the post from his father in 1966, vehemently denied Greene's accusations. However, the author's prophecies proved correct when Jacques fled to Uruguay in 1990 after the Justice Department uncovered a swindle involving funds for the Nice Opéra being siphoned off into his personal bank account. He was arrested by Interpol in 1993 and now faces charges involving the misuse of millions of francs of public money.

Jewel-heists and bombs Outside of Nice the *milieu* continues to operate with impunity. Kickbacks on big projects are a way of life (see panel). A popular and successful nightclub in Hyères was recently destroyed by a bomb — attributed to Mafia rivals. The Mafia were also suspected when Hollywood mogul Marvin Davis's gold Cadillac was hijacked in 1993 and he was robbed of $10 million worth of jewels at Cap d'Antibes. But worse was to come…

Death of a "saint" In February 1994 Yann Piat, dubbed "Yann d'Arc" by the French press for her relentless campaign against Mafia corruption, was murdered near her home in Hyères. Two masked gunmen shot Mme Piat from a motorcycle as she was being driven home — the murder bore all the hallmarks of a classic contract killing and shocked the nation not just for its brutality but because the assassination of a prominent member of the National Assembly was seen as a direct challenge to the French state. Just prior to her death, Mme Piat claimed to have uncovered evidence of Mafia money being laundered through Hyères's casino and various real estate projects.

Unanswered allegations Three months after Yann Piat's death an employee of the right-wing PACA administration was found dead just before he was due to hand over to a magistrate documents naming politicians involved in corruption along the coast. Fernand Saincène, who claimed trade tax exemptions were being traded for political favors, had apparently "committed suicide."

Mafia-sur-Mer
The dockyards of La Seyne near Toulon have been derelict since 1985, but a recent attempt to revitalize 75 acres of docks has been scuppered by greedy local *milieu* bosses. A British consortium had spent three years planning an innovative maritime and business complex, the World Sea Centre, but the $195 million Franco-British deal was called off in 1994 after demands for $1.6 million in bribes were turned down by the project's backers. Now the dockyards will remain empty in La Seyne, which has been dubbed Mafia-sur-Mer by the French media.

Gene Hackman in French Connection II

▶▶▶ **Parc National du Mercantour** *200C4*

Covering the highest peaks and the most dramatic scenery of the Alpes-Maritimes, the Parc National du Mercantour stretches for over 80 miles along the Italian border. Established in 1979, it is the most recently designated national park in France.

Covering over 168,000 acres, the park lies mostly in the *département* of the Alpes-Maritimes (131,000 acres), with the rest in the Alpes de Haute-Provence (37,000 acres). It is divided between a central protected zone (a core strip of the most inaccessible areas, including the Vallée des Merveilles, see page 246) and the peripheral access zone surrounding it.

The landscapes of the Mercantour are highly varied, ranging from pastureland and alpine forests to glacial lakes, canyons, and picturesque peaks. The park starts at an altitude of 1,600 feet and as you climb upward the pines and larches of the lower slopes give way to beautiful Alpine meadows and rock-strewn scree, before reaching permanent snow on peaks around 10,000 feet high.

Above these wild landscapes circle birds of prey such as golden eagles, kestrels, and falcons — and the rare lammergeyer vulture, successfully reintroduced after becoming extinct here. Other feathered fauna include the ptarmigan, which changes its summer plumage of mottled brown for a winter plumage of pure white, the great spotted woodpecker, hoopoe, citril finches, ortolan, and rock buntings.

The small Alpine marmot can be seen sitting on its haunches in meadowlands — until it spots a predator, and disappears in a flash down its burrow. Mouflons (wild mountain sheep) were reintroduced from Italy in the 1950s, and the chamois, ibex, and boar populations are all now increasing. There are also foxes, stoats, and hares — including the mountain hare which, like the ptarmigan, changes color to white in winter.

The flora of the park is equally remarkable, with around 2,000 of the 4,200 species found in France represented, including 40 that are endemic to the region. In springtime the meadows are ablaze with bellflowers and blue gentians. There is also the elusive edelweiss, and, rarest of all, the big, spiky saxifrage (*Saxifraga florulenta*), which has become the symbol of the park.

Reunited reserve
The Mercantour was originally a hunting reserve, created by Italian royalty in 1859; it remained an Italian enclave until after World War II. In 1946 it was split, with Italy gaining the major part and France the rest. The two were symbolically joined together again with the creation of the Aregentera National Park in Piedmont in 1980, forming a huge and unique protected area for alpine flora and fauna.

Park rules
Picking flowers is forbidden in the park, as are camping, fires, and dogs. There are park information centers at Allos, Barcelonnette, Entraunes, St-Dalmas-de-Tende, St-Étienne-de-Tinée, St-Martin-Vésubie, and St-Sauveur-sur-Tinée. Any of these bureaux can provide information on walking and "VTT" (mountain bike) trails, as well as guided tours.

The Parc National du Mercantour is a region of unspoiled wilderness and imposing peaks

►► Peille *201D2*

An unspoiled *village perché* with a great deal of character, Peille has several lovely old buildings in cobbled alleys and passageways. Inside the **Église Ste-Mairie►** (ask at the hospice for the key) is an interesting painting of the village in medieval times, with its castle (now in ruins) which once belonged to the Counts of Provence, and a fine 16th century *Polyptych of the Rosary* by Honoré Bertone of the Niçois school.

A typical medieval street in the village perché *of Peille*

► Peillon *201D2*

Peille's twin and neighbor, Peillon enjoys a spectacular setting high above the Paillon valley. The vaulted alleys and steep steps that climb up through the village are lined by carefully restored houses, many looking older than their 16th-century origins. The **Chapelle des Pénitents Blancs►** is decorated with dramatic frescoes depicting *The Passion of Christ*, painted in 1485 by Giovanni Canavesio.

► Puget-Théniers *200B3*

This attractive old town straddles the confluence of the Var and the Roudoule rivers and is dominated by the ruins of the Château des Trainières, which belonged to the Grimaldis until it was pulled down in 1691.

On the west bank of the Roudoule the old town, centered around the place A-Conil, was once the Templars' quarter and features many fine old doorways with carved shields on the lintels. On the other side of the river is the parish church of **Notre-Dame-de-l'Assumption►** which contains a couple of remarkable 16th-century altarpieces, the *Polyptyque de Notre-Dame-de-Secours* by Antoine Ronzen, and the carvings of the *Passion* by Mathieu d'Anvers.

Nearby A short detour from Puget-Théniers (3.4 miles along D116) brings you to the small village of Puget-Rostang whose main attraction is the excellent **Écomusée du Pays de la Roudoule►►**. Unlike many "ecomuseums" which have simply jumped on the bandwagon by adding the éco tag to their names, this écomusée plays an active role in the surrounding area and runs guided tours based on themes such as architecture, geology, and botany (tel. 93 05 07 38 for details). In the *Maison de l'Écomusée* itself (open Easter to September daily, winter on demand) there are a series of exhibitions on local heritage topics.

Auguste Blanqui

A monument in the town square of Puget-Théniers (*L'Action enchaînée* by Aristide Maillol) commemorates the town's most famous son, Auguste Blanqui. Born in 1805, Blanqui was one of the leaders of the Paris Commune of 1871.

Cap Ferrat, crowned by the Italianate Villa Ephrussi de Rothschild

► Roquebrune-Cap-Martin *201D2*

Sandwiched between Menton and Monte-Carlo, **Cap Martin** and the village of **Roquebrune** seem to have merged into one big suburb of Menton. The medieval village of Roquebrune is a maze of steps and passageways, covered by arches and vaults, culminating at the **château** (open daily, closed Friday and November; admission).

Cap Martin, an exclusive enclave of fenced-off villas among the cypresses, pines, and mimosa, had its heyday toward the end of the last century when aristocrats fluttered like moths around the socialites Empress Eugenie and Elizabeth, Empress of Austria. W. B. Yeats died here in 1939, and Le Corbusier also met his maker while swimming off the cape in 1965. The superb coastal path among the rocks and battered pine trees has since been named in his honor.

►► St-Jean-Cap-Ferrat *201D2*

Like the Cap d'Antibes and Cap Martin, Cap Ferrat was long ago taken over by luxurious mansions and villas hidden away behind tall gates and impenetrable hedges. The peninsula's past residents have included Leopold II of Belgium, Otto Preminger, Somerset Maugham, and David Niven. It is, however, a little more welcoming than some of the other privacy-obsessed capes, with a tourist office of its own which is happy to point you in the direction of the **Zoo** (open daily; admission), the little harbor area at **St-Jean-Cap-Ferrat** itself, or the marked walking trails around its 9-mile coastline.

The highlight of Cap Ferrat is the amazing **Villa Ephrussi de Rothschild**►►► (open daily except Monday in summer, weekends in winter; admission). An avid art collector, Beatrice de Rothschild built this Italianate-style villa after marrying the banker Baron Ephrussi — the choice of site was because he liked to gamble at nearby Monte Carlo.

The villa was built over a period of seven years, with around 40 different architects having worked on it (some did not last more than a few hours, thanks to the Baroness' capriciousness), and contains something in the region of 5,000 art treasures. Critics say that the Baroness had more money than taste but this is not borne out by either her background or the many exquisite pieces she assembled here, ranging from Beauvais tapestries to Sèvres porcelain, Renaissance furniture, rare Chinese chests, and vases, frescoes, paintings...the list goes on and on. Don't miss the lovely tearoom, with its huge bay windows framing the Bay of Villefranche. The villa was bequeathed to the Académie des Beaux-Arts on the death of the Baroness in 1934.

Visits to the villa are by guided tour only, but you are free to wander around the extraordinary gardens (see page 245) on your own.

►► St-Martin-Vésubie *201D4*

This cool mountain retreat at the head of the Vésubie valley, the only substantial town in the area, is a popular base for excursions into the Parc National du Mercantour (see page 236). From the Mercantour, the streams of le Boréon and la Madone de Fenestre descend and meet at St-Martin to form the Vésubie itself.

Swiss-style houses overhang the main street of rue Dr-Cagnoli, where another torrent is channeled through a conduit between the cobbles creating a lovely effect — not the original intention, since the channel once carried the village sewage.

Descending rue Dr-Cagnoli from place Félix-Faure, the main square, you pass the **Chapelle des Pénitents-Blancs** with its bulb-shaped bell tower, the **Église** (which has an altarpiece from the Bréa school), and a massive Gothic mansion, the **Maison des Contes de Gubernatis**.

The polychrome wooden statue of the Madonna only stays in the parish church for part of the year: at the beginning of July it is carried in procession up to the **Sanctuaire de la Madone de Fenestre►** 7 miles northeast of St-Martin and brought back again in September. An ancient refuge, the chapel gets its name from a natural window in the rocks above it through which you can see the sky.

Nearby walks Following the Boréon 5 miles upstream from St-Martin-Vésubie leads you to the charming resort village of **le Boréon**, whose specialty is fresh trout pulled from the mountain streams in the vicinity (the season is from mid-March to early September). Some of the wild and beautiful landscapes of the Mercantour Park can be explored on a four-hour circular walking tour of the Haut-Boréon area above the village, skirting the isolated Lac de Trecoulpes.

St-Martin-Vésubie is a popular base for exploring the neighboring mountains

Sculpture is just one of the strengths of the Fondation Maecht. Above: a Giacometti piece

► St-Paul 200C2

Probably the only medieval village in the country with compulsory underground car parking, St-Paul is another of those tourist honeypots that have become so overrun with boutiques that their identity has been totally swamped. Proudly proclaiming 18 ateliers, 15 art galleries, 17 artisans, seven antique and gift shops, and 12 restaurants and hotels, it is a wonder that St-Paul does not come to a complete standstill with shoppers clogging the narrow streets in the summer months.

There is a small but interesting **Musée►** (open daily; admission) housed in a 12th-century keep next to the town hall. At the exit, hundreds of photographs record the numerous celebrities who have visited or lived in this overblown village.

A must is the **Fondation Maecht►►►** (see panel on opposite page, open daily; admission) set on a wooded hill just outside St-Paul. Incorporated into the grounds and the outside of the building are mosaics by Braque and Chagall, a moving tubular fountain by Pol Bury, a stick-like cat by Giacometti and a Calder mobile. Also within the grounds is the small Chapelle St-Bernard, with stained glass windows by Braque. The vast permanent collection includes major works by the most important artists of the last 50 years, as well as temporary exhibitions of young artists and retrospectives.

Also here are a huge arts library, a bookstore, workshops and studios, and a cinema screening films (at 3P.M. daily) on the lives of artists represented here.

The Colombe d'Or
St-Paul was no doubt a much more peaceful place in the 1920s when a clutch of artists settled here after World War I and ended up paying their checks at the famous *La Colombe d'Or* restaurant with paintings which are now priceless: the walls are hung with works by Picasso, Matisse, Vlaminck, Léger, Dufy, Bonnard, Derain, and Modigliani — but you will have to part with a small fortune for a meal to be able to eat in these rarified surroundings.

► St-Vallier-de-Thiey 200B2

This small town set in wooded hills 7 miles above Grasse has few attractions of its own, but nearby are three of the best cave systems in Provence (see map, page 219).

The **Grotte de Baume Obscure►►** (open daily from Easter to September; admission), is signposted off D5 west of town. Inside a 2,300 foot-long path climbs and winds up and down through vast galleries and caverns

The baroque interior of the Église St-Sauveur in Saorge

draped with stalagmites and stalactites; the caves descend to around 200 feet and are beautifully lit, with fluorescence fed into some of the cascades for added effect.

Continue on down the same road and turn left onto D613 for the **Grottes de St-Cézaire►** (open daily, closed November to mid-February; admission). The circuit here is only 660 feet long, but is known for the unusual red coloring of its iron-rich stalactites and stalagmites.

Finally, there is the **Grotte des Audides►** (open daily; admission). The cave descends almost vertically (with 279 steps!) to a depth of 200 feet, and has some unusual and very beautiful formations. There is also a jolly **Parc Prehistorique** in the woodland setting around the cave mouth, with life-size mockups of the prehistoric settlements that existed here.

►► Saorge *201E3*

The next village up the Roya valley after Breil-sur-Roya (see page 208), Saorge is set on a steep slope high above the river: seen from below it seems amazing that this jumble of houses clinging to the rock does not just slide gracefully down the hillside. The tortuous drive up to the village is well worth it to see how this peculiar place has been built, with houses piled one on top of the other and connected by obscure stairways and alleys where daylight never penetrates.

In this semitroglodytic world, the inhabitants of Saorge have retained some of their own, ancient dialect which contains elements of Provençal and Ligurian Italian. The site was an important defensive post in the Middle Ages, guarding the approach to the Col de Tende, but the fort was destroyed by Napoleon.

At the center of the village the **Église St-Sauveur** contains *trompe l'oeil* frescoes and an organ built in Genoa and brought here by packmules. From the village a track leads across the terraces to a 17th-century **Franciscan convent** and the adjoining 11th-century chapel of **la Madone del Poggio►** containing some fine 15th-century works.

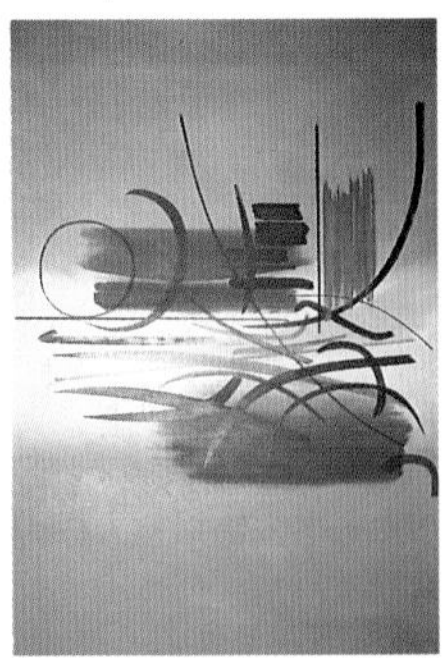

Modern art at the Fondation Maecht

Playful rhythms
The Maecht foundation was established by collectors Aime and Marguerite Maecht, who commissioned the building from Spanish architect Jose-Luis Sert (a protégé of Le Corbusier) in the 1960s, with numerous contemporary artists contributing to the ornamentation: the result is an extraordinary temple to modern art where the structure itself is "a play between the rhythms of the interior and exterior spaces," as Sert himself put it.

Sophia-Antipolis 200C1

Dubbed "France's answer to Silicon Valley," Sophia-Antipolis was the nation's first Science Park and now covers a huge area — 12,500 acres, and another 6,000 acres are to be added soon — behind Vallauris and Antibes on the Plateau de Valbonne. Created in the 1970s, this futuristic complex amid rolling hills has attracted around 830 businesses, employing around 15,000 people, working in information technology, life sciences, pharmaceuticals, robotics, and other high-tech areas.

The whole complex (which includes residential areas, schools, and stores) is linked up by fiber optics and France Telecom has recently built a huge new training and research center for advanced telecommunications here.

►► Sospel 201D3

A charming Alpine-Italianate town on the banks of the river Bévéra, Sospel thrived from the Middle Ages to the 18th century when it was an important crossroads on the trade routes between Haute Provence, the coast, and Piedmont via the Col de Tende.

The tollgate through which travelers then had to pass sits in the middle of an 11th-century **bridge►►** connecting the two halves of the town. Damaged during the war, it was restored in 1947 and now houses a small tourist office. From the road bridge downstream, there is a fabulous view of the medieval/Italianate houses on the right bank of the river, with the tollgate bridge and the mountains behind.

In the western half of the town, the narrow streets unexpectedly open up into the **place St-Michel►►**, a large square surrounded by magnificent, colorful baroque facades. The main building is the vast Église St-Michel, built in the 17th century and incorporating, somewhat incongruously, the Romanesque bell tower of the 12th-century church which it replaced. Inside, there is a magnificent Bréa altarpiece, the *Annunciation*.

To the left of St-Michel are the chapels of the Pénitents Gris and Pénitents Rouges (helpfully color-coded gray and red respectively) and, to the right, the Palais Ricci with *trompe l'oeil* windows.

Underground fort
Just outside of Sospel on D2204 there is an old Maginot Line fortress, the *Fort St-Roch*. Built in 1932 against the threat of an Italian invasion, it was put to effective use toward the end of the war and has nearly a mile of underground tunnels, complete with accommodations for over 200 soldiers, to explore (open daily in summer except Monday; admission).

The lovely old medieval bridge and tollgate spanning the Bévéra river at Sospel

Intricate paintwork on Sospel's riverside houses

Tende 201D4

Once the capital of the Upper Roya, Tende is the last town before the Col de Tende and once played an important role guarding the route across to Piedmont. Tende's tall, gaunt houses and bell towers cling to the side of the valley, with a terraced, slightly depressing cemetery high above the town.

Many of the houses are roofed with stone slabs (*lauzes*) in the local green schist, with door lintels dating back to the 15th century and bearing coats of arms and the symbols of old trades. The **Collégiale Ste-Marie des Bois** has a handsome Renaissance doorway and a 17th century organ.

The tourist office here (tel. 93 04 67 00) can provide information and bookings for tours to the *Vallée des Merveilles* (see page 246).

▶▶ la Turbie 201D2

The chunky silhouette of the monument for which this village is famous, the **Trophée des Alpes▶▶▶**, is an unmistakable landmark. Situated at the loftiest point of the main Roman highway (the *Via Julia*) between Cimiez and Italy 1,570 feet above sea level, the trophy was built to commemorate Augustus' triumphs over the Alpine tribes. Originally topped off with a statue of Augustus, it stood 164 feet high and 124 feet wide: despite being vandalized, turned into a fortress in the Middle Ages, partly dismantled on the orders of Louis XIV in 1705, and then finally quarried to build the neighboring church in the last century, enough of it survived to make partial restoration feasible — even though it is now "only" 115 feet high. The long inscription on its base, listing all 44 tribes conquered by Augustus, has also been restored.

In the gardens surrounding the trophy (open daily; admission) there is a small museum documenting its restoration, financed by an American, Edward Tuck, and from the terrace behind there is a wonderful panorama of Monaco and the coastline from Italy to the Esterel.

Next to the trophy, the baroque **Église St-Michel-Archange** contains works attributed to, or from the schools of, Veronese, Raphael, Bréa, Ribera, and Murillo.

The Roman monument that put la Turbie on the map, the Trophée des Alpes

Provençal gardens

■ Water gardens, stone gardens, secret gardens, kitchen-gardens — there is almost no end to the different types of garden you can find in Provence. Here is a selection of just a few, all of which can be visited.....■

A perfumed garden
One of the most charming books ever written about Provençal gardens is the classic *Perfume from Provence* by Lady Winifred Fortescue, first published in 1935. Lady Fortescue and her husband, Sir John, settled in a small stone house outside Grasse between the wars and set about trying to tame the terraced landscape of vines, roses, lavender, and wild flowers that surrounded them. The book's patronizing attitude to Provençals now seems very dated, but this warm-hearted account (it was an instant bestseller) conveys the magic of Provençal gardens very convincingly.

Cacti (below and right) flourish in the hot, dry climate

Châteaux gardens The castles of Provence have not always had a great deal of space surrounding them in which to plant gardens. The garden was often an afterthought, squeezed on to a terrace between the castle and the village streets surrounding it.

Such is the case with the Château de Sabran at Ansouis, where the stone-walled terraces were filled in during the 17th century (the castle itself dates back to the 10th century): on the west side of the château, hemmed in by the adjoining chapel, the Paradise garden displays an elegant pattern of clipped box hedges in the northern French style.

At Entrecasteaux the castle sits on a small knoll with its garden (with magnolias, box hedges, and eucalyptus surrounding a small pool) some way beneath. The garden was designed by Le Notre, who created the gardens of Versailles; he also designed the gardens at the château of Gourdon (spectacularly perched on the edge of the hillside) and those at the **Château de la Barben▶** outside Salon (open 10–12, 2–6 daily in summer, closed Tuesday in winter and during January; admission). Rebuilt many times over the centuries, the château is remarkable for its elegant 18th-century ceilings; also on display is the bedroom which belonged to Pauline Borghese, Napoléon's sister, who once lived here. The formality of the flower borders, statues, and basins is emphasized by the untamed woodland that surrounds them. In the grounds there is a large zoo and a children's playground.

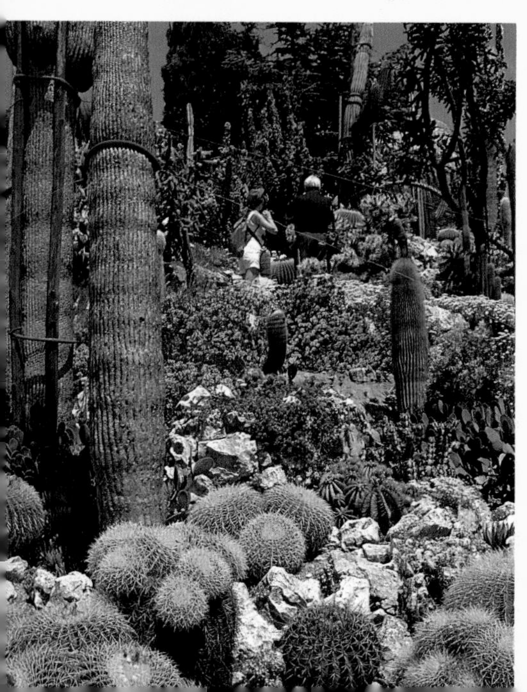

Herb gardens Although herbs are a vital part of Provençal cuisine and folk medicine, herb gardens are rare for the good reason that most herbs grow wild. But there are two exceptions: the first is at the Ethnological Conservatory of Haute Provence (Conservatoire du Patrimoine Ethnologique de la Haute Provence) in the old Prieuré de Salagon near Mane, where they have planted a medicinal herb garden with over 100 of the most commonly used species; there is also a medieval monastery garden with ornamental, edible, and herbal plants.

The second is the *Harmas* of the entomologist J-H Fabre at Sérignan-du-Comtat, a little wilderness which

Fabre allowed to grow untended simply so that he could study the insect inhabitants. This untamed botanic park contains more than 800 plant species.

Exotic gardens In the 18th century the first botanic gardens were opened in Aix and Salon to nurture exotic plants brought back from Africa and the Orient. Palm trees arrived in Hyères in 1867, and palms — along with a multitude of other exotic species — form an important part of the huge Jardin Olbius Riquier on the outskirts of Hyères. In contrast, thousands of species of cacti are the main feature of the Jardin Exotique in Monaco, and papyrus, ferns, and pineapple plants are interspersed with thousands of orchids in Provence Orchidées just outside Barbentane. The Parc Naturel de Mugel at la Ciotat is predominantly Mediterranean, with *garrigue* species and wild flowers, but it also contains cacti and thickets of wild bamboo.

City gardens Framed by monumental ruins or grand buildings, city gardens often have a dramatic setting. The Rocher des Doms in Avignon, for example, is perched above the Rhône with the Palais des Papes rising up beside it. Its leafy paths, rock gardens, lawns, and splashing fountains offer a respite from the hurly-burly below. In Nîmes, the best-loved public park is the Jardin de la Fontaine, which incorporates not only the Temple of Diana but also the old Roman baths and the spring itself, landscaped into a series of balustrades and monumental steps beneath the shade of chestnuts and hackberries. Aix has its French-style gardens in the Pavillon de Vendome and Arles its charming Jardin d'Été on the boulevard des Lices with enormous cedars backing on to the Théâtre.

Unusual gardens One of the most extraordinary gardens is that of the Villa Ephrussi de Rothschild on St-Jean-Cap-Ferrat, created by Baroness Ephrussi de Rothschild from 1905 onward. The Île de France garden in the center, created in the form of a boat, is flanked on either side by a series of smaller gardens designed in Japanese, Spanish, Florentine, Oriental, and Provençal styles: an instant tour of the world's gardens, completely mad and great fun.

Colette in Nîmes
Writing of her "Elysian refuge, the Gardens of the Fountain" in Nîmes, Colette says, "the baths of Diana, over which I lean, still, as always, reflect Judas trees, the terebinths, the pines, the paulownias with their mauve flowers and the double purple thorns. A whole garden of reflections is spread out there below me, turning, as it decomposes in the aquamarine water, dark blue, the violet of a bruised peach, and the maroon of dried blood. Oh beautiful garden and beautiful silence, where the only sound is the muted splashing of the green, imperious water, transparent and dark, blue and brilliant as a bright dragon."

Pottery is one of the mainstays of Vallauris

► Vallauris *200C1*

Vallauris is a fairly hideous town — the modern part, at least — which is stuffed to the gunwales with pottery and ceramic shops of variable quality which owe their popularity (if not their style) to Picasso's stay here in the 1940s and 1950s. He got hooked on a new passion when he started working with clay in the Poterie Madoura (giving fresh impetus to an industry which has existed here since Roman times.) Pottery-making thrived here during the Middle Ages, was knocked out by the plague and then re-invigorated by the arrival of Genoese potters in the 16th century. After World War II it suffered at the expense of the aluminum industry, only to take off again thanks to Picasso's ten-year stay here.

Picasso-inspired designs can be purchased at the Poterie Madoura (off rue 19 Mars 1962); many of his originals are in the **Musée Municipal►** (closed Tuesday; admission) housed in a Renaissance château on place de la Libération. The same ticket allows you entry to the **Musée National Picasso►►** which is in fact a small, deconsecrated chapel which Picasso decorated in 1952 with his seminal paintings *La Guerre et La Paix.*

►►► Vallée des Merveilles *201D4*

Part of the Mercantour National Park (see page 236), the Vallée des Merveilles contains one of the richest collections of open-air petroglyphs (rock carvings) in Europe. Lying on the western flank of Mont Bégo between Lac du Basto and Lac Long, the valley covers over 11 square miles and contains an estimated 30,000 carvings.

The carvings may be the work of pilgrims (see panel) but since latter-day visitors with less reverential attitudes have also left their mark the two most important areas are now protected, and you must stick to the marked paths unless accompanied by an official guide.

Although there are thousands of symbols they are not easily visible to the untrained eye, which is another good reason for visiting with a guide. *Destination Merveilles* (tel. 93 89 88 98) organizes regular guided visits from

Mysterious markings
Little is known about the purpose of the carvings of the Vallée des Merveilles, which represent human figures, animals, and tools, and include many mysterious symbols, but they are thought to date from between 1500 and 1800B.C. It is possible that the valley was an ancient sacred site, and that the symbols were made by pilgrims. However, the tools which were used to carve them have never been found and it has even been whispered that they may be fake. The first systematic investigation of the site was carried out earlier this century by an Englishman, Clarence Bicknell.

June through to October, with the main access point being St-Dalmas-de-Tende south of Tende (see page 243).

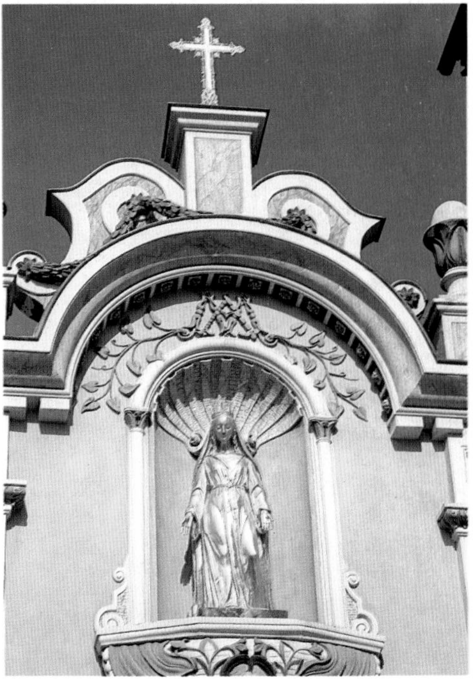

►►► Vence *200C2*

Although only 6 miles from the coast this lively town has more in common with its counterparts in inland Provence than with the frenetic resorts of the Riviera. Vence was popular with artists and the intelligentsia during the 1920s (including the likes of Dufy, André Gide, Paul Valery, and D. H. Lawrence — the latter dying here of tuberculosis in 1930). Matisse moved here in 1941 to escape the bombings on the coast but fell dangerously ill; he was nursed back to health by the Dominican sisters and in thanks to them he started work in 1946 on his famous **Chapelle du Rosaire►►►** (open Tuesday and Thursday).

"I think it is my masterpiece" declared Matisse after five years of work. The white tiled walls of the chapel are covered in black line drawings of the Stations of the Cross, the Virgin and Child, the Crucifixion, and St. Dominic — the only color to intrude on the simple, stark interior comes from the stained glass windows which throw patterns of yellow, green, and blue across these surprising murals.

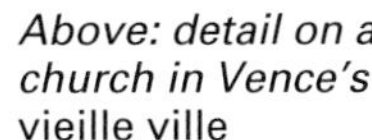

Above: detail on a church in Vence's vieille ville

The *vieille ville* of Vence is an enjoyable place to wander — starting off at the **place du Peyra** where there is an obligatory stop to taste the mineral-rich waters from the urn-shaped fountain. From here, head down the lively **rue du Marché** which is crammed with mouth-watering food shops — little *patisseries*, fish shops with sacks of *moules* and mounds of fresh-cooked *crevettes*, charcuteries, cheese shops and *poulet grillé à la flame* wafting tempting aromas down the narrow street.

The rue du Marché leads to the central place Clemenceau, where you can see Roman tombstones incorporated into the walls of the **cathédrale►**. As well as a mosaic by Chagall (in the baptistry at the back), there are all sorts of odds and ends inside including finely carved Gothic choirstalls, the sarcophagus of St. Veran, and stone reliefs from the 5th-century church that it replaced.

A Picasso ceramic (1953) from his Vallauris period

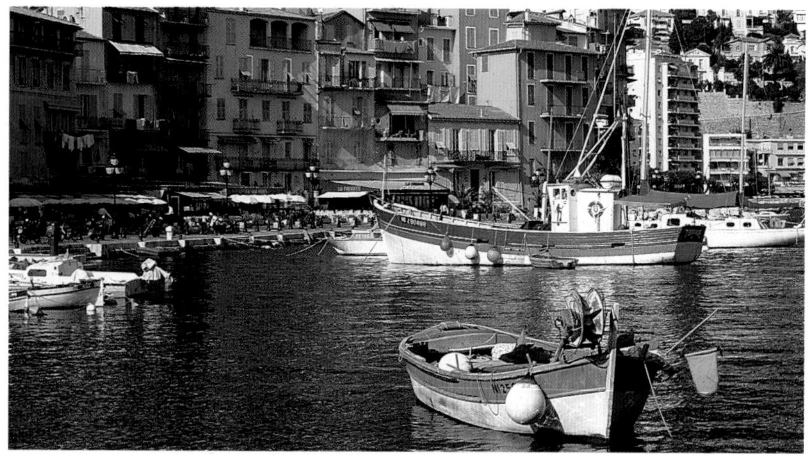

Villefranche harbor and fishing boats

The harbor
Protected by the Cap Ferrat peninsula, Villefranche harbor has a long history. Its deep waters (over 200feet in places) sheltered galleys in Roman times, when it was known as *Olivula*. In the 14th century the Comte de Provence, Charles II of Anjou, declared it a duty-free port, *Villam-Francam* — hence its name today. In the 16th century Charles V moored his imperial galley here: one tale has it that when his sister (then Queen of France) came to visit, the entire entourage — dukes, Queen, and all — was plunged into the sea when his gangplank collapsed.

Cocteau's chapel

▶▶▶ Villefranche-sur-Mer *201D2*

Just around the Boron headland east of Nice, Villefranche is a small "fishing village" which the Niçois visit at the slightest opportunity for a meal out in one of the harborside restaurants. It is indeed one of the most delightful spots on the Riviera to spend a summer's evening dining on the quayside, with fishing boats and yachts bobbing about in the harbor.

Villefranche has been a military port for many centuries and although warships sometimes still put in to the deep, sheltered harbor it was the small fishing community which inspired Villefranche's most famous resident, Jean Cocteau, when he lived here.

In homage to them he decorated the **Chapelle St-Pierre▶▶▶** (open daily in summer, closed Friday and mid-November–mid-December; admission) just near the waterfront; depicting the fisherwomen of Villefranche, gypsies and the life of St. Peter, these extraordinary, luminuous frescoes are suffused with Cocteau-esque symbolism. Above the chapel the Galerie Jean-Cocteau (open daily) is one of the few outlets for his original drawings, lithographs, and ceramics. Changing exhibitions also feature his work.

Within the massive walls of the **Citadelle St-Elme▶▶** above the port is the *mairie* (town hall) and, tucked away in various corners, an open-air theater and two museums. The **Fondation-Musée Volti▶** (open daily except Sunday morning and Tuesday in summer, afternoons in winter except Tuesday, Saturday, and Sunday; admission) is dedicated to the provocative sculptures of local artist Volti. The **Musée Goetz-Boumeester** (same hours) contains two works by Picasso and one by Miró.

At the entrance to the citadel there is a display of maritime archaeological finds from the wreck of a Genoese trading ship that went down in the harbor in a violent storm in 1516.

Behind the port is the **rue Obscure▶**, a vaulted passageway that has altered little since the 13th century; this dark, cavernous alleyway has sheltered the inhabitants of the port from bombardments throughout history, including during World War II.

TRAVEL FACTS

Arriving and departing

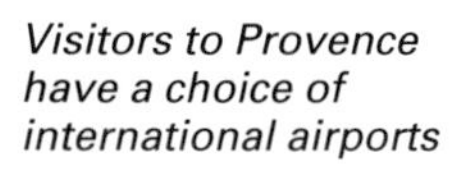

Visitors to Provence have a choice of international airports

By air Nice and Marseille are Provence's two main international gateways. Nice is the second busiest airport in France after Paris, with about 5.5 million passengers annually. Over 30 airlines have scheduled flights into Nice, with 92 direct flights to 34 countries. During the summer months, the best deals are on charter flights. If you are heading primarily for the Vaucluse, the Bouches-du-Rhône, or the Var it is more convenient to fly into Marseille–Provence airport (previously Marseille–Marignane). With around 4.4 million annual passengers, Marseille caters mostly to business traffic and is France's third busiest airport.

By sea The classiest way to arrive on the coast is on your own yacht, and with over 125 marinas and ports and 57,000 berths there is no shortage of mooring space. An average of between 120,000 and 130,000 annual passengers arrive on cruise ships, with the principal ports of call being Cannes, Marseille, Nice, Toulon, St-Tropez, and Villefranche.

Regular ferry services operate between Marseille and Tunisia and Algeria.

By train French National Railways (SNCF) operates an efficient and comfortable service from Paris right the way down the coast.

The fastest option is the high-speed TGV (Train à Grand Vitesse) that plunges southward at 170mph and reaches Avignon in just under 4hrs. and Marseille in 4hrs. 40mins. The dedicated TGV track at present only reaches Valence, after which the train runs at normal speeds, but SNCF is planning the TGV Mediterranéen which will push the high-speed track farther south (due for completion in 1998). TGV tickets are slightly more expensive than normal tickets, and you will need to reserve a seat in advance or before boarding the train. If you are traveling to northeast Provence you can take the TGV to Grenoble or Valence and change to local trains from there.

Another option is an overnight sleeper train from Paris, which is one of the most relaxing and evocative ways to arrive as the Provençal landscapes unfold outside your window in the early morning hours.

If you are taking a car or motorcycle the Motorail service operates from Channel ports to Avignon, Fréjus/St-Raphaël, and Nice, and from Paris to the same stations plus Marseille and Toulon. Again, these are overnight trains with couchettes (berths) for sleeping, and although ticket prices are fairly exorbitant it is safer and more relaxing than driving all the way there.

For further information and bookings, contact the overseas branches of SNCF in major cities in the United States, Canada, or Europe. Discounts on rail tickets are available for students and senior citizens and with train passes (see **Getting around** page 255).

Bus Regular long-distance bus services connect Provence with European cities such as Paris, London, Brussels, Madrid, Geneva, and elsewhere.

Car Traveling down from Paris the quickest route is on the *Autoroute du Soleil* (A6 from Paris, then A7 from

❏ Although the *autoroute* is fast it is not cheap: toll charges from Calais to Nice add up to about 450 francs ($90). An alternative is to take N7 south from Paris to Lyon. Both should be avoided in July and August. ❏

Lyon) which goes to Marseille. However, if you are continuing down the coast you will need to branch off at Aix along the *Autoroute la Provençale* (A8) which runs all the way to the Italian border. If you are coming from the UK the quickest route is via A26 to Reims and Troyes, followed by A5 and A31 to Dijon, after which you join up again with the *Autoroute du Soleil*. This completely avoids the nightmare of the *Boulevard Périphérique* around Paris.

Customs There are no limits on the import or export of tax-paid goods between EU countries (provided they are for personal use). For duty-free goods, see table.

Insurance Travel insurance should cover medical expenses, loss of luggage or money, cancellation of your vacation or flight, delayed departure and delayed baggage. If

❏ **Duty-free allowances**
Allowances are for bringing into France goods bought duty-free or from outside the EU:

Cigarettes	200
or Cigars	50
or Tobacco	250g
Table wine	2 liters
Alcohol over 22 proof	1 liter
or	
Alcohol under 22 proof	2 liters
or Additional table wine	2 liters
Perfume	60ml
Eau de Toilette	250ml

❏

you are taking a car, breakdown and accident insurance is recommended (third party insurance is compulsory).

Visas A valid passport only is required for citizens of the EU, US, or Canada. Other nationals vary: check with a travel agent or the French Government Tourist Office.

Departing There is an airport departure tax of 17 francs for international flights, and 10 francs for internal flights.

Made in Provence

Climate and when to go Although renowned for its temperate weather and sunshine, Provence is a land of climatic extremes — veering between blistering hot summers and freezing winters during which the *mistral* can blow for days on end. What's more, normal weather patterns are no longer as predictable as they once were, with extensive flooding in 1993 and 1994 of some coastal areas.

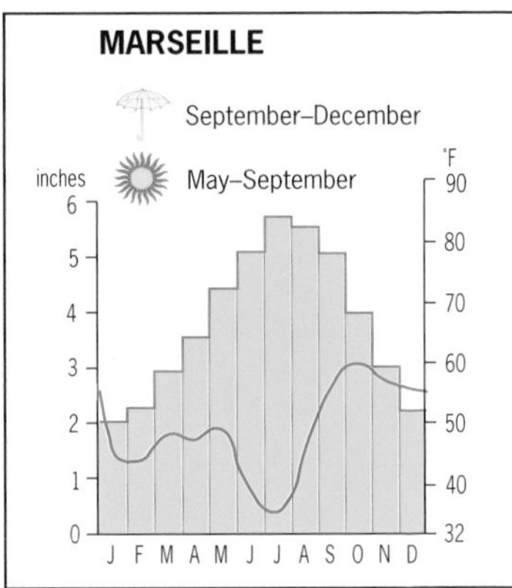

Spring A delightful time to be in Provence, with wild flowers in profusion and mimosa and almonds blossoming on the coast from March onward. In April and May it is warm enough to sit out in the sunshine in restaurants and cafés, although the sea is still a bit chilly for swimming.

Summer Peak season throughout Provence, hot and dry with minimal rainfall and temperatures that rarely drop below 70°F between June and September (summer heat waves can push temperatures much higher). The sea is warm enough for swimming from June onward, and the crowds not yet unbearable.

Avoid the coast in July and August. It is at its worst then, with overcrowding, traffic jams, overinflated prices and short-tempered service. Festivals, however, are in full swing.

If you are planning on hiking (particularly on any of the long-distance paths), wooded areas and sometimes entire hill ranges are closed off from July 1 through to September 12 if they are in a high-risk Red Fire Zone. Summer is the ideal time to be in the Alpes de Haute-Provence, where cooler temperatures favor outdoor activities.

Autumn September and October can be extremely pleasant — you can still sunbathe although there are occasional rainstorms. The vineyards and forests take on their mantle of

Dining al fresco

Harvesting grapes in the late summer

autumn colors and, after early September, resorts start to empty when French school vacations end.

Winter In November colder weather settles in and most museums (as well as many hotels and restaurants) close. Still, you can have some surprisingly mild and sunny days. Snow starts to settle on the Alps from late November onward, with the ski season in the high altitude resorts lasting through March/April.

A predominant feature of the winter months is the dreaded *mistral*, which whips down the Rhône valley and can make life unpleasant for days on end. However, it can be avoided by moving further east down to the Côte d'Azur.

National holidays (*jours fériés*) January 1, Easter Sunday, Easter Monday, May 1 (Labor Day), May 8 (VE Day), Ascension Day (40 days after Easter), Pentecost (7th Sunday after Easter) and the following Monday, July 14 (Bastille Day), August 15 (Assumption Day), November 1 (All Saints' Day), November 11 (Armistice Day), and Christmas Day.
Banks, businesses, and most shops and museums are closed.

Time differences France operates according to Central European Time, which is six hours ahead of Eastern time, with daylight saving lasting from March 29 to September 25.

Money matters The unit of currency is the French franc (denoted as F or FF) which is divided into 100 centimes. There are banknote denominations of 20, 50, 100, 200, and 500 francs; coins of 1, 2, 5, 10, 20 francs, and 5, 10, and 20 centimes.

Unlimited currency can be imported, but you must declare amounts over 50,000F being reexported.

Traveler's checks are one of the safest ways of carrying your vacation money. Foreign currency, traveler's checks and Eurocheques can be changed at banks and bureaux de change. You can also change currency in hotels and some tourist offices.

Banks generally open 9–12, 1:30–4, close Sundays, public holidays, and often Saturdays or Mondays. Bureaux de change (in main train stations and in major town centers) open longer hours and sometimes on holidays. It is sensible to buy some French francs before leaving home, in case there is nowhere open.

Exchange rates fluctuate widely, as do commissions on changing traveler's checks (hotels and bureaux de change usually have the worst rates or take the highest commission). If changing large amounts, always shop around.

Credit cards such as Visa/ Barclaycard (Carte Bleu in France), MasterCard/Access (Eurocard), American Express, and Diners Club are widely accepted. In remote places or small, family-run restaurants cards may not be accepted.

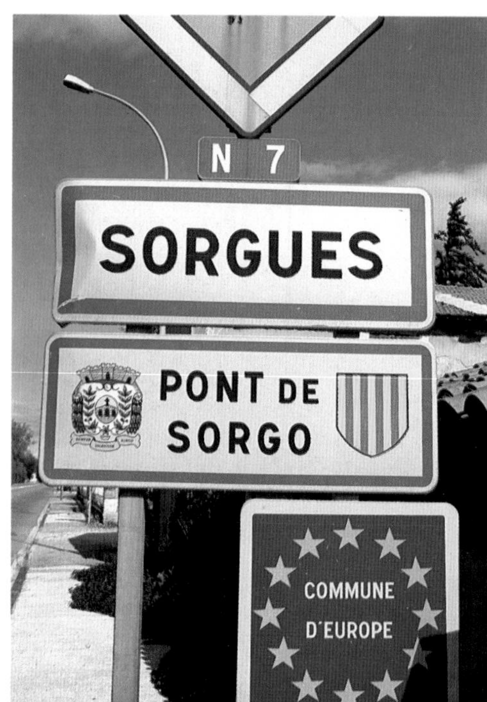

You will need a car if you wish to seek out the best of Provence

Driving Provence lends itself to gentle exploration by car, with many unexpected sights and delightful corners of the countryside that are accessible only with your own transportation. Unfortunately the public transportation network cannot cater to the needs of most visitors unless you are planning on staying put in a coastal resort with just the occasional excursion to major tourist sights. Over 70 percent of overseas visitors (and nearly 80 percent of French tourists) travel around by car.

Driving documents If you are taking a car to France, it is compulsory to carry a full driver's license, current insurance certificate, and the original vehicle registration document (plus a letter of authorization from the owner of the vehicle if it is not registered in your name). A spare set of headlight bulbs is a good idea, since driving with faulty lights is illegal. A red warning triangle is advisable, although not compulsory if your car is fitted with hazard warning lights.

Car Rental There are plenty of car rental agencies but the major drawback is price, with costs that exceed most other European countries. Renting a car locally is the most expensive option. Usually the best deals are fly-drive packages arranged by a travel agent or tour operator in your home country, or train/car rental arrangements with SNCF. Sometimes competitive rates can be obtained by booking in advance through major car rental companies (such as Hertz, Avis, Budget or Europcar, all of which are represented in Provence).

The minimum age to rent a car is 18 years old, although many international firms have now raised this to 20 or even 23 years old (with the national license having been held for at least a year). A valid license and credit card are required for local bookings.

Car breakdown A warning triangle must be placed 50m (165ft.) behind the car in case of breakdown. On *autoroutes* emergency telephones are located every 2km (1.2mi.), with breakdown services provided by nearby garages 24 hours a day, seven days a week (including holidays). Tow and repair rates are fixed by the government, and carry a 25 percent surcharge at night and on Saturdays, Sundays, and holidays. These rates are shown on the emergency telephones, and start at around 335 francs (420 francs with surcharge).

Public transportation Air Air Inter, the French domestic airline, has frequent flights connecting Paris with local airports such as Cannes, Toulon, Fréjus, and Nîmes, as well

Parking can be a problem in the coastal resorts

❑ SNCF discount rail passes include:

France Vacances: 15- or 30-day railpass, must be bought in your home country.
Carte Jeune: For under-26-year-olds.
Carte Couple: Half-price for second person on some trains.
Carte Vermeil: For over-60-year-olds, half-price on some trains.
Carte Kiwi: Family card, gives discount for parents and other children. ❑

as Nice and Marseille. Obtain information from Air France or travel agents.

Rail The main SNCF line links towns in the Rhône valley with Marseille and coastal resorts. Trains are clean, efficient, reliable, and an excellent way of avoiding summer traffic along the coast (the Metrazur service links Riviera resorts with trains at half-hourly intervals in peak season). All tickets must be date stamped in the orange machines on station platforms, and you will face a surcharge if you forget to *compostez votre billet* (stamp your ticket).

Information from tourist offices or SNCF stations (tel. Nice 93 87 50 50; Marseille 91 08 50 50; Avignon 90 82 50 50).

There is a wonderful narrow-gauge railway that winds up through mountain scenery from Nice to Digne, operated by the Chemins de Fer de la Provence (tel. Nice 93 82 10 17; Digne 92 31 01 58).

Bus The bus network is not ideal. Where they exist at all, buses in rural areas are geared to school runs and market days. Between towns and cities, they tend to duplicate the rail services and are not necessarily cheaper or faster. In addition, timetables are not coordinated because services are run by so many different private companies. Most large towns have a *gare routière* (bus station), usually near the train station. SNCF also operates buses to various places on the rail routes where trains no longer stop.

❑ The most efficient bus network in Provence is in Nice, where computerized signboards at every bus stop let you know the exact time of arrival of your service. ❑

Driving tips

Keep to the right (*serrez à droite*). The most common cause of confusion (and accidents) is the rule of giving priority to traffic coming from the right (*priorité à droite*) at any intersection unless indicated otherwise. It does not matter how small the - side-turning is, you must give way. In any town, treat junctions with the utmost caution. On main roads outside towns main roads usually have priority — which is indicated by roadsigns with a yellow diamond or marked *passage protégé*. Beware a yellow diamond crossed-out, which signals that you do not have right of way. Traffic already on traffic circles has priority over other vehicles.

In rural areas driving behavior is normally fairly sedate; the main hazard in small villages is locals suddenly stopping their cars in the middle of the road to lean out of the window and talk to friends in cars coming the other way. On the Côte d'Azur different standards apply, with tempers and the blare of car horns reaching a crescendo in July and August that probably equals Parisian driving conditions (possibly because many of them are Parisians).

In villages and small towns many streets are now closed off to cars *sauf riverains* (except for residents). Although these restrictions can usually be disregarded out of season, in peak season only foolish drivers would ignore them. Pay attention to signs in village centers indicating not be popular if you leave your car overnight and block stallholders setting up in the early hours.

Old-style road markers even give the altitude

Parking Finding somewhere to park can be a headache in peak months although most large towns have sufficient underground car parking (follow the blue "P" signs). If you lose your parking lot ticket be warned that you will need to produce your vehicle registration document to exit (they will reluctantly let foreigners off the hook if they do not have it with them) as well as having to pay the full day price. If you can find a space, on-street parking is cheaper for short periods in *stationement paymant* zones (you will need change for the ticket machines).

Gas stations These are plentiful, and most sell unleaded petrol (*sans plomb*). However, be careful on weekends (many are closed on Sundays) and in mountainous areas, where there are far fewer of them.

Rules and regulations Speed limits are 130kph (80mph) on the *autoroutes*, 110kph (68mph) on divided highways, 90kph (56mph) on other roads, and 50kph (31mph) in urban areas. These limits are lower in poor weather conditions. Signs saying *Rappel* (reminder) mean that the speed restriction has not ended.

Fines for speeding or other violations are levied on the spot, with only cash or a check drawn on a French bank account accepted: the minimum fine for speeding is 1,300 francs and for exceeding the drink/drive limit 2,500 to 5,000 francs.

Accidents If you are involved in an accident take the registration number of the other car and exchange insurance details with the other driver: try and take the names and addresses of witnesses. Once you have contacted the police, you will be required to fill in a statement (a *constant aimable*), but if your French is not good enough to do this you will have to find someone to translate.

Autoroutes The *autoroutes à péage (highways with tolls)* generally offer safe, hassle-free driving (at a price, except for limited stretches near urban areas which are free) and service stations are plentiful — and are obliged to provide free tire checks, oil checks, and windshield washes in the interests of highway safety. Most have small supermarkets (where you can buy everything from snacks to souvenirs) and usually also a café/restaurant. Payments at *autoroute* tollbooths can be made using credit cards; if you are planning multiple trips you can apply for the *Carte Voie Libre* which can only be used on *autoroutes*.

To avoid holiday weekends and regular traffic jams a leaflet obtainable from *autoroute* offices lists all the seasonal blockages, or you can call the Centre d'Information Routière (tel. 91 78 78 78 for Provence, open 24 hours).

❑ To tell whether you should be honking someone or politely waiting, local car registration codes are:
Vaucluse: 84
Bouches-du-Rhône: 13
Var: 83
Alpes de Haute-Provence: 04
Alpes-Maritimes: 06 ❑

*Tollbooths (*péages*) on an* autoroute

Media Local papers include *La Marseillaise*, *Le Provençal*, *Le Méridional*, *Var-Matin*, and *Nice-Matin*. All these carry details on local events and entertainment. Hotels usually carry copies of pamphlets such as the monthly *Farandole* or the weekly *Semaine des Spectacles*, that cover exhibitions and events. The *Riviera Reporter* serves the expatriate community on the coast, but one of the best magazines is the quarterly *Vivre en Provence* which has color features on a wide range of regional topics. The *International Herald Tribune* is widely available, as are London newspapers and other foreign publications, in most big towns and holiday resorts.

French television relies heavily on game shows and foreign films. There is a wide selection of radio stations including France Inter (1829 long wave), which has English-language news bulletins twice daily in summer. At the eastern end of the coast Radio Riviera (104FM) broadcasts in English. BBC World Service and Voice of America can be picked up.

Post Offices Known as the *PTT* (*Poste et Telecommunications*), *Bureau de Poste* or simply *la Poste*, post offices (which deal with both

The post is usually efficient

telephone and mail services) are usually open 8A.M.–7P.M. weekdays, 8A.M.–12P.M. Saturdays in large towns, while in villages they may have shorter hours and close for lunch.

The range of services includes selling stamps and phonecards, *poste restante*, and in some cases fax-sending and check-cashing facilities. Stamps (*timbres de poste*) can also be bought in tobacconists' kiosks (*tabacs*).

Telephone and fax France has no area codes, so you simply dial the number wherever you are calling (the exception is Paris, which needs the code 161 before the usual eight-digit number if you are calling from within France. The majority of public phone booths (*cabines*) are now card-operated, and phonecards (*telecartes*) can be bought in post offices, *tabacs*, and newsstands in denominations of 40F (50 units) or 96F (120 units).

Some post offices and major hotels offer fax facilities, but it is cheaper to use a newsagent or other fax bureaux.

Language guide

English is spoken by many people involved in tourism (campsites, hotels, etc.) and in upscale shops and restaurants. In rural areas this is less often the case, and your attempts at French will be appreciated — even if you master only "B*onjour,*" "*monsieur,*" "*madame*" and "*s'il vous plaît,*" it will get you off to the right start.

Basic vocabulary

yes	oui
no	non
hello/good morning	bonjour
good evening	bonsoir
goodbye	au revoir
please	s'il vous plaît
how are you?	comment allez-vous?
thank you (very much)	merci (beaucoup)
sorry	pardon/excusez-moi
I understand	je comprends
I do not understand	je ne comprends pas
I don't know	je ne sais pas
please help me	aidez-moi, s'il vous plaît
help!	au secours!
toilets	les toilettes
no smoking	défense de fumer
entrance	entrée
exit	sortie
at what time?	à quelle heure?
today	aujourd'hui
tomorrow	demain

yesterday hier
the morning le matin
the afternoon l'après midi
the evening le soir
the night la nuit
now maintenant
later plus tard
closed fermé
open ouvert
prohibited interdit
when? quand?
why? pourquoi?
with avec
without sans
big grand
small petit
good bon
bad mauvais
hot chaud
cold froid
inexpensive bon marché
expensive cher

Shopping

stores les magasins
market le marché
bakery la boulangerie
pharmacy la pharmacie
food shop l'alimentation
butcher la boucherie
newsdealer/stationers la libraire
supermarket le supermarché
I would like je voudrais…
this one ceci
that one cela
that's enough ça suffit
how much…? combien...?

Eating and drinking

to eat manger
to drink boire
breakfast le petit déjeuner
lunch le déjeuner
dinner le dîner
coffee/tea café/thé
beer (draft) une bière (pression)
wine (white/red) le vin (rouge/blanc)
wine list la carte des vins
the check, please l'addition, s'il vous plaît

Directions

where is...? où se trouve...?
left à gauche
right à droite
near/not far près/pas loin
far loin
straight on tout droit
there là

behind derrière
in front of devant
opposite en face de
before avant
after après

Numbers

one un/une
two deux
three trois
four quatre
five cinq
six six
seven sept
eight huit
nine neuf
ten dix
eleven onze
twelve douze
twenty vingt
fifty cinquante
one hundred cent
one thousand mille

Days of the week

Monday lundi
Tuesday mardi
Wednesday mercredi
Thursday jeudi
Friday vendredi
Saturday samedi
Sunday dimanche

A public phone booth

Shopping

Provence offers an enormous variety of things to buy, ranging from local produce such as olives and garlic to handicrafts or brightly printed clothes. Provençal markets are not be missed (local tourist offices can provide lists of nearby market days) and often feature crafts alongside traditional products such as honey, cheeses, and olive oil.

Clothes Block-print fabrics were first produced in Provence in the 17th century after the import of cheap Indian prints was banned: Provençals responded by producing their own cotton prints, still known today as *indiennes*. These colorful prints can either be bought by the length or ready-made into skirts, tops, scarves or furnishing items. The two most famous retail chains for traditional prints are Souleiado and Les Olivades, both of which have numerous outlets throughout Provence.

Superb traditional costumes, flamboyant vests, *gardians'* jackets, and hats and other items can be found at Les Indiennes de Nîmes/Mistral (4 rue Collège du Roure, Avignon) and Bandido (12 rue Pasteur, Aigues-Mortes). Provençal and Camarguais clothes and fabrics can also be found at L'Arlesienne (12 rue du Président Wilson, Arles).

Haute couture boutiques are plentiful in Monte Carlo and Cannes, with a fair smattering in Nice and St-Tropez. Many of the Riviera hill villages also have designer boutiques hidden away down their narrow streets.

Clothes are not cheap in France, but if you need something essential then large markets (such as in Toulon, Avignon and elsewhere) are the best place to look.

Crafts The small figurines known as *santons* are one of the most typical traditional crafts. Local tourist offices can provide addresses of *santonniers*; well-known workshops include those of Sylvette Amy (Aubagne), Atelier Fouque (Aix), Santons Reboulins (l'Isle-sur-la-Sorgue), Elizabeth Ferriol (Arles), and the Atelier Carbonel (Marseille).

Olive-wood carvings can be found in most souvenir shops and basketry, cork bowls and hand-woven woolen garments are also popular. Hundreds of different kinds of pipes are sold in Cogolin, and traditional handmade paper products in Fontaine-de-Vaucluse.

Souvenirs of Provence

Herbs, scents, and soaps Small sachets of herbs de Provence and potpourri are ubiquitous, although a much wider selection of dried and fresh herbs and herbal products is available at L'Herbier de Provence (34 blvd Victor Hugo, St-Rémy-de-Provence), La Parfumerie Artisanale de St-Rémy-de-Provence (34 blvd Mirabeau, St-Rémy), Le Musée des Aromes et du Parfum (near Graveson), and the Maison de la Lavande (58 blvd Gassendi, Digne). All the perfume factories in Grasse have retail outlets.

Marseille soap was once exported worldwide, with the industry reaching its peak in the 17th century. With the advent of washing powders manufacturing declined, but it is now enjoying a revival thanks to the pure, biodegradable properties of the soaps (which are often scented with mountain herbs). Beautifully packaged Marseille soaps (as well as bath oils, perfumes, and herbal essences) are available at the Éco-Musée du Savon (5.5 miles from Mane at Les Fours à Chaux, Volx, in the Alpes de Haute-Provence). Another traditional manufacturer is Rampal-Patou (71 rue Félix-Pyat, Salon; visits by appointment, tel. 90 56 07 28).

Pottery, ceramics, and glassware Practically every *village perché* has its share of pottery shops, with the quality varying widely and prices which are in many cases unjustified. However, you can often find original pieces that are well worth the investment. Hand-crafted enameled tiles can be found at the Établissements Vernin (Les Carreaux d'Apt, le Pont Julien, Bonnieux); good value, rustic cookware is available at the Poterie Provençale (avenue des Goms, Aubagne).

Moustiers-Ste-Marie is the Provençal capital for *faïences* (fine, glazed ceramics) and among the more reputable establishments are Michèle Blanc, Bondil à Moustiers, Lallier à Moustiers, le Grillon, and Ségriès (all within the village center).

Finally, an extensive range of hand-blown glassware is on sale at the Verrerie de Biot (chemin des Combes, Biot).

❑ Provence is a great place for the sweet-toothed, with candied fruits in Apt, *calissons* (almond cookies) in Aix, nougat in Vence, *berlingots* (mint-flavoured caramels) in Carpentras, and *marrons glacés* (glazed chestnuts) in Collobrières. The best jam in Provence is the sensational Les Merveilles range, which includes bilberry, black fig, apricot, and plum. ❑

Sports

Provence has a well-developed infrastructure providing first-rate facilities for outdoor activities and sports. As well as sports listed here, you can also find locations for hang-gliding, gliding, water skiing, scuba diving, and skiing.

Canoeing and kayaking There are numerous locations for canoeing and kayaking, the two most spectacular of which are the Grand Cañon du Verdon and the Ubaye valley in the Alpes de Haute-Provence, where they also organize "hydrospeed" (white-water swimming with wetsuit and floats). Canoeing is also possible on the Durance and the Sorgue.

Note that many rivers in Provence are harnessed to hydroelectric power schemes and therefore subject to sudden changes in water level as barrages are opened or closed: always seek local advice before setting off on your own.

Climbing The top climbing regions are the Grand Cañon du Verdon, the Calanques of Cassis, and the Dentelles

Bicycles can be rented in many areas

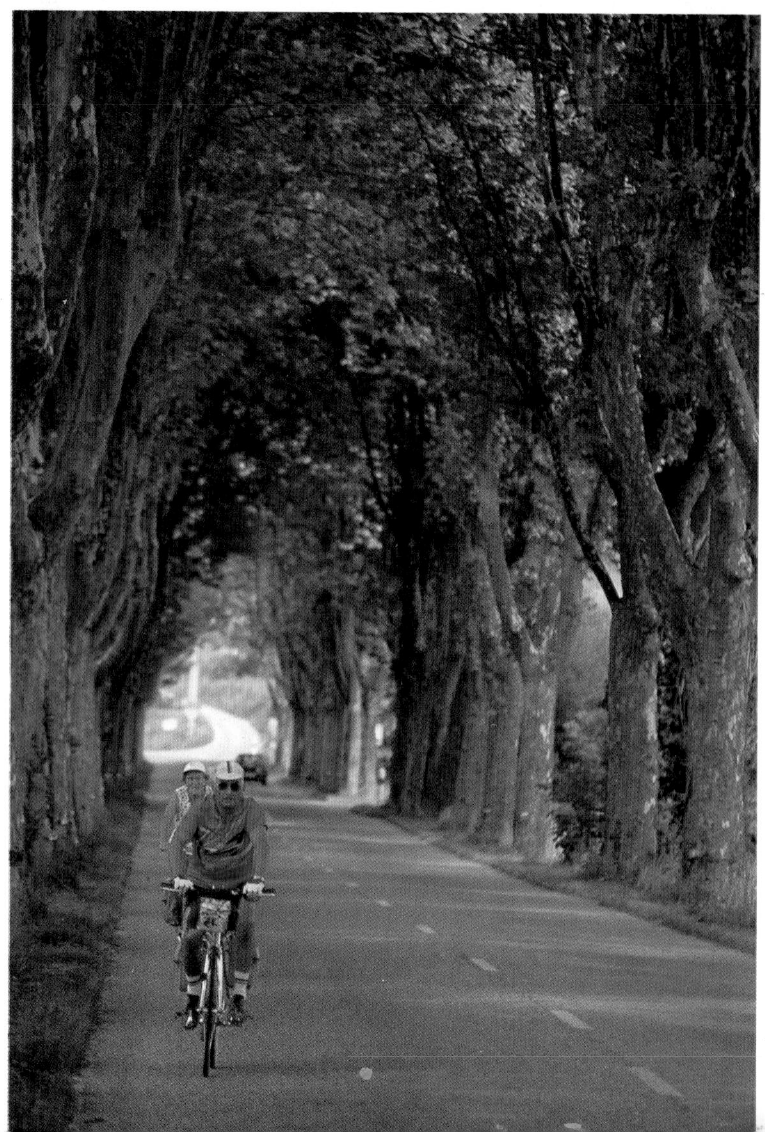

of Montmirail and the cliffs at Buoux in the Vaucluse. Contact either the Club Alpine Français or the Fédération Française de la Montagne et de l'Escalade, both at 14 avenue Mirabeau, 06000 Nice (tel. 93 62 59 99).

Biking The French have always been avid cyclists and they have taken to mountain bikes (called VTT – *Vehicules Tout Terrain*) like ducks to water. Daily or weekly rentals are available in coastal resorts as well as the more spectacular (and demanding) mountain areas. Many of the long-distance hiking paths (see below) have now been marked with a VTT logo indicating permitted routes (in some forestry areas and fragile environments VTT is prohibited).

One of the most stunning areas near the coast is the Esterel *massif*, which has 56 miles of VTT tracks; some of the most extensive trails are in the Alpes de Haute-Provence, and a color brochure in English detailing biking tours of several days' duration, plus guides and rental outlets, is available from the Comité Départemental du Tourisme, 19 rue du Dr Honnorat, 04000 Digne-les-Bains (tel. 92 31 57 29).

Golf Golfers have plenty of choice in Provence with dozens of courses to play on — particularly on the coast. Some of the best are the Golf de Fregate near Bandol, the Golf d'Esterel near Fréjus (designed by Robert Trent Jones), Golf de Ste-Maxime (a challenging new course), the Golf de Fuveau in the Bouches-du-Rhône (one of the biggest courses in Europe), and the prestigious Pont Royal at Mallemort in the Lubéron.

Other good courses include those at Cannes, Mandelieu, Ste-Baume, and Barbaroux.

Full details are obtainable from the Ligue de Golf de Provence-Alpes Côte d'Azur, Domaine de Riquetti, 13290 les Milles (tel. 42 39 86 83).

Hiking There is a comprehensive network of hiking trails throughout Provence, starting with the long-distance footpaths, the *sentiers de grande randonnée* (known as GRs for short) which crisscross the mountains and coastal hinterland. Each GR is described in a detailed *Topoguide*, published by the Comité National des Sentiers de Grande Randonnée (8 ave Marceau, Paris) and available in local bookstores.

National and regional parks also have their own signposted trails, and guides can usually be hired if required (details from local tourist offices).

Horseback riding Particularly popular in the Camargue, although there are many short- and long-distance trails throughout Provence and numerous *centres équestres* where you can hire horses (as well as *gîtes* (lodges) and *relais équestres* that provide board and lodging as well). Details from the Direction National du Tourism Équestre, 170 blvd de Stalingrad, 92130 Issy les Moulineaux.

Sailing With 125 ports and marinas along 516 miles of coastline, Provence offers plenty of opportunities for the nautically inclined. Most ports and marinas have sailing schools and boats for rent. For a complete list of marina facilities write to: Office Régional de la Mer, CMCI, 2 rue Henri-Barbusse, 13001 Marseille.

Sailing (as well as water skiing and windsurfing) is also popular on the big mountain lakes of the Alpes de Haute-Provence such as Lac de Quinson, Lac du Castillon and Lac de Serre-Ponçon. For details contact the Comité Departmental de Voile des Alpes de Haute-Provence, 322 les Aliziers, 04100 Manosque (tel. 92 72 27 93).

Windsurfing With the benefit of the *mistral*, which gusts at over 60 miles an hour, it is perhaps not surprising that world windsurfing records have been broken here; but beginners will also find plenty of gentler spots along the coast. Two world-class locations are les Saintes-Maries-de-la-Mer and l'Almanarre near Hyères, both of which have staged championship events. You can rent boards in many resorts, with week-long courses costing around 500 francs.

Crime and police Although crime gangs (the *milieu*) operate in Marseille and on the Côte d'Azur you are unlikely to be affected unless you are in the seriously rich category and a target for a jewel-heist. The most common causes of theft from tourists are pickpockets and car break-ins.

Always leave valuables locked up or in the hotel safe, and be particularly careful when parking in remote tourist spots where car break-ins are common — never leave cameras or valuables in your car. Burglars tend to target rented villas: always secure the house at night or if going out, and do not leave anything on the terrace overnight — thieves often terrace-hop between villas to see what they can quickly pick up.

In 1993 a spate of "highway robberies" took place on the *autoroutes* near Lyon, with tourists being forced off the road at night and then robbed. French police since claim to have caught the gang responsible.

Make sure you have adequate travel insurance, carry traveler's checks rather than cash, and keep a separate record of credit card numbers, check numbers and emergency phone numbers for canceling credit cards and traveler's checks.

If you are the victim of a theft report it to the nearest *gendarmerie* and keep a copy of the statement if you intend to claim on your insurance.

Pharmacists will give first aid

Police In cities and towns police duties are the responsibility of the Police Municipale while the Gendarmes (part of the national police force) cover smaller places and the countryside. You are unlikely to encounter the fearsome CRS (*Compagnies Républicains de Securité*), a special force that deals with riots and civil unrest, although strangely they also look after security on public beaches. The *Garde Mobile* or *Police de la Route* look after highway security.

Embassies and consulates
Embassies in Paris
US: 2 ave Gabriel, 75382 Paris cedex 08 (tel. (1) 42 96 12 02).
Canada: 35 ave Montaigne, 75008

Paris cedex 08 (tel. (1) 44 43 29 00).
UK: 35 rue du Fauborg St-Honoré, 75383 Paris cedex 08 (tel. (1) 42 66 91 42).

Consulates in Provence:
US: 31 rue Maréchal Joffre, 06000 Nice (tel. 93 88 89 55).
UK: 24 ave du Prado, 13006 Marseille (tel. 91 53 43 32).

Emergency telephone numbers
Police: 17
Fire (*sapeurs pompiers*): 18
Ambulance: 18

❑ The French passion for wild mushrooms means that inevitably dozens of people fall ill or die every year eating poisonous varieties: during the autumn, pharmacists' windows display mushroom identification data to help prevent this and anyone can take in a mushroom so that the pharmacist can check if it is an edible variety. ❑

Lost property
Serious losses should be reported to the police (keep a copy of the statement for your insurance). Lost passports should be reported to the nearest embassy or consulate (see left), who will be able to issue emergency documents. Report loss of credit cards and traveler's checks to the relevant company immediately.

Health and pharmacies
France does not require any vaccinations, and health care standards are high. Water is safe everywhere except for taps marked *eau non potable*.

All EU citizens are entitled to reciprocal health care (British citizens should bring with them form E111, which allows you to claim back expenses: apply at main post offices in Britain).

If you need a doctor urgently, contact SOS Médecins (telephone numbers are in the directory under *Urgences* or call information, tel. 12). Otherwise, pharmacies can provide addresses.

Pharmacists (marked by a green cross) are trained to administer first aid and can also dispense advice on minor ailments. On weekends or holidays pharmacies operate in rotation (addresses are posted in the window or in local papers) or you can call the *gendarmerie* for the nearest *pharmacie de garde* (on-duty pharmacist).

A local resident finds time for a pause in the sunshine

Campsites in popular areas can be crowded

Camping Camping is extremely popular in Provence, particularly among the French themselves. Campsites are well organized and graded from one to four stars depending on the facilities provided. The best have swimming pools, sports facilities, supermarkets or shops, and a restaurant/bar.

Camping municipals are the most basic, run by local authorities and found in nearly every town; other possibilities include *camping à la ferme*, where you can pitch your tent on farmland, although generally there will be no facilities. Camping outside recognized sites (*camping sauvage*) is sometimes possible but often forbidden (*interdit*) by local authorities (always check with the town hall first). Never camp in the forests in summer because of the fire risk.

In July and August campsites on the Côte d'Azur are notoriously over-crowded (and can be unsanitary). Always phone ahead to check space availability.

Lists of campsites are available from local tourist offices or French Government Tourist Offices. A guide to the country's campsites is published by the Fédération Française de Camping et de Caravaning (78 rue de Rivoli, 75004 Paris, tel. (1) 42 72 84 08). They'll send it to you directly for 70 francs plus shipping.

Preplanned camping packages are an increasingly popular option for budget vacations.
UK holiday firms include: Eurocamp Travel, tel. (01565) 626262; Eurosites, tel. (01706) 830888; Canvas Holidays, tel. (01383) 621000; Keycamp Holidays, tel. (0181) 395 4000.

Villa rentals There are numerous options for renting in Provence, ranging from isolated *mas* (farmhouses) to beach apartments and grand villas on the Côte d'Azur. Good value rentals in or near small country villages are offered by the Gîtes de France organization, with properties ranging from village houses to converted farm outbuild-ings or country cottages.

❑ There are approximately 700 campsites in Provence, providing a total of around 98,000 individual sites with room for 275,000 people. The majority are in the Var (279), followed by Alpes-Maritimes (128), Alpes de Haute-Provence (116), Bouches-du-Rhône (92,) and Vaucluse (84). In France as a whole there are more than 9,000 campsites. ❑

Membership will provide you with a full list of properties and discount offers on ferry crossings (in France, contact the Fédération National Gîtes de France, 35 rue Godot-de-Mauroy, 75009 Paris, tel. (1) 49 70 75 75).

In the U.S., the following companies can provide information on villa rentals in France:
At Home Abroad, 405 E. 56th St., Suite 6H, New York, NY 10022, tel. (212) 421-9165, Europa-Let, 92 N. Main St., Ashland, OR 97520, tel. (503) 482-5806 or (800) 462-4486, Interhome Inc., 124 Little Falls Rd., Fairfield, NJ 07004, tel. (201) 882-6864, Overseas Connection, 31 North Harbor Dr., Sag Harbor, NY 11963, tel. (516) 725-9308, Property Rentals International, 1 Park West Circle, Suite 108, Midlothian, VA 23113, tel. (804) 378-6054 or (800) 220-3332, Rent a Home International, 7200 34th Ave. NW, Seattle, WA 98117, tel. (206) 789-9377 or (800) 488-7368, Vacation Home Rentals Worldwide, 235 Kensington Ave., Norwood, NJ 07648, tel (201) 767-9393 or (800) 633-3284, Villas and Apartments Abroad, 420 Madison Ave., Suite 1105, New York, NY 10017, tel. (212) 759-1025 or (800) 433-3020, and Villas International, 605 Market St., Suite 510, San Francisco, CA 94105, tel. (415) 281-0910 or (800) 221-2260.

Student and youth accommodations Budget accommodations are available in dormitory rooms in youth hostels (*Auberges de Jeunesse*) in most towns; contact your home branch of the International Youth Hostel Federation (IYHF) or the Fédération Unie des Auberges de Jeunesse (6 rue Mesnil, 75116 Paris, tel. (1) 42 61 84 03). Some places also have more comfortable accommodations in *Foyers des Jeunes Travelleurs/euses* which usually provide individual rooms.

For discounts on museum admissions, entertainment and public transportation anyone under 26 can apply for a special youth card (*Carte Jeune*); details at tourist offices or post offices.

Visitors with disabilities France is no better or worse than other EU countries in providing access facilities for travelers with disabilities, although the situation is gradually improving and ramps and other forms of access are now provided at many museums and tourist sites (nearly all new museums and public buildings are wheelchair-friendly). There are accessible hotels in most major towns and resorts. Public transportation is difficult; Hertz is the only car rental company to offer rental cars with hand controls.

Nice Airport, one of France's busiest

Information on accommodations, transportation and other topics is covered in a booklet, *Touristes quand même*, available from the bigger tourist offices or from the Comité National Française de Liaison pour la Réadaption des Handicapés, 30–32 quai de la Loire, 75019 Paris (tel. (1) 45 48 90 13). The red *Guide Michelin* lists hotels with facilities for the handicapped.

Opening times Lunch is a serious business in Provence (as elsewhere in France) — almost everything closes for two hours at midday. Normal working hours are 8A.M.–noon, 2–6P.M. Food shops usually open at 7:30A.M., closing at lunchtime and not reopening in some cases until 3 or 4P.M. but they then stay open until 7:30 or 8P.M. Shops and supermarkets in large towns and resorts often don't close in the lunch hour, but may not open until 10A.M. Sunday and Monday (or sometimes Tuesday) are the standard closing days, although food shops are usually open on Sunday mornings until noon. Food markets (weekly in villages, daily in cities) operate mornings only.

Museums and monuments are normally open from 9 or 10A.M. to noon, then 2 or 3P.M. to 5 or 6P.M. depending on the season. The longer hours are during the summer (mid-May or early June until September), when some also remain open over lunchtime. Closing days are usually Monday (for municipal museums) or Tuesday (national museums and monuments), sometimes both. Many tourist sights close altogether during November, with some of the smaller ones staying closed all winter.

Churches and cathedrals are usually open for tourists all day except during services, although a handful spurn tourists altogether and are only open during Mass (sometimes you can request the key from the priest's house, the *presbytère*).

On national holidays (see page 253) shops, banks, and businesses are closed; some museums stay open (apart from Christmas Day and New Year's Day) and you can be sure that restaurants will usually be open.

Places of worship Nearly every town or village has a Catholic church, with the times of Mass usually pinned on the door. Anglican churches with English-language services are found in Nice, St-Raphaël and Menton. There are synagogues in Avignon, Carpentras, Nice and Cavaillon, and Greek and Russian Orthodox churches in Nice.

Toilets There is no such thing as a free toilet in France, since you either have to pay to use one of the coin-operated, self-cleansing public toilets found on the streets or buy a coffee or drink to use the facilities in a bar or café — you are not obliged to, but signs indicating that the WC is *strictement réserve pour la clientèle* indicate that it's frowned on not to do so. Occasionally you do still come across old-fashioned type toilets with footrests where you have to squat. Public toilets (other than the automatic ones) usually have a dish for small change. Women's are labeled *Dames*, men's *Hommes* or *Messieurs*. If you have to ask, request the WC ('vay-say').

Electricity Usually 220V; two round-pin plugs; adaptors are needed for foreign appliances. In some remote areas the supply is still 110V.

Women travelers Women travelers should take all the normal precautions if traveling alone and hitchhiking is not recommended. You will probably find the French courteous and charming and it is quite normal to be offered a drink without the expectation that it will lead any further than a pleasant chat. Topless swimming is perfectly acceptable and doesn't provoke harassment.

Tourist offices

Overseas Overseas branches of the French Government Tourist Office can provide reams of information on every aspect of traveling in France. However, getting through by telephone is often difficult.

- Australia: French Tourist Bureau, BNP Building, 12th Floor, 12 Castlereagh Street, Sydney, NSW 2000 (tel. 02 231 5244).
- Canada: Representation Française du Tourisme, 1981 Avenue McGill College, Suite 490, Montreal, Quebec H3A 2W9 (tel. 514/288-4264).
- Ireland: FGTO, 35 Lower Abbey Street, Dublin 1 (tel. 01 77 1871).
- UK: FGTO, 178 Piccadilly, London W1V 0AL (tel. (0891) 244123 (premium rate service).
- USA: FGTO, 610 Fifth Avenue, New York, NY 10020–2452 (tel. 212/757-1125).

In Provence Tourist offices are called either Offices du Tourisme or Syndicats d'Initiatives. Larger towns have tourist offices called Accueil de France (which can also make hotel

CONVERSION CHARTS

FROM	TO	MULTIPLY BY
Inches	Centimeters	2.54
Centimeters	Inches	0.3937
Feet	Meters	0.3048
Meters	Feet	3.2810
Yards	Meters	0.9144
Meters	Yards	1.0940
Miles	Kilometers	1.6090
Kilometers	Miles	0.6214
Acres	Hectares	0.4047
Hectares	Acres	2.4710
Gallons	Liters	4.5460
Liters	Gallons	0.2200
Ounces	Grams	28.35
Grams	Ounces	0.0353
Pounds	Grams	453.6
Grams	Pounds	0.0022
Pounds	Kilograms	0.4536
Kilograms	Pounds	2.205
Tons	Tonnes	1.0160
Tonnes	Tons	0.9842

MEN'S SUITS

US	36	38	40	42	44	46	48
UK	36	38	40	42	44	46	48
Rest of Europe	46	48	50	52	54	56	58

DRESS SIZES

US	6	8	10	12	14	16
UK	8	10	12	14	16	18
France	36	38	40	42	44	46
Italy	38	40	42	44	46	48
Rest of Europe	34	36	38	40	42	44

MEN'S SHIRTS

US	14	14.5	15	15.5	16	16.5	17
UK	14	14.5	15	15.5	16	16.5	17
Rest of Europe	36	37	38	39/40	41	42	43

MEN'S SHOES

US	8	8.5	9.5	10.5	11.5	12
UK	7	7.5	8.5	9.5	10.5	11
Rest of Europe	41	42	43	44	45	46

WOMEN'S SHOES

US	6	6.5	7	7.5	8	8.5
UK	4.5	5	5.5	6	6.5	7
Rest of Europe	38	38	39	39	40	41

A Provençal view, with Mont Ventoux in the background

bookings for requests in person on the same day or up to eight days in advance). The quality of information available varies widely from office to office, and many have the habit of keeping some brochures under the counter instead of on open display

Provence's **regional tourist offices** accept written inquiries only. Comité Régional du Tourisme du Languedoc-Roussillon, 27 rue Aiguillerie, 34000 Montpellier, tel. 67 22 81 00 will provide information on all towns west of the River Rhône, while the other towns covered in this book are handled by the Comité Régional du Tourisme de Provence-Alpes – Côte d'Azur, Immeuble C.M.C.E., 2 rue Henri-Barbusse, 13241 Marseille, tel. 91 39 38 00, and the Chambre Départmentale de Tourisme de Vaucluse (La Balance, Place Campana, B.P. 147, 84008 Avignon cedex, tel. 90 86 43 42.

Local tourist offices are:
Aix-en-Provence: 2 place Général de Gaulle, 13100 (tel: 42 16 11 61)
Arles: esplanade des Lices, 13200 (tel: 90 96 29 35)
Avignon: 41 cours Jean-Jaurès, 8400 (tel: 90 82 65 11)
Cannes: Gare SNCF (tel: 93 99 19 77)
Digne-les-Bains: le Rond-Pont (tel: 92 31 42 73)
Fréjus: 325 rue Jean-Jaurès (tel: 94 17 19 19)
Marseille: 4 la Canabière (tel: 91 54 91 11)
Montpellier: Place René-Devic (tel. 67 58 67 58.Nice: avenue Thiers (tel: 93 87 07 07)
Nîmes: 6 rue Auguste (tel: 66 67 29 11)
Toulon: 8 avenue Colbert (tel: 94 22 08 22)

HOTELS AND RESTAURANTS

ACCOMMODATIONS

The following hotels have been divided into three price categories:

Budget $
Moderate $$
Expensive $$$

VAUCLUSE

Ansouis

Le Jardin d'Ansouis ($) rue du Petit Portail, 84240 (tel. 90 09 89 27). Small, friendly *chambre d'hôte* with rooms overlooking the garden, where lunch and tea (including home-made *pâtisseries* and ice creams) are served.

Apt

Auberge du Lubéron ($$–$$$) 17 quai Léon Sagy, 84400 (tel. 90 74 12 50). Conveniently located on the river bank the best hotel in Apt.

Avignon

Hôtel de l'Angeleterre ($–$$) 29 boulevard Raspail, 84000 (tel. 90 86 34 31). Good-sized rooms, good value in a quiet location.

Hôtel d'Europe ($$$) 12 place Crillon, 84000 (tel. 90 82 66 92). Royalty and celebrities by the dozen have all enjoyed the first-class service and antique-furnished rooms in Avignon's chicest hotel.

Hôtel Mignon ($$) 12 rue Joseph Vernet, 84000 (tel. 90 82 17 30). As the name ("Hotel Dainty") implies, sweetly decorated rooms; reasonable prices.

Hôtel de Mons ($$) 5 rue de Mons, 84000 (tel. 90 82 57 16). Converted from an old chapel; comfortable and central.

Hôtel du Palais des Papes ($$–$$$) 1 rue Gérard Philippe, 84000 (tel. 90 86 04 13). Old-style furnishings but with modern comforts and a great view of the Palais des Papes.

Hôtel Provençal ($$) 13 rue Joseph Vernet, 84000 (tel. 90 85 25 24). Centrally located.

Carpentras

Hôtel le Coq Hardi ($$) 36 place de la Marotte, 84200 (tel. 90 63 00 35). Modern hotel but well-situated in the center of town, with a pleasant terrace.

Hôtel du Fiacre ($$) 153 rue Vigne, 84200 (tel. 90 63 03 15). Housed in an elegant 18th-century mansion with an attractive courtyard. Good value.

Hôtel du Théâtre ($) 7 avenue Albin Durand, 84200 (tel. 90 63 02 90). Unpretentious and friendly; budget prices for the town center.

Cavaillon

Hôtel du Parc ($$–$$$) 40 place Francois Tourel, 84300 (tel. 90 71 57 78). Opposite the *arc de triomphe*; old-fashioned but comfortable.

Fontaine-de-Vaucluse

Hôtel le Château ($$) quartier Petit Place, 84800 (tel. 90 20 31 54). On the riverbank, with reasonable rates.

Hôtel du Parc ($$) les Bourgades, 84800 (tel. 90 20 31 57). Also within earshot of the river; reasonable prices for the location.

Gordes

Auberge de Carcarille ($$–$$$) les Gervais, 84220 (tel. 90 72 02 63). Old restored *mas* just outside of town in a peaceful location. Pool.

Hôtel la Mayanelle ($$$) rue de la Combe, 84220 (tel. 90 72 00 48). Stylish, comfortable rooms; fabulous views from the terrace.

L'Isle-sur-la-Sorgue

Le Bassin ($$) avenue du Général de Gaulle, 84800 (tel. 90 38 03 16). Reasonable value in the center of town — request a room with view over the river.

Hôtel Restaurant Le Pescador ($$) le Partage des Eaux, 84800 (tel. 90 38 09 69). Good location next to the weir where the Sorgue divides. Ten rooms (reservations essential).

Malaucène

Hôtel Origan ($$) Cours des Isnards, 84340 (tel. 90 65 27 08). Clean and friendly hotel right on the main street.

Orange

Hôtel Arcôtel ($) 8 place aux Herbes, 84100 (tel. 90 34 09 23). Centrally situated and inexpensive.

Hôtel Arène ($$$) place de Langes, 84100 (tel. 90 34 10 95). Overlooking a small, quiet square in the heart of town, the Arène has a long-standing reputation as Orange's finest hotel.

Hôtel de la Gare ($) 60 avenue Frédéric Mistral, 84100 (tel. 90 34 00 23). Ten minutes' walk from the center, but reasonable prices.

Hôtel Louvre et Terminus ($) 89 avenue Frédéric Mistral, 84100 (tel. 90 34 10 08). Opposite the above; also reasonable.

Vaison-la-Romaine

Hostellerie Le Beffroi ($$$) rue de l'Évêché, 84110 (tel. 90 36 04 71). Housed in a lovely old 16th-century building in the narrow streets of the *haute ville*; not cheap but well worth it for the atmosphere.

Hôtel Burrhus ($$) place Montfort, 84110 (tel. 90 36 00 11). Comfortably furnished rooms right in the heart of town.

Hôtel Restaurant du Théâtre Romain ($–$$) avenue Général de Gaulle, 84110 (tel. 90 36 05 87). Simply furnished rooms; a good budget choice.

BOUCHES-DU-RHÔNE

Aix

Hôtel des Augustins ($$$) 3 rue de la Masse, 13100 (tel. 42 27 28 59). Recently renovated to a very high standard, the hotel is housed inside the 15th-century Convent of Grand Augustins right in the heart

of town. The spacious and tastefully decorated rooms all have their own Jacuzzis.
Hôtel de France ($–$$) 63 rue Espariat, 13100 (tel. 42 27 90 15). In a busy part of Vieil Aix, this old-fashioned hotel is reasonable value.
Hôtel Le Manoir ($$$) 8 rue d'Entrecasteaux, 13100 (tel. 42 26 27 20). Housed inside a 14th-century monastery, the hotel is furnished in period style but with all modern comforts. The cloister itself has been turned into an atmospheric outdoor dining area.
Grand Hôtel Nègre Coste ($$–$$$) 33 cours Mirabeau, 13100 (tel. 42 27 74 22). An old hotel with a long history and plenty of character, although rooms are on the small side.
Hôtel St-Christophe ($$) 2 avenue Victor Hugo, 13100 (tel. 42 26 01 24). Basic, no-frills hotel just off the cours Mirabeau. Good value for Aix.
Le Moulin ($$) 1 avenue Robert Schuman, 13090 (tel. 42 59 41 68). A modern building, but quiet and not overpriced.
Le Pigonnet ($$$) 5 avenue du Pigonnet, 13090 (tel. 42 59 02 90). Set in a wooded park five minutes' drive to the southwest of the center of Aix, this old Provençal farmhouse (where Cezanne once painted in the grounds) has been lovingly converted into a luxury hotel. Pool.

Aigues-Mortes

Les Mas des Sables ($$–$$$) On the CD979, 30220 (tel. 66 53 79 73). Just outside Aigues-Mortes, with rooms furnished in Provençal style opening out onto lovely gardens. Pool.
St-Louis ($$$) 10 rue Amiral Courbet 30220 (tel. 66 53 72 68). Comfortable rooms in a wonderful old building right in the heart of Aigues-Mortes.

Arles

Grand Hôtel Nord-Pinus ($$$) place du Forum, 13200 (tel. 90 93 44 44). Full of character, and very attractively decorated throughout.
Hôtel D'Arlatan ($$$) 26 rue du Sauvage, 13200 (tel. 90 93 56 66). Delightful hotel in a converted 15th-century mansion with a patio and walled garden just off the place du Forum. Rooms are all individually furnished, with many distinctive features (four-poster beds, beamed ceilings, etc.). Parts of the old Roman baths are visible through a glass floor in the reception area.
Hôtel du Forum ($$–$$$) 10 place du Forum, 13200 (tel. 90 93 48 95). Modern hotel in a restored mansion, in need of refurbishment but the lower price range rooms are reasonable value for the location.
Hôtel Gauguin ($) 5 place Voltaire, 13200 (tel. 90 96 14 35). Simple and friendly hotel with basic rooms at budget prices.
Hôtel Jules César ($$$) 5 boulevard des Lices, 13200 (tel. 90 93 43 20). Gracious and elegant hotel, top of the range for Arles with spacious reception areas and very comfortable rooms.
Hôtel du Musée ($–$$) 11 rue du Grand Prieuré, 13200 (tel. 90 93 88 88). Pleasant traditional-style hotel opposite the Musée Reattu; good value for Arles center.
Hôtel St-Trophime ($–$$) 16 rue de la Calade, 13200 (tel. 90 96 88 38). Reasonable value.

les Baux-de-Provence

La Benvengudo ($$$) Vallon de L'Arcoule, 13520 les Baux (tel. 90 54 32 54). Traditional-style converted farmhouse in a delightful setting. Pool.
La Cabro d'Or ($$$) Val d'Enfer, 13520 les Baux (tel. 90 54 33 21). Sister hotel to L'Oustau de Baumanière; slightly less luxurious but also set in lovely gardens (with pool).
Le Mas d'Aigret ($$$) 13520 les Baux (tel. 90 54 33 54). Delightful old converted farmhouse with 7.5 acres of gardens and a pool, just below the village. Most rooms have their own private terrace, balcony or garden.
L'Oùstau de Baumanière ($$$) Val d'Enfer, 13520 les Baux (tel. 90 54 33 07). Luxury and refinement are the hallmarks of this famous hotel with its immaculate gardens, pool, flowered terraces, and elegant guest rooms.

Cassis

Les Jardins du Campanile ($$$) rue Favier, 13260 (tel. 42 01 84 85). Stylish hotel in an old Provençal farmhouse. Pool and garden.
Les Roches Blanches ($$$) route des Calanques, 13260 (tel. 42 01 09 30). Set on a promontory 0.5mi. west of Cassis, this converted villa has fine views of the sea and Cap Canaille. Pool and private beach.

la Ciotat

Ciotel Le Cap ($$$) corniche du Liouquet, 13600 (tel. 42 83 90 30). 4mi. east of town in a parkland setting with two pools, tennis, private beach.
Provence Plage ($$$) 3 avenue de Provence, 13600 (tel. 42 83 09 61). 500ft. from the beach, shaded terrace, reasonable rates.
La Rotonde ($$) 44 boulevard République, 13600 (tel. 42 08 67 50). Modern but pleasant hotel above the old town; very reasonable.

Marseille

Grand Hôtel de Genève ($$$) 3b rue Reine-Elisabeth, 13001 (tel. 91 90 51 42). In the pedestrian zone a few minutes' walk from the old port. Attractive rooms.
Hôtel Caravelle ($) 5 rue Guy-Moquet, 13001 (tel. 91 48 44 99). Centrally located, family-run hotel with a friendly atmosphere and basic rooms at budget prices.
Hôtel Estérel ($$) 124–125 rue Paradis, 13006 (tel. 91

37 13 90). Recently renovated with pleasant, modern rooms.
Hôtel Le Corbusier ($$) 280 boulevard Michelet, 13008 (tel. 91 77 18 15). Incorporated into Le Corbusier's famous *Unité d'Habitation*; good value for money (reservations advisable).
Hôtel Montgrand ($) 50 rue Montgrand, 13006 (tel. 91 33 33 81). Behind the Opéra in a quiet street; clean, comfortable, and very popular — reservations necessary.
New Hôtel Bompard ($$$) 2 rue des Flots Bleus, 13007 (tel. 91 52 10 93). Set in its own grounds 1.2mi. east of the city; a peaceful retreat.
New Hôtel Select ($$$) 4 allées Gambetta, 13001 (tel. 91 50 65 50). Modern hotel with good prices for its central location.
Pullman Beauvau ($$$) 4 rue Beauvau, 13001 (tel. 91 54 91 00). Overlooking the Vieux Port with comfortable, sound-proofed rooms.

Nîmes
Le Cheval Blanc ($$$) 1 place des Arènes, 30000 (tel. 66 76 32 32). Right opposite the arena, ultra-chic hotel with individually designed furniture in the comfortable, modern rooms.
Hôtel Imperator Concorde ($$$) quai de la Fontaine, 30900 (tel. 66 21 90 30). Right in the heart of Nîmes opposite the Jardin de la Fontaine, with its own enclosed terrace and garden. Deluxe rooms; top of the range in Nîmes.
Hôtel Le Louvre ($$) 2 square de la Couronne , 30000 (tel. 66 67 22 75). Centrally located, a lovely 17th-century mansion with a courtyard/garden.
Hôtel de la Mairie ($$) 11 rue des Greffes, 30000 (tel. 66 67 65 91). Basic rooms at reasonable prices right in the town center.
Hôtel Plazza ($–$$) 10 rue Roussy, 30000 (tel. 66 76 16 20). Characterful hotel, recently renovated with small but tastefully furnished rooms.
Hôtel de Provence ($–$$) 5/7 square de la Couronne, 30000 (tel. 66 67 28 64). Basic rooms but good rates for the town center.
Le Lisita ($) 2 boulevard des Arènes, 30000 (tel. 66 67 29 15). Bullfighting decor and personalized rooms; good value.

St-Rémy-de-Provence
Auberge de la Reine Jeanne ($$) 12 boulevard Mirabeau, 13210 (tel. 90 92 15 33). Just 10 rooms above the restaurant in this charming little hotel, which is reasonably priced.
Le Castelet des Alpilles ($$) 6 place Mireille, 13210 (tel. 90 92 07 21). Reasonable value for the levels of comfort provided in this old mansion with an enclosed garden.
Grand Hôtel de Provence ($) 36 boulevard Victor Hugo, 13210 (tel. 90 92 06 27). Huge old building right on the main boulevard, old-fashioned and charming with a rambling garden out the back. Bargain prices in a town not known for them.
Hôtel du Cheval Blanc ($$) 6 avenue Fauconnet, 13210 (tel. 90 92 09 28). Stylish rooms in the heart of St-Rémy; modest prices.
Villa Glanum ($$) 46 avenue Vincent van Gogh, 13210 (tel. 90 92 03 59). Just next to the Roman ruins, a welcoming hotel with a pool and gardens.

Saintes-Maries-de-la-Mer
Chez Kiki ($) route de Cacharel, 13460 (tel. 90 97 83 27). Modern and functional, with reasonably priced rooms.
L'Etrier Carmarguais ($$) chemin Bas-des-Launes, 13460 (tel. 90 97 81 14). Popular hostelry outside town; large rooms in bungalows in the grounds. Pool, tennis, horseback riding.
Le Galoubet ($$$) route de Cacharel, 13460 (tel. 90 97 82 17). Modern hotel with rustic touches, close to the beach and the old port.
Mas des Rièges ($$$) route de Cacharel, 13460 (tel. 90 97 85 07). Just outside town in a quiet location, small but attractively furnished rooms. Small garden and pool.

Salon-de-Provence
Abbaye de Ste-Croix ($$$) Val de Cuech, 13300 (tel. 90 56 24 55). Set in a woodland park 3mi. north-east of Salon, this converted abbey is one of the region's top hotels. Sweeping views from the terrace. Pool, horseriding. The rooms (former monks' cells) are small but tastefully furnished; the apartments have private gardens.
Hôtel Angleterre ($–$$) 98 cours Carnot, 13300 (tel. 90 56 01 10). Recently renovated and good value. Centrally located.
Hôtel du Midi ($–$$) 518 allées Craponne, 13300 (tel. 90 53 34 67). On the southern outskirts of town; good-sized, modern rooms at decent prices.

Tarascon
Hôtel du Rhône ($) place Colonel Bérrurier, 13150 (tel. 90 91 03 35). Old-fashioned hotel with rooms at budget prices.
Provence ($$) 7 boulevard Victor-Hugo, 13150 (tel. 90 91 06 43). Huge rooms (with equally large bathrooms), most with balconies. Quiet and tasteful; good value for the facilities provided.
Le St-Jean ($–$$) 24 boulevard Victor-Hugo, 13150 (tel. 90 91 13 87). Large, comfortable rooms at reasonable prices.

VAR
Bandol
La Ker-Mocotte ($$$) 103 rue Raimu, 83150 (tel. 94 29 46 53). Lovely old house with a Provençal garden and private beach.
L'Oasis ($$–$$$) 15 rue des Écoles, 83150 (tel. 94 29 41 69). Small, friendly hotel halfway between the port and the beach. Large shady garden, terrace.
La Réserve ($$$) route de

Sanary, 83150 (tel. 94 29 30 00). Directly on the beach; popular for its restaurant.
Splendid Hôtel ($$) plage de Renécros, 83150 (tel. 94 29 41 61). Quiet, peaceful hotel right on Bandol's best beach.

Brignoles
Le Caramy ($) 11 place Caramy, 83170 (tel. 94 69 11 08). Budget prices in the center of town.
Château de Brignoles ($$) avenue Dréo, 83170 (tel. 94 69 06 88). On the outskirts of town, comfortable and quiet. Pool, tennis.
Hôtel Ibis ($$) chemin du Val, 83170 (tel. 94 69 19 29). Part of a chain; moderately priced. Pool.

la Cadière
Hostellerie Bérard ($$$) rue Gabriel-Peri, 83740 (tel. 94 90 11 43). Right in the heart of the village, this converted monastery has comfortable rooms at reasonable prices.

le Castellet
Le Castel Lumière ($$–$$$) rue Portail, 83330 (tel. 94 32 62 20). There are just six rooms above this well-known restaurant next to the gateway into the village. Good value.

Draguignan
Hôtel le Dracenois ($–$$) 14 rue du Cros, 83300 (tel. 94 68 14 57). Just off the market square, this small, friendly hotel has decent rooms at budget prices.
Hôtel du Parc ($$) 21 boulevard de la Liberté, 83300 (tel. 94 68 53 84). The best and quietest rooms overlook a courtyard at the back.

Fréjus
Auberge du Vieux Four ($–$$) 49 rue Grisolle, 83600 (tel. 94 51 56 38). Budget-priced rooms above an excellent restaurant; homey atmosphere.
Hôtel il etait un fois ($$) 254 rue Frédéric Mistral, 83600 (94 17 19 69). The "once upon a time" hotel is about 500 yards from the beach with its own flourishing gardens around a charming Provençal farmhouse. Good value.
Hôtel La Riviera ($) 90 rue Grisolle, 83600 (tel. 94 51 31 46). Budget choice in the heart of the old town.
Residence du Colombier ($$$) route de Bagnols, 83600 (tel. 94 51 45 92). A good choice for families, with individual bungalows spread out in a woodland setting. Pool, tennis.

Grimaud
Hostellerie du Côteau Fleurie ($$$) place des Pénitents, 83360 (tel. 94 43 20 17). Pleasant Provençal auberge on the outskirts of the village with views over the Massif des Maures.

Hyères
Hôtel-Pension de la Poste ($) 7 avenue Lyautey, 83400 (tel. 94 65 02 00). A popular budget option; small and friendly.
Hôtel du Soleil ($$) 2 rue Rampart, 83400 (tel. 94 65 16 26). In a quiet location just near the Parc St-Bernard; reasonable value.
La Reine Jane ($–$$) le port de l'Augade, 83400 (tel. 94 66 32 64). Excellent value down by the seaside.
Relais Bon Accueil ($$) Presqu-île des Giens, 83400 (tel. 94 58 20 48). A member of the *Relais du Silence* group, set in a large garden out on the peninsula past Hyères. Pool, tennis, horseriding.

le Lavandou
L'Escapade ($–$$) 1 chemin du Vannier, 83980 (tel. 94 71 11 52). Small hotel in a peaceful location; good value.
Hôtel Belle-Vue ($$) St-Clair, 83980 (tel. 94 71 01 06). Peaceful hotel overlooking the Corniche des Maures; lovely gardens, reasonable prices.
Les Roches ($$$) Aiguebelle, 83980 (tel. 94 71 05 07). Top-notch hotel on the beach in neighboring Aiguebelle; superb rooms. Pool, tennis.
Les Tamaris ($$) plage de St-Clair, 83980, (tel. 94 71 07 22). A few steps from the beach, unpretentious yet classy food at the right prices.

St-Raphaël
Hôtel Golf de Valescure ($$$) avenue Pierre Lermite, 83700 (94 82 40 31). 3mi. from town, set in woodlands with easy access to the golf course. Pool, tennis.
Hôtel La Potiniere ($$–$$$) 169 avenue de Boulouris, 83700 (tel. 94 95 21 43). Very peaceful location 3mi. from St-Raphaël, 300 yards from the sea, set in pine woods and has a pool, tennis, sauna, etc.
Le Provençal ($$) 197 rue de la Garonne, 83700 (tel. 94 95 01 52). Not far from the port; standard rooms at budget prices.
Les Templiers ($) place de la République, 83700 (tel. 94 95 38 95). Cheap and cheerful hotel in the town center.

St-Tropez
Le Byblos ($$$) avenue Paul Signac, 83990 (tel. 94 97 00 04). Chic hotel with luxuriously decorated rooms and a fabulous pool.
Les Chimères ($$–$$$) quartier du Pilon, 83990 (tel. 94 97 02 90). Ten minutes' walk from the port, very reasonable for St-Tropez. Request a room overlooking the garden.
La Ferme d'Augustin ($$$) plage de Tahiti, 83350 (tel. 94 97 23 83). Quiet location just a few yards from Tahiti beach; deluxe rooms in traditional style.
Lou Cagnard ($$–$$$) rue Paul Roussel, 83990 (tel. 94 97 04 24). Not far from the town center; reasonable prices considering the location.
La Ponche ($$$) place du Révelin, 83990 (tel. 94 97 02 53). Just off the port, this small, romantic hotel converted from a row of

fishermen's cottages is popular with celebrities.

Ste-Maxime

Hostellerie de la Belle Aurore ($$$) 4 boulevard Jean Moulin, 83120 (tel. 94 96 02 45). Ste-Maxime's most prestigious hotel, on the edge of the sea with views of the St-Tropez Gulf. Pool.
Hôtel de la Poste ($$–$$$) 7 boulevard Frédéric Mistral, 83120 (tel. 94 96 18 33). Modern hotel with a pool and gardens; reasonably priced rooms.

Toulon

La Corniche ($$$) 1 littoral Frédéric Mistral, 83000 (tel. 94 41 35 12). A modern hotel near the beach with views over the bay. Good value.

Hôtel St-Nicolas ($$) 49 rue Jean Jaurès, 83000 (tel. 94 91 02 28). Centrally located, soundproofed rooms at reasonable rates.
Le Jaurès ($) 11 rue Jean Jaurès, 83000 (tel. 94 92 83 04). Right in the town center, budget rooms all with bathrooms.

ALPES DE HAUTE-PROVENCE

Allos

Hôtel Pascal ($) center village, 04260 (tel. 92 83 00 04). Small, friendly hotel with clean and very reasonably priced rooms.

Annot

Hôtel du Parc ($) place du Germe, 04240 (tel. 92 83 20 03). An old hotel with a large garden; reasonable value.
Hôtel Restaurant de l'Avenue ($$) avenue de la Gare, 04240 (tel. 92 83 22 07). Small but comfortable rooms at the right price.

Barcelonnette

Choucas Bar-Hôtel ($) 4 place Manuel, 04400 (tel. 92 81 15 20). On the central square, basic rooms at budget prices.
Le Grand Hôtel ($$) 6 place Manuel, 04400 (tel. 92 81 03 14). On the central square, old-fashioned but good value.
Hôtel Azteca ($$–$$$) 3 rue François Arnaud, 04400 (tel. 92 81 46 36). Decorated in Mexican style with every available comfort.
Hôtel La Grand Epervière ($$$) 18 rue des 3 Frères Arnaud, 04400 (tel. 92 81 00 70). Peaceful location with mountain views from all the rooms.

Castellane

Hôtel Restaurant du Commerce ($$–$$$) place de l'Église, 04120 (tel. 92 83 61 00). Not much atmosphere but comfortable rooms.
Ma Petite Auberge ($$–$$$) 8 boulevard de la République, 04120 (tel. 92 83 62 06). Just 16 rooms in this welcoming inn.

Chateau-Arnoux

La Bonne Étape ($$$) chemin du Lac, 04160 (tel. 92 64 00 09). Lovely rooms, garden, pool.
Hôtel Restaurant du Lac ($$–$$$) 12/14 allées des Érables, 04160 (tel. 92 64 04 32). Pleasant rooms; good value. It is worth paying extra for a room overlooking the lake.
La Taverne Jarlandine ($) montée de l'Oratoire, 04160 (tel. 92 64 04 49). Very reasonable prices, right in the center of the village.

Digne-les-Bains

Hôtel Central ($$) 26 boulevard Gassendi, 04000 (tel. 92 31 31 91). Stylish and comfortable hotel in the mid-price range.
Hôtel L'Origan ($) 6 rue du Pied de Ville, 04000 (tel. 92 31 62 13). Friendly budget hotel.
Hôtel Restaurant de Grand Paris ($$–$$$) 19 boulevard Thiers, 04000 (tel. 92 31 11 15). Luxurious hotel housed in a former convent. Garden, garage parking.
Hôtel Restaurant Le Petit St-Jean ($) 14 cours des Arès, 04000 (tel. 92 31 30 04). An old hotel with very attractive rooms at budget prices.

Forcalquier

Le Grand Hôtel ($–$$) 10 boulevard Latourette, 04300 (tel. 92 75 00 35). Large rooms at reasonable rates. Garden with panoramic views.
Hostellerie des Deux Lions ($$–$$$) 11 place du Bourguet, 04300 (tel. 92 75 25 30). Top choice in town, this ancient hotel has been welcoming travelers since the 18th century. Extremely comfortable and atmospheric rooms. Excellent value.

Gréoux-les-Bains

La Crémaillère ($$–$$$) route de Riez, 04800 (tel. 92 74 22 29). Modern but comfortable rooms, gardens, pool.
Hôtel Restaurant Villa Borghese ($$–$$$) avenue des Thermes. 04800 (tel. 92 78 00 91). Charming hotel with flower-filled balconies and delightful rooms. Pool, tennis, spa, gardens.

Manosque

Le François-1er ($–$$) 18 rue Guilhempierre, 04100 (tel. 92 72 07 99). Central and reasonably priced.
Le Provence ($$) route de la Durance, 04100 (tel. 92 72 39 38). Modern rooms but comfortable and good value. Pool.

Moustiers-Ste-Marie

Bonne Auberge ($–$$) route du Castellane, 04360 (tel. 92 74 66 18). Adequately comfortable and not too expensive.

Riez

Hôtel Carina ($$) rue Hilarion Bourret, 04500 (tel. 92 77 85 43). Smart new hotel; comfortable if lacking in atmosphere.
Hôtel Restaurant des Alpes ($$) 2 avenue de Verdon, 04500 (tel. 92 77 80 03). Old-fashioned but reasonable value.

Sisteron

Grand Hôtel du Cours ($$–$$$) place de l'Église, 04200 (tel. 92 61 04 51). Centrally located and very comfortable.

Hostellerie Provençale ($) 2 avenue Jean Moulin, 04200 (tel. 92 61 02 42). Central and inexpensive.
Hôtel Restaurant de la Citadelle ($$) 126 rue Saunerie, 04200 (tel. 92 61 13 52). Well-run hotel where some rooms have excellent views over the river valley.
Hôtel Restaurant Tivoli ($$) place de Tivoli, 04200 (tel. 92 61 15 16). Spacious rooms; good value.

CÔTE D'AZUR/ALPES MARITIMES

Antibes

L'Auberge Provençale ($$–$$$) 61 place Nationale, 06600 (tel. 93 34 13 24). Popular small hotel (it only has five rooms) on a shady square in the heart of the old town. Booking essential.
Mas Djoliba ($$–$$$) 29 avenue de Provence, 06600 (tel. 93 34 02 48). Lovely old Provençal farmhouse set in 7.5 acres of grounds within walking distance of the town and the beach. Pool. *Demi-pension* (i.e. inc. dinner) obligatory in season; reserve.
La Méditerranée ($$) 6 avenue du Maréchal-Reille, 06600 (tel. 93 34 14 84). Agreeable mid-price-range hotel with some rooms overlooking a delightful small garden.
Modern Hôtel ($–$$) 1 rue Fourmillière, 06600 (tel. 93 34 03 05). Clean and economic hotel, although some rooms can be noisy.

Beaulieu-sur-Mer

Le Havre Bleu ($$) 29 boulevard de Maréchal-Joffre, 06310 (tel. 93 01 01 40). Lovely old hotel with attractive rooms.
Hôtel Select ($) 1 montée des Myrtes, place Général de Gaulle, 06310 (tel. 93 01 05 42). Clean, simple rooms at bargain prices.
Metropole ($$$) boulevard Maréchal-Leclerc, 06310 (tel. 93 01 00 08). Splendid *belle époque* hotel with bright and cheerful rooms. Terrace, pool and gardens overlooking the sea and private beach.
Réserve de Beaulieu ($$$) boulevard Maréchal-Leclerc, 06310 (tel. 93 01 00 01). Fabulous old hotel on the seafront, pool, private beach;very expensive but well worth it.

Breil-sur-Roya

Le Castel du Roy ($$–$$$) route de Tende, 06540 (tel. 93 04 43 66). Modern but extremely comfortable hotel, impeccable rooms, heated pool.

la Brigue

Auberge St-Martin ($$–$$$) place St-Martin, 06430 (tel. 93 04 62 17). Charming family-run hotel in the village center.

Cannes

Carlton Inter-Continental ($$$) 58 la Croisette, 06400 (tel. 93 68 91 68). The magnificent facade of this grand old hotel is a familiar Riviera landmark. Inside, the keynote is luxury on a palatial scale — and you will need a princely sum to stay here.
Le Chanteclair ($–$$) 12 rue Fortville, 06400 (tel. 93 39 68 88). In a quiet location just back from the seafront.
Hôtel de Provence ($$) 9 rue Molière, 06400 (tel. 93 38 44 35). Small, comfortable hotel with reasonably priced rooms.
Majestic ($$$) 14 la Croisette, 06400 (tel. 92 98 77 00). Another classic hotel. Extremely comfortable, heated pool, private beach.
Martinez ($$$) 73 la Croisette, 06400 (tel. 92 98 73 00). Flamboyant *belle époque* hotel; rooms are well equipped. Heated pool and tennis.

Èze

Château de la Chèvre d'Or ($$$) rue Barri, 06360 (tel. 93 41 12 12). A converted castle with 15 rooms and eight suites, all with fabulous sea views. Pool and terrace.

Grasse

Hôtel Panorama ($$–$$$) 2 place du Cours, 06130 (tel. 93 36 80 80). Centrally located, modern hotel with rooms at reasonable rates.
Hôtel du Patti ($$–$$$) place du Patti, 06310 (tel. 93 36 01 00). Extremely comfortable and central.
Pension Michele ($) 6 rue du Palais-du-Justice, 06130 (tel. 93 36 06 37). In the heart of town, welcoming and well-kept little establishment with a small garden. *Demi-pension* compulsory.

Juan-les-Pins

La Marjolaine ($$) 15 avenue du Docteur-Fabre, 06160 (tel. 93 61 06 60). Large old house in a quiet street; comfortable but reasonably priced.
Pré-Catalan ($$$) 22 avenue des Lauriers, 06160 (tel. 93 61 05 11). Small, comfortable hotel behind the casino. *Demi-pension* compulsory in season.

Menton

Hôtel Pension Beauregard ($$) 10 rue Albert 1er, 06500 (tel. 93 35 74 08). Superb little hotel surrounded by gardens; good value.

Monaco

Hôtel Cosmopolite ($$) 4 rue de la Turbie, MC 98000 (tel. 93 30 16 95). One of the few "budget" hotels in Monaco; basic but pleasant rooms.
Hôtel de France ($$) 6 rue de la Turbie, MC 98000 (tel. 93 30 24 64). Pleasant hotel; good value for Monaco.
Hôtel Hermitage ($$$) square Beaumarchais, MC 98000 (tel. 92 16 40 00). Perched up above the town with splendid views, the Hermitage is another magnificent *belle époque* hotel which many consider to be at least the equal of the Hôtel de Paris.

Hôtel de Paris ($$$) place du Casino, MC 98000 (tel. 92 16 30 00). The most prestigious hotel in Monte-Carlo, frequented by gamblers and aristocrats for over a hundred years. Superb rooms, many with views over the harbor and the old town.

Nice

La Belle Meunière ($–$$) 21 avenue Durant, 06000 (tel. 93 88 66 15). Close to the station, comfortable and very hospitable hotel with a shaded garden.
Hôtel Central ($) 10 rue de Suisse, 06000 (tel. 93 88 85 08). Small, simple rooms at budget prices.
Hôtel Mercure Opéra ($$–$$$) quai des États-Unis, 06000 (tel. 93 85 74 19). Despite the forbidding façade, the hotel's rooms are attractive and sound-proofed with sea views.

Hôtel Windsor ($$–$$$) 11 rue Dalpozzo, 06000 (tel. 93 88 59 35). Characterful hotel, with rooms decorated in different styles, just near the beach. Pool and garden.
Negresco ($$$) 37 promenade des Anglais, 06000 (tel. 93 88 39 51). Nice's flagship hotel, one of the great landmarks of the Riviera. Impeccable service and luxurious rooms decorated with original art works.
Relais de Rimiez ($$) 128 avenue de Rimiez, 06000 (tel. 93 81 18 65). Peaceful hotel 10 minutes from the city center with views of Nice and the sea.

St-Paul

La Colombe d'Or ($$$) place des Ormeaux, 06570 (tel. 93 32 80 02). This famous hostelry needs to be booked months in advance despite the exorbitant cost of the rooms.
Les Orangers ($$–$$$) route de la Colle, 06570 (tel. 93 32 80 95). Tranquil location with a view over the village.

Sospel

Hôtel des Etrangers ($$–$$$) 7 boulevard de Verdun, 06380 (tel. 93 04 00 09). Comfortable rooms overlooking the river. Terrace and pool.

Vence

La Closerie des Genets ($–$$) 4 impasse Maurel, 06140 (tel. 93 58 33 25). Small hotel in a peaceful location right in the town center; nine rooms at surprisingly reasonable prices.
La Rosaraie ($$–$$$) 14 avenue Henri Giraud, 06140 (tel. 93 58 02 20). Small hotel on the edge of town with a pretty terrace and pool.

Villefranche-sur-Mer

Hôtel Provencal ($$) avenue Maréchal Joffre, 06230 (tel. 93 01 71 42). Family-run hotel with attractive rooms (ask for a sea view) at reasonable prices.
Hôtel Welcome ($$$) 1 quai Amiral Courbet, 06230 (tel. 93 76 76 93). Famous hotel on the seafront that has included many artists and writers among past guests. Well-furnished, air-conditioned rooms.

RESTAURANTS

The following restaurants have been divided into three price categories:

Budget $
Moderate $$
Expensive $$$

VAUCLUSE

Avignon

Christian Étienne ($$$) 10 rue Mons, 84000 (tel. 90 86 16 50). Housed in an old building overlooking the Palais des Papes, sophisticated restaurant with a long-standing reputation. Imaginative vegetarian menu available.
Hiély ($$$) 5 rue République, 84000 (tel. 90 86 17 07). With its long-standing gourmet reputation, Hiély never fails to please with dishes such as *feuillete de légumes aux truffes, pistou d'homard* and *cassoulet des moules aux épinards.*
Le Pain Bis ($) 6 rue Armand de Pontmartin 84000. Vegetarian meals served with considerable flair in this popular little bistro.
Le Petit Bedon ($) 70 rue Joseph Vernet, 84000 (tel. 90 82 33 98). Generous portions of Provençal cuisine with innovative touches; good value lunchtime menu.
Tache d'Encre ($) 22 rue des Teinturiers, 84000 (tel. 90 85 46 03). Friendly café-theater (live music Friday and Saturday nights) with excellent value set meals such as cod *aioli.*
Le Venaissin ($$) place de l'Horloge, 84000 (tel. 90 86 20 99). The best value restaurant on the central square, with good quality food that is not compromised by their very reasonable prices. Neighboring restaurants live by the trade turned away from this busy restaurant, but standards are low elsewhere by comparison. Arrive early to be sure of a table.
Le Vernet ($$) 58 rue Joseph Vernet, 84000 (tel. 90 86 64 53). The perfect setting on a summer's evening, with tables set under the trees in the walled back garden of this ancient townhouse. Specialties include fish dishes and vegetarian meals.

Bonnieux

Hostellerie du Prieuré ($$–$$$) rue J B Aurard, 84480 (tel. 90 75 80 78). 18th century building at the bottom of the ramparts. Meals are eaten in front of open fire or in the garden.

Carpentras

Le Marijo ($) 73 rue Raspail, 84200 (tel. 90 60 42 65). Cheerful, intimate little restaurant close to for the town center. Regional menu includes *crevettes* and

salade niçoise followed by *filet de dorade Mistral.* Excellent value evening menu.
L'Orangerie ($$) 26 rue Duplessis, 84200 (tel. 90 67 27 23). Original cooking in a pleasant atmosphere (outside on the terrace in summer). Good value for the price.
La Vert Galant ($$) 12 rue Clapiès, 84200 (tel. 90 67 15 50). Imaginative cuisine with local seafood a specialty.

Cavaillon

La Fin du Siècle ($$) 46 place de Clos, 84300 (tel. 90 71 12 27). Café-restaurant embellished with brass and glass in *fin de siècle* style serving tempting dishes at very reasonable prices.
Restaurant Pantagruel ($–$$) 5 place Philippe-de-Cabassole, 84300 (tel. 90 76 11 30). Atmospheric and lively restaurant, with an attractive terrace for warm days. Specialties include char-grilled *gigôt d'agneau.* Inexpensive with plentiful portions.

Fontaine-de-Vaucluse

Hostellerie le Château ($$) quartier Petit Place, 84800 (tel. 90 20 31 54). Restaurant on a shady terrace on the river's edge; specialties include trout, *lotte moutarde à l'ancienne* and *canard avec cèpes.*
Restaurant Philip ($$) 'au pied des cascades', 84800 (tel. 90 20 31 81). On a prime site opposite the soothing cascades on the footpath up to the source. Seafood and grills plus snacks and sandwiches in the bar.

Gigondas

Les Florets ($$) route des Dentelles, 84190 (tel. 90 65 85 01). 2mi. outside Gigondas in the middle of a pine forest, this popular local restaurant is excellent value for money. Specialties include *noisettes d'agneau à la crème d'ail.*

Gordes

Chez Tante Yvonne ($–$$) place Genty-Panataly, 84220 (tel. 90 72 02 54). Cozy restaurant with an original menu featuring specialties such as *terrine d'épinards au thon* or *tarte au roquefort.*
La Mayanelle ($$) 6 rue de la Colombe, 84220 (tel. 90 72 00 28). Classic Provençal cooking with lovely views of the Lubéron from the outside terrace.

L'Isle-sur-la-Sorgue

La Guinguette ($$) le Partage des Eaux, 84800 (tel. 90 38 10 61). Outside of town in a tranquil setting next to the "parting of the waters" where the Sorgue divides; reasonable value with fresh fish and seafood (such as *filet de perche au beurre blanc* and *croustade de moules*) the mainstay.
Le Pescador ($$) le Partage des Eaux, 84800 (tel. 90 38 09 69). Smarter and slightly more expensive than its neighbor La Guinguette and not so well positioned, but with a longstanding reputation for fish dishes.
La Saladelle ($) 33 rue Carnot, 84800 (tel. 90 20 68 59). Simple menus at very reasonable prices.

Malaucène

Hostellerie La Chevalerie ($) center ville, 84340 (tel. 90 65 11 19). In a charming location with a garden below the medieval ramparts, good value and very popular with locals.
L'Origan ($–$$) center ville, 84340 (tel. 90 65 27 08). Well-presented Provençal cooking at prices which will not hurt your wallet.

Ménerbes

Clémentine ($–$$) place Albert Roux, 84560 (tel. 90 72 32 81). Fabulous panoramic views from the terrace; menus featuring *soupe de poissons, daube Provençale* and other classics.

Orange

Le Français ($–$$) 34 rue des Lilas, 84100 (tel. 90 34 67 65). Traditional brasserie food such as *couscous* and *bouillabaisse* as well as pizzas; sometimes there is a floor show.
Le Parvis ($$–$$$) 3 cours Pourtoules, 84100 (tel. 90 34 82 00). Elegant restaurant, Provençal cooking with innovative touches. Specialties include *escalope de loup au fenouil.*
Le Pigraillet ($$) colline St-Eutrope, 84100 (tel. 90 34 44 25). Set in a wooded park at the top of the St-Eutrope hill above Orange, a delightful setting, and you can also use the large swimming pool to work up an appetite before lunch. The menu includes grills, fish, salads, and dessert.
Le Yaca ($) 24 place Sylvian, 84100 (tel. 90 34 70 03). Near the theater, this restaurant in an old vaulted chamber is cheerful and good value.

Roussillon

La Gourmandine ($) place de l'Abbé-Avon, 84220 (tel. 90 05 68 86). Lovely panoramic terrace; good value.
Restaurant David ($$) place de la Poste, 84220 (tel. 90 05 60 13). Provençal cooking, tables outdoors in the summer, popular with locals. Specialties include *cassolette de moules* and *pintade aux cerises.*

Séguret

Domaine de Cabasse ($$–$$$) route de Sablet, 84110 (tel. 90 46 91 12). Just outside of the village, this renowned gastronomic restaurant is extravagant but well worth it.

Vaison-la-Romaine

Le Bataleur ($$) place Theo Aubanel, 84110 (tel. 90 36 28 04). Small and cozy restaurant just near the bridge, with a fixed-price menu with a choice of eight appetizers and ten main

courses. Specialty is *carré d'agneau frisée aux amandes.*

La Pomme Crêperie ($) Haute-ville, 84110 (tel. 90. 36 38 80). Inexpensive savory and sweet *crêpes*, salads, ice creams. Breezy terrace with views over the river.

Restaurant du Vieux Vaison ($–$$) Haute-ville, 84110 (tel. 90 36 19 45). Terrace with panoramic views down from the old town; *pizza au feu du bois* and reasonably priced menus.

BOUCHES-DU-RHÔNE

Aigues-Mortes

Restaurant Chez Laurette ($) 9 rue Alsace-Lorraine, 30220 (tel. 66 53 62 67). Small, cozy restaurant serving traditional Camarguais specialties such as *taureau à la gardienne* and seafood at exceptionally reasonable prices.

Aix

Le Bistro Latin ($$) 18 rue de la Couronne, 13100 (tel. 42 38 22 88). Well-cooked food at reasonable prices.

La Brocherie ($$) 5 rue Fernand Dol, 13100 (tel. 42 38 33 21). Rustic atmosphere with game roasted on a spit in the large chimney. Fish also a specialty.

Le Grillon ($–$$) 49 Cours Mirabeau, 13100 (tel. 42 25 58 81). Good but simple food in café setting frequented by locals. Efficient service.

Clos de la Violette ($$–$$$) 10 avenue Violette, 13100 (tel. 42 23 30 71). One of Aix's best restaurants; essential to book. Specialties include *petits farcis Provençaux, rougets de roche et caillettes d'herbes.*

Les Deux Garcons ($$) 53 cours Mirabeau, 13100 (tel. 42 26 00 51). Wonderful *fin de siècle* atmosphere, at least worth visiting for a morning *cafe crème* and *croissants.* Otherwise, the brasserie-style dishes (which include seafood) tend to be on the expensive side.

L'Hacienda ($) 7 rue Merindol, 13100 (tel. 42 27 00 35). Very good value Spanish restaurant.

Keops ($) 28 rue de la Verrèrie, 13100 (tel. 42 96 59 05). Aix has a number of ethnic restaurants and this Egyptian eatery is one of the best, serving traditional cuisine (*falafel*, etc.) at reasonable prices.

Arles

Hostellerie des Arènes ($) 62 rue du Réfuge, 13200 (tel. 90 96 13 05). Home-style cooking presented with panache; good value.

Hôtel-Restaurant d'Arlatan ($) 7 rue de la Cavaleire, 13200 (tel. 90 96 24 85). The hotel's restaurant serves a basic, well-priced three-course menu; reservations advisable.

Lou Marques ($$) Hôtel Jules César, boulevard des Lices, 13200 (tel. 90 93 43 20). Traditional gourmet food in Arles' top hotel; monkfish soup and *carré d'agneau* with artichokes are two notable specialties.

Le Tourne-Broche ($) 6 rue Balze, 13200 (tel. 90 96 16 03). Pasta and seafood at affordable prices.

Le Vaccarès ($$) place du Forum, 13200 (tel. 90 96 06 17). Inventive variations on traditional Provençal dishes using seasonal produce.

Vitamine ($) 16 rue du Docteur-Fanton, 13200 (tel. 90 93 77 36). Inexpensive restaurant with 50 different salads plus 15 varieties of pasta.

les Baux

Le Mas d'Aigret ($$–$$$) 13520 les Baux (tel. 90 54 33 54). This charming hotel also has a very good restaurant, with imaginatively prepared food.

L'Oustau de Baumanière ($$$) Val d'Enfer, 13520 les Baux (tel. 90 54 33 07). This renowned restaurant is expensive, but with its two Michelin rosettes you may feel it is worth the extravagance. Specialties include *ravioli de truffes* and *filets de rougets au basilic.*

Cassis

César ($) 21 quai des Baux, 13260 (tel. 42 01 75 47). Cassis' seafront restaurants are not renowned for their budget prices and this is one of the very few where you can enjoy the port's famous seafood without overspending.

Chez Gilbert ($$) 19 quai des Baux, 13260 (tel. 42 01 71 36). *Bouillabaisse* (which must be ordered in advance) is a specialty of this reliable restaurant on the seafront.

El Sol ($) 23 quai des Baux, 13260 (tel. 42 01 76 10). Similarly priced to César's; deservedly popular — book a table or get there early.

la Ciotat

Ciotel Le Cap ($$) corniche du Liouquet, 13600 (tel. 42 83 90 30). The gourmet restaurant in this hotel serves classic dishes with regional touches — *bourride de chapon* is a specialty.

Restaurant Les Flots ($) 3 rue Gueymard, 13600 (tel. 42 08 24 61). La Ciotat has a good selection of inexpensive restaurants and this is one of the better ones.

Marseille

Les Arcenaulx ($$) 25 cours d'Estienne d'Orves. 13001 (tel. 91 54 77 06). Housed inside an ancient arsenal with massive stone walls and lined with books, this atmospheric restaurant serves regional food with *nouvelle cuisine* overtones (such as *compote d'agneau aux amandes, gigot aux artichauts*, etc.). Lunchtime menus are budget-priced and good value.

Le Chaudron Provençal ($$) 48 rue Caisserie, 13002 (tel. 91 91 02 37). *Bouillabaisse* and other fish dishes are the

mainstay of this reputable restaurant; fairly expensive but worth it.
Chez Angèle ($–$$) 50 rue Caisserie, 13002 (tel. 91 90 63 35). Inexpensive and small but lively bistro near the old port. Good portions of Provençal dishes and friendly service.
Michel-Brasserie des Catalans ($$$) 6 rue des Catalans, 13007 (tel. 91 52 30 63). Traditional *bouillabaisse* restaurant.
Le Petit Nice ($$$) corniche Kennedy, Anse de Maldorme, 13007 (tel. 91 59 25 92). Beautifully decorated villa overlooking the sea, Marseille's top restaurant with a very inventive menu.
Le Rascasse-Dauphin ($) 6 quai de Rive-Neuve, 13000 (tel. 91 33 17 25). One of the most reasonable seafood restaurants on the old harbor, with interesting menus.

Martigues

Chez Marraine ($$) 6 rue des Cordonniers, 13500 (tel. 42 49 37 48). Delicious fresh fish and superb *bouillabaisse* made the traditional way (for the latter, you must phone to order in advance).
Restaurant Pascal ($) 3 quai Lucien Toulmond, 13500 (tel. 42 42 16 89). Martigues is Provence's premier fishing port so you can always be sure that the fish in this inexpensive restaurant is absolutely fresh. Good value.

Maussane

Ou Ravi Provencau ($$) avenue Vallée des Baux, 13520 (tel. 90 54 31 11). Small restaurant with a big reputation; recommended.

Nîmes

La Belle Respire ($) 12 rue de l'Étoile, 30000 (tel. 66 21 27 21). Good value in the heart of the old town.
Le Cheval Blanc ($$$) place Arènes, 30000 (tel. 66 76 32 32). Elegant, top of the range restaurant right opposite the arena.
L'Enclos de la Fontaine ($$$) Hôtel Imperator Concorde, quai de la Fontaine, 30900 (tel. 66 21 90 30). Reckoned by many to be Nîmes's best restaurant, with imaginative dishes and classic cuisine served overlooking the delightful courtyard garden.
Lou Mas ($) 5 rue du Sauve, 30900 (tel. 66 23 24 71). Pleasant rustic-looking restaurant serving a selection of Catalan-style dishes at reasonable prices.

St-Rémy-de-Provence

Café des Arts ($) 30 boulevard Victor-Hugo, 13210 (tel. 90 92 08 50). Fashionable watering hole with a wide selection of bistro-type food.
La Gousse d'Ail ($$) 25 rue Carnot, 13210 (tel. 90 92 16 87). Intimate restaurant, good value for money with some interesting dishes such as *noix d'entrecôte à la crème d'ail* and *escargots à la Provençale*.
Lou Grillado ($) impasse Jaume Conte, 13210 (tel. 90 92 21 04). Hidden away down a side street, busy and welcoming pizzeria.
Le Marceau ($$) 13 boulevard Marceau, 13210 (tel. 90 92 37 11). Refined decor; excellent food for the price.

Salon-de-Provence

Abbaye de Ste-Croix ($$$) val de Cuech, 13300 (tel. 90 56 24 55). The hotel has a superb restaurant featuring classic Provençal cuisine with innovative touches.
Le Mas du Soleil ($$) 38 Chemin St-Côrne, 13300 (tel. 90 56 06 53). This restaurant has a long-standing reputation and is not outrageously expensive for its excellent cooking.

Tarascon

Le St-Jean ($) 24 boulevard Victor-Hugo, 13150 (tel. 90 91 13 87). Simple, regional cooking at affordable prices; interesting atmosphere.

VAR

Bandol

Auberge du Port ($$) 9 allées Jean-Moulin, 83150 (tel. 94 29 42 63). Seafood restaurant on the port with a long-standing reputation, with *langoustines*, *rouget*, *rascasse* and *loup* among the many fish dishes available on the extensive menu.
Au Fin Gourmet ($$) 16, rue de la République, 83150 (tel. 94 29 41 80). Popular restaurant with a choice of three reasonably priced menus.

le Beausset

La Grange ($–$$) 34 boulevard Chanzy, 83330 (te. 94 90 40 22). Busy local restaurant with an open-spit fire; good value.

Bormes-les-Mimosas

La Bellevue ($–$$) opposite the hotel La Terrasse, place Gambetta, 83230 (tel. 94 71 15 15). Good regional cooking at budget prices, with views of the coast.
La Tonnelle des Délices ($$) place Gambetta, 83230 (tel. 94 71 34 84). Delightful setting, with tables beneath hanging vines. Even more delightful *nouvelle cuisine*, using the freshest of local ingredients, at prices which are a pleasant surprise.

la Cadière

Hostellerie Bérard ($$$) rue Gabriel-Peri, 83740 (tel. 94 90 11 43). Extensive menu with regional specialties on a panoramic terrace overlooking the valley.

le Castellet

Le Castel Lumière ($$–$$$) rue Portail, 83330 (tel. 94 32 62 20). A gastronomic treat, the Castel Lumière features s*uprême du loup aux truffes* and *l'agneau au basilic* among the many other mouth-watering choices.

Fréjus

Cadet Rousselle ($) 25 place Agricola, 83600 (tel. 94 53

36 92). Popular crêperie in the heart of town.
Lou Grillado ($) 80 place Agricola, 83600 (tel. 94 53 48 27). Copious pizzas and lasagna, as well as a well-priced *plat du jour.*
Les Potiers ($–$$) 135 rue des Potiers, 83600 (tel. 94 51 33 74). In the heart of the old town, very popular and atmospheric restaurant featuring standard dishes with a touch of *nouvelle cuisine.*

Grimaud
Restaurant du Café de France ($$) place Neuve, 83310 (tel. 94 43 20 05). Large outdoor terrace for eating in the summer; very reasonable menu (featuring steak or *lapin au moutarde*).

Hyères
La Bergerie ($) 16 rue de Limans, 83400 (tel. 94 65 57 97). Inexpensive and tasty salads and pizzas in a friendly atmosphere.
La Reine Jane ($) le port de l'Aygade, 83400 (tel. 94 66 32 64). Good cooking at good prices.

le Lavandou
Auberge Provençale ($–$$) 11 rue du Patron-Ravello, 83980 (tel. 94 71 00 44). Busy Provençal-style restaurant with well-thought-out menus.
Les Lavandou La Bouée ($) 2 rue Charles Cazin, 83980 (tel. 94 71 11 88). Good value and friendly. Lobster a specialty.

St-Tropez
La Cascade ($) 5 rue de l'Église, 83990 (tel. 94 54 83 46). Lively restaurant with food oriented toward the Caribbean as well as *soupe de poissons* and other local staples. Good value.
L'Échalote ($$) 35 rue Allard, 83990 (tel. 94 54 83 26). Attractive little restaurant with a pretty garden for eating out on warm nights. *Boeuf grillé à l'échalote* is a specialty; very reasonably priced menus.
Les Oliviers ($$) rue des Carles, 83990 (tel. 94 97 20 13). In a lovely garden just outside the town center, with a menu which is terrific value for the area.
Lou Revelen ($$) 4 rue des Ramparts, 83990 (tel. 94 97 06 34). Just behind the port this restaurant offers honest, well-cooked menus, plus an exceptional, well-priced seafood menu. Bookings essential in summer.

Toulon
Le Cellier ($) 52 rue Jean-Jaurès, 83000 (tel. 94 92 64 35). Friendly and welcoming bistro.
La Corniche ($$$) 17 littoral Frédéric Mistral, 83000 (tel. 94 41 35 12). On the outskirts of Toulon, gastronomic cooking with prices to match but well worth it.
Le Galion ($$) 10 rue Jean-Jaurès, 83000 (tel. 94 93 02 52). Pleasant atmosphere and an extensive menu at reasonable prices.
Madeleine ($$) 7 rue des Tombades, 83000 (tel. 94 92 67 85). Homey restaurant with good, solid country cooking. Very popular; reservations advisable.

ALPES-DE-HAUTE-PROVENCE

Annot
Hôtel de l'Avenue ($–$$) avenue de la Gare, 04240 (tel. 92 83 22 07). Family-run restaurant with a three-course menu and a "gourmet" menu. Generous portions; honest cooking.

Barcelonnette
La Mangeoire ($$) place Quatre-Vents, 04400 (tel. 92 81 01 61). Atmospheric restaurant in an old sheep barn; lovingly prepared food at a reasonable cost.

Château-Arnoux
La Bonne Étape ($$$) chemin du Lac, 04160 (tel. 92 64 00 09). One of the top restaurants in Provence, inside this château-hotel. Exceptionally high quality — and high prices, but you may feel it is worth it for a splurge. Fresh, local ingredients prepared with imagination and flair are the hallmarks of chef Pierre Gleize's cooking.
la Taverne Jarlandine ($) montée de l'Oratoire, 04160 (tel. 92 64 04 49). The rustic-style restaurant in this budget hotel serves copious meals with a reasonably priced menu which includes *médaillon de sanglier* or *terrine de langoustines*, followed by *entrecôte maître d'hôtel* or *brochette de boeuf grillé*, salad, cheese, and dessert. Recommended.

Digne-les-Bains
Le Grand Paris ($$–$$$) 19 boulevard Thiers, 04000 (tel. 92 31 11 15). A distinguished restaurant with imaginative and well-presented menus.
Restaurant Mistre ($$) 63 boulevard Gassendi, 04000 (tel. 92 31 00 16). One of Digne's longest established and best-loved restaurants, serving regional specialties at reasonable prices.

Forcalquier
Hostellerie des Deux Lions ($$–$$$) 11 place du Bourguet, 04300 (tel. 92 75 25 30). The restaurant in this renowned hotel is noted for its excellent cooking, particularly game and fish. Booking essential.

Manosque
Chez André ($) 21 bis place des Terraux, 04100 (tel. 92 72 03 09). Basic menus at budget prices.

Riez
Les Abeilles ($) allées Louis-Gardiol, 04500 (tel. 92 77 89 29). Pleasant little café serving local staples (such as *aïoli*) as well as original dishes at highly affordable prices.

Sisteron
Hôtel Restaurant de la Citadelle ($$) 126 rue Saunerie, 04200 (tel. 92 61 13 52). Wonderful views from the terrace restaurant

of this hotel, with a choice of two reasonably priced menus.

CÔTE D'AZUR/ALPES MARITIMES

Antibes

Le Caméo ($) 5 place Nationale, 06600 (tel. 93 34 24 17) in the old town. Unpretentious restaurant with a terrace; specialties include *sardines fraîches à l'espagnole* and grilled *daurade.*

La Clafoutis ($$) 18 rue Thuret, 06600 (tel. 93 34 66 70). Popular restaurant with a menu featuring *terrine de crustaces* and *filet de canard* followed by *fromage blanc* and *clafoutis aux kiwis.*

La Marmite ($) 20 rue James Close, 06600 (tel. 93 34 56 79). Attractive little restaurant with good value menus.

Biot

Auberge du Jarrier ($$–$$$) "au village," 06410 (tel. 93 65 11 68). Excellent restaurant inside an old converted jar factory, with a superb terrace. Classic cooking with a regional slant; particularly good value is the four-course *menu du marché Provençale.*

Cannes

Le Au Bec Fin ($) 12 rue du 24-Août, 06400 (tel. 93 38 35 86). The decor might not be inspiring but almost every dish is appetizing and well presented. Generous portions and interesting *plats du jour.*

Lou Souleou ($$) 16 boulevard Jean-Hibert, 06400 (tel. 93 39 85 55). This restaurant with a nautical theme overlooks the sea and the Esterel *massif* and serves consistently good food at cheerful prices.

La Palme d'Or ($$$) Hôtel Martinez, 73 boulevard de la Croisette, 06400 (tel. 92 98 74 14). Rating two Michelin rosettes, this renowned restaurant is well worth considering for a special treat despite the cost. Chef Jacques Chibois' specialties include *pigeonneau de ferme en crépinette de laitue, crème de févettes à la sarriette,* and other carefully prepared delights.

Èze

Le Troubadour ($$) 'au village', 06360 (tel. 93 41 19 03). Pleasant, welcoming restaurant with a menu featuring *saumon fumé artisanal, magret de canard à la compôte d'oignons,* goat's cheese, and desserts.

Grasse

Maître Boscq ($–$$) 13 rue de la Fontette, 06130 (tel. 93 36 45 76). Provençal and local specialties (such as Grassois stuffed cabbage, *sous fassoun*) of a consistently high standard.

Juan-les-Pins

Auberge de l'Esterel ($$) 21 rue des Îles, 06160 (tel. 93 61 86 55). Excellent menu; attractive outdoor terrace for summer eating. Booking essential.

Lou Capitole ($) 26 avenue Amiral-Courbet, 06160 (tel. 93 61 22 44). Good value.

Menton

L'Oursin ($$–$$$) 3 rue Trenca, 06500 (tel. 93 28 33 62). Seafood of every conceivable variety is the specialty of this popular restaurant, just near the covered market.

Monaco

Bar-restaurant Bacchus ($) 13 rue de la Turbie, 98000 (tel. 93 30 19 35). Family-run café near the station; generous helpings of basic, decent cooking.

Le Louis XV ($$$) Hôtel de Paris, place du Casino, 98000 (tel. 92 16 30 01). Three Michelin rosettes indicate that the food here is as sumptuous and ornate as the gilded restaurant itself. It will cost a king's ransom, but you might find yourself seated next to royalty.

Polpetta ($) 6 avenue Roqueville, 98000 (tel. 93 50 67 84). Rustic Italian-style restaurant with a good selection of reasonably priced pasta dishes.

Nice

Acchiardo ($) 38 rue Droite, 06300 (tel. 93 85 51 16). Popular and busy little restaurant with red oil-cloth tablecloths, serving a variety of excellent regional dishes at incredibly reasonable prices. Recommended.

Atmosphère ($$) 36 cours Saleya, 06000 (tel. 93 80 52 50). Long-established seafood restaurant with a delightful ambience and classic cooking at affordable prices.

Chez Les Pêcheurs ($$) 18 quai des Docks, 06300 (tel. 93 89 59 61). Famous for its wonderful *bouillabaisse* and *bourride.*

Misa Socca ($) 5 rue de Ste-Réparate, 06000 (tel. 93 80 18 35). In the old town, enormously popular for Niçois specialties such as *socca* (a savory cake made from chickpea flour), *ravioli* and *beignet d'aubergines.* Get there early.

La Toque Blanche ($$$) 40 rue Buffa, 06000 (tel. 93 88 38 18). This small restaurant has a growing reputation for carefully prepared fish dishes. Due to its size, booking is advisable.

Vence

La Farigoule ($$) 15 rue Henri-Isnard, 06140 (tel. 93 58 01 27). Genuine Provençal country cooking of a consistently high standard.

Villefranche-sur-Mer

La Mère Germaine ($$$) quai Courbet, 06230 (tel. 93 01 71 39). One of the largest and most popular waterfront seafood restaurants, with *bouillabaisse* and a reasonably priced set menu based on the day's catch.

Le Nautic ($$) 1 quai Courbet, 06230 (tel. 93 01 94 45). Good value for seafood overlooking the port.

Index

A

B

C

P

R

S

T

The Automobile Association would like to thank the following photographers, libraries and associations for their assistance in the preparation of this book.

COURTAULD GALLERIES 107 Cézanne *Still life with apples, bottle and chairback*, 112b Vincent Van Gogh *Self Portrait with Bandaged Ear*
MARY EVANS PICTURE LIBRARY 28 Greek heptareme, 32 Troubadour, 36/37 Louis XIV, 37 Bishop of Marseille, 39a Execution of Robespierre, 40 Somerset Maugham
FOOTPRINTS COLOUR PICTURE LIBRARY 13b Cassis, 141/5, 15 Farmhouse, 116 *Gardian's cabane*, Camargue, 117a Trees, Camargue, 124 Walkers (N Hanna)
RONALD GRANT ARCHIVES 210/11 *The Monte Carlo Story*, 210b *And Woman was Created*, 235 *French Connection II*
E NAGELE Cover, Abbaye de Senanque
PICASSO MUSEUM *Nature Morte* (A Ramie)
PICTURES COLOUR LIBRARY LTD 17 Lavender, 18/19 Gypsy festival, 117 Horses
BARRIE SMITH 133 Bullfight
SPECTRUM COLOUR LIBRARY 19 Procession of *Gardians*, 20/21 St-Raphaël, 132 Bullfight, 170 St-Raphaël
THE MANSELL COLLECTION 35 Pope Benedict XII, 38/39 Ships of war, 60/1 Mistral and his wife, 61 Mistral

The remaining photographs are held in the Automobile Association's own library (AA PHOTO LIBRARY). Adrian Baker took all the pictures except pages 112a (P Kenward), 157 (E Meacher), 23, 182, 184, 185, 186, 187, 195, 207a, 207b, 208, 209b, 234, 236, 239, 240/41, 242, 243a, 246, 258, 259, 264, 266 (R Moss), 49a, 93, 220 (T Oliver), 211, 232, 232/33 (N Ray), Spine 12/13, 42/43, 133, 146/47, 160, 196/97, 213, 256 (B Smith), back flap, 4b, 5b, 6/7, 10/11, 10, 11, 13a, 161/7, 27, 28/29, 30/31, 30b, 33, 34/35, 40/41, 41, 44, 46, 47, 49b, 73a, 74a, 78, 80/81, 81, 92a, 95, 96, 98/99, 104a, 104b, 105, 106, 107, 114/15, 115, 119, 120/21, 121, 122, 123, 132b, 138, 140, 151, 153, 156, 158b, 164, 168, 169, 172a, 172b, 175b, 202, 212a, 212b, 222, 223a, 225, 229b, 238, 243b, 247a, 248a, 248b, 250, 253, 261, 265, 271 (R Strange).

Contributors

Series adviser: Christopher Catling **Joint series editor**: Susi Bailey
Copy editor: Lynn Bresler **Designer**: PPD Design
Verifier: Laurence Phillips **Indexer**: Marie Lorimer